Boris Johnson: Why is England not a Scam?

Deluded Richard Dawkins: A Closeted White Supremacist Antichrist Briton

Dr Benjamin Bedford Ayres

"The Negro is an animal, the Negro is bad, the Negro is mean, the Negro is ugly; look, a nigger ……... Mama the nigger's going to eat me up ……. Where shall I hide? Frantz Fanon

DEDICATION:

Dedicated to Great K (1933 – 2021).

The colour bar was crude and cruel. The reasoning bar is spineless cowardice.

"I hate a fellow who pride, or cowardice, or laziness drives into a corner, and who does nothing when he is there but sit and growl; let him come out as I do, and bark." - Dr Samuel Johnson

"Masonry ought forever to be abolished. It is wrong - essentially wrong - a seed of evil which can never produce any good." President John Quincy Adams (1767 – 1848).

C of E raises serious concerns about Christian Freemasons
https://www.theguardian.com › uk-news › feb › c-of-e-...

8 Feb 2018 — Church of England warning that secret society may not be compatible with Christianity echoes concerns from 1987.

3

INTRODUCTION:

Boris Johnson: Why is England not a scam?

"When one is dirty, one is black whether one is thinking of physical dirtiness or of moral dirtiness ....The black man is the equivalent of a sin." Frantz Fanon

Then, there, the archetypal Judge, top Police Officer, Vicar of a Church, and other members of the Society were white, male, members of the Charitable Antichrist Closeted Racist Freemasonry Quasi-Religion (Mediocre Mafia/New Pharisees), and closeted white supremacists, and some of them were thicker than a gross of planks - Habakkuk. Then, they were a very powerful network, the true rulers of the State, and they were unelected, and they never leave. They were instinctively white supremacists and racists. Elected Politicians come and go.

One of the most important tasks of a Freemason is to pay regularly into the coffers of the Satanic fraternity, quasi protection money.

One of the most important expectations of members of churches overseen by Masons is the regular payment of tithe, quasi protection money.
Then, churches were mere branches of the closeted Satanic Cult that believes in 'FAITHS': Dissenters of John 14:6.

4

Freemasonry and the doctrine of the Church of England
https://anglican.ink › Op-Ed
25 Jun 2015 — The Church of England's official stance on masonry was set by the June 1987 meeting of General Synod in York, which held Christianity and ...

Freemasonry in the Church of England | Thinking Anglicans
https://www.thinkinganglicans.org.uk › ...

15 May 2011 — A bit like pipe-smoking and beating your children, being a Freemason has gone from being almost compulsory for Church of England bishops to ...

Freemasons are very active within most churches, and they believe in 'FAITHS, and they are more intolerant to other views than Jihadists.

FREEMASONS: There people are everywhere, they are closeted white supremacists, and their huge network controls almost everything, and some Africans believe that the closeted white Supremacists' network has devised a method of killing blacks and members of the ethnic minority, albeit hands-off, and legally.

Google: Dr Richard Bamgboye, GP.

Google: Dr Anand Kamath, dentist.

They do vulgar Pharisees' charitable works, so what, and in exchange for what?

BORIS JOHNSON: Let me tell you, theirs is a bribe, and it is not a good deal.

Then, He rejected the grandest bribe of their ruler – Matthew 4:9.

OYINBO OLE: RIGHTEOUS DESCENDANTS OF ULTRA-RIGHTEOUS THIEVES AND OWNERS OF STOLEN CHILDREN OF DEFENCELESS POOR PEOPLE (BLACK AFRICAN ANCESTORS OF MEGHAN MARKLE AND HER WHITE CHILDREN) – HABAKKUK.

Jonathan Wynne-Jones implied that Archbishop Rowan William, an open detractor of the Charitable Antichrist Racist Freemasonry Religion (Mediocre Mafia/New Pharisees) allows freemason to be bishop.

Dr Rowan Williams, whose father was a Freemason, endorsed a believer of Faiths (dissenter of John 14:6) when he nominated the Rev Jonathan Baker as the next Bishop of Ebbsfleet despite knowing he was an active and senior mason.

Dr Williams who had previously said that Freemasonry was "incompatible" with Christianity and had refused to promote Masons to senior posts.

Freemasonry is absolutely incompatible with the exceptionalism of Christ (John 14:6), so it is irreconcilably opposed to Christianity.

Many clergy and members of the General Synod are familiar with the sacrosanct exceptionalism of Christ – John 14:6.

The Church of England views on Freemasonry:

"July 1987 General Synod considered a report Freemasonry and Christianity: Are they compatible?

'That this Synod endorses the Report of the Working Group (GS 784A), including its final paragraph, and commends it for discussion by the Church.'

At national level, there have been no formal developments since the 1987 debate.

The final paragraph of the report referred to in the motion reads as follows:

'This Report has identified a number of important issues on which, in the view of the Working Group, the General Synod will have to reflect as it considers 'the compatibility or otherwise of Freemasonry with Christianity'. The reflections of the Working Group itself reveal understandable differences of opinion between those who are Freemasons and those who are not. Whilst the former fully agree that the Report shows that there are clear difficulties to be faced by Christians who are Freemasons, the latter are of the mind that the Report points to a number of very fundamental reasons to question the compatibility of Freemasonry and Christianity.'

Freemasonry Quasi-Religion is absolutely incompatible with the exceptionalism of Christ.

"I joined freemasonry as an undergraduate in Oxford, before ordination. Over the years I have found it to be an organisation admirably committed to community life and involvement, with a record of charitable giving second to none, especially among, for example, unfashionable areas of medical research. Had I ever encountered anything in freemasonry incompatible with my Christian faith I would, of course, have resigned at once. On the contrary, freemasonry is a secular organisation, wholly supportive of faith, and not an alternative to, or substitute for it. In terms of the Church of England, its support, for example, for cathedral fabric is well documented. Last year HRH the Duke of Kent invited me to serve as an assistant Grand Chaplain, an invitation which I was pleased to accept. This appointment was for one year and ceased in April. To be a bishop requires one to review commitments across every area of life; indeed, Archbishop Rowan had invited me, in discussion, to re-consider, amongst other commitments, my membership of freemasonry. I had intended to discuss the issue more fully with friends and colleagues. I have, however, decided to take the decision now. My absolute priority is the new ministry to which I have been called and to the people who will be in my care. I wish nothing to distract from the inauguration of that ministry. I wish to pay tribute to the aims and objectives of freemasonry and the work which it carries out. I am thankful for the part it has played in my life and for the many friendships it has nurtured. I have concluded that, because of the particular charism of episcopal ministry and the burden that ministry bears, I am resigning my membership of freemasonry." Reverend Jonathan Baker, bishop designate of Ebbsfleet.

"Had I ever encountered anything in freemasonry incompatible with my Christian faith I would, of course, have resigned at once." Reverend Jonathan Baker, bishop designate of Ebbsfleet.

What about the question of 'THE FAITH' and 'FAITHS'?

'The Faith' depicts the exceptionalism of Christ.

'Faiths' is the byword for Freemasonry, dissenters of John 14:6.

Lambeth Palace does not know the number of bishops who are Freemasons.

Then, there, Judges, nearly all, were White, Christian, and Freemasons, and some of them were thicker than a gross of planks – Habakkuk 1:4; John 8:44; John 10:10.

"I joined freemasonry as an undergraduate in Oxford, before ordination." Reverend Jonathan Baker, bishop designate of Ebbsfleet.

MEANING: I was not stupid when I joined the Masons, I mean I was at Oxford.

"The first class at Oxford, where I have examined is an overrated mark." Trevor Hugh-Roper

"Someone must be trusted. Let it be the Judges." Lord Denning (1899 – 1999), a closeted white supremacist.

Judges are human beings. Some human beings are RACISTS.

"All sections of the UK Society are institutionally racist." Sir Bernard Hogan – Howe.

Freemasonry is part of the UK Society.
The Judiciary is part of the UK Society.

Then, there, white Judges who were members of the Charitable Antichrist Closeted Racist Freemasonry Religion (Mediocre Mafia/New Pharisees), were like mice, and like mice they loved to act without being seen, but like mice, they were excessively stupid, as they defecated everywhere, and on everything, and left tell-tale signs.

OYINBO OLE: IGNORANT DESCENDANTS OF ULTRA-RIGHTEOUS THIEVES AND OWNERS OF STOLEN CHILDREN.

They see higher class white people (Freemasons), the Negro sees white imbeciles; if they are not excessively stupid white people, the Negro must be mad.

https://www.youtube.com/watch?v=BlpH4hG7m1A&feature=youtu.be

"They may not have been well written from a grammatical point of view but I am confident I had not forgotten any of the facts." Dr Geraint Evans, Postgraduate Tutor, Oxford

AN IMBECILE: AN ADULT WITH THE BASIC SKILL'S OF A CHILD.

Based on available, GDC, Geraint Evans, Postgraduate Tutor, Oxford, unrelentingly lied under implied oath.

They foresaw that an imbecile will be a postgraduate tutor, Oxford, they embarked on armed robbery and dispossession raids in Africa: Whenever the racist bastards mercilessly slaughtered, they dispossessed, and wherever they robbed, they took possession.

OYINBO OLE: THIEVES - HABAKKUK

Closeted racist bastards do not believe in His exceptionalism (John 14:6), so they are not deterred by His Justice (John 5:22; Matthew 25: 31-46).

https://youtu.be/rayVcfyu9Tw

"Why, Sir, Sherry is dull, naturally dull; but it must have taken him a great deal of pains to become what we now see him. Such an excess of stupidity, Sir, is not in Nature." DR SAMUEL JOHNSON

-----Original Message-----
From: George Rothnie <georgerothnie@hotmail.com>
To: adeolacole@aol.com
Sent: Mon, 8 Mar 2010 20:19
Subject: Re Meeting 9th March

Hi Ola,

We are scheduled to meet tomorrow evening at my surgery about 5.30ish.
Unfortunately something has cropped up which necessytates me having to
postpone the meeting. I'm really sorry it's such short notice.
I will contact you in the week to arrange another date.
Once agaim my apologies.
George.

AN IMBECILE: AN ADULT WITH THE BASIC SKILLS OF A CHILD.
GDC: Dr George Rothnie, our Edinburgh University Educated Deputy Postgraduate Dean, Oxford unrelentingly lied under implied oath.

Then, there, it was a crime only if it were not prior authorised by the FREEMASONS.

Then, there, white Judges, nearly all, were Freemasons; some of them were thicker than a gross of planks.

Closeted racist bastards who use very expensive aprons to decorate the temples of their powerless and useless fertility tools do not believe in His exceptionalism (John 14:6), so they are not deterred by His Justice (John 5:22; Matthew 25: 31-46).

Facts are sacred; they cannot be overstated.

Our Edinburgh University Educated Prime Minister, the scholar from Fife, couldn't spell, in a country of the blind, the partially sighted is the torchbearer.

"By definition therefore there needs to be a contact order for Mr B so that he knows when he is going to see his son. It is absolutely essential that this occurs and mother agrees with that. She said so several times in her evidence. Mrs Waller agreed that not only should a child have the opportunity of developing relationship with both parents, any sibling should also be there so that inter- sibling relationship could be fostered and nurtured. Obviously in this particular case the children reside in different places. That immediately puts a strain on the children having limited contact with each other. F's sister is very much older than him and she will be further advanced into her adult life. Thus it is not a matter that that sibling relationship can only be fostered by the children being together. Indeed as we all know absence sometimes makes

the heart grow fonder. F should have an opportunity of seeing his sister. Wherever he does that it should be done in a friendly and loving environment. If the time comes that his sister goes to university of course his contact with her will be restricted to the time that she is home from university. In years to come when they have both grown up, with their own family they will see less of each other. But it doesn't mean that they don't still love and adore each other as much as they would if they saw each other every day." District Judge Paul Ayers of Bedford County Court, 3, St Paul Square, MK40 1SQ, the Senior Vice President of the Association of Her Majesty's District Judges – proofed and approved Judgement.

Brainless nonsense: An intellectually impotent white nonentity. A racist descendant of racists, ultra-righteous white thieves, and owners of stolen black children of defenceless poor people (the black ancestors of Meghan Markle and her white children).

AN IMBECILE: AN ADULT WITH THE BASIC SKILLS OF A CHILD.

"Yes, Sir, it does *her* honour, but it would do nobody else honour. I have indeed, not read it all. But when I take up the end of a web, and find it packthread, I do not expect, by looking further, to find embroidery." Dr Samuel Johnson.

The yield of poly-educated very, very elementary intellect; the spinal cord District Judge Paul Ayers of Bedford County Court, 3, St Paul Square, MK40 1SQ, the Senior

14

Vice President of the Association of Her Majesty's District Judges seemed to be his highest centre.

PERCEPTION IS GRANDER THAN REALITY.

Everything is baselessly and brainlessly assumed in favour of the irrefutably superior skin colour that the wearer neither made nor chose.

Then, there, Judges were White, Christian, closeted white supremacists, and Freemasons, and some of them were thicker than a gross of planks. Freemasons taught their members s handshakes, not grammar, and the former was considerably easier to master.

District Judge Paul Ayers of Bedford County Court, 3, St Paul Square, MK40 1SQ, the Senior Vice President of the Association of Her Majesty's District Judges approved and immortalised what his functional semi-illiterate white mother and father spoke (deductible), the type of stories his functional semi-illiterate (deductible) white father used to tell when he returned home from QUEEN VICTORIA, after a long day, and at very odd hours, stoned, and which his poly-educated white supervisors in Luton authorised.

"To survive, you must tell stories." Umberto Eco

His Honour Judge Perusko studied Law at Poly, not at a Russell Group Proper University: Lower Class Alternative Education – Proverbs 17:16.

"I believe that what we become depends on what our fathers teach us at odd moments, when they aren't trying to teach us. We are formed by little scraps of wisdom. " — Umberto Eco

GDC: Richard Hill fabricated reports and unrelentingly lied under oath. A white man. A dishonest racist. It is a crime only if the Freemasons did not prior authorise it.

GDC: Kevin Atkinson (NHS) unrelentingly lied under oath. A white man. A dishonest racist. It is a crime only if the Freemasons did not prior authorise it.

GDC: Jonathan Martin unrelentingly lied on record. A white man. A dishonest racist. It is a crime only if the Freemasons did not prior authorise it.

GDC: Helen Falcon (MBE) unrelentingly lied on record. A white woman. A dishonest racist. It is a crime only if the Freemasons did not prior authorise it.

GDC: George Rothnie (NHS) unrelentingly lied on record. A white man. A dishonest racist. It is a crime only if the Freemasons did not prior authorise it.

GDC: Stephanie Twiddle, TD, (NHS) unrelentingly lied under oath. A white woman. A dishonest racist. It is a crime only if the Freemasons did not prior authorise it.

GDC: Sue Gregory, (NHS), Officer of the Most Excellent Order of our Empire, unrelentingly lied on record. A white woman. A dishonest racist. It is a crime only if the Freemasons did not prior authorise it.

GDC: Rachael Bishop (NHS) unrelentingly lied under oath. A white woman. A dishonest racist. It is a crime only if the Freemasons did not prior authorise it.

GDC: Geraint Evans (NHS) unrelentingly lied on record. A white man. A dishonest racist. It is a crime only if the Freemasons did not prior authorise it.

OYINBO OLE: Righteous descendants of ultra-righteous WHITE THIEVES and owners of stolen children of defenceless poor people (the black ancestors of Meghan Markle and her white children) - Habakkuk

CROOKED IMBECILES: ADULTS WITH THE BASIC SKILLS OF A CHILD.

In exchange for vulgar Pharisees' charitable works, closeted white supremacist thugs who use very expensive aprons to decorate the temples of the powerless and useless fertility tools, remove their masks, reveal their 'FANGS', and display seemingly hereditary prejudice.

Ignorant racist FOOLS.

They were all white, including the Judges, and they were all RACISTS, and incompetent liars — Habakkuk

The closeted racist white bastards were not deterred by His Justice (John 5:22; Matthew 25: 31 – 46), as they did not believe in His glaring exceptionalism – John 14:6.

Based on very proximate observations and direct experiences, the white man is the devil; he is as greedy as the grave, and like death, he is never satisfied – Habakkuk 2:5.

<u>The white man is the devil - Columbia University</u>
https://ccnmtl.columbia.edu › mmt › mxp › concepts

Referring to Whites as "devils" originates with the teachings of Master W.D. Fard and the legend of Yakub. Fard taught Elijah Muhammad who preached the ...

"Of black men, the numbers are too great who are now repining under English cruelty." Dr Samuel Johnson

A bastardised, indiscreetly dishonest, unashamedly mediocre, vindictive, potently weaponised, and

18

institutionally RACIST legal system that is overseen by members of the very Charitable Antichrist Racist FREEMASONRY RELIGION (Mediocre Mafia/ New Pharisees) — Habakkuk 1:4; John 8:44; John 10:10.

Vulgar Pharisees' charitable works in exchange for what?

BORIS JOHNSON: Let me tell you, theirs is a SATANIC BRIBE, and it is not a good deal; then, the grandest bribe of their father, the father of lies, was rejected by our own Messiah – John 8:44; Matthew 4:9.

Facts are sacred, and they cannot be overstated.

BORIS JOHNSON: Let me tell you, the psychologically and intellectually insecure closeted racist bastards who use very, very expensive aprons to decorate the temples of their powerless and useless fertility tools are incompetent liars, and they tell the mother of lies, and all the time, and they lie that they don't lie – Psalm 144.

BORIS JOHNSON: Give us the legal tools, and we will deal with the vulgarly charitable closeted racist bastards who use very, very expensive aprons, with vulgar embroideries, to decorate the temples of their powerless and useless fertility tools.

"Lies are told all the time." Sir Michael Havers (1923 – 1992)

BORIS JOHNSON: "Give us the tools, and we will finish the job." Churchill

"To deny or belittle this good is, in this dangerous century when the resources and pretensions of power continue to enlarge, a desperate error of intellectual abstraction. More than this, it is a self-fulfilling error, which encourages us to give up the struggle against bad laws and class bound procedures and to disarm ourselves before power. It is to throw away a whole inheritance of struggle about the law and within the forms of law, whose continuity can never be fractured without bringing men and women into immediate danger." — E. P Thompson.

A white Prime Minister implied that he had very good reasons to suspect that white Judges, not all, were RACIALISTS.

Then, there, Judges were White, Christians, closeted racist, and Freemasons.

Facts are sacred.

"The truth allows no choice." Dr Samuel Johnson

"British Prime Minister attacks racial bias in Universities and the Justice System. 'David Cameron has persuaded a leading labour MP to 'defect' by launching a government investigation into why black people make up such a high proportion of the prison population. Mr Cameron said Mr Lammy would examine why blacks and ethnic minorities make up nearly a quarter of Crown Court defendant – compared to 14 per cent of the population. He added: 'If you are black, you are more likely to be in a prison cell than studying in a university. And if you are black, it seems you're more likely to be sentenced to custody for a crime than if you are white. 'We should investigate why this is and how we can end this possible discrimination. That's why I have asked David Lammy to lead a review. Mr Lammy, who is a qualified barrister, said: 'I am pleased to accept the Prime Minister's invitation." Mr Paul Dacre, Daily Mail, 31.01.2016

"They say the UK isn't racist. Yesterday routing home from training we got pulled over because @MetPoliceUK assumed the car was driving suspiciously. They put out a fabricated report so here is the full story and my reply. The UK is a very racist country." Bianca Williams, British Athlete

"Meghan Markle was the subject of explicit and obnoxious RACIAL HATRED." John Bercow

https://www.youtube.com/watch?v=BlpH4hG7m1A&feature=youtu.be

"They may not have been well written from a grammatical point of view but I am confident I had not forgotten any of the facts." Dr Geraint Evans, Postgraduate Tutor, Oxford

AN IMBECILE: AN ADULT WITH THE BASIC SKILLS OF A CHILD.

https://youtu.be/rayVcfyu9Tw

"Why, Sir, Sherry is dull, naturally dull; but it must have taken him a great deal of pains to become what we now see him. Such an excess of stupidity, Sir, is not in Nature." DR SAMUEL JOHNSON

NIGERIA: SHELL'S DOCILE CASH COW: Urhobo Children with huge oil wells and gas fields near their huts eat only 1.5/day in Nigeria, a Welsh imbecile whose white father and mother have never seen crude oil, and whose white ancestors were fed like battery hens with the yields of stolen children of defenceless poor people (black ancestors of Meghan Markle and her white children) – is a postgraduate tutor, Oxford.

There are no oil wells or gas fields in the Valleys of Wales, there, there are thousands of white sheep and people, and all the white sheep, but not all the people were incestuously conceived, and all the white sheep, but not all the people were excessively stupid.

The very highly luxuriant soil of Bishop's Stortford yields only food.

Cecil Rhodes (1853 – 1902) was a thief.

OYINBO OLE: THIEVES – HABAKKUK.

"We shall deal with the racist bastards when we get out of prison." Comrade Robert Mugabe

-----Original Message-----
From: George Rothnie <georgerothnie@hotmail.com>
To: adeolacole@aol.com
Sent: Mon, 8 Mar 2010 20:19
Subject: Re Meeting 9th March

Hi Ola,

We are scheduled to meet tomorrow evening at my surgery about 5.30ish.
Unfortunately something has cropped up which necessytates me having to
postpone the meeting. I'm really sorry it's such short notice.
I will contact you in the week to arrange another date.
Once agaim my apologies.
George

Dr George Rothnie, Deputy Postgraduate Dean, Oxford

AN IMBECILE: AN ADULT WITH THE BASIC
SKILLS OF A CHILD.

Facts are sacred, they can't be overstated.

Based on very, very proximate observations and direct
experiences, everything about closeted racist bastards is
superior except their brains, so it is the job of white
Freemason Judges to conceal the truth in pursuance of
white privilege and white supremacy.

Based on available evidence, Dr George Rothnie, Deputy
Postgraduate Dean, Oxford unrelentingly lied under
implied oath.

Then, there, it was a lie only if white Freemason Judges,
the direct descendants of the father of lies, did not prior
authorise the mother of lies – John 8:44
The white ancestors of Dr George Rothnie, Deputy
Postgraduate Dean, Oxford, economically cannibalistic
Scottish racist bastards, were incompetent Negrophobic
liars too: They were industrial-scale professional WHITE
THIEVES and owners of stolen children of defenceless
poor people (Black African ancestors of Meghan Markle
and her white children) – Habakkuk.

"Many Scots masters were considered among the most
brutal, with life expectancy on their plantations averaging a
mere four years. We worked them to death then simply
imported more to keep the sugar and thus the money

flowing. Unlike centuries of grief and murder, an apology cost nothing. So, what does Scotland have to say?" Herald Scotland: Ian Bell, Columnist, Sunday 28 April 2013

They want superiority, their brainless and baseless birth right, but they don't want Freedom of Expression because they don't want their mentally very gentle children to know that for several continuous centuries, their white ancestors were merciless racist murderers and THIEVES – Habakkuk

OYINBO OLE: THIEVES – HABAKKUK.

"Sometimes people don't want to hear the truth because they don't want their illusions destroyed." Friedrich Nietzsche.

The report, by the OECD, warns that the UK needs to take significant action to boost the basic skills of the nation's young people. The 460-page study is based on the first-ever survey of the literacy, numeracy and problem-solving at work skills of 16 to 65-year-olds in 24 countries, with almost 9,000 people taking part in England and Northern Ireland to make up the UK results. The findings showed that England and Northern Ireland have some of the highest proportions of adults scoring no higher than Level 1 in literacy and numeracy - the lowest level on the OECD's scale. This suggests that their skills in the basics are no better than that of a 10-year-old.

AN IMBECILE: AN ADULT WITH THE BASIC SKILLS OF A CHILD.

BORIS JOHNSON: Let me tell you, based on very proximate observations and direct experiences, then, privileged dullards who believed that daily dialogues with IMBECILES was a worthwhile, meaty, and manly job were scammers, and those who demanded and accepted valuable considerations in exchange for daily dialogues with IMBECILES were racketeers.

"By definition therefore there needs to be a contact order for Mr B so that he knows when he is going to see his son. It is absolutely essential that this occurs and mother agrees with that. She said so several times in her evidence. Mrs Waller agreed that not only should a child have the opportunity of developing relationship with both parents, any sibling should also be there so that inter- sibling relationship could be fostered and nurtured. Obviously in this particular case the children reside in different places. That immediately puts a strain on the children having limited contact with each other. F's sister is very much older than him and she will be further advanced into her adult life. Thus it is not a matter that that sibling relationship can only be fostered by the children being together. Indeed as we all know absence sometimes makes the heart grow fonder. F should have an opportunity of seeing his sister. Wherever he does that it should be done in a friendly and loving environment. If the time comes that his sister goes to university of course his contact with her will be restricted to the time that she is home from university. In years to come when they have both grown up, with their own family they will see less of each other.

But it doesn't mean that they don't still love and adore each other as much as they would if they saw each other every day." District Judge Paul Ayers of Bedford County Court, 3, St Paul's Square, MK40 1SQ, the Senior Vice President of the Association of Her Majesty's District Judges – proofed and approved Judgement.

Tortuous gibberish.

Shocking!

"Why, that is, because, dearest, you are a dunce." Dr Samuel Johnson

AN IMBECILE: AN ADULT WITH THE BASIC SKILLS OF A CHILD.

OYINBO OLODO: A CLOSETED RACIST FOOL'S APPROVAL.

"Yes, Sir, it does *her* honour, but it would do nobody else honour. I have indeed, not read it all. But when I take up the end of a web, and find it packthread, I do not expect, by looking further, to find embroidery." Dr Samuel Johnson.

The yield of a very, very elementary intellect; the spinal cord of District Judge Paul Ayers of Bedford County Court, 3, St Paul's Square, MK40 1SQ, the Senior Vice

President of the Association of Her Majesty's District Judges seemed to be his highest centre.

Then, there, Judges, were white, closeted racists, Christians, and FREEMASONS; some of them were THICKER than a gross of planks.

"The truth allows no choice." Dr Samuel Johnson

LATENT, BUT VERY POTENT TURF WAR:
Descendants of undocumented refugees (genetic aliens) from Eastern Europe, with camouflage English names, oppress, we, the descendants of the robbed with the yield of the armed robbery - Habakkuk.

"It was our arms in the river of Cameroon, put into the hands of the trader, that furnished him with the means of pushing his trade; and I have no more doubt that they are British arms, put into the hands of Africans, which promote universal war and desolation that I can doubt their having done so in that individual instance. I have shown how great is the enormity of this evil, even on the supposition that we take only convicts and prisoners of war. But take the subject in another way, and how does it stand? Think of 80,000 persons carried out of their native country by we know not what means! For crimes imputed! For light or inconsiderable faults! For debts perhaps! For crime of witchcraft! Or a thousand other weak or scandalous pretexts! Reflect on 80,000 persons annually taken off! There is something in the horror of it that surpasses all bounds of imagination." – Prime Minister William Pitt the Younger.

Then, the white man was the devil.

Then, the white man was as greedy as the grave, and like death, he was never satisfied – Habakkuk 2:5.

'The white man is the devil' – what the Nation of Islam taught ...
https://www.independent.co.uk › World

5 Jun 2016 — In 1974, Muhammad Ali told Michael Parkinson and a stunned chat show audience that the white man of America was "the blue-eyed, blond-headed ...

OYINBO OLE: RIGHTEOUS DESCENDANTS OF ULTRA-RIGHTEOUS WHITE THIEVES: HABAKKUK.

"Those who know the least obey the best." George Farquhar

Then, there, closeted racist bastards feared the untamed mind of the self-educated African more than Putin's poisons.

The colour bar was crude and cruel. The reasoning bar is spineless cowardice,

Herod, the intolerant lunatic removed John's head only because John spoke; Herod was a Jew. John was not

29

punished for speaking, he was permanently prevented from speaking – Matthew 14.

He was lynched like Gadhafi and crucified only because He disclosed pictures His unbounded mind painted. Christ was not punished for speaking, He was prevented from speaking.

BORIS JOHNSON: The closeted white supremacist thugs who use very expensive aprons to decorate the temples of their powerless and useless fertility tools are intellectually disorientated and mentally imbalanced, and they are psychologically and intellectually insecure; they are quasi-voodoo men.

BORIS JOHNSON: Let me tell you, the vulgar Pharisees' charitable workers are closeted white supremacists, scammers, impostors, and experts of deception who, without measurable objectivity, awarded themselves the supreme knowledge, but see only molecules.

BORIS JOHNSON: Give us the legal tools, and we will deal with the demented or dementing geriatrics, and we will openly uncover part of His face, and we will show the narrow and shallow believers of Faiths and dissenters of John 14:6, atoms.

BORIS JOHNSON: "Give us the tools, and we will finish the job." Churchill

FREEMASONS: They are psychologically and intellectually insecure, and they are more intolerant to other views than lunatic Jihadists. Anyone, especially a mere Negro, who refuses to fall in line with their Satanic Mumbo quasi-voodoo religion will be destroyed with the mother of LIES by the direct descendants of the father of lies – John 8:44.

Half-educated school dropouts and their superiors who decorate the temples of their powerless and useless fertility tools with very expensive aprons, with vulgar embroideries, and who have informal access to some very powerful white Judges, are not our God, and they are not the only creation of Almighty God, and they are not immortal, and the irrefutably superior skin colour that they neither made nor chose is not the only wonder of our world: Based on very, very proximate observations and direct experiences, the closeted racist direct descendants of the father of lies always tell the mother of lies, and the closeted lie that they don't lie – Psalm 144; John 8:44.

"Lies are told all the time." Sir Michael Havers (1923 – 1992).

"A typical English man, usually violent and always dull." Wilde

They know how to steal money for their people, but they don't how to repair their scatter-heads.

"This statement is about a series of letters and emails I have been recieving. I am the above named person. I live at an address provided to police. In this statement I will also mention XXXXXXXXXXXXXXXXXXXXXXXXXXX a leaseholder for a property I manage at my place work. I am the company director of DOBERN properties based in Ilford. These emails have been sent to my company email address of mail@debern.co.uk, and also letters have been sent to myself at our company ADDress of P.O BOX 1289, ILFORD, IG2 7XZ over the last Two and a half years, I have recieving a series of letters and emails from DR BAMGeLu. DR BAMGBELU is a leasholder for a property I manage at my place of work. Over the period of his leaseholding, DR BAmGelu has continually failed to pay arrears for the property. In march 2016 my company took DR to court and he was ordered to pay outstanding costs of around £20000 since that time and lead up to the case, DR BaMGBelu has been emailing me and posting me letters that are lengthy and accuses me repeatedly of being a racist in emails and letters tact are regularly Ten to twelve pages long, DR BAMGBELU. lists numerous quots from google searches all refrencing ham I am a bigot and a racist. The most recent letter I received from DR BAMGBELU opens with you are jealous and racist Evil combination you hate us we know it" he goes on to say "I would not have knowingly had anything to do with white supremicists." In the last email I recieved from him on 02/09/2016 DR BaMGBELU stated "you are restricted by poor Education within one of the least literate countries in the world". I would be perfectly happy for DR BAMGBElu to contact myself or my company if he has relevant

enquiries to his lease holding, however these continuous letters and emails are causing me distress and I feel intimidated. I am not a racist and these accusatios make uncomfortable. All I want is to conduct between us in a normal manner. I want BambGlu to stop emailing me and sending me letters accusing me of being racist and harassing me." MR ROBERT KINGSTON, SOLICITOR, ACCOUNTANT, AND COMPANY DIRECTOR.
AN IMBECILE: AN ADULT WITH THE BASIC SKILLS OF A CHILD.

Irreversibly intellectually disorientated and mentally imbalanced: A scatter-head white man.

If one's skin colour is irrefutably superior and one's brain is not, Freedom of Expression is not one's friend, and if one has power, one will stifle or ban it.

Like Herod, Saddam Hussein, Putin, Kim, MBS, and babies, closeted racist bastards expect everyone to love them unconditionally, and say and/or print only what they want to hear.

NEW HEROD, MATTHEW 2:16: Closeted racist bastards deceive to their mentally very, very gentle children that they are geniuses, and the kill, albeit hands off, all those who know that they are brainless racist bastards.

The very, very intolerant lunatic Jew (Herod) removed John's head only because he spoke. John was not punished for speaking, he was permanently prevented from speaking.

Based on available evidence, the white man, Mr Robert Kingston, unrelentingly lied under implied oath - Habakkuk.

They were all white. It is a crime only if the Freemasons did not prior authorise it.

Sons and daughters of the father of lies always tell incompetent mother of all racist lies with impunity, and all the time – John 8:44.

"Those who have the power to do wrong with impunity seldom wait long for the will." Dr Samuel Johnson

SONS AND DAUGHTERS OF THE DEVIL: The very charitable closeted white supremacist thugs who use very expensive aprons to decorate the temples of their powerless and useless fertility tools belong to their father, the devil, and they always carry out their father's desires. Their father was a murderer from the beginning, not holding to the truth, for there is no truth in him. When he lies, he speaks his native language, for he is a liar and the father of lies – John 8:44.

CHAPTER ONE:

BORIS JOHNSON: Why is England not a scam?

FREEMASONS: Very intolerant Defenders of FAITHS, and Dissenters of John 14:6, are undeterred by His Justice (John 5:22), because they do not believe in His Exceptionalism – John 14:6.

"The supreme vice is shallowness." Wilde

LUCIANS STORY: Jupiter and a countryman were walking together, conversing with great freedom and familiarity upon the subject of heaven and earth. The countryman listened with attention and acquiescence, while Jupiter strove only to convince him …... but happening to hint a doubt, Jupiter turned hastily around and threatened him with his THUNDER. 'Ah! Ah!' says the countryman, 'now, Jupiter, I know that you are wrong, you are always wrong when you appeal to your thunder.'

BORIS JOHNSON: Vulgar Pharisees' charitable works in exchange for what?

BORIS JOHNSON: Let me tell you, theirs is not a good deal. The grandest offer of their ruler, the father of lies (John 8:44), was rejected – Matthew 4:9.

He didn't like their ancestors, so he blessed them with the irrefutably superior skin colour, and in protest, the closeted racist bastards used extreme violence to steal almost everything He gave to others: Movable and immovable - Habakkuk

"I know of no evil that has ever existed, nor can imagine any evil to exist, worse than the tearing of eighty thousand persons annually from their native land, by a combination of the most civilised nations inhabiting the most enlightened part of the globe, but more especially under the sanction of the laws of that Nation which calls herself the most free and the most happy of them all." Prime Minister William Pitt the Younger

Then, for sure, the white man was the devil.

'The white man is the devil' – what the Nation of Islam taught ...
https://www.independent.co.uk › World

5 Jun 2016 — In 1974, Muhammad Ali told Michael Parkinson and a stunned chat show audience that the white man of America was "the blue-eyed, blond-headed ...

OYINBO OLE: WHITE THIEVES - HABAKKUK.

"All have taken what had other owners and all have had recourse to arms rather than quit the prey on which they were fastened." Dr Samuel Johnson

Based on available evidence, District Judge Paul Ayers of Bedford County Court, 3, St Paul's Square, Bedford, MK40 1SQ, a mere former debt-collector Solicitor in Norwich, the Senior Vice President of the Association of Her Majesty's District Judges, implied that like his own functional semi-illiterate white mother and father (deductible), the functional semi-illiterate mothers and fathers (deductible) - of Edinburgh University Educated, Dr George Rothnie, a Deputy Postgraduate Dean, Oxford, Mr Robert Kingston, Director Dobern Property Limited, and Dr Geraint Evans, Postgraduate Tutor, Oxford, did not have very, very strong views about education.

Why should we come all the way from very far Africa to give a 'FORK' whether the white fathers and mothers of closeted racist bastards had very, very strong views about education?

Then, racist bastards carried and sold millions of stolen children (black African ancestors of Meghan Markle and her white children), now, they carry natural resources.

OYINBO OLE: THIEVES – HABAKKUK.

Substitution is fraudulent emancipation.

"Moderation is a virtue only among those who are those to have found alternatives." Henry Kissinger.

"They may not have been well written from a grammatical point of view but I am confident I had not forgotten any of the facts." Dr Geraint Evans, Postgraduate Tutor, Oxford

AN IMBECILE: AN ADULT WITH THE BASIC SKILLS OF A CHILD.

Facts are sacred, they can't be overstated

The Welsh man from the Valleys is the product of the educational system of one of the richest nations on earth; had he been the product of one of the poorest nations on earth, the closeted racist bastard mightn't be able to read properly.

"The earth contains no race of human beings so totally vile and worthless as the Welsh ----" Walter Savage Landor

GDC: Based on available evidence, Dr Geraint Evans, Postgraduate Tutor, Oxford, unrelentingly lied under implied oath. His Welsh ancestors were incompetent racist liars too, they were WHITE THIEVES and owners of stolen children of defenceless poor people (Black African ancestors of Meghan Markle and her white children) – Habakkuk.

"Why, Sir, Sherry is dull, naturally dull; but it must have taken him a great deal of pains to become what we now see him. Such an excess of stupidity, Sir, is not in Nature." DR SAMUEL JOHNSON

Then, dementing or demented closeted racist bastards who use very expensive aprons to decorate the temples of their powerless and useless fertility tools were impostors and experts of deception.

If one were to ask all the white master builders (33rd Degree Freemasons) at the Grand Bedfordshire Masonic Temple to Baal, the Keep, Bedford, MK 42, and at the Mother Temple to Baal, **60** Great Queen St, London WC2B 5AZ, to handwrite short essays, many of the closeted racist bastards wouldn't be able to write legibly, and of the rest, most of them wouldn't be able to spell.

PERCEPTION IS GRANDER THAN REALITY.

Everything is assumed in favour of the irrefutably superior skin colour that the very, very fortunate wearer neither made nor chose.

Then, racist bastards mercilessly flogged stolen children who disagreed with them until they succumbed to sadistic tyranny or frogmarched stolen human beings, to the woods, at gunpoint, and viciously hanged them from tall trees, without hoods.

Then, for sure, the white man was the devil.

'The white man is the devil' – what the Nation of Islam taught ...
https://www.independent.co.uk › World

5 Jun 2016 — In 1974, Muhammad Ali told Michael Parkinson and a stunned chat show audience that the white man of America was "the blue-eyed, blond-headed ...

-----Original Message-----
From: George Rothnie <georgerothnie@hotmail.com>
To: adeolacole@aol.com
Sent: Mon, 8 Mar 2010 20:19
Subject: Re Meeting 9th March

Hi Ola,
We are scheduled to meet tomorrow evening at my surgery about 5.30ish.
Unfortunately something has cropped up which necessytates me having to
postpone the meeting. I'm really sorry it's such short notice.
 I will contact you in the week to arrange another date.
Once agaim my apologies.
George

AN IMBECILE: AN ADULT WITH THE BASIC
SKILLS OF CHILD.

Edinburgh University Educated George Rothnie (Scottish George), the Deputy Postgraduate Dean, Oxford.

Based on available evidence, our Prime Minister, the Edinburgh University Educated Scholar from Fife, couldn't spell.

In a Country of the blind, the partially sighted is the torchbearer.

Based on available evidence, Edinburgh University Educated George Rothnie (Scottish George), the Deputy Postgraduate Dean, Oxford, unrelentingly lied under implied oath. His white Scottish ancestors were incompetent racist liars too, they were WHITE THIEVES, murderers, racists, and owners of stolen children of defenceless poor people (Black African ancestors of Meghan Markle and her white children).

"Sometimes people don't want to hear the truth because they don't want their illusions destroyed." Friedrich Nietzsche

Why should the white mother and father of District Judge Ayers of Bedford County Court, 3, St Paul's Square, Bedford, MK40 1SQ, the Senior Vice President of the Association of Her Majesty's District Judges need very, very strong views about education if there is absolutely irrefutable evidence that white ancestors of his white mother and father were very hardened racists, WHITE

THIEVES, murderers, drug dealers (opium merchants), and owners of stolen children of defenceless poor people (Black African ancestors of Meghan Markle and her white children) – Habakkuk?

"Find the truth and tell it." Harold Pinter

"Many Scots masters were considered among the most brutal, with life expectancy on their plantations averaging a mere four years. We worked them to death then simply imported more to keep the sugar and thus the money flowing. Unlike centuries of grief and murder, an apology cost nothing. So, what does Scotland have to say?" Herald Scotland: Ian Bell, Columnist, Sunday 28 April 2013

Based on available evidence, then, the white man was the devil.

OYINBO OLE: IGNORANT DESCENDANTS OF ULTRA-RIGHTEOUS THIEVES – HABAKKUK

"Mr Bamgbelu clearly has very, very strong views about education and I understand those views are based upon the fact that he is a successful dentist here in Bedford which he attributes to the fact that his parents cared for him and his education when he was young. They ensured that he had a proper fee paying education……...." District Judge Ayers of Bedford County Court, 3, St Paul's Square, Bedford, MK40 1SQ, the Senior Vice President of the Association of Her Majesty's District Judges – proofed and approved Judgement.

When irreversible innate RACIAL HATRED (hereditary), and uncontrollable, and unconcealable envy copulate, insanity is their offspring

Financial disclosure in a divorce: 'How can a mere Negro have what I do not have?'

OYINBO ODE: A CLOSETED RACIST DUNCE.

Indiscreet envy.

Envy is a thief.

"Envy is weak." Yul Brynner.

Poly-educated class elementary, opportunistic brainless sarcasm.

Then, the closeted racist white man will be floored for the opportunistic insult, in man-to-man fist fight, in less than 8.47, and whether he got up will depend on how he fell and/or what he fell on.

Had he not been our District Judge in Bedford, one wouldn't know him. What can a functional semi-illiterate, white, former debt-collector Solicitor in Norwich have that one will voluntarily buy?

"By definition therefore there needs to be a contact order for Mr B so that he knows when he is going to see his son.

It is absolutely essential that this occurs and mother agrees with that. She said so several times in her evidence. Mrs Waller agreed that not only should a child have the opportunity of developing relationship with both parents, any sibling should also be there so that inter- sibling relationship could be fostered and nurtured. Obviously in this particular case the children reside in different places. That immediately puts a strain on the children having limited contact with each other. F's sister is very much older than him and she will be further advanced into her adult life. Thus it is not a matter that that sibling relationship can only be fostered by the children being together. Indeed as we all know absence sometimes makes the heart grow fonder. F should have an opportunity of seeing his sister. Wherever he does that it should be done in a friendly and loving environment. If the time comes that his sister goes to university of course his contact with her will be restricted to the time that she is home from university. In years to come when they have both grown up, with their own family they will see less of each other. But it doesn't mean that they don't still love and adore each other as much as they would if they saw each other every day." District Judge Paul Ayers of Bedford County Court, the Senior Vice President of the Association of Her Majesty's District Judges – proofed and approved Judgement.

AN IMBECILE: AN ADULT WITH THE BASIC SKILLS OF A CHILD.

"Yes, Sir, it does *her* honour, but it would do nobody else honour. I have indeed, not read it all. But when I take up the end of a web, and find it packthread, I do not expect, by looking further, to find embroidery." Dr Samuel Johnson.

Facts are sacred, and they can't be overstated.

Like his mentally very, very gentle white children, the imbeciles who sit before him (adults with the basic skills of a child) do not know that the last time he passed through the filter of colour blind and measurable objectivity was when he studied 5th rate law at Poly, and that everything else is subjective packaging, embellishments, and Freemasons' froth.

"Those who know the least obey the best." George Farquhar

His mentally very gentle white children are not curious, so they do not know that the Christ granted talent of their white father and the yield of the highly luxuriant soil of Norwich could not sustain their standard of living, and they do not know that for several continuous centuries, the white ancestors of their white father were ultra-righteous WHITE THIEVES, white racists, white murderers, and white owners of stolen poor black children of defenceless poor people (Black African ancestors of Meghan Markle and her white children) – Habakkuk

OYINBO OLE: THIEVES – HABAKKUK.

They see a Senior District Judge, the Negro sees a white imbecile (an adult with the basic skills of a child), an impostor, and an expert of deception, if they are not excessively stupid, the Negro must be mad.

"There is no sin except stupidity." Wilde.

Sheep unnaturally shepherd sheep.

Shepherds know that sheep are imbeciles (adults with the basic skills of a child), sheep do not know that shepherds are imbeciles too.

"Mediocrity weighing mediocrity in the balance, and incompetence applauding its brother ...." Wilde

Our incontrovertibly functional semi-illiterate Freemason District Judge of our Empire of Stolen Affluence approved what his functional semi-illiterate (deductible) white father and mother spoke, the type of stories his functional semi-illiterate (deductible) white father used to tell when he returned home, after a very long day at QUEEN VICTORIA, and at very odd hours, stoned, and which his Poly-educated supervisors in Luton authorised.

"To survive you must tell stories." Umberto Eco

Based on available evidence, His Honour Judge Perusko studied law at Poly: Lower Class Alternative Education (Not Russell Group) - Proverbs 17:16

Facts are sacred.

"The truth allows no choice." Dr Samuel Johnson.

"I believe that what we become depends on what our fathers teach us at odd moments, when they aren't trying to teach us. We are formed by little scraps of wisdom. — Umberto Eco

It is plainly deductible that the white father and mother of District Judge Paul Ayers of Bedford County Court, the Senior Vice President of the Association of Her Majesty's District Judges did not have very, very strong views about education, and they did not care about their white son, had they, their incontrovertibly functional semi-illiterate white son would not have approved and immortalised excessive stupidity at 16, and he would be a properly educated lawyer, privately educated Anthony Julius, Anthony Blair, Geoff Hoon, and Rabinder Singh's Class, and he might practice proper law in STRAND instead of daily dialogues with imbeciles (adults with the basic skills of a child) in BEDFORD.

Just as it was in Professor Stephen Hawking's School, then, at the University of Lagos, the brightest students did mathematics, physics, and chemistry, and did not attend lectures at the Faculty of Law.

"In my school, the brightest boys did math and physics, the less bright did physics and chemistry, and the least bright did biology. I wanted to do math and physics, but my father made me do chemistry because he thought there would be no jobs for mathematicians." Dr Stephen Hawking.

A grossly overrated, overhyped, overpopulated broad church that admits geniuses and imbeciles (adults with the basic skills of a child) alike, and an unashamedly mediocre trade that is dying slowly and imperceptibly, and is overseen by the Charitable Antichrist Racist Freemasons (Mediocre Mafia) - Habakkuk 1:4; John 8:44; John 10:10.

"The legal system lies at the heart of any society, protecting rights, imposing duties, and establishing a framework for the conduct of almost every social, political, and economic activity. Some argue that the law is in its death throes while others postulate a contrary prognosis that discerns numerous signs of law's enduring strength. Which is it?" Professor Raymond Wacks.

Closeted white supremacist bastards seemed to have paid for the right to choose those who thrive or die within their Antichrist Satanic System.

Based on very proximate observations and direct experiences, the administration of English Law is a weapon of war: Race and Religious War.

Based on available evidence, English Law is equal, but its administration is not.

"Rightful liberty is unobstructed action according to our will within limits drawn around us by the equal rights of others. I do not add 'within the limits of the law' because law is often but the tyrant's will, and always so when it violates the rights of the individual." Thomas Jefferson

☐ BEDFORD, ENGLAND: ANTICHRIST RACIST FREEMASONS: | by ...
https://olubamgbelu21.medium.com/bedford-england-antichrist-racist...
01/01/2021 · Bedford. Justice, 04/01/21. District Judge Ayers, 04/01/21. Her Honour Judge Gargan ... Family; District Judge Murch Yinka Bamgbelu (Daring Truths, Non-Fiction Writer) on Twitter ... twitter.com › adeadeolacole1 › status 28 Nov 2018 — JUDGE AYERS,you're a bad human being,a RACIST,and a COWARD.The JUDICIARY that made you a JUDGE isn't

☐ BASED ON AVAILABLE EVIDENCE, THE JUDGE LIED; YES, ...
https://medium.com/@yinkabamgbelu45/based-on-available-evidence-the...
28/09/2021 · District Judge, Bedford, the Senior Vice President of the Association of Her Majesty's District Judges approved and immortalised the type of stories his functional semi-illiterate father used to...

☐ Daringtruths - DISTRICT JUDGE AYERS OF BEDFORD …

https://www.facebook.com/Daringtruths01/posts/district-judge-ayers-of...

DISTRICT JUDGE PAUL AYERS, prior to the European commerce in STOLEN HUMAN BEINGS, there weren't very many proper houses in BEDFORD. In that era, JUDGES like you were complicit in MERCILESS RACIST EVIL (SLAVERY); they were fed like battery hens with its yields

☐ Creeping DPRK: Builders want to ban the expression of …

https://medium.com/@yinkabamgbelu45/creeping-dprk-builders-want-to-ban...

29/09/2021 · Sir Winston Churchill Based on accessible information, it is the absolute truth that District Judge Ayers of Bedford County Court in Bedfordshire, England,

☐ This judgment was delivered in private. The judge has …

https://www.judiciary.uk/wp-content/uploads/2021/04/G00LU644-Bp... · PDF file
18/03/2021 · Judge Ayers of Bedford that " Upon the defendants agreeing that the interim injunction order and power of arrest be made final, And Upon the Defendants acknowledging in open court that they were aware of the terms of the injunction order and the power of arrest and acknowledging that although they will not take a copy of the orders away with them, they …

☐ Olu Bamgbelu – Medium

https://olubamgbelu21.medium.com

14/06/2021 · Daily Cause District Judges, 08/06/21 …
District Judge Stone Barrow … Bedford. District Judge
Ayers, 08/06/21. Justice, 08/06/21. Her
Honour Judge Gargan. Daringtruths — His
Honour Judge Perusko studied at Poly… | Facebook
https://en-gb.facebook.com › Daringtruths01 › …

☐ CourtServe - Live Court Listings

https://www.courtserve.net/courtlists/current/county/indexv
2county.php?...

18/11/2021 · Bedford: District Judge Ayers 13/12/21
Justice 13/12/21 Birkenhead: Daily Cause 14/12/21 Daily
All Judges 17/12/21 Daily All Judges 16/12/21 Daily
All Judges 15/12/21 Daily All Judges 14/12/21: 2: Daily
All Judges 14/12/21 Daily All Judges 13/12/21
Birmingham: Honourable Mr Justice Saini 13/12/21
Recorder Verduyn 13/12/21: 2: Recorder Verduyn
13/12/21 Dep. …

☐ Facebook

https://www.facebook.com/Daringtruths01/photos/district-
judge-ayers-of...

district judge ayers of bedford county court: a brainless
white man; a racist descendant of professional thieves and
owners of stolen human beings

☐ Daringtruths - Daringtruths - DISTRICT JUDGE
AYERS OF ...

https://www.facebook.com/1053403758117551/posts/darin
gtruths-district...
DISTRICT JUDGE AYERS OF BEDFORD COUNTY
COURT: A BRAINLESS WHITE MAN; A RACIST
DESCENDANT OF PROFESSIONAL THIEVES AND ...
Daringtruths - Posts | Facebookwww.facebook.com ›
Daringtruths01 › posts District Judge Ayers, 15/12/20. ...
NEW HEROD: They lied to their children that they are
geniuses; they kill all those who ... Her Honour ...

☐ Yinka Bamgbelu – Medium
https://yinkabamgbelu441.medium.com
DISTRICT JUDGE AYERS OF BEDFORD COUNTY
COURT: A BRAINLESS WHITE MAN; A RACIST
DESCENDANT OF PROFESSIONAL THIEVES AND ...
The Law Paralysed by Michael Coleade —

"All sections of the UK Society are institutionally racist."
Sir Bernard Hogan-Howe

The Judiciary and the Police Force are parts of the UK
Society.

Then, there, closeted racist white Judges and Policemen,
nearly all, were FREEMASONS.

GDC: Dr Kevin Atkinson (NHS), a white man,
unrelentingly lied under oath. His white ancestors were
incompetent racist liars too, they were THIEVES and
owners of stolen children of defenceless poor people

(African ancestors of Meghan Markle and her white children) - Habakkuk

GDC: Jonathan Martin, a white man, unrelentingly lied under implied oath. His white ancestors were incompetent racist liars too, they were THIEVES and owners of stolen children of defenceless poor people (African ancestors of Meghan Markle and her white children) - Habakkuk

GDC: Helen Falcon (MBE) a white woman, unrelentingly lied under implied oath. Her white ancestors were incompetent racist liars too, they were THIEVES and owners of stolen children of defenceless poor people (African ancestors of Meghan Markle and her white children) – Habakkuk

GDC: George Rothnie (NHS), a white man, unrelentingly lied under implied oath. His white ancestors were incompetent racist liars too, they were THIEVES and owners of stolen children of defenceless poor people (African ancestors of Meghan Markle and her white children) - Habakkuk

GDC: Stephanie Twiddle, TD, (NHS), a white woman, unrelentingly lied under oath. Her white ancestors were incompetent racist liars too, they were THIEVES and owners of stolen children of defenceless poor people (African ancestors of Meghan Markle and her white children) – Habakkuk. Based on very proximate contacts, Stephanie Twiddle had a very distinct body odour, the white woman stank.

"The truth allows no choice." Dr Samuel Johnson

"Britons stank." W.S.

W.S: Wole Soyinka, not William Shakespeare.

He should know; at least one of his wives, the mother of his Mulatto son, and many of his concubines, were Britons.

GDC: Sue Gregory (OBE), a white woman, unrelentingly lied under oath. Her white ancestors were incompetent racist liars too, they were THIEVES and owners of stolen children of defenceless poor people (African ancestors of Meghan Markle and her white children) – Habakkuk

GDC: Rachael Bishop (NHS), a white woman, unrelentingly lied under oath. Her white ancestors were incompetent racist liars too, they were THIEVES and owners of stolen children of defenceless poor people (African ancestors of Meghan Markle and her white children) – Habakkuk

GDC: Geraint Evans (NHS), a white man, unrelentingly lied under implied oath. His white ancestors were incompetent racist liars too, they were THIEVES and owners of stolen children of defenceless poor people (African ancestors of Meghan Markle and her white children) - Habakkuk

GDC: Richard Hill (NHS), a white man, fabricated reports and unrelentingly lied under oath. His white ancestors were incompetent racist liars too, they were THIEVES and owners of stolen children of defenceless poor people (African ancestors of Meghan Markle and her white children) – Habakkuk

No brain.

Poor in natural resources.

Several continuous centuries of stealing and slavery preceded the stolen trust fund.

Only the skin colour is irrefutably superior, and the very, very fortunate wearer neither made nor chose it.

OYINBO OLE: RIGHTEOUS DESCENDANTS OF ULTRA-RIGHTEOUS THIEVES – HABAKKUK

Based on very proximate observations and direct experiences, the white man is the devil.

God Almighty did not place Africans in the back row, white men did.

God Almighty does not place Africans in the back row, white men do.

"Of black men, the numbers are too great who are now repining under English cruelty." Dr Samuel Johnson

OYINBO OLE: THIEVES – HABAKKUK

The white man is the devil - Columbia University

Referring to Whites as "devils" originates with the teachings of Master W.D. Fard and the legend of Yakub. Fard taught Elijah Muhammad who preached the ...

Then, closeted racist bastards carried and sold millions of stolen children of defenceless poor people (Black African ancestors of Meghan Markle and her white children); now, they carry natural resources.

SUBSTITUTION IS FRAUDULENT EMANCIPATION.

"Moderation is a virtue only among those who are thought to have found alternatives." Henry Kissinger

DELUDED PAPER TIGERS: "England will fight to the last American." American saying

Their hairs stand on end when they are challenged by our people (Africans); we and our type are the ones the closeted racist bastards will beat up without the support of the YANKS.

"Ethical foreign policy." Robin Cook (1946 -2005).

If FREEMASONS are as brave and as ethical as they imply, they should use guns to evict Putin from Crimea; he stole it with guns.

Putin sits on the largest gas reserves in the world, did he poison Bob Dudley?

They must win because superiority is their brainless and baseless birth right, but only their skin colour and the ascent they use to speak their own language, are superior, their intellects are not superior, so the direct descendants of the father of lies (John 8:44) use the mother of lies, and racist Judicial terrorism to criminally balance the unbalanced.

OYINBO OLE: IGNORANT DESCENDANTS OF ULTRA-RIGHTEOUS THIEVES – HABAKKUK.

Like Christ's universe, our Empire did not evolve from NOTHING, then, almost everything was actively and deliberately stolen with guns.

"Sometimes people don't want to hear the truth because they don't want their illusions destroyed." Friedrich Nietzsche

He does not like the closeted racist bastards, so He gave them the irrefutably superior skin colour, and in protest, the direct descendants of the father of lies (John 8:44) used the mother of all racist lies to steal the yield of the Christ granted talents of black Africans.

Closeted racist bastards persecute our people because of the dark coat that we neither made nor chose, and cannot change, and they impede our ascent from the bottomless crater into which their armed ancestors threw ours, in the African bush, unprovoked, during several centuries of the greediest economic cannibalism and the evilest racist terrorism the world will ever know, and they steal the yield of our Christ granted talent - Habakkuk.

A nri nile inu nbi elesin.

OYINBO OLE: RIGHTEOUS DESCENDANTS OF ULTRA-RIGHTEOUS THIEVES – HABAKKUK.

Based on very proximate observations and direct experiences, the white man is the devil – John 8:44

The white man is the devil - Columbia University
https://ccnmtl.columbia.edu › mmt › mxp › concepts

Referring to Whites as "devils" originates with the teachings of Master W.D. Fard and the legend of Yakub. Fard taught Elijah Muhammad who preached the ...

Truths are sacred, and they can't be overstated.

Closeted racist bastards want to eat all their own cakes, and eat all other people's cakes, and they want to have everything.

Based on very proximate observations and direct experiences, closeted racist bastards are greedier than the grave, and like death, they are never satisfied – Habakkuk 2:5.

They love Africa, but only Africa's money, not Africans.

OYINBO OLE: THIEVES – HABAKKUK.

Then, racist bastards carried and sold millions of stolen children of defenceless poor people (Black African ancestors of Meghan Markle and her white children); now, they carry natural resources – Habakkuk

SUBSTITUTION IS FRAUDULENT EMANCIPATION.

"Moderation is a virtue only among those are thought to have found alternatives." Henry Kissinger

OYINBO OLE: RIGHTEOUS DESCENDANTS OF ULTRA-RIGHTEOUS THIEVES – HABAKKUK.

Like Herod, Saddam Hussein, Putin, Kim, MBS, and babies, they expect everyone to love them, and say and/or print only what they want to hear.

There is Freedom of Expression in DPRK, there, one is free to say and/or print only what Kim wants to hear.

The ancestors of Kim did not kidnap the people of North Korea overnight, they did gradually, and the basic right to disclose pictures painted by the mind was the first to be withdrawn.

"Freedom of Expression is a basic right." Lady Hale

Everything about them is superior except their brains, and the concealment of that truth is one of the most important objectives of white Freemason Judges.

The very, very intolerant lunatic Jew removed John's head only because he spoke: King Herod did not punish John for speaking, John was permanently prevented from speaking.

He was lynched like Gadhafi and crucified only because He spoke; He disclosed pictures that His unbounded mind painted.

Facts are sacred, and they can't be overstated.

Based on very, very proximate observations and direct experiences, closeted racist bastards believe that progressive colour-blind merit should be subservient to the irrefutably superior skin colour that they neither made nor chose, and the superior accent they use to speak their own language.

APARTHEID BY STEALTH: WHITE PRIVILEGE

Based on very, very proximate observations and direct experiences, the natural instinct of the privileged dullard is the soft but durable Apartheid by stealth.

OYINBO ODE: IGNORANT RACIST MORONS, AND RIGHTEOUS DESCENDANTS OF ULTRA-RIGHTEOUS THIEVES, AND OWNERS OF STOLEN CHILDREN OF DEFENCELESS POOR PEOPLE (BLACK AFRICAN ANCESTORS OF MEGHAN MARKLE AND HER WHITE CHILDREN) – HABAKKUK.

CONFLICT OF INTEREST: Based on very proximate observations and direct experiences, Freemasons, through their very, very vulgar Pharisees' charitable works, believe that they have paid for the right to be the true rulers of the state, and they believe that they have also paid for the right to resort to uncivilised, unintelligent, and educated racist criminality in pursuance of their own best interest.

"The rulers of the state are the only persons who ought to have the privilege of lying, either at home or abroad; they may be allowed to lie for the good of the state." Plato

They know their law so well, they can destroy any Negro with it, but that is only the theory: Their chief of tools is incompetent racist lies; the direct descendants of the father of lies always tell incompetent mother of lies – John 8:44.

OYINBO OLE: THIEVES – HABAKKUK.

"Lies are told all the time." Sir Michael Havers (1923 – 1992)

Then, there, the most important task of Freemason Judges was to steady the ship, and guide and guard RACIST CRIMINALITY – Habakkuk 1:4; John 8:44; John 10:10.

There, then, white Judges, nearly all, were FREEMASONS; some of them were thicker than a gross of planks.

Facts are sacred.

"The truth allows no choice." Dr Samuel Johnson

The report, by the OECD, warns that the UK needs to take significant action to boost the basic skills of the nation's young people. The 460-page study is based on the first-ever survey of the literacy, numeracy and problem-solving at work skills of 16 to 65-year-olds in 24 countries, with almost 9,000 people taking part in England and Northern Ireland to make up the UK results. The findings showed that England and Northern Ireland have some of the highest proportions of adults scoring no higher than Level 1 in literacy and numeracy - the lowest level on the OECD's scale. This suggests that their skills in the basics are no better than that of a 10-year-old.

AN IMBECILE: AN ADULT WITH THE BASIC SKILLS OF A CHILD.

They foresaw that their descendants will be imbeciles (adults with the basic skills of a child), so they, directly and indirectly used, made in Birmingham, guns to loot Africa, and they used the yield of several centuries of the greediest economic cannibalism, and the evilest racist terrorism the world will ever know, to create an Eldorado for millions of white imbeciles, and they decommissioned natural selection, and they reversed evolution, and they made it affordable for millions of imbeciles, of all shades, to breed irresponsibly - Habakkuk.

Apart from creating very cushy salaried jobs for incontrovertibly functional semi-illiterate white Judges

(predominantly) who foreseeably FAILED in the practice of their grossly overrated, overpopulated, and mediocre trade (quasi-communism), what do imbeciles (adults with the basic skills of a child)
need very expensive administration of the law for?

BORIS JOHNSON: Let me tell you, then, there, Judges who believed that daily dialogues with imbeciles (adults with the basic skills of a child) was a properly meaty and manly job, were SCAMMERS, and Judges who demanded and accepted very valuable considerations in exchange for daily dialogues with imbeciles (adult with the basic skills of a child) are RACKETEERS (Thieves).

"Natural selection will not remove ignorance from future generations." Dr Samuel Johnson

Adults with the basic skills of a foetus will succeed imbeciles (adults with the basic skills of a child), and they will need only food and shelter, not very expensive administration of English Law.

Their excessively stupid lunatic professor (Psalm 53), Lala's husband, believes that the supernatural does not exist because Christ does not disclose Himself to him, and if He discloses Himself to others, they must be lying or mad. An excessively stupid white man, Oxford university educated closeted white supremacist descendant of industrial-scale professional thieves, and owners of stolen children of defenceless poor people (Black African ancestors of Meghan Markle) baselessly awarded himself the supreme of knowledge – Habakkuk

"There is no sin except stupidity." Wilde

If Lala's husband, the closeted white supremacist Antichrist Briton, and a John 14:6 dissenter, Dr Clinton Richard Dawkins, and the British Premier, The Right Honourable Boris Johnson, and the Prime Minister of India, His Excellency, Narendra Modi, and the Prime Minister of Israel, His Excellency Naftali Bennett, and Cambridge University Educated rich man's son, Sir, Mr Justice Haddon-Cave, QC, KBE, and the Mayor of London, His Excellency Sadiq Khan could prove that District Judge Paul Ayers of Bedford County Court, 3, St Paul's Square, Bedford, MK40 1SQ, was not a functional semi-illiterate and an incompetent liar, and if they could prove that Mr Robert Kingston was not a functional semi-illiterate and an incompetent liar, and if they could prove that Dr Shiv Pabary, Member of the Most Excellent Order of our Empire (MBE), Justice of Peace (JP), and the archetypal GDC Committee Chairman, was not a functional semi-illiterate and an incompetent liar, and if they could prove that GDC: Dr Kevin Atkinson (NHS), a white man, did not unrelentingly tell lies under oath, and if they could prove that GDC - Executive: Jonathan Martin, a white man, did unrelentingly tell lies under implied oath, and if they could prove that GDC: Helen Falcon, Member of the Most Excellent Order of our Empire (MBE), a Rotarian, a Member of the GDC Committee, and a white woman, did not unrelentingly tell lies under implied oath, and if they could prove that GDC: George Rothnie (NHS), a white man, did not unrelentingly tell lies under implied oath, and if they could prove that GDC: Stephanie Twidale, a British Soldier, TD, (NHS), and a white woman, did unrelentingly tell lies under oath, and if they could prove that GDC: Sue Gregory, Officer of the Most Excellent Order of our Empire (OBE), and a white woman, did unrelentingly tell lies under oath, and if they could prove that GDC: Rachael Bishop (Senior NHS Nurse), a white woman, did unrelentingly tell lies under oath, and if they could prove that GDC: Geraint Evans (NHS), a white man, did not unrelentingly tell lies under implied oath, and if they could prove that GDC: Richard Hill (NHS), a white man, did not fabricate reports and unrelentingly told lies under oath, they will confirm the belief of billions of people in our world, which is that dissenters of John 14:6, believers of 'FAITHS', Antichrist Islam, Antichrist Judaism, Charitable Antichrist Freemasonry Quasi-Religion, and all other motley assemblies of exotic religions and faiths under the common umbrella of the Defender of The Faith and the Governor of the Church of England, are not intellectually flawed Satanic Mumbo Jumbo, and they will also confirm that reasoning and vision have boundaries. If reasoning and vision have boundaries, He must have deceived Jews, in the Council, when He disclosed parts of the pictures His unbounded painted, and He must have also lied when He audaciously stated that He was exceptional – John 14:6.

"The first quality that is needed is audacity." Churchill

If the fellow told the truth, we are FORKED, as His Knights attacks Queens and Kings simultaneously, and only the Queens can move, and any belief that is not aligned with John 14:6 is travelling in the wrong direction and heading straight for the rocks.

He reveals Himself to those He wants, not through their righteousness, but only true His unsolicited and underserved kindness.

Only stupid people believe that the probability that we are alone in the universe – is 100%, and only stupider people believe that what they can't see does not exist, and those who say they see what deluded racist bastards can't see – must be lunatics.

"It does no harm to throw the occasional man overboard, but it does not do much good if you are steering full speed ahead for the rocks." Sir Ian Gilmour (1926 – 2007)

Ignorance is bliss.

"Too often the strong, silent man is silent only because he does not know what to say and is reputed strong only because he has remained silent." - Churchill

CHAPTER TWO:

Boris Johnson: Why is England not a scam?

Boris Johnson: Defenders of Faiths (Dissenters of John 14:6) – are busted, and they will do whatever it takes to conceal and protect their Satanic Mumbo Jumbo.

"Masonry ought forever to be abolished. It is wrong - essentially wrong - a seed of evil which can never produce any good." President John Quincy Adams (1767 – 1848).

Their system is fundamentally institutionally ANTICHRIST, and it is, in its entirety, based on incompetent myopic self-defeating racist lies, and it is not deterred by His Justice (John 5:22), as they do not believe in his exceptionalism – John 14:6.

Why should closeted racist bastards (devils) be deterred by His Justice (John 5:22; Matthew 25: 31-46), if they do not believe in His exceptionalism (John 14:6)?

"There is no sin except stupidity." Wilde

"It is incumbent upon the court and all those professionals involved to conclude court proceedings as quickly as possible. This hopefully ensures that a child has stability, love and affection and the parents working together to ensure that he has the best opportunity of developing academically and emotional." District Judge Paul Ayers of

Bedford County Court, 3, St Paul's Square, MK40 1SQ, the Senior Vice President of the Association of Her Majesty's District Judges – proofed and approved Judgement

A CLOSETED RACIST FOOL'S APPROVAL!

Our incontrovertibly functional semi-illiterate white Senior District Judge of our Empire of Stolen Affluence - Habakkuk.

There, then, all functional semi-illiterate white Judges were racists.

Before Slavery, what?

Then, there, white Judges who expended their professional life on daily dialogues with white imbeciles (predominantly), were affected by their regular encounters.

Based on available evidence, those who nearly passed or just passed the A/Level could do Law in Great Britain.

District Judge Paul Ayers of Bedford County Court, the Senior Vice President of the Association of Her Majesty's District Judges, which part of mediocrity and confusion is the great in Great Britain?

Facts are sacred.

Just as it was in Professor Stephen Hawking's School, then, at Akoka and Idi-Araba (the University of Lagos), where the author was a student in the late 70s and early 80s, the brightest students did mathematics, physics, and chemistry, and did not attend lectures at the Faculty of Law.

"In my school, the brightest boys did math and physics, the less bright did physics and chemistry, and the least bright did biology. I wanted to do math and physics, but my father made me do chemistry because he thought there would be no jobs for mathematicians." Dr Stephen Hawking.

"Sometimes even lawyers need lawyers." Billy Carter

Their grossly overrated, overhyped, overpopulated, and mediocre trade that is dying slowly and imperceptibly, and is overseen by the members of the Charitable Antichrist Racist Freemasonry Quasi-Religion (Mediocre Mafia/ New Pharisees) - Habakkuk 1:4; John 8:44; John 10:10.

"The legal system lies at the heart of any society, protecting rights, imposing duties, and establishing a framework for the conduct of almost every social, political, and economic activity. Some argue that the law is in its death throes while others postulate a contrary prognosis that discerns numerous signs of law's enduring strength. Which is it?" Professor Raymond Wacks.

If closeted racist bastards know what some self-educated Africans truly feel, and say behind their backs, they will kill them, albeit hands-off.

"The truth allows no choice." Dr Samuel Johnson

If the closeted racist, incontrovertibly functional semi-illiterate white man, District Judge Paul Ayers of Bedford County Court, the Senior Vice President of the Association of Her Majesty's District Judges, read his approved judgement, he was a FOOL, and if he didn't, he lied, as he implied that he did. His white ancestors were incompetent racist liars too, they were ultra-righteous, armed, and industrial-scale professional thieves, and owners of stolen children of defenceless poor people (the African ancestors Meghan Markle and her white children) – Habakkuk

OYINBO OLE: THIEVES – HABAKKUK.

FREEMASONS (Defenders of Faiths and dissenters of John 14:6): Like Putin, MBS, Kim, Saddam Hussein, Herod, and babies, they expect everyone to love them unconditionally, and they expect everyone to see our world only from their perspective, and the intolerant closeted racist bastards expect everyone to say and/or print only what they want to hear.

There is Freedom of Expression in DPRK and KSA, the freedom to write and print only what Kim and MBS likes.

There was Freedom in the African bush, including the basic natural right to disclose pictures painted by minds, for thousands of years before Europeans' commerce in millions of stolen children of defenceless poor people (Meghan Markle and her white children's African ancestors) – Habakkuk

They want superiority, and they can have whatever they want, but based on progressive, colour blind, ad measurable objectivity; what's wrong with that?

They are not the only creation of Almighty God, and they are not immortal, and the irrefutably superior skin colour that they neither made nor chose is not the only wonder of our world.

Then, on the plantations, racist bastards used to sadistically flog our people who disagreed with them, until they died, and/or from march children, at gunpoint, to the woods, and, often, strip them naked, and hang them from tall trees, without hoods.

Then, the white man was the devil.

'The white man is the devil' – what the Nation of Islam taught ...
https://www.independent.co.uk › World

5 Jun 2016 — In 1974, Muhammad Ali told Michael Parkinson and a stunned chat show audience that the white man of America was "the blue-eyed, blond-headed ..

They were extremely wicked people, and they were greedier than the grave, and like death, the closeted racist bastards were never satisfied – Habakkuk 2:5.

They were not deterred by His Justice (John 5:22) because they did not believe in His exceptionalism. They are no longer here, but their direct descendants remain. They are not the only creation of Almighty God, and they are not immortal, and the irrefutably superior skin colour that they neither made nor chose is not the only wonder of our world.

Facts are sacred, and they can't be overstated.

OYINBO OLE: RIGHTEOUS DESCENDANTS OF ULTRA-RIGHTEOUS THIEVES – HABAKKUK.

The nemesis is not extinct and the fact that it tarries isn't proof that it will never come – Habakkuk.

The sadistic white savages are no longer here, but it will be naïve and reckless not to expect their sadistic genes to continue to flow through the veins of their descendants who remain here.

OYINBO OLE: THIEVES – HABAKKUK.

"Individual liberty is not an asset of civilisation. It was greatest before there was any civilisation ……" Sigmund Freud

****

From: Nikivorovic, Blazo
[mailto:Blazo.Nikivorovic@hmcts.x.gsi.gov.uk]
Sent: 12 March 2015 13:34
To: ADEOLACOLE@AOL.COM; Clerks
Subject: CO000672015–0005.doc * OFFICIAL *

Dear Clerks

Please find attach appointment to fix letter regarding the above matter.

Also can all clerks attend the upcoming appointment with a time estimate.

Kind Regards

Blazo

Blazo Nikivorovic | Listing Office | Royal Courts of Justice | Strand | London WC2A 2LL | Telephone: 020 7947 6655 | Fax: 020 7947 6802

If replying by email, please use the following address:
Administrativecourtoffice.listoffice@hmcts.x.gsi.gov.uk

*****

RE: CO000672015–0005.doc * OFFICIAL *

Thu, 12 Mar 2015 13:41

Joe Martin (jmartin@2bedfordrow.co.uk)To:you + 2 more
Details

THANKS KINDLY

*****

From: adeolacole [mailto:adeolacole@aol.com]
Sent: 12 March 2015 17:04
To: Joe Martin
Subject: Re: CO000672015–0005.doc * OFFICIAL *

Dear Joe Martin,

What exactly does 'THANKS KINDLY' mean?

If the Royal High Court sends me a correspondence that it
copied to you, 13.34, and you resend the same
correspondence only seven minutes later, with 'THANKS
KINDLY', may I ask you to kindly expatiate?

******

RE: CO000672015–0005.doc * OFFICIAL *

Thu, 12 Mar 2015 17:24

Joe Martin (jmartin@2bedfordrow.co.uk)To:you Details

Thanks to the person whom sent the email ......

******

Hi Ola,

We are scheduled to meet tomorrow evening at my surgery
about 5.30ish.
Unfortunately something has cropped up which
necessytates me having to
postpone the meeting. I'm really sorry it's such short
notice.
I will contact you in the week to arrange another date.
Once agaim my apologies.

George

******

AN IMBECILE: AN ADULT WITH THE BASIC
SKILLS OF A CHILD.

"To disagree with three – fourths of the British public on
all points is one of the first elements of sanity, one of the
deepest consolations in all moments of spiritual
doubt." Wilde

https://www.youtube.com/watch?v=BlpH4hG7m1A&featu
re=youtu.be

"They may not have been well written from a grammatical point of view but I am confident I had not forgotten any of the facts." Dr Geraint Evans, Postgraduate Tutor, Oxford

BORIS JOHNSON: The administration of English Law is white supremacist charade; it is, almost in its entirety, a purified confusion.

https://youtu.be/rayVcfyu9Tw

"Why, Sir, Sherry is dull, naturally dull; but it must have taken him a great deal of pains to become what we now see him. Such an excess of stupidity, Sir, is not in Nature." DR SAMUEL JOHNSON

They were all white: Homogeneity in the administration of English Law is the impregnable secure mask of merciless, hereditary (innate) RACIAL HATRED - Habakkuk.

APARTHEID BY STEALTH: They want superiority, their brainless and baseless birth right, they don't want Freedom of Expression because they don't want their mentally very gentle children to know that the centuries-old unspoken myth that intellect is related to the irrefutably superior skin colour that the very fortunate wearer neither made nor chose is the mother of all racist scams, and they don't want their simpler children to know that their ancestors were THIEVES and owners of stolen children of defenceless poor people (the African ancestors of Meghan Markle and her white children) – Habakkuk.

The report, by the OECD, warns that the UK needs to take significant action to boost the basic skills of the nation's young people. The 460-page study is based on the first-ever survey of the literacy, numeracy and problem-solving at work skills of 16 to 65-year-olds in 24 countries, with almost 9,000 people taking part in England and Northern Ireland to make up the UK results. The findings showed that England and Northern Ireland have some of the highest proportions of adults scoring no higher than Level 1 in literacy and numeracy - the lowest level on the OECD's scale. This suggests that their skills in the basics are no better than that of a 10-year-old.

AN IMBECILE: AN ADULT WITH THE BASIC SKILLS OF A CHILD.

BORIS JOHNSON: Then, there, based on very proximate observations and direct experiences, privileged dullards who believed that having daily dialogues with imbeciles (adults with the basic skills of a child) - was a proper job, were SCAMMERS, and those who demanded and accepted valuable consideration in exchange for daily dialogues with imbeciles are RACKETEERS (Thieves) – Habakkuk.

"The best argument against democracy is a five-minute conversation with the average voter." Churchill

Then, closeted racist bastards accurately foresaw that the majority of their descendants will be imbeciles (adults with the basic skills of a child), so they used guns, made in Birmingham, to loot Africa, and the very wicked racist bastards used the yield of several centuries of the greediest economic cannibalism and the evilest racist terrorism to create an Eldorado for millions of white imbeciles and others, and they decommissioned progressive natural selection, and they reversed progressive evolution, and they made it possible for millions of imbeciles, of all shades, and others, to breed irresponsibly.

OYINBO OLE: THIEVES - HABAKKUK

FREEMASONS: If one is an imbecile, one wouldn't discern imbecility, and most Britons can't see Freemasons as they truly are.

"To disagree with three – fourths of the British public on all points is one of the first elements of sanity, one of the deepest consolations in all moments of spiritual doubt." Wilde

If one could see the closeted racist bastards as they truly are, one will bow to white devils and/or play devils like chess only if one believes in FAITHS and one is a dissenter of John 14:6.

Defenders of Faiths (Dissenters of John 14:6):

They know that they are devils, and they know that most people don't know, and they know that those who know must bow to devils, or play devils like chess, in pursuance of regular bread – Matthew 4:9.

The closeted racist bastards who use very expensive aprons to decorate the temples of their powerless and useless fertility tools are more intolerant than lunatic Jihadists, and anyone who refuses to bow to them, or who doesn't know how to play them like chess, or who, otherwise, refuses to align with their Satanic voodoo Religion that is based on 'FAITHS' – will be killed, albeit hands off.

Their people are everywhere, particularly with the Judiciary and the Police Force, and they control everything.

Then, there, white Judges, nearly all, were members of the Charitable, Antichrist Racist Freemasonry Quasi-Religion; some of them were thicker than a gross of planks.

Then, like MBS, Kim, and Herod, their white ancestors were intolerant lunatic butchers who regularly removed the heads of those who disagreed with them.

The last decapitation, with a very sharp axe, in England, was in 1817, and decapitation was removed from the Statute book in 1973. The same year, 1973, Kenneth Baker banned flogging.

Based on very proximate observations and direct experiences, the white man is the devil; every other devil is an imitation (fake).

"There is now less flogging in our great schools than formerly, but then less is learned there; so that what the boys get at one end, they lose at the other." Dr Samuel Johnson.

Why remove the heads of those who disagree with you if it is illegal to flog them?

Then, disagreeing with the closeted racist bastards, who baselessly awarded themselves the supreme knowledge, and who oversaw the administration of the law, especially by a mere Negro, was treasonous, and a very high crime.

BORIS JOHNSON: We do not believe in Satanic Mumbo Jumbo, and we do not believe in FAITHS; gives us the tools and will reveal the existence of 'atoms' to the closeted racist brainless bastards who see only molecules, and vulgarly use very expensive aprons to decorate the temples of their powerless and useless fertility tools, and lie that they don't lie – Psalm 144

Your Majesty: We believe only in THE FAITH, not because we are subjects of the Defender of the Faith, but solely because of His vivid revelation, and through His unsolicited and undeserved kindness – Romans 11: 1 John 4:4.

BORIS JOHNSON: The Negro is a foetus only because what he sees is clearer than dreams, prophesies, and visions – Act 2:17.

BORIS JOHNSON: Freemasons are our irreconcilable religious enemies, and they oversee the administration of English law. Give us the legal tools, and we have the courage and conviction to defend ourselves against the Charitable, Antichrist, and closeted white supremacist thugs who vulgarly use very expensive aprons to decorate the temples of their powerless and useless fertility tools and lie that they don't lie – Psalm 144.

BORIS JOHNSON: "Give us the tools, and we will finish the job." Churchill

Then, their ancestors were as wicked as the devil, and they were greedier than the grave, and like death, the closeted racist bastards were never satisfied – Habakkuk 2:5.

OYINBO OLE: THIEVES – HABAKKUK.

Then, the Defender of those who believed in THE FAITH had only a few to defend, as almost everyone, including the successor of the Defender of those who believed in THE FAITH, became a believer of FAITHS – Romans 11.

"You will bow. You can't beat the system." Kemi Daramola

Esu!

Luciferians speak.

Imported devil.

Omo alata.

Nouveau riche: Nigerian contractor's daughter. A parasite who found a host. A glorified prostitute and a thief.

A deliberate, properly schooled, and calculative glorified prostitute, and a THIEF.

Like her mother, she liked what her mother couldn't afford, so she used her tubes and the improperly cooked Ibadan Dentistry to get it.

"A woman is the only hunter who uses herself for bait." Confucius

She prays to Christ and pays tithe (about £100,000 since she joined the Satanic Church that is overseen by the Freemasons), and members of the Charitable Antichrist Racist Freemasonry – Religion in Kempston answer her prayers.

WE MUST BOW TO ENORMOUSLY ADVANTAGEOUS WHITE PRIVILEGE IN EXCHANGE FOR REGULAR BREAD – MATTHEW 4:9.

Bow to a brainless tall dwarf, the son of white plebeians, a mere poly-educated, former debt-collector Solicitor in Norwich, whose most valuable asset as a human being is the irrefutably superior skin colour that he neither made nor chose, and who WILL BE considerably diminished as a human being without it.

"Those who know the least obey the best." George Farquhar.

Ignorance is bliss.

"Someone must be trusted. Let it be the Judges." Lord Denning (1899 – 1999).

White Judges are human beings. Some human beings are RACISTS,

It is not the truth that white Judges are Superhuman, who cannot tell lies, and cannot be racialist.

Based on very proximate observations and direct experiences, the most important hallmark of 'FAITHS' is

82

incompetent racist lies – Habakkuk 1:4; John 8:44; John 10:10.

"Lies are told all the time." Sir Michael Havers (1923 – 1992).

"All sections of the UK Society are institutionally racist." Sir Bernard Hogan-Howe

The Judiciary is part of the UK Society.

Bedfordshire Police is part of the UK Society.

"Racism is rife throughout most organisations across Britain." The Mayor of London.

"Meghan Markle was the subject of explicit and obnoxious racial hatred." John Bercow

THE JUDICIARY IS NOT A BRANCH OF FREEMASONRY QUASI-CULT

"Racism is alive and well and living in Tower Hamlets, in Westminster and, yes, sometimes in the judiciary." Judge Peter Herbert, Officer of the Most Excellent Order of the British Empire (OBE).

"White supremacy is real, and it needs to be shattered." Dr Cornel West

I shan't. I know who will – Romans 11; 1 John 4:4

Kemi Daramola prays to Christ, and regularly pays very handsome tithe (quasi-protection money) at Brickhill

Baptist Church, Bedford, and members of the Charitable Antichrist Racist Freemasonry Quasi-Religion (Mediocre Mafia/New Pharisees) in Kempston answer her prayers – Habakkuk 1:4; John 8:44; John 10:10.

Facts are sacred.

"The truth allows no choice." Dr Samuel Johnson

Those she pays tithe to must protect the financial interest of the tithe payer.

CONFLICT OF INTEREST: A BLATANTLY FRAUDULENT ARRANGEMENT.

"A government that robs Peter to pay Paul can always depend on the support of Paul." George Bernard Shaw

"You should play them like chess." Dr Resh Diu

Playing closeted racist bastards who use very expensive aprons to decorate the temples of their powerless and useless fertility tools, like chess, is a variant of bowing to the closeted white supremacist thugs – Matthew 4:9.

OYINBO OLE: RIGHTEOUS DESCENDANTS OF ULTRA-RIGHTEOUS THIEVES – HABAKKUK.

They were all white, including the Judges.

'Ultra-righteousness' without equitable reparation is continuing racist fraud - Habakkuk.

OYINBO OLE: THIEVES – HABAKKUK.

They are not the only creation of Almighty God, and they are not immortal, and their irrefutably superior skin colour is not the only wonder of our world.

OYINBO OLE: STRAIGHT-FACED DESCENDANTS OF VERY, VERY HARDENED ULTRA-RIGHTEOUS PROFESSIONAL THIEVES – HABAKKUK.

"Many Scots masters were considered among the most brutal, with life expectancy on their plantations averaging a mere four years. We worked them to death then simply imported more to keep the sugar and thus the money flowing. Unlike centuries of grief and murder, an apology cost nothing. So, what does Scotland have to say?" Herald Scotland: Ian Bell, Columnist, Sunday 28 April 2013

Then, the white man was the devil; he was wickeder than the devil, and greedier than the grave, and like death, he was never satisfied – Habakkuk 2:5.

Facts are sacred.

"The truth allows no choice." Dr Samuel Johnson

-----Original Message-----
From: resh diu <rdiu@me.com>
To: adeolacole <adeolacole@aol.com>
Sent: Fri, 11 Apr 2014 9:28
Subject: Re:

It's sad Ola
I kept telling you to play the game of chess rather than fight it

You take care
If you wish to dispose of 24 park road let me know
Regards
Resh
Dr Resh Diu BDS
www.oradi.co.uk

Only atheist and those whose belief align with 'FAITHS' can thrive under FREEMASONS' rule.

CREEPING DPRK.

"By definition therefore there needs to be a contact order for Mr B so that he knows when he is going to see his son. It is absolutely essential that this occurs and mother agrees with that. She said so several times in her evidence. Mrs Waller agreed that not only should a child have the opportunity of developing relationship with both parents, any sibling should also be there so that inter- sibling relationship could be fostered and nurtured. Obviously in this particular case the children reside in different places. That immediately puts a strain on the children having limited contact with each other. F's sister is very much older than him and she will be further advanced into her adult life. Thus it is not a matter that that sibling relationship can only be fostered by the children being together. Indeed as we all know absence sometimes makes the heart grow fonder. F should have an opportunity of seeing his sister. Wherever he does that it should be done in a friendly and loving environment. If the time comes that his sister goes to university of course his contact with her will be restricted to the time that she is home from university. In years to come when they have both grown up, with their own family they will see less of each other. But it doesn't mean that they don't still love and adore each other as much as they would if they saw each other every day." District Judge Paul Ayers of Bedford County Court, 3, St Paul's Square, Bedford, MK40 1SQ, the Senior Vice President of the Association of Her Majesty's District Judges – proofed and approved Judgement.

TORTUOUS GIBBERISH!

A brainless white man, a closeted racist descendant of ultra-righteous white thieves and owners of stolen children of defenceless poor Africans (the ancestors of Meghan Markle and her white children) – Habakkuk.

AN IMBECILE: AN ADULT WITH THE BASIC SKILLS OF A CHILD.

The yield of a very, very elementary intellect; his spinal cord seemed to be his highest centre.

PERCEPTION IS GRANDER THAN REALITY.

"Yes, Sir, it does *her* honour, but it would do nobody else honour. I have indeed, not read it all. But when I take up the end of a web, and find it packthread, I do not expect, by looking further, to find embroidery." Dr Samuel Johnson.

White Privilege: It is universally acknowledged that the skin colour that the very, very fortunate wearer neither made nor chose is irrefutably superior, and it is his most valuable asset as human beings; apart from it, what?

Before SLAVERY, what?

Our functional semi-illiterate closeted racist Freemason District Judge of our Empire of stolen affluence. Our Empire did not evolve from NOTHING; then, almost everything was actively and deliberately stolen with tools.

"Affluence is not a birth right." David Cameron

Facts are sacred.

"The truth allows no choice." Dr Samuel Johnson

Had the white man, District Judge Paul Ayers of Bedford County Court, 3, St Paul's Square, Bedford, MK40 1SQ, the Senior Vice President of the Association of Her Majesty's District Judges, written that in a proper examination where there would be no direct or indirect marks for his irrefutably superior skin colour, and his association with Her Majesty would not favour him, he would have FAILED.

Then, there, some white privileged dullards attach unashamed mediocrity and confusion to revered sovereigns, and they sell them to the undiscerning for valuable consideration.

District Judge Paul Ayers of Bedford County Court, 3, St Paul's Square, Bedford, MK40 1SQ, the Senior Vice President of the Association of Her Majesty's District Judges is the product of the educational system of one of the richest nations on earth, and had he been the product of one of the poorest nations on earth, the white man, albeit England's Class Senior Judge, might not be able to read properly.

A properly proofed and approved Judgement by a properly educated Judge, should pass through at least four separate filters: The transcript writers, the proof-readers, the court clerks, and the Judge.

In an open dialogue with Justice Ruth Bader Ginsburg (1933 – 2020), Lady Hale lamented funding.

My Lady, what is the value of several layers of unashamed mediocrity and confusion?

Our Parliament should rewrite our law: 'Freedom of expression for imbeciles (adults with the basic skills of a child) should replace 'Freedom of Expression for all'.

"Our government is valuable because it is free. What, I beg gentlemen to ask themselves, are the fundamental parts of a free government? I know there are differences of opinion upon this subject, but my own opinion is that freedom does not depend upon the executive government, or upon the administration of justice, or upon anyone particular or distinct part, or even upon forms so much as it does on general freedom of speech and writing. What I mean is this: that any man may write and print what he pleases, although he is liable to be punished if he abuses that freedom; this I call perfect freedom in the first instance. I say, it is not the written law of the constitution of England; it is not the law that is to be found in books, that has constituted the true principle of freedom of any country, at any time. No! It is the energy, the boldness of a man's mind, which prompts him to speak, not in private, but in large and popular assemblies, that constitutes, that creates, in a state, the spirit of freedom. This is the principle which gives life to liberty; without, the human character is a stranger to freedom. If you suffer the liberty of speech to be wrested from you; you will then have lost the freedom, the energy, and the boldness of the British character." The Right Honourable Charles James Fox, English Politician

Closeted racist bastards love the irrefutably superior skin colour that they neither made nor chose, their brainless and baseless birth right, but they do not love Freedom of Expression because they don't want their mentally very gentle children to know that they are excessively stupid closeted racist bastards.

"Freedom to report the truth is a basic right to which the court gives a high level of protection, and the author's right to his story includes the right to tell it as he wishes." Lord Toulson

Members of the Charitable Antichrist Racist Freemasonry Quasi-Religion (Mediocre Mafia/New Pharisees) want to guide the education of our black children, with what?

Irrefutably superior skin colour that the very, very fortunate wearer neither made nor chose, stolen trust fund, and what else?

OYINBO OLE: THIEVES – HABAKKUK.

"Those who know the least obey the best." George Farquhar

Charity should 'FORKING' begin at home, in the very beautiful Shires – Matthew VII.

Everything, absolutely everything, is assumed in favour of the irrefutably superior skin colour that the very, very fortunate wearer neither made nor chose.

They are not the only creation of Almighty God, and they are not immortal, and the irrefutably superior skin colour that the very fortunate wearer neither made nor chose is not the only wonder our world.

GIGANTIC yields of millions of stolen children of defenceless poor people (Meghan Markle and her white children's African ancestors) seemed to have distorted the realities of closeted racist bastards, descendants of undocumented refugees, genetic Eastern Europeans, with camouflage English names, whose ancestors crossed the

English Channels, in dinghy boats, not that long ago, without luggage or decent shoes, and who seem to oversee the potently weaponised Judiciary and Police Force.

"All sections of the UK Society are institutionally racist."
Sir Bernard Hogan-Howe

The Police Force and the Judiciary are part of the UK society.

Seemingly motivated by uncontrollable innate (hereditary) RACIAL HATRED, they damaged the boy, and passed him back to his parent to repair.

Unlike her little brother, age saved the child's sister (100% genetic Nigerian) from racist and evil clutches of the Closeted-Racist-Dylan–Roof- Freemason- District-Judge of our Empire of stolen affluence - Habakkuk.

Like our Universe, our Empire did not evolve from NOTHING; then, almost everything was actively and deliberately stolen with GUNS - Habakkuk.

Facts are sacred; they cannot be overstated.

"Sometimes people don't want to hear the truth because they don't want their illusions destroyed." Friedrich Nietzsche

OYINBO OLE: THIEVES - HABAKKUK

"Affluence is not a birth right." David Cameron

Like death, the closeted racist bastards will never be satisfied because they are wickeder than the devil, and greedier than the grave – Habakkuk 2:5.

The child's sister (100% genetic Nigerian) thanks her stars that the incontrovertibly functional semi-illiterate, closeted racist white man, District Judge Paul Ayers of Bedford County Court, 3, St Paul's Square, MK40 1SQ, the Senior Vice President of the Association of Her Majesty's District Judges, did not have anything to do with her education.

In her GCSE, she gained the following grades:
English Language A*
English Literature A*
Mathematics A*
Additional Mathematics A*
Physics A*
Chemistry A*
Biology A*
History A*
Latin A
Spanish A
Advanced Level Mathematics A

Two years later, she gained 6 A grades in the A/Level.

Members of the Antichrist Racist Freemasonry Quasi-Religion (Mediocre Mafia/New Pharisees) want to guide the education of our children (100% genetic Nigerians);

charity should 'FORKING' begin at home, in the very beautiful Shires – Matthew VII.

Envy is a thief.
Indiscreet envy.
"Envy is weak." Yul Brynner.

Gigantic yields of millions of stolen and destroyed children of defenceless poor people (Meghan Markle and her white children's African ancestors) seemed to have distorted the realities closeted racist bastards: Ignorant descendants of THIEVES and owners of stolen human beings.

He rides a very powerful tiger, and deluded, he thinks he is it, dismounted, he'd instantly revert to the functional semi-illiterate debt-collector Solicitor in Norwich that he once was (PURIFIED NOTHING).

Everything, absolutely everything, is assumed in favour of the irrefutably superior skin colour that the very fortunate wearer neither made nor chose.

The only part of Africa that closeted racist bastards truly love is MONEY; everything else is incompetent art that incompetently imitates life.

OYINBO OLE: THIEVES – HABAKKUK.

Then, they carried and sold millions of stolen children of defenceless poor people (the African ancestors of Meghan

94

Markle and her white children; now, they carry natural resources.

Substitution is fraudulent emancipation.

"Moderation is a virtue only among those who are thought to have found alternatives." Henry Kissinger

The academic height that the white father and mother of the closeted racist white District Judge Paul Ayers of Bedford County Court, 3, St Paul's Square, MK40 1SQ, the Senior Vice President of the Association of Her Majesty's District Judges, CANNOT know, and which the natural talents of his own white children WILL NOT exploit.

PERCEPTION IS GRANDER THAN REALITY.

Based on very proximate observations and direct experiences, the white man is scared; he fears the untamed mind of the self-educated Negro more than wicked Putin's poisons.

WHITE PRIVILEGE: The centuries-old unspoken myth that intellect is related to the irrefutably superior skin colour that the very fortunate wearer neither made nor chose is the mother of all racist scams.

They are not the only creation of Almighty God, and they are not immortal, and the irrefutably superior skin colour that they neither made nor chose is not the only wonder of our world - Habakkuk.

Closeted racist bastards are more familiar with the descendants of the Plantation Negroes (Blacks of Caribbean extraction): Descendants of stolen children who were unnaturally selected, genetically reversed, artificially bred for labour, and reared like cattle of stolen land - by very highly civilised, enlightened, and righteous white Christians - Habakkuk.

If we are not very, very smart, why are we very, very rich?

MOTHER TERESA OF AFRICA: Shepherds did not bring stolen children of defenceless poor people home (African ancestors of Meghan Markle and her white children), they deceived their mentally very, very gentle children that they were paragons of wisdom and virtue who, like TARZAN, did only virtuous works in AFRICA.

OYINBO OLE: THIEVES - HABAKKUK

"All men are created equal." Abraham Lincoln.

Abraham Lincoln: A closeted white supremacist and an incompetent liar.

"White supremacy is real, and it needs to be shattered." Dr Cornel West

WHITE SUPREMACY IS IMMORTAL.

Only foolish Africans expect others to relinquish stolen advantageous positions in exchange for NOTHING. Stolen advantageous positions can only be vacated through overwhelming violence or in exchange for very valuable consideration. Since theirs found ours in the African bush in the 15th, things have not turned out well for Africa and Africans. Africans are powerless, and Africa, and Africans have been robbed penniless.

OYINBO OLE: THIEVES – HABAKKUK.

"No advance in wealth, no softening of manners, no reform or revolution has ever brought human equality a millimeter nearer. George Orwell.

If Lala's husband, the mere Science Journalist (Dr E.O Wilson), and England's Class Biology genius, Dr Clinton Richard Dawkins, and all the White Master Builders (33rd Degree Freemasons - Scottish Rite), they're all white, at the Bedfordshire Masonic Temple to Baal, the Keep, Bedford Road, Kempston, Bedford MK42, and the highest ranking Freemasons at the Grand Masonic Temple to Baal, 60 Great Queen St, London WC2B 5AZ, and Cambridge University Educated rich man's son, Sir, Mr Justice Haddon-Cave, QC, KBE, could prove that all the white children of District Judge Paul Ayers of Bedford County Court, 3, St Paul's Square, MK40 1SQ, the Senior Vice President of the Association of Her Majesty's District Judges, were not less favoured by Almighty God, certainly intellectually, and if they could prove that GDC-Witness,

Richard William Hill did not fabricate reports and unrelentingly told lies under oath, and if they could prove that GDC: Kevin Atkinson (NHS) did not unrelentingly tell lies under oath, and if they could prove that GDC: Jonathan Martin did not unrelentingly tell lies on record, and if they could prove that GDC: Helen Falcon (MBE) did not unrelentingly tell lies on record, and if they could prove that GDC: George Rothnie (NHS) did not unrelentingly tell lies on record, and if they could prove that GDC: Stephanie Twiddle, TD, (NHS) did not unrelentingly tell lies under oath, and if they could prove that GDC: Sue Gregory (OBE) did not unrelentingly tell lies on record, and if they could prove that GDC: Rachael Bishop (NHS) did not unrelentingly tell lies under oath, and if they could prove that GDC: Geraint Evans (NHS) did not unrelentingly tell lies on record, it should confirm the belief of billions of people, which is that Antichrist Freemasonry Quasi-Religion, Antichrist Islam, Antichrist Judaism, and all other motley assemblies of exotic religions and faiths under the Common Umbrella of the Governor of the Church of England and the Defender of the FAITH - are not intellectually flawed Satanic Mumbo Jumbo, and it will also confirm that reasoning and vision have boundaries. If reasoning and vision have finite boundaries, He must have lied when, before the Council, He disclosed pictures His unbounded mind painted, and He must have also lied, when He audaciously stated: "I am the way and the truth and the life. No one comes to the Father except through me" (John 14:6).

"The first quality that is needed is audacity." Churchill

If the fellow told the truth before the Council, everything that is not aligned to John 14:6 is traveling in the wrong direction and heading straight for very hard rocks.

OYINBO ODE: IGNORANT DESCENDANTS OF RIGHTEOUS THIEVES – HABAKKUK.

Ignorance is bliss.

BORIS JOHNSON: Based on available evidence, the administration of English law is bastard, indiscreetly racist, unashamedly mediocre, vindictive, potently weaponised, and institutionally racist weapon of race and religious war – that is overseen by members of the Charitable Antichrist Racist Freemasonry Quasi-Religion (Mediocre Mafia/New Pharisees) – Habakkuk 1:4; John 8:44; John 10:10.

BORIS JOHNSON: The Negro is a foetus because what he can see is clearer than a dream, a prophesy, and a vision – combined – Acts 2:17.

BORIS JOHNSON: We are travelling in the wrong direction and heading straight for the rocks, and we are FORKED, as His Knights attacks Kings and Queens simultaneously, and only the Queens can move.

"It does no harm to throw the occasional man overboard, but it does not do much good if you are steering full speed ahead for the rocks." Sir Michael Havers (1923 – 1992)

CHAPTER THREE:

BORIS JOHNSON: Why is England not a scam?

BORIS JOHNSON: The Negro's mind is finer than the system you serve. We are not alone. It will be treachery not to uncover part of His face, and reveal the truth, which is that we are travelling in the wrong direction.

NIGERIA: SHELL'S DOCILE CASH COW.

Children with huge oil wells and gas fields near their huts eat only 1.5/day in NIGERIA; a closeted racist functional semi-illiterate former debt-collector Solicitor in NORWICH whose white mother and father have never seen crude oil, and whose white ancestors, including self-righteous John Bunyan, were fed like battery hens with the yields of stolen children of defenceless poor people (African ancestors of Meghan Markle and her white children) is our District Judge in Bedford.

OYINBO OLE: THIEVES – HABAKKUK.

Irrefutably superior skin colour that the wearer neither made nor chose, stolen trust fund, and what else?

Before SLAVERY, what?

The brain isn't skin colour; then, closeted racist bastards, directly and indirectly, robbed us with guns.

WHITE PRIVILEGE: The centuries-old unspoken myth that intellect is related to their irrefutably superior skin colour is the mother of all racist scams.

Facts are sacred; they cannot be overstated.

Those who shipped millions of guns to Africa during several continuous centuries (about 200,000 made in Birmingham guns annually) of the greediest economic cannibalism, and the evilest racist terrorism (in comparison, Nazi Holocaust was a storm in a tea cup) the world will ever know, among those who had no means of treating penetrative gunshot wounds and internal injuries, were not intelligent, and they were not enlightened, and they were not civilised, and they were not Christians; they were devils: Murderers and the fathers of racist lies – John 8:44.

"Many Scots masters were considered among the most brutal, with life expectancy on their plantations averaging a mere four years. We worked them to death then simply imported more to keep the sugar and thus the money flowing. Unlike centuries of grief and murder, an apology cost nothing. So, what does Scotland have to say?" Herald Scotland: Ian Bell, Columnist, Sunday 28 April 2013

"It was our arms in the river of Cameroon, put into the hands of the trader, that furnished him with the means of pushing his trade; and I have no more doubt that they are British arms, put into the hands of Africans, which promote universal war and desolation that I can doubt their having done so in that individual instance. I have shown how great is the enormity of this evil, even on the supposition that we take only convicts and prisoners of war. But take the subject in another way, and how does it stand? Think of 80,000 persons carried out of their native country by we know not what means! For crimes imputed! For light or inconsiderable faults! For debts perhaps! For crime of witchcraft! Or a thousand other weak or scandalous pretexts! Reflect on 80,000 persons annually taken off! There is something in the horror of it that surpasses all bounds of imagination." – Prime Minister William Pitt the Younger

The armed closeted racist bastards and arm-dealers were devils; they were greedier than the grave, and like death, they were never satisfied – Habakkuk 2:5.

"I know of no evil that has ever existed, nor can imagine any evil to exist, worse than the tearing of eighty thousand persons annually from their native land, by a combination of the most civilised nations inhabiting the most enlightened part of the globe, but more especially under the sanction of the laws of that Nation which calls herself the most free and the most happy of them all." Prime Minister William Pitt the Younger

If we are not very, very smart, why are we very, very rich?

Then, the closeted racist bastards fed their children with the yield of extreme violence; now, the direct descendants of the fathers of lies (John 8:44) feed their children with the yield of the mother of incompetent racist lies and Negrophobic Judicial Terrorism – Habakkuk 1:4; John 10:10.

GDC: A white man, Richard Hill fabricated reports and unrelentingly lied under oath: A dishonest racist.

GDC: A white man, Kevin Atkinson (NHS) unrelentingly lied under oath. A dishonest racist Scotchman.

GDC: A white man, Jonathan Martin unrelentingly lied on record. A dishonest racist Englishman

GDC: A white woman, Helen Falcon (MBE) unrelentingly lied on record. A dishonest racist cougar.

GDC: A white man, George Rothnie (NHS) unrelentingly lied on record. A dishonest racist Scotchman.

GDC: A white woman, Stephanie Twiddle (TD), unrelentingly lied under oath. A dishonest racist cougar.

GDC: A white woman, Sue Gregory (OBE) unrelentingly lied on record. A dishonest racist cougar.

GDC: A white woman, Rachael Bishop (Senior NHS Nurse) unrelentingly lied under oath. A dishonest racist cougar.

GDC: A white man, Geraint Evans (NHS) unrelentingly lied on record. A dishonest racist Welshman.

They hate our people with merciless racist venom; we know.
They persecute our people for the dark coat that we neither made nor chose and cannot change, and closeted racist bastards steal the yields of our Christ granted talents, and they impede our ascent from the bottomless crater into which their ancestors threw ours, in the African bush, during several centuries of the greediest economic cannibalism, and the evilest racist terrorism the world will ever know.

Based on very proximate observations and direct experiences, the white man is a devil and a thief – Habakkuk 1:4; John 8:44; John 10:10.

The foundation of their system is the mother of racist lies, and closeted racist bastards are direct descendants of the father of lies – John 8:44.

They were all white, including the Judges, and they were all incompetent racist liars.

"Lies are told all the time." Sir Michael Havers (1923 - 1992).

A bastardised, vindictive, potently weaponised, indiscreetly dishonest, unashamedly mediocre, and institutionally racist legal system that is overseen by the FREEMASONS (Mediocre Mafia/New Pharisees) - Habakkuk 1:4; John 8:44; John 10:10.

Closeted racist bastards want superiority, particularly intellectual superiority. They can have everything they want but only on merit, what's strong with that?

He doesn't like them, so He gave them the irrefutably superior skin colour, and in protest, the closeted racist bastards, the direct descendants of the father of lies used incompetent mother of racist lies and Judicial Terrorism to steal the yield of what He gave to others – John 8:44, Habakkuk.

Based on very proximate observations and direct experiences, the closeted racist bastards are wickeder than the devil, and they are as greedy as the grave and like death, they are never satisfied – Habakkuk 2:5.

"To deny or belittle this good is, in this dangerous century when the resources and pretensions of power continue to enlarge, a desperate error of intellectual abstraction. More than this, it is a self-fulfilling error, which encourages us to give up the struggle against bad laws and class bound procedures and to disarm ourselves before power. It is to throw away a whole inheritance of struggle about the law and within the forms of law, whose continuity can never be fractured without bringing men and women into immediate danger." - E. P Thompson.

They do not believe in His exceptionalism (John 14:6), and they do not believe in His Justice (John 5:22); we do.

If they are better than us, not only in terms of the irrefutable superior skin colour that they neither made nor chose, as they seem to believe, why do they steal the yield of our Christ granted talents with blatantly crude and cruel Judicial Terrorism?

OYINBO OLE: THIEVES - HABAKKUK

Based on very proximate observations, the white man is the devil; every other devil is a mere imitation (a fake).

The white man is the devil - Columbia University
https://ccnmtl.columbia.edu › mmt › mxp › concepts

Referring to Whites as "devils" originates with the teachings of Master W.D. Fard and the legend of Yakub. Fard taught Elijah Muhammad who preached the ...

Closeted racist bastards persecute our people for the dark coat we neither made nor chose, and cannot change, and they steal the yield of our Christ granted talent, and they mercilessly impede our ascent from the bottomless crater into which their sadistic ancestors threw ours, in the African bush, during several continuous centuries of the greediest economic cannibalism and the evilest racist terrorism the world will ever know - Habakkuk.

NEW HEROD, Matthew 2:16: They lied to their mentally very gentle children that they are geniuses, and they kill, albeit hands-off, all self-educated Africans who know they are brainless, closeted racist bastards.

Google: Dr Richard Bamgboye.

The intolerant lunatic bastard, a Jew, removed John's head only because he spoke; King Herod did not punish John for speaking, John was permanently prevented from speaking – Matthew 14.

He was lynched like Gadhafi, and crucified only because He spoke, He disclosed pictures His unbounded mind painted; had the intolerant lunatic bastards had guns, they would have shot him like Gadhafi. The only real Judge (John 5:22; Matthew 25: 31 - 46) was not punished for speaking, He was prevented from speaking.

Like Herod, Saddam Hussein, Putin, Kim, MBS, and babies, intolerant lunatic bastards expect everyone to love them unconditionally, and say and/or print only what they want to hear: Demigods.

Then, like the Jew (King Herod), Kim, and MBS, highly civilised, enlightened, Christian, and intolerant lunatic bastards used to butcher those who stated and/or printed what they did not like: The last decapitation of a human being, with an axe, in England, was in 1817, and beheading was removed from the Statute book in 1973.

"Of black men, the numbers are too great who are now repining." Dr Samuel Johnson

The DNA of their closeted racist system is the mother of incompetent racist lies guided and guarded by the direct descendants of the father of lies (John 8:44), Mediocre Mafia/New Pharisees who use very expensive aprons to decorate the temples of their powerless and useless fertility tools and lie that they don't lie – Psalm 144.

A bastardised, potently weaponised, vindictive, unashamedly mediocre, indiscreetly dishonest, and institutionally RACIST legal system that is overseen by the FREEMASONS – Habakkuk 1:4; John 8:44; John 10:10.

BORIS JOHNSON: Why is England not a scam?

OYINBO OLE: RACIST THIEVES - HABAKKUK

District Judge Paul Ayers of Bedford County Court, 3, St Paul's Square, Bedford, MK40 1SQ: He righteously sat on bones of stolen children of defenceless poor people (The African ancestors of Meghan Markle and her white children), more bones than the millions of skulls at the doorstep of Comrade Pol Pot, destroyed lives of innocent children yielded his court, future flats.

"I know of no evil that has ever existed, nor can imagine any evil to exist, worse than the tearing of eighty thousand persons annually from their native land, by a combination of the most civilised nations inhabiting the most enlightened part of the globe, but more especially under the sanction of the laws of that Nation which calls herself the most free and the most happy of them all." Prime Minister William Pitt the Younger

OYINBO OLE: STRAIGHT-FACED DESCENDANTS OF ULTRA-RIGHTEOUS THIEVES – HABAKKUK

"Many Scots masters were considered among the most brutal, with life expectancy on their plantations averaging a mere four years. We worked them to death then simply imported more to keep the sugar and thus the money flowing. Unlike centuries of grief and murder, an apology cost nothing. So, what does Scotland have to say?" Herald Scotland: Ian Bell, Columnist, Sunday 28 April 2013

OYINBO OLE: THIEVES – HABAKKUK.

It's plainly deductible that the white man was the devil.
'The white man is the devil' – what the Nation of Islam taught ...
https://www.independent.co.uk › World

5 Jun 2016 — In 1974, Muhammad Ali told Michael Parkinson and a stunned chat show audience that the white man of America was "the blue-eyed, blond-headed ...

Then, there were laws as there are laws now. Then, the yield of stolen children of defenceless poor people (the African ancestors of Meghan Markle and her white children) were used to build Magnificent Courts and pay wages of white Judges who sent white people who stole money to prisons built with the yield of stolen lives – Habakkuk.

The child sister (100% genetic Nigerian) has since gained a First-Class Science Degree, with Honours, from one of the topmost Universities in the UK, and she's gainfully engaged, batting for her Country.

BORIS JOHNSON: Why is the Negro not a patriot?

Ohun ti a kii nta lo ja ni omo eru kii je.

What they want for our children is very different from what we want for our children; what they want for their children is very different from what they want for our children.

OYINBO OLE: THIEVES – HABAKKUK.

"White supremacy is real, and it needs to be shattered." Dr Cornel West

Christ saved the child's sister from the evil clutches of the Charitable, Antichrist, Closeted Racist members of the Freemasonry Quasi-Religion (Mediocre Mafia/New Pharisees) - Habakkuk 1:4; John 8:44; John 10:10.

It's plainly deductible that all the white children of District Judge Paul Ayers of Bedford County Court, 3, St Paul's Square, MK40 1SQ, the white Senior Vice President of the Association of Her Majesty's District Judges were less favoured by Almighty God, certainly intellectually - OECD.

"Racism is rife throughout most organisations across Britain." The Mayor of London

"Someone must be trusted. Let it be the Judges." Lord Denning

Judges are human beings. Some human beings are racists.

Facts are sacred.

https://www.youtube.com/watch? v=BlpH4hG7m1A.

The closeted racist former debt-collector white Solicitor in Norwich, District Judge Paul Ayers of Bedford County Court, 3, St Paul's Square Bedford, MK401SQ, the Senior Vice President of the Association of Her Majesty's District Judges, should be asked to bring out all his own white children and white grandchildren, if he agrees, they should be asked to handwrite short essays, if they agree and could write legibly, Dr Richard Dawkins and OECD implied that all his white children and white grandchildren should be mentally gentler than their closeted racist, functional semi-illiterate, high ranking Freemason, white father.

Before SLAVERY, what?

OYINBO OLE: THIEVES – HABAKKUK.

"The fact is, that civilisation requires slaves. The Greeks were quite right there. Unless there are slaves to do the ugly, horrible, uninteresting work, culture and contemplation become almost impossible. Human slavery is wrong, insecure, and demoralising......" Wilde

CREEPING DPRK.

The ancestors of Kim did not kidnap and imprison all the people of North Korea, body, and mind, overnight, they did gradually, and the basic right to disclose pictures painted by the mind was the first to be withdrawn.
"Natural selection will not remove ignorance from future generations." Dr Richard Dawkins.

England's young people are near the bottom of the global league table for basic skills. OECD finds 16- to 24-year-olds have literacy and numeracy levels no better than those of their grandparents' generation.

England is the only country in the developed world where the generation approaching retirement is more literate and numerate than the youngest adults, according to the first skills survey by the Organisation for Economic Co-operation and Development.

In a stark assessment of the success and failure of the 720-million-strong adult workforce across the wealthier economies, the economic thinktank warns that in England, adults aged 55 to 65 perform better than 16- to 24-year-olds at foundation levels of literacy and numeracy. The survey did not include people from Scotland or Wales.

The OECD study also finds that a quarter of adults in England have the maths skills of a 10-year-old. About 8.5 million adults, 24.1% of the population, have such basic levels of numeracy that they can manage only one-step tasks in arithmetic, sorting numbers or reading graphs. This is worse than the average in the developed world, where an average of 19% of people were found to have a similarly poor skill base.

PERCEPTION IS GRANDER THAN REALITY.

They are not the only creation of Almighty God, and they are not immortal, and the irrefutably superior skin colour that they neither made nor chose is not the only wonder of our world - Habakkuk.

NORTHAMPTON, ENGLAND: Based on available evidence, GDC-WITNESS, Dr Geraint Evans, Postgraduate Tutor, Oxford, unrelentingly lied under implied oath - Habakkuk 1:4; John 8:44; John 10:10.

A RACIST CROOK. A DISHONEST WHITE MAN.

Based on available evidence, English law is equal; its administration is not.

"Why kill white babies in South Africa, because when they grow up, they will oppress black children." Dr Khalid Mohammed (1948 – 2001)

In the same analogy as that of Dr Khalid Mohammed, closeted racist bastards impose inferior educational culture on our children in order to make it easy for their children to oppress ours in the future.

Closeted racist bastards are more familiar with the descendants of plantation Negroes (Africans of Caribbean extraction): Descendants of stolen human beings who were unnaturally selected, genetically reversed, artificially paired up, bred for labour, and reared like cattle on the stolen plantations of highly civilised, enlightened, and Christian Europeans.

Percentage of children in the UK hitting educational targets at 5, in descending order:
1. Asian (Indian)
2. Asian (Any other Asian)
3. White (British)
4. White (Irish)
5. Mixed (any other)
6. Mixed (white and black African)
7. Chinese
8. Mixed (White and black Caribbean)
9. Black (African heritage)

10. Asian (Any other Asian)
11. Black (Caribbean heritage)
12. Black (other)
13. Asian (Bangladeshi)
14. White (Any other white)
15. Any other ethnic group
16. Asian (Pakistani)
17. White (Traveller of Irish heritage)
18. White (Gypsy/ Roma)
Source: Centre Forum, Daily Mail, 04.04.2016

Children in the UK hitting educational targets at 16, in descending order:
1. Chinese
2. Asian (Indian)
3. Asian (Any other Asian)
4. Mixed (White and Asian)
5. White (Irish)
6. Mixed (Any other)
7. Any other ethnic group
8. Asian (Bangladeshi)
9. Parent/pupil preferred not to say
10. Mixed (White and black African)
11. White (Any other white)
12. Black (African heritage)
13. White (British)
14. Asian (Pakistani)
15. Black (other)
16. Mixed (White and black Caribbean)
17. Black (Caribbean heritage)

18. White (Traveller of Irish heritage)
19. White (Gypsy/ Roma)
Source: Centre Forum, Daily Mail, 04.04.2016

Genetic damage is the most enduring residue of several centuries of European Christians' sadistic commerce in millions of stolen children of defenceless poor people (Black African ancestors of Meghan Markle and her white children) - Habakkuk.

Based on very proximate observations and direct experiences, the white man is the devil.

Facts are sacred; they cannot be overstated.

Based on available evidence, when their people commit racist crimes against our people, closeted racist bastards who oversee the administration of their law (FREEMASONS) criminally bury RACIAL HATRED – Habakkuk 1:4; John 8:44; John 10:10.

Only stupid Negroes do not know that white Judges measure white people with a very, very different yardstick, and only stupider Negroes expect demons to cast out demons – Matthew 12:27.
"Sometimes people don't want to hear the truth because they don't want their illusions destroyed." Friedrich Nietzsche

******

A NEGRO'S TWEETS:

GDC: A white man, Richard Hill (NHS) unrelentingly fabricated reports

OYINBO OLE: A RIGHTEOUS DESCENDANT OF ULTRA-RIGHTEOUS THIEVES—HABAKKUK

"The best opportunity of developing academically and emotional." District Judge Paul Ayers of Bedford County Court, 3, St Paul's Square, Bedford, MK40 1SQ, the Senior Vice President of the Association of Her Majesty's District Judges.

Our semi-illiterate Freemason Judge of our Empire of stolen affluence

GDC: A white man, Richard Hill (NHS) lied under oath

OYINBO OLE: A RIGHTEOUS DESCENDANT OF ULTRA-RIGHTEOUS THIEVES—HABAKKUK

"The best opportunity of developing academically and emotional." District Judge Paul Ayers of Bedford County Court, 3, St Paul's Square, Bedford, MK40 1SQ, the Senior Vice President of the Association of Her Majesty's District Judges.

Our semi-illiterate Freemason Judge of our Empire of stolen affluence

GDC: A white man, Kevin Atkinson (NHS)unrelentingly lied under oath

OYINBO OLE: A RIGHTEOUS DESCENDANT OF ULTRA-RIGHTEOUS THIEVES—HABAKKUK

"The best opportunity of developing academically and emotional." District Judge Paul Ayers of Bedford County Court, 3, St Paul's Square, Bedford, MK40 1SQ, the Senior Vice President of the Association of Her Majesty's District Judges.

Our semi-illiterate Freemason Judge of our Empire of stolen affluence

GDC: A white man, Jonathan Martin unrelentingly lied on record

OYINBO OLE: A RIGHTEOUS DESCENDANT OF ULTRA-RIGHTEOUS THIEVES—HABAKKUK

"The best opportunity of developing academically and emotional." District Judge Paul Ayers of Bedford County Court, 3, St Paul's Square, Bedford, MK40 1SQ, the Senior Vice President of the Association of Her Majesty's District Judges.

Our semi-illiterate Freemason Judge of our Empire of stolen affluence

GDC: A white woman, Helen Falcon (MBE) unrelentingly lied on record

OYINBO OLE: A RIGHTEOUS DESCENDANT OF ULTRA-RIGHTEOUS THIEVES—HABAKKUK

"The best opportunity of developing academically and emotional." District Judge Paul Ayers of Bedford County Court, 3, St Paul's Square, Bedford, MK40 1SQ, the Senior Vice President of the Association of Her Majesty's District Judges.

Our semi-illiterate Freemason Judge of our Empire of stolen affluence

GDC: A white man, George Rothnie (NHS)unrelentingly lied on record

OYINBO OLE: A RIGHTEOUS DESCENDANT OF ULTRA-RIGHTEOUS THIEVES—HABAKKUK

"The best opportunity of developing academically and emotional." District Judge Paul Ayers of Bedford County Court, 3, St Paul's Square, Bedford, MK40 1SQ, the Senior

Vice President of the Association of Her Majesty's District Judges.

Our semi-illiterate Freemason Judge of our Empire of stolen affluence

GDC: A white woman, Stephanie Twidale (NHS) unrelentingly lied under oath

OYINBO OLE: A RIGHTEOUS DESCENDANT OF ULTRA-RIGHTEOUS THIEVES—HABAKKUK

"The best opportunity of developing academically and emotional." District Judge Paul Ayers of Bedford County Court, 3, St Paul's Square, Bedford, MK40 1SQ, the Senior Vice President of the Association of Her Majesty's District Judges.

Our semi-illiterate Freemason Judge of our Empire of stolen affluence

GDC: A white woman, Sue Gregory (OBE) unrelentingly lied on record

OYINBO OLE: A RIGHTEOUS DESCENDANT OF ULTRA-RIGHTEOUS THIEVES—HABAKKUK

"The best opportunity of developing academically and emotional." District Judge Paul Ayers of Bedford County Court, 3, St Paul's Square, Bedford, MK40 1SQ, the Senior

Vice President of the Association of Her Majesty's District
Judges.

Our semi-illiterate Freemason Judge of our Empire of
stolen affluence

GDC: A white woman, Rachael Bishop
(NHS)unrelentingly lied under oath

OYINBO OLE: A RIGHTEOUS DESCENDANT OF
ULTRA-RIGHTEOUS THIEVES—HABAKKUK

"The best opportunity of developing academically and
emotional." District Judge Paul Ayers of Bedford County
Court, 3, St Paul's Square, Bedford, MK40 1SQ, the Senior
Vice President of the Association of Her Majesty's District
Judges.

Our semi-illiterate Freemason Judge of our Empire of
stolen affluence

GDC: A white man, Geraint Evans (NHS) unrelentingly
lied on record

OYINBO OLE: A RIGHTEOUS DESCENDANT OF
ULTRA-RIGHTEOUS THIEVES—HABAKKUK

"The best opportunity of developing academically and emotional." District Judge Paul Ayers of Bedford County Court, 3, St Paul's Square, Bedford, MK40 1SQ, the Senior Vice President of the Association of Her Majesty's District Judges.

Our semi-illiterate Freemason Judge of our Empire of stolen affluence

******

"Time for Scots to say sorry for slavery

Herald Scotland:
Ian Bell, Columnist / Sunday 28 April 2013 / Opinion
Sunday 28 April 2013
According to the American founding father, the son of a Caithness Kirk minister had about him "an air of great simplicity and honesty'". The likes of James Boswell and Laurence Sterne also enjoyed the merchant's company. To his contemporaries, he was, as the author Adam Hochschild has written, '"a wise, thoughtful man who embodied the Scottish virtues of frugality, sobriety, and hard work'". Oswald was a scholar of theology, philosophy, and history. He collected art, particularly Rubens and Rembrandt, and gave handsomely to charity. Oswald, who learned his trade in Glasgow, also represented Britain in negotiations with the Americans after their war of liberation. He was the cosmopolitan epitome of Enlightenment success. But when he wasn't busy with good works, Oswald waded in blood. The precise number of deaths that can be laid at his door is

impossible to calculate. As the leading figure in Grant, Oswald & Co, he had investments in each corner of the "'triangular trade'". In his own name, Oswald trafficked at least 13,000 Africans, although he never set foot on their continent. By the time he bought Auchincruive House and 100,000 acres in Ayrshire in 1764, he was worth £500,000. Writing in 2005, Hochschild thought this was "'roughly equivalent'" to $68 million (about £44m). This is conservative.

Oswald was remarkable, but not unique. Where Glasgow and its merchants in sugar, tobacco, and human life are concerned, there are plenty of names and no shortage of monuments: Dennistoun, Campbell, Glassford, Cochrane, Buchanan, Hamilton, Bogle, Ewing, Donald, Speirs, Dunlop. One way to understand what they wrought is simple: take pleasure in the city's architecture today and you are likely to be admiring the fruits of slavery. Glasgow is not alone in that. London, Liverpool and Bristol also have their stories to tell. Edinburgh's once-great banks grew from foundations built on bones. The first Scottish venture into slavery set out from the capital in 1695. Montrose, Dumfries, Greenock and Port Glasgow each tried their hands. In the language of the present age, they were all in it together.

When commerce was coursing around the triangle, most of polite Scotland was implicated. The nobility (and country) rendered bankrupt in 1700 in the aftermath of the Darien Venture was by the mid-1760s contemplating big elegant townhouses and 100,000-acre estates. You could call that a reversal of fortune. Contrary to self-serving myth, it did not happen because of "'frugality, sobriety, and hard work'".

Certain things need to be remembered about Scotland and slavery. One is that the mercantile class got stinking rich twice over: despite fortunes made from stolen lives, they were quick to demand compensation when slavery was ended in 1833. Britain's government decided that £20m, a staggering sum, could be raised. In his 2010 book, The Price of Emancipation, Nicholas Draper reckons Glasgow's mob got £400,000 – in modern terms, hundreds of millions. Compensation cases also demonstrated that Scots were not merely following an English lead. According to Draper, a country with 10% of the British population accounted for at least 15% of absentee slavers. By another estimate, 30% of Jamaican plantations were run by Scots. For all the pride taken in the abolitionist societies of Glasgow and Edinburgh, the slave-holders did not suffer because of abolition. They were '"compensated"'.

And that wasn't the worst of it. Thanks to Hollywood movies, the slave economy of the American South is still taken as barbarism's benchmark. Few realise that the behaviour of Scots busy getting rich in the slave-holders'' empire was actually worse – routinely worse – than the worst of the cottonocracy. You need only count the corpses……………."

OYINBO OLE: THIEVES – HABAKKUK

Based on available evidence, the white man was the devil.

"Of black men, the numbers are too great who are now repining under English cruelty." Dr Samuel Johnson

Facts are sacred.

We must all align with the belief of the Defenders of Faiths (Dissenters of John 14:6), or be subservient to their Mumbo Jumbo Quasi-Religion, or else we will be destroyed by their huge network of closeted white supremacist thugs; they are more intolerant than lunatic Jihadists, and they are everywhere, and they control almost everything, and they are not deterred by His Justice (John 5:22) because they do not believe in His exceptionalism (John 14:6).

White Privilege: Closeted racist bastards love the enormous advantage that automatically comes with the irrefutably superior skin colour that they neither made nor chose, their brainless and baseless birth right, but they do not love Freedom of Expression because they do not want their mentally very gentle children to know that they are excessively stupid, and they don't want their simpler wards to know the truth, which is that their white ancestors were racists, devils, owners of stolen children of defenceless poor people (the African ancestors of Meghan Markle and her white children), and professional thieves - Habakkuk.

OYINBO OLE: RIGHTEOUS DESCENDANTS OF PROFESSIONAL THIEVES – HABAKKUK.

"Freedom of Expression is the cornerstone of our democracy." The Right Honourable Jacob Rees-Mogg.

"Freedom of Expression is a basic right." Lady Hale

Facts are sacred.

"It does no harm to throw the occasional man overboard, but it does not do much good if you are steering full speed ahead for the rocks." Sir Ian Gilmour (1926 – 2007).

CHAPTER FOUR:

Boris Johnson: Why is England not a scam?

They (FREEMASONS) control everything except the intellect.

The good shepherd was lynched like Gadhafi, and He was crucified only because He disclosed pictures His unbounded mind painted. He was not punished for speaking, He was prevented from speaking. They were not His sheep, and they didn't hear His voice, and they didn't listen to Him – John 10

For shepherds (FREEMASONS) to control their sheep, and for sheep to obey their shepherds, the sheep must believe that shepherds have the supreme knowledge, and anyone who interferes with the brainless and baseless arrangement between shepherd and sheep will be destroyed.

NEW HEROD, MATTHEW 2:16: Shepherds deceive sheep that they are geniuses who have the supreme knowledge, and they kill all those who know that they are brainless racist bastards.

FREEMASONS: Closeted white supremacist thugs want a world where everything is primarily subservient to the irrefutably superior skin colour that the very fortunate wearer neither made nor chose, and where those with the superior skin colour are graded according to the vulgar

127

embroidery on the very expensive aprons, they use to decorate their powerless and useless fertility tools.

BORIS JOHNSON: Defenders of Faiths (Dissenters of John 14:6): Freemasons brainlessly and baselessly awarded themselves the supreme knowledge, and anything that is aligned to their voodoo religion must be inferior to it, and everything that is not aligned to their Satanic Mumbo Jumbo – will be destroyed by their huge network. Their people are everywhere, and they control almost everything, and they lie that the don't lie – Psalm 144.

Vulgar Pharisees' charitable works in exchange for what?

BORIS JOHNSON: Theirs is a satanic bribe, and it is not a good deal; then, the grandest satanic bribe of their ruler was rejected – Matthew 4:9.

"Masonry ought forever to be abolished. It is wrong - essentially wrong - a seed of evil which can never produce any good." President John Quincy Adams (1767 – 1848).

C of E raises serious concerns about Christian Freemasons
https://www.theguardian.com › uk-news › feb › c-of-e-...

8 Feb 2018 — **Church of England** warning that secret society may not be compatible with Christianity echoes concerns from 1987.

BORIS JOHNSON: Give us the legal tools, and we will deal with the charitable closeted white supremacist thugs and anarchist who use very expensive aprons to decorate the temples of their powerless and useless fertility tools.

The very, very, shallow closeted white supremacist thugs and anarchists see molecules, we will show them atoms.

"The supreme vice is shallowness." Wilde

They are not the only creation of Almighty God, and they are not immortal, and their irrefutably superior skin colour is not the only wonder of our world.

Then, the indiscreetly white thugs were wickeder than the devil, and greedier than the grave, and like death, the sadistic racist bastards were never satisfied—Habakkuk 2:5.

OYINBO OLE: THIEVES - HABAKKUK

Then, the greediest economic cannibals and the meanness racist terrorists the world will ever know, carried and sold millions of stolen children of defenceless poor people (Meghan Markle's African ancestors); now, they carry natural resources.

SUBSTITUTION IS FRAUDULENT EMANCIPATION.

"Moderation is a virtue only among those who are thought to have found alternatives." Henry Kissinger.

"Jews are very good with money." President Donald Trump

Whose money?

Judas Iscariot, King Herod, Bernard Madoff, and Ján Ludvík Hyman Binyamin Hoch (Ghislaine Maxwell's father).

OYINBO OLE: THIEVES – HABAKKUK.

GDC: A white man, Richard Hill (NHS) fabricated reports and unrelentingly lied under oath. If there is irrefutable evidence that one's white ancestors were THIEVES and owners of stolen children of defenceless poor people (African ancestors of Meghan Markle and her white children) it will be naïve not to expect RACIAL HATRED complicated by incompetent mendacity to be part of one's genetic inheritances. OYINBO OLE: A WHITE CROOK-HABAKKUK.

GDC: A white man, Kevin Atkinson (NHS) unrelentingly lied under oath. If there is irrefutable evidence that one's white ancestors were THIEVES and owners of stolen children of defenceless poor people (African ancestors of Meghan Markle and her white children) it will be naïve not to expect RACIAL HATRED complicated by incompetent mendacity to be part of one's genetic inheritances. OYINBO OLE: A WHITE CROOK- HABAKKUK.

GDC: A white woman, Helen Falcon (MBE) unrelentingly lied on record. If there is irrefutable evidence that one's white ancestors were THIEVES and owners of stolen children of defenceless poor people (African ancestors of Meghan Markle and her white children) it will be naïve not to expect RACIAL HATRED complicated by incompetent mendacity to be part of one's genetic inheritances. OYINBO OLE: A WHITE CROOK- HABAKKUK.

GDC: A white man, George Rothnie (NHS) unrelentingly lied on record. If there is irrefutable evidence that one's white ancestors were THIEVES and owners of stolen children of defenceless poor people (African ancestors of Meghan Markle and her white children) it will be naïve not to expect RACIAL HATRED complicated by incompetent mendacity to be part of one's genetic inheritances. OYINBO OLE: A WHITE CROOK- HABAKKUK.

GDC: A white woman, Stephanie Twiddle (TD), British Soldier – Territorial Defence, lied under oath. If there is irrefutable evidence that one's white ancestors were THIEVES and owners of stolen children of defenceless poor people (African ancestors of Meghan Markle and her white children) it will be naïve not to expect RACIAL HATRED complicated by incompetent mendacity to be part of one's genetic inheritances. OYINBO OLE: A WHITE CROOK- HABAKKUK.

GDC: A white woman, Sue Gregory (OBE) unrelentingly lied on record. If there is irrefutable evidence that one's white ancestors were THIEVES and owners of stolen children of defenceless poor people (African ancestors of Meghan Markle and her white children) it will be naïve not to expect RACIAL HATRED complicated by incompetent mendacity to be part of one's genetic inheritances. OYINBO OLE: A WHITE CROOK- HABAKKUK.

GDC: A white woman, Rachael Bishop (NHS) unrelentingly lied under oath. If there is irrefutable evidence that one's white ancestors were THIEVES and owners of stolen children of defenceless poor people (African ancestors of Meghan Markle and her white children) it will be naïve not to expect RACIAL HATRED complicated by incompetent mendacity to be part of one's genetic inheritances. OYINBO OLE: A WHITE CROOK- HABAKKUK.

GDC: A white man, Geraint Evans (NHS) unrelentingly lied on record. If there is irrefutable evidence that one's white ancestors were THIEVES and owners of stolen children of defenceless poor people (African ancestors of Meghan Markle and her white children) it will be naïve not to expect RACIAL HATRED complicated by incompetent mendacity to be part of one's genetic inheritances. OYINBO OLE: A WHITE CROOK- HABAKKUK.

OYINBO OLE: RIGHTEOUS DESCENDANTS OF ULTRA-RIGHTEOUS THIEVES – HABAKKUK.

Closeted racist bastards want superiority, He doesn't like them, so He gave them the irrefutably superior skin colour, and in protest, they used Judicial Terrorism to steal what He gave to Africans. They are not deterred by His Justice (John 5:22; Matthew 25: 31-46) because they do not believe in His exceptionalism (John 14:6).

Facts are sacred, they cannot be overstated,

"The highest reach of injustice is to be deemed just when you are not." Plato

Facts are sacred; they cannot be overstated.

"I don't think anyone will dispute that lots and lots of people are denied Justice." Sir David Napley (1915 – 1994).

FREEMASONS: A properly organised racist crime syndicate impersonates impartial administrators of English Law. Dissenters of John 14:6 and Defenders of Faiths are not deterred by His Justice (John 5:22) because they do not believe in His exceptionalism (John 14:6).

The closeted racist bastards were all white, including the Judges, and they were all racists and incompetent liars.

The closeted racist bastards stalk our people (Africans) like prey, and they hunt in packs.

133

They are not the only creation of Almighty God, and they are not immortal, and the irrefutably superior skin colour that they neither made nor chose is not the only wonder of our world.

If they know what we truly feel, and say behind their backs, the closeted racist bastards will kill us, albeit hands-off.

NEW HEROD, MATTHEW 2:16: They deceive their mentally very gentle children that they are geniuses, and they kill all those who know that they are brainless racist bastards.

CREEPING DPRK.

There is Freedom of Expression in DPRK, there one is free to say and/or print only what Kim wants to hear.

True feeling rarely discloses its intentions, so it shuns display – Lord Byron paraphrased.

Had Nikolai Ceausescu realised what Romanians truly felt, he would have dealt with them, so when he was cornered and summarily dealt with, millions of his enemies believed he deserved it.

"If a sovereign oppresses his people to a great degree, they will rise and cut off his head. There is a remedy in human nature against tyranny, that will keep us safe under every form of government." Dr Samuel Johnson

Christ does not place Africans in the back row, white men do.

"The truth allows no choice." Dr Samuel Johnson

-----Original Message-----
From: George Rothnie <georgerothnie@hotmail.com>
To: adeolacole@aol.com
Sent: Mon, 8 Mar 2010 20:19
Subject: Re Meeting 9th March

Hi Ola,

We are scheduled to meet tomorrow evening at my surgery about 5.30ish.
Unfortunately something has cropped up which necessytates me having to
postpone the meeting. I'm really sorry it's such short notice.

I will contact you in the week to arrange another date.

Once agaim my apologies.

George

AN IMBECILE: AN ADULT WITH THE BASIC SKILLS OF A CHILD.

Irrefutably superior skin colour that the very fortunate wearer neither made nor chose seemed to conceal dark black brain.

An ignorant descendant of WHITE THIEVES and owners of stolen children of defenceless poor people (African ancestors of Meghan Markle and her white children) - Habakkuk

Edinburgh University Educated Dr George Rothnie, Deputy Postgraduate Dean, Oxford, within one of the dullest adult populations in the industrialised world (the least literate and the least numerate) - OECD.

"Natural selection will not remove ignorance from future generations." Dr Richard Dawkins

"Sometimes people don't want to hear the truth because they don't want their illusions destroyed." Friedrich Nietzsche.

The report, by the OECD, warns that the UK needs to take significant action to boost the basic skills of the nation's young people. The 460-page study is based on the first-ever survey of the literacy, numeracy and problem-solving at work skills of 16 to 65-year-olds in 24 countries, with almost 9,000 people taking part in England and Northern Ireland to make up the UK results. The findings showed that England and Northern Ireland have some of the highest proportions of adults scoring no higher than Level

1 in literacy and numeracy - the lowest level on the OECD's scale. This suggests that their skills in the basics are no better than that of a 10-year-old.

AN IMBECILE: AN ADULT WITH THE BASIC SKILLS OF A CHILD.

BORIS JOHNSON: Let me tell you, and based on very proximate observations and direct experiences, privileged dullards who believed that daily dialogues with IMBECILES was a worthwhile, meaty manly job were scammers, and those who demanded and accepted valuable consideration in exchange for daily dialogues with IMBECILES were racketeers (thieves).

Natural selection was decommissioned, and retrogressively, Nuclear Bombs are used to guard the continuing propagation of adults with the basic skills of a child, those who natural selection would have decommissioned had it not been decommissioned.

"Natural selection will not remove ignorance from future generations." Dr Richard Dawkins
"We have decommissioned natural selection and must now look deep within ourselves and decide what we wish to become." Dr Edward O Wilson

WHITE PRIVILEGE: Closeted racist bastards love the gigantic advantage that comes with the irrefutably superior skin colour that they neither made nor chose; they don't love Freedom of Expression because they don't want their mentally very gentle children to know that they are innately (hereditary) very, very dull, and excessively stupid – Habakkuk 1:4; John 8:44; John 10:10.

"Why, Sir, Sherry is dull, naturally dull; but it must have taken him a great deal of pains to become what we now see him. Such an excess of stupidity, Sir, is not in Nature." Dr Samuel Johnson

Adults with the basic skills of a foetus will succeed adults with the basic skill of a child (IMBECILES), and the former will need only food and shelter, not very, very expensive administration of the law – Habakkuk 1:4; John 8:44; John 10:10.

Then, the successors of Boris Johnson will guard the continuing propagation of the successors of hereditary imbeciles (adults with the basic skills of a foetus) with sticks and stones.

"I do not know with what weapons World War III will be fought, but World War IV will be fought with sticks and stones." – Albert Einstein.

******

RE: Outstanding statutory annual registration fee invoice: payment due – FINAL REMINDER
Thu, 3 Sep 2015 20:00
cqc (NHS SHARED BUSINESS SERVICES LTD (BRISTOL)) (SBS-B.cqc@nhs.net)To:you Details

Hello,

Thank you for your below email

Kindly request you to provide your contact details (telephone number) so we can contact you and explain.

If any query please let me know

Thanks and Regards,

Kanchan Jaisinghani

Collections
Debt Management Team

Shared Business Services

Tel 0303-123-1155

Fax 0117-933-8890

E-mail: sbs-b.cqc@nhs.net

Website: www.sbs.nhs.uk

Government Business Award Winner

Central Government Supplier of the Year 2011.

AN IMBECILE: AN ADULT WITH THE BASIC
SKILLS OF A CHILD.

"I think I will ask our legal adviser for any advice he may have. My view is that there are six or seven of us here who had the admission down, but we cannot find it in the transcript and there is wordings that imply that there was, but it is not in black and white ….." Shiv Pabary, Member of the Most Excellent Order of our Empire (MBE) and Justice of Peace (JP).

AN IMBECILE: AN ADULT WITH THE BASIC SKILLS OF A CHILD.

MMBE: Mediocre Member of our Empire.
JIRL: Justice of Incompetent Racist Lies.

His cousins go to the bush to defecate in Punjab, here, he is 'somebody'.

Based on very proximate observations and direct experiences, the Indian is happy with every position underneath very beautiful white women, if white men place him above all Negroes in the pecking order.

"One witness at a Royal Commission in 1897 said the ambition of Indians in Trinidad was 'to buy a cow, then a shop, and say: "We are no Niggers to work in cane fields." Patrick French, The World Is What It Is: The Authorized Biography of V.S Naipaul

Five years earlier, in 1892, after several centuries of the greediest economic cannibalism and the evilest racist terrorism the world will ever know, racist white bastards, and the naked Muslims they found in the African bush, tamed, and armed, - returned to our tribe in the African

140

bush, Ijebu, only a walking distance from the Atlantic Ocean, and they, mercilessly, used heavy guns, on wheels, to sadistically slaughter almost everyone in our tribe, and they evicted our King (The Awujale of Ijebu Kingdom) from his palace and converted it to their Garrison, and in 1893, many pretty Ijebu girls, including beautiful children, gave birth to Mulattos.

Libidinous European Christians were sex machine in the African bush; they were inter-racial rapists. The libidinous racist white bastards (sex machines) were greedier than the grave and like death, they were never satisfied – Habakkuk 2:5.

GOOGLE: IMAGBON 1892.

SHIV PABARY: They find a very, very dull, and incompetently mendacious Indian, and they adorn him with very, very high titles, and he becomes Freemasons' zombie private soldier (IRA of Sinn Fein).

Prince Charles wants to shake up honours system when he ...
https://www.dailymail.co.uk › news › article-2933738

30 Jan 2015 — Charles wants to shake up honours: Gongs are handed out 'to the wrong people for the wrong reasons' ... Prince Charles will demand a total ...

BORIS JOHNSON: Legalise the disclosure of all truths, including all true pictures minds paint, and we will uncover their centuries-old Satanic Mumbo Jumbo. We will show closeted racist bastards who use very expensive aprons to decorate the temples of their powerless and useless fertility tools, and lie that they don't lie (Psalm 144), and who see molecules, atoms.

BORIS JOHNSON: Believe me, any adult who does not recognise Satanic Mumbo Jumbo when she sees one is an imbecile.

Closeted white supremacists who use very, very expensive aprons to decorate the temples of their powerless and useless fertility tools are psychologically and intellectually insecure: They kill all those who disagree with them. Dr Rowan Williams appointed a Freemason as a Bishop.

Freemasons fear truths more than Putin's poisons.

"There is not a truth existing which I fear or would wish unknown to the whole world." Thomas Jefferson

BORIS JOHNSON: "Give us the tools, and we will finish the job." Churchill

BRAINLESS NONSENSE: White Judges are geniuses, and they are superhuman, they cannot tell lies, and they cannot be racists.

"All sections of the UK Society are institutionally racist."
Sir Bernard Hogan-Howe.

The Judiciary is part of the UK Society.

"Lies are told all the time." Sir Michael Havers (1923 – 1992).

Then, there, White Judges, nearly all, were devout Christians, closeted white supremacists, and FREEMASONS (Mediocre Mafia/New Pharisees); some of them were THICKER than a gross of planks – Habakkuk 1:4; John 8:44; John 10:10.

https://www.youtube.com/watch?v=BlpH4hG7m1A

Why should the white mother and father of District Judge Paul Ayers of Bedford County Court, 3, St Paul's Square, MK 40 1SQ, the Senior Vice President of the Association of Her Majesty's District Judges, need very, very strong views about education if there is irrefutable evidence that the white ancestors of his white mother and father were ultra-righteous WHITE PROFESSIONAL THIEVES and owners of stolen children of defenceless poor people (Black African ancestors of Meghan Markle and her white children) – Habakkuk?

OYINBO OLE: THIEVES – HABAKKUK.

Ignorance is bliss.

Facts are sacred.

They want superiority, their brainless and baseless birth right, but they don't want Freedom of Expression because they don't want their mentally very gentle children to know that they are excessively stupid, and that their white ancestors were THIEVES and owners of stolen children of defenceless poor people (Black African ancestors Meghan Markle and her white children) - Habakkuk.

Percentage of children in the UK hitting educational targets at 5, in descending order:
1. Asian (Indian)
2. Asian (Any other Asian)
3. White (British)
4. White (Irish)
5. Mixed (any other)
6. Mixed (white and black African)
7. Chinese
8. Mixed (White and black Caribbean)
9. Black (African heritage)
10. Asian (Any other Asian)
11. Black (Caribbean heritage)
12. Black (other)
13. Asian (Bangladeshi)
14. White (Any other white)
15. Any other ethnic group
16. Asian (Pakistani)
17. White (Traveller of Irish heritage)
18. White (Gypsy/ Roma)
Source: Centre Forum, Daily Mail, 04.04.2016

Children in the UK hitting educational targets at 16, in descending order:

1. Chinese
2. Asian (Indian)
3. Asian (Any other Asian)
4. Mixed (White and Asian)
5. White (Irish)
6. Mixed (Any other)
7. Any other ethnic group
8. Asian (Bangladeshi)
9. Parent/pupil preferred not to say
10. Mixed (White and black African)
11. White (Any other white)
12. Black (African heritage)
13. White (British)
14. Asian (Pakistani)
15. Black (other)
16. Mixed (White and black Caribbean)
17. Black (Caribbean heritage)
18. White (Traveller of Irish heritage)
19. White (Gypsy/ Roma)

Source: Centre Forum, Daily Mail, 04.04.2016

Facts are sacred; the truth cannot be overstated.

The closeted racist white supremacist thugs who use very expensive aprons to vulgarly draw attention to, and decorate, temples of their powerless and useless fertility tools – are more familiar with the descendants of plantation Negroes (Africans of Caribbean extraction): Descendants of stolen children (African ancestors of Meghan Markle and her white children) who were unnaturally selected, genetically reversed, artificially paired up, bred for labour, and reared like cattle on stolen Indian land - Habakkuk.

If Yellow People (Chinese Ethnic Group) who were first on the list of those meeting academic targets at age 16 were granted Freedom of Choice, they would not allow members of the so called White British Ethnic Group (Descendants of Genetic Aliens (undocumented refugees from Eastern Europe), with camouflage English names) to have a say in the education of their Yellow Children, why should NIGERIANS (Africans) who were above White British ethnic group on the list of those meeting academic targets at age 16, allow a White Gypsy District Judge of our Empire of Stolen Affluence, whose ethnic group, White Gypsy/Roma, were last on the list of those meeting academic targets at age 16, to impose an inferior educational culture on their genetically NIGERIAN child?

Genetic damage is the most enduring residue of several centuries of highly civilised and enlightened Europeans' barbarously racist traffic in millions of stolen children of defenceless poor people (Meghan Markle's ancestors) - Habakkuk.

"By definition therefore there needs to be a contact order for Mr B so that he knows when he is going to see his son. It is absolutely essential that this occurs and mother agrees with that. She said so several times in her evidence. Mrs Waller agreed that not only should a child have the opportunity of developing relationship with both parents, any sibling should also be there so that inter- sibling relationship could be fostered and nurtured. Obviously in this particular case the children reside in different places. That immediately puts a strain on the children having limited contact with each other. F's sister is very much older than him and she will be further advanced into her adult life. Thus it is not a matter that that sibling relationship can only be fostered by the children being together. Indeed as we all know absence sometimes makes the heart grow fonder. F should have an opportunity of seeing his sister. Wherever he does that it should be done in a friendly and loving environment. If the time comes that his sister goes to university of course his contact with her will be restricted to the time that she is home from university. In years to come when they have both grown up, with their own family they will see less of each other. But it doesn't mean that they don't still love and adore each other as much as they would if they saw each other every day." District Judge Paul Ayers of Bedford County Court, 3, St Paul's Square, MK40 1SQ, the Senior Vice President of the Association of Her Majesty's District Judges – proofed and approved Judgement.

Charitable Antichrist Racist Freemasonry Religion (Mediocre Mafia/New Pharisees) taught white Freemason Judges secret handshakes, not grammar, as the former was considerably easier to master.

AN IMBECILE: AN ADULT WITH THE BASIC SKILLS OF A CHILD.

The yield of a very, very elementary intellect; his spinal cord seemed to be his highest centre.

"Yes, Sir, it does *her* honour, but it would do nobody else honour. I have indeed, not read it all. But when I take up the end of a web, and find it packthread, I do not expect, by looking further, to find embroidery." Dr Samuel Johnson.

"Someone must be trusted. Let it be the Judges." Lord Denning (1899 – 1999).

White Judges are human beings and members of the Society.

Some human beings are RACISTS.

Then, there, Judges were white, Christian, and Freemasons; some of them were thicker than a gross of planks - Habakkuk.

C of E raises serious concerns about Christian Freemasons
https://www.theguardian.com › uk-news › feb › c-of-e-...

8 Feb 2018 — Church of England warning that secret society may not be compatible with Christianity echoes concerns from 1987.

Based on very proximate observations and direct experiences, functional semi-illiterate white Judges, nearly all, are RACIALISTS.

"Racism is rife throughout most organisations across Britain." The Mayor of London

"All sections of the UK Society are institutionally racist." Sir Bernard Hogan-Howe

The Judiciary is part of the UK Society.

Based on available evidence, those who nearly passed or just passed the A/Level could do Law.

Just as it was in Dr Stephen Hawking's School, then, at the University of Lagos (UNILAG), the smartest students did mathematics, physics, and chemistry, and did not attend lectures at the Faculty of Law.

"In my school, the brightest boys did math and physics, the less bright did physics and chemistry, and the least bright did biology. I wanted to do math and physics, but my father made me do chemistry because he thought there would be no jobs for mathematicians." Dr Stephen Hawking.

THE LEGAL TRADE: Based on very proximate observations and direct experiences, a grossly overrated, overhyped, overpopulated, and institutionally mediocre trade that is dying slowly and imperceptibly, and is overseen by members of the Charitable Antichrist Racist

Freemasonry Quasi-Religion (Mediocre Mafia/New Pharisees) - Habakkuk 1:4; John 8:44; John 10:10.

"The legal system lies at the heart of any society, protecting rights, imposing duties, and establishing a framework for the conduct of almost every social, political, and economic activity. Some argue that the law is in its death throes while others postulate a contrary prognosis that discerns numerous signs of law's enduring strength. Which is it?" Professor Raymond Wacks.

GENETICS: The Holy Grail.

If there is absolutely irrefutable evidence that the white ancestors of District Judge Paul Ayers of Bedford County Court, 3, St Paul's Square, MK40 1SQ, were very greedy economic cannibals and extremely nasty racist terrorists, it will be naïve not to expect racial hatred to be part of his genetic inheritances.

"Study history, study history, in history lies all the secrets of statecraft." Churchill

Based on available evidence, the white ancestors of District Judge Paul Ayers of Bedford County Court, 3, St Paul's Square, MK40 1SQ, the Senior Vice President of the Association of Her Majesty's District Judges were greedier than the grave, and like death, they were never satisfied – Habakkuk 2:5.

"Sometimes people don't want to hear the truth because they don't want their illusions destroyed." Friedrich Nietzsche

It is brainless nonsense, and a deliberate deceit that Judges are ultra-righteous superhuman who cannot tell lies and cannot be racists - Habakkuk.

"Lies are told all the time." Sir Michael Havers (1923 – 1992).

It is not the truth that RACIAL HATRED is a myth, and it is not extinct, and it is considerably more common than ordinarily realised.

"Meghan Markle was the subject of explicit and obnoxious racial hatred." John Bercow

"All sections of the UK Society are institutionally racist." Sir Bernard Hogan-Howe

The Judiciary is part of the UK Society.

Bedfordshire Police is part of the UK Society.

"I know of no evil that has ever existed, nor can imagine any evil to exist, worse than the tearing of eighty thousand persons annually from their native land, by a combination of the most civilised nations inhabiting the most enlightened part of the globe, but more especially under the sanction of the laws of that Nation which calls herself the most free and the most happy of them all." Prime Minister William Pitt the Younger

OYINBO OLE: THIEVES – HABAKKUK.

151

Christ didn't place Africans in the back row, white men did.

Then, the white man was the devil.

"Of black men, the numbers are too great who are now repining under English cruelty." Dr Samuel Johnson

BORIS JOHNSON: Then, the Prime Minister, The Right Honourable William Pitt the Younger lied, because it is not the truth that those who shipped millions of, made in Birmingham, guns to Africa, in exchange for millions of stolen children of defenceless poor people (Meghan Markle's African ancestors), during several centuries of the greediest economic cannibalism and the evilest racist terrorism the world will ever know, and among those who, then, had no means of treating penetrative gunshot wounds and internal injuries, were the most civilised and the most enlightened.

They did not believe in His exceptionalism (John 14:6), so they were not deterred by His Justice (John 5:22).

They hate us, and we know, but they hate our creator more. Had closeted racist bastards been our God and creator, the innately racist bastards would have created us to be mentally very dull, and compliant, and we wouldn't know that the aggressors, oppressors, subjugators, and persecutors were created excessively stupid, and, more importantly, we will not have the mental power to resist racist tyranny by turning against our 'creators'.

"We have the power to turn against our creators." Dr Richard Dawkins.

Then, on the plantations, kidnapped Africans who turned against their captors, who acted like their creators, were unnaturally deselected (killed) by very highly civilised and enlightened European Christians.

"To disagree with three – fourths of the British public on all points is one of the first elements of sanity, one of the deepest consolations in all moments of spiritual doubt." Wilde

Then, armed racist white bastards frogmarched unarmed Negroes who disagreed with them to the woods, at gunpoint, and those who openly disagreed with merciless racist tyranny were unnaturally deselected (killed); they were stripped naked, flogged, and sadistically hanged from tall trees, without hoods.

"Of black men, the numbers are too great who are now repining under English cruelty.

Facts are sacred, and they cannot be overstated.
They were wickeder than the devil, and greedier than the grave, and like death, the racist bastards were never satisfied – Habakkuk 2:5.

Properly rehearsed civilised decorum and deceptively schooled ultra-righteousness were preceded by several centuries of the greediest economic cannibalism and the evilest racist terrorism the world will ever know – Habakkuk

"England is like a prostitute who, having sold her body all her life, decides to quit and close her business, and then tells everybody that she wants to be chaste and protect her flesh as if it were Jade." He Manzi, Chinese Politician.

OYINBO OLE: THIEVES – HABAKKUK.

He didn't like them, so He gave them the irrefutably superior skin colour, and in protest, their ancestors used extreme violence to steal almost everything He gave to others: Movable and immovable – James 4; Habakkuk

"All have taken what had other owners, and all have had recourse to arms rather than quit the prey on which they were fastened." Dr Samuel Johnson

"Many Scots masters were considered among the most brutal, with life expectancy on their plantations averaging a mere four years. We worked them to death then simply imported more to keep the sugar and thus the money flowing. Unlike centuries of grief and murder, an apology cost nothing. So, what does Scotland have to say?" Herald Scotland: Ian Bell, Columnist, Sunday 28 April 2013
Then, for sure, the white man was the devil.

154

'The white man is the devil' – what the Nation of Islam taught ...
https://www.independent.co.uk › World
5 Jun 2016 — In 1974, Muhammad Ali told Michael Parkinson and a stunned chat show audience that the white man of America was "the blue-eyed, blond-headed ...

OYINBO OLE: THIEVES - HABAKKUK

WHITE PRIVILEGE: Based on very proximate observations and direct experiences, only the irrefutably superior skin colour that District Judge Paul Ayers of Bedford County Court, 3, St Paul's Square, MK 40 1SQ, the Senior Vice President of the Association of Her Majesty's District Judges, neither made nor chose is truly good, and without it, he will be considerably diminished as a human being.

PERCEPTION IS GRANDER THAN REALITY: EVERYTHING IS BASELESSLY AND BRAINLESSLY ASSUMED IN FAVOUR OF THE IRREFUTABLY SUPERIOR SKIN COLOUR THAT THE WEARER NEITHER MADE NOR CHOSE.

OYINBO OLE: STRAIGHT-FACED DESCENDANTS OF THIEVES – HABAKKUK

"Sometimes people don't want to hear the truth because they don't want their illusions destroyed." Friedrich Nietzsche

FREEMASON DIPSTICKS WANT TO CONSTRUCTIVELY BAN THE EXPRESSION OF THE TRUTH BECAUSE IT DOES NOT FAVOUR THEM.

The very, very powerful half-educated school dropouts and their superiors who have informal access to some powerful white Judges, and who use very expensive aprons to decorate the temples of their powerless and useless fertility tools, and who seem to want human beings to be graded according to the skin colour that the neither made nor chose and the vulgar embroidery on their expensive aprons, awarded themselves the supreme knowledge, but the closeted racist bastards see molecules, so they kill all those who see atoms, especially if they were mere Negroes.

Like Herod, Kim, Putin, MBS, Saddam Hussein, and babies, they (FREEMASONS) expect everyone to love them, and they kill those who don't, albeit hands-off.

FREEMASONS: They do vulgar Pharisees' charitable works in exchange for what? He rejected the grandest offer of their ruler – Matthew 4:9.

Based on very proximate observations and direct experiences, FREEMASONRY is Antichrist, and a white supremacist quasi-religion that wears vulgar Pharisees' charitable works as a cloak of deceit.

Only the very shallow and undiscerning do not know that charitable works of closeted white supremacist thugs are akin to throwing flares, a properly rehearsed and deliberate instrument of deceit.

Then, He rejected the grandest of the ruler of the Builders – Matthew 4:9.

The stone that the Builders rejected is now the cornerstone – Psalm 118:22; Luke 20:17.

OYINBO OLE: THIEVES – HABAKKUK.

The colour bar was crude and cruel. The reasoning bar is spineless cowardice.

They are not the only creation of Almighty God, and they are not our God because they are not immortal, and the irrefutably superior skin colour that they neither made nor chose is not the only wonder of our world.

"Affluence is not a birth right." David Cameron.

SLAVERY IS NOT HEREDITARY: SUPERIORITY IS NOT THEIR INVIOLABLE BIRTH RIGHT.

"It must be agreed that in most ages many countries have had part of their inhabitants in a state of slavery; yet it may be doubted whether slavery can ever be supposed the natural condition of man. It is impossible not to conceive that, men, in their original state were equal; and very difficult to imagine how one would be subjected to another but by violent compulsion. An individual may, indeed, forfeit his liberty by a crime; but he cannot by that crime forfeit the liberty of his children. What is true of a criminal seems true likewise of a captive. A man may accept life from a conquering enemy on condition of perpetual servitude; but it is very doubtful whether he can entail that servitude on his descendants; for no man can stipulate without commission for another. The condition which he

157

himself accepts, his son or grandson would have rejected."
DR SAMUEL JOHNSON

GDC: Richard Hill fabricated reports and unrelentingly lied under oath.

A WHITE MAN. A DISHONEST RACIST BASTARD

GDC: Jonathan Martin lied on record

A WHITE MAN. A DISHONEST RACIST BASTARD

GDC: Helen Falcon (MBE) lied on record

A WHITE WOMAN. A DISHONEST RACIST COUGAR.

GDC: George Rothnie (NHS) lied on record

A WHITE MAN. A DISHONEST RACIST BASTARD

GDC: Stephanie Twidale lied under oath

A WHITE WOMAN. A DISHONEST RACIST COUGAR.

GDC: Sue Gregory (OBE) lied on record

A WHITE WOMAN. A DISHONEST RACIST COUGAR.

GDC: Rachael Bishop lied under oath

A WHITE WOMAN. A DISHONEST RACIST
COUGAR.

GDC: Geraint Evans (NHS) lied on record

A WHITE MAN. A DISHONEST RACIST BASTARD

They were all white; had they been black, they would have
been in trouble.

A properly organised racist crime syndicate that is
overseen by the FREEMASONS, impersonates a
competently administered impartial administration of the
Law.

"The highest reach of injustice is to be deemed just when
you are not." Plato

Based on very proximate observations and direct
experiences, the administration of their Law is the tyrant's
tool.

OYINBO OLE: THIEVES – HABAKKUK

"Rightful liberty is unobstructed action according to our
will within limits drawn around us by the equal rights of
others. I do not add 'within the limits of the law' because
law is often but the tyrant's will, and always so when it
violates the rights of the individual." Thomas Jefferson

They were all white, including the Judges, and they were
all closeted racist white bastards - Habakkuk.

Facts are sacred, and they can't be overstated.

Closeted racist white bastards stalk our people
(AFRICANS) like prey and the hunt in packs.

They want superiority, their brainless and baseless birth
right, but they don't want Freedom of Expression because
they don't want their mentally very gentle children to know
that they are crooked racist white bastards – Habakkuk 1:4;
John 8:44; John 10:10.

Extremely greedy racist white bastards want to eat all their
cakes, and eat all our cakes, and they want to have
everything: They are not the only creation of Almighty
God, and they are not immortal, and their irrefutably
superior skin colour is not the only wonder of our world.

He didn't like them, so He gave them the irrefutably
superior skin colour, so in protest, they greedily used, made
in Birmingham, GUNS to steal almost everything He gave
to others: Movable and immovable - Habakkuk.

OYINBO OLE: THIEVES – HABAKKUK.

160

Are we at the beginning of the end-game.

"It was our arms in the river of Cameroon, put into the hands of the trader, that furnished him with the means of pushing his trade; and I have no more doubt that they are British arms, put into the hands of Africans, which promote universal war and desolation that I can doubt their having done so in that individual instance. I have shown how great is the enormity of this evil, even on the supposition that we take only convicts and prisoners of war. But take the subject in another way, and how does it stand? Think of 80,000 persons carried out of their native country by we know not what means! For crimes imputed! For light or inconsiderable faults! For debts perhaps! For crime of witchcraft! Or a thousand other weak or scandalous pretexts! Reflect on 80,000 persons annually taken off! There is something in the horror of it that surpasses all bounds of imagination." – Prime Minister William Pitt the Younger

OYINBO OLE: THIEVES - HABAKKUK

Only stupid Negroes expect white Judges to measure whites with the same yardstick they use to measure our people, and only stupider Negroes do not know that demons cannot cast out demons – Matthew 12:27.

Christ did not place black people in the back rows, white men did.

The white man was the devil.

Christ does not place black people in the back rows, white men do.

The white man is the devil.

Facts are sacred, they cannot be overstated.

Closeted racist bastards want to beat us up illegally, and the intellectually ungifted closeted racist bastards want to prevent our people from screaming, naturally, in excruciating pain: Cane Plantation Justice.

"I hate a fellow who pride, or cowardice, or laziness drives into a corner, and who does nothing when he is there but sit and growl; let him come out as I do, and bark."—Dr Samuel Johnson

Omi fin, o daran, o be mi, times two – African bush saying

"Too often the strong, silent man is silent only because he does not know what to say and is reputed strong only because he has remained silent."—Sir Winston Churchill

Then, theirs used to strip ours naked, and mercilessly flog them, sometimes until they die.

Then, theirs used to frog march ours to the woods, at gunpoint, and sadistically hang them from tall trees, without hoods.

"To disagree with three – fourths of the British public on all points is one of the first elements of sanity, one of the deepest consolations in all moments of spiritual doubt." Wilde

OYINBO OLE: IGNORANT DESCENDANTS OF
EXTREMELY NASTY RACIST BASTARDS –
HABAKKUK.

The very crude and very, very cruel sadistic savages, and
murderous racist bastards, are no longer here, it will be
naïve not to expect their sadistic genes to remain in some
of their descendants who remain here.

Ignorance is bliss.

"It is incumbent upon the court and all those professionals
involved to conclude court proceedings as quickly as
possible. This hopefully ensures that a child has stability,
love and affection and the parents working together to
ensure that he has the best opportunity of developing
academically and emotional." District Judge Paul Ayers,
Senior Vice President of the Association of Her Majesty's
District Judges – proofed and approved Judgement

AN IMBECILE: AN ADULT WITH THE BASIC
SKILLS OF A CHILD.

"Yes, Sir, it does *her* honour, but it would do nobody else
honour. I have indeed, not read it all. But when I take up
the end of a web, and find it packthread, I do not expect, by
looking further, to find embroidery." Dr Samuel Johnson

A CLOSETED RACIST FOOL'S APPROVAL!

PURIFIED ROT!

"Gentlemen, you are now about to embark on a course of studies which will occupy you for two years. Together, they form a noble adventure. But I would like to remind you of an important point. Nothing that you will learn in the course of your studies will be of the slightest possible use to you in after life, save only this, that if you work hard and intelligently you should be able to detect when a man is talking rot, and that, in my view, is the main, if not the sole, purpose of education." John Alexander Smith, Oxford University Professor of MORAL PHILOSOPHY.

Based on very proximate observations and direct experiences, the incontrovertibly functional semi-illiterate white man, albeit England's Class Senior Judge, seemed so totally vile and intellectually worthless.

"The earth contains no race of human beings so totally vile and worthless as the Welsh." Walter Savage Landor.

Based on observations and direct experiences, all functional semi-illiterate white Judges are racists.

What District Judge Paul Ayers, Senior Vice President of the Association of Her Majesty's District Judges immortalised on record is very consistent with being a very senior Judge within one of the dullest adult populations in the industrialised world: Among the least literate and the least numerate adults in the industrialised world - OECD.

——-Original Message——- -From: cqc (NHS SHARED BUSINESS SERVICES LTD (BRISTOL)) <SBS-B.cqc@nhs.net>

To: adeolacole <adeolacole@aol.com>
Sent: Thu, 3 Sep 2015 20:00
Subject: RE: Outstanding statutory annual registration fee
invoice: payment due—FINAL REMINDER

Hello,
Thank you for your below email

Kindly request you to provide your contact details
(telephone number) so we can contact you and explain.

If any query please let me know

Thanks and Regards,

Kanchan Jaisinghani

Collections
Debt Management Team

Shared Business Services

Tel 0303–123–1155

Fax 0117–933–8890

E-mail: sbs-b.cqc@nhs.net

Website: www.sbs.nhs.uk

Government Business Award Winner

AN IMBECILE: AN ADULT WITH THE BASIC SKILLS OF A CHILD.

The report, by the OECD, warns that the UK needs to take significant action to boost the basic skills of the nation's young people. The 460-page study is based on the first-ever survey of the literacy, numeracy and problem-solving at work skills of 16 to 65-year-olds in 24 countries, with almost 9,000 people taking part in England and Northern Ireland to make up the UK results. The findings showed that England and Northern Ireland have some of the highest proportions of adults scoring no higher than Level 1 in literacy and numeracy - the lowest level on the OECD's scale. This suggests that their skills in the basics are no better than that of a 10-year-old.

NIGERIA: SHELL'S DOCILE CASH COW.

There are no oil wells and/or gas fields in LUTON.
Then, all the people of LUTON, including white Judges and white Freemasons were fed like battery hens with the yields of stolen children of defenceless poor Africans (Meghan Markle's ancestors)

NIGERIA: Babies with huge oil wells and gas fields near their huts eat only 1.5/day; a closeted racist former debt-collector Solicitor in Norwich whose white mother and father have never seen crude oil, and whose white ancestors were fed like battery hens with the yields of stolen children of defenceless poor people (Meghan Markle's ancestors) is our District Judge in BEDFORD – Habakkuk

Then, there, white Judges, nearly all, were Freemasons; some of them were THICKER than a gross of planks.

Based on available evidence, their own Money, NIGERIA (oil/gas) is by very far more relevant to the economic survival of the white mother, white father, white spouse, and all the white children of District Judge Paul Ayers of Bedford County Court, 3, St Paul's Square, MK 401SQ, the Senior Vice President of the Association of Her Majesty's District Judges – than Kempston.
The only evidence of his very high IQ is the stolen affluence that his white ancestors crossed the English Channels, without luggage or decent shoes, to latch onto.

OYINBO OLE: RIGHTEOUS DESCENDANTS OF ULTRA-RIGHTEOUS THIEVES AND OWNERS OF STOLEN CHILDREN OF DEFENCELESS POOR PEOPLE (MEGHAN MARKLE'S ANCESTORS) – HABAKKUK.

They want superiority, their baseless and brainless birth right, but they don't want Freedom of Expression.

"A typical English man, usually violent and always dull."
Wilde

BASED ON OBSERVATIONS AND DIRECT EXPERIENCES, IN ORDER TO EXCHANGE UNASHAMED CONFUSION FOR VALUABLE CONSIDERATION, SOME CLOSETED RACIST WHITE FREEMASONS ATTACH IT TO A DEVOUT JOHN 14:6 CHRISTIAN - SOVEREIGN.

JUDICIAL DIVERSITY: ACCELERATING CHANGE. Sir Geoffrey Bindman, QC Karon Monaghan QC "The near absence of women and Black, Asian and minority ethnic judges in the senior judiciary, is no longer tolerable. It undermines the democratic legitimacy of our legal system; it demonstrates a denial of fair and equal opportunities to members of underrepresented groups, and the diversity deficit weakens the quality of justice. GDC: A white man, Richard William Hill fabricated reports and unrelentingly lied under oath.

A WHITE MAN. A DISHONEST RACIST.

GDC: A white man, Jonathan Martin unrelentingly lied under implied oath.

A WHITE MAN. A DISHONEST RACIST.

GDC: A white man, Geraint Evans, Postgraduate Tutor Oxford, unrelentingly lied under implied oath

A WHITE MAN. A DISHONEST RACIST.

"The truth allows no choice." Dr Samuel Johnson

Facts are sacred, and they can't be overstated.

Christ does not place Africans in the back row, white men do. The white man is the devil: The white man is the thief.

The most potent racists are white supremacist Freemason Judges, they have enormous Judicial power, and motivated by RACIAL HATRED, they can manipulate the lae to injure black people.

Based on available evidence, SEXED-UP legal transcripts are not uncommon in the administration of English Law.

Christ did not place Africans in the back row, white men did. The white man was the devil. The white was the thief.

BEDFORD, ENGLAND: A white man, Senior District Judge Paul Ayers, the Senior Vice President of the Association of Her Majesty's District Judges - explicitly lied or he otherwise deviated from the truth when he stated that the Negro took part in a hearing on July 01, 2013, at Bedford County Court, 29, Goldington Road, Bedford, MK40 3NN

A WHITE MAN. A DISHONEST RACIST BASTARD.

Based on very proximate observations and direct experiences, the white man is the devil.

'The white man is the devil' – what the Nation of Islam taught ...
https://www.independent.co.uk › World

5 Jun 2016 — In 1974, Muhammad Ali told Michael Parkinson and a stunned chat show audience that the white man of America was "the blue-eyed, blond-headed ...

Case No: 2YL06820

Bedford County Court
May House
29 Goldington Road
Bedford
MK40 3NN

Monday, 1st July 2013

B E F O R E:

DISTRICT JUDGE AYERS

DOBERN PROPERTY LIMITED
(Claimants)

v.

DR. ABIODUN OLA BAMGBELU
(Defendant)

-

Transcript from an Official Court Tape Recording.

Transcript prepared by:

MK Transcribing Services

29 The Concourse, Brunel Business Centre,

Bletchley, Milton Keynes, MK2 2ES

Tel: 01908-640067 Fax: 01908-365958

DX 100031 Bletchley

Official Court Tape Transcribers.

MR. PURKIS appeared on behalf of THE CLAIMANTS.

THE DEFENDANT appeared in PERSON.

JUDGMENT

(As approved)

An approved Judgement by a properly educated Judge, including in NIGERIA, depicts a wilful statement in its purest term.

There were laws then, as there are laws now. Then, the yield of stolen and destroyed children of defenceless poor people (African ancestors of Meghan Markle and her white children) were used to build Magnificent Courts and pay the wages of white Judges who sent white people who stole money to Great Prisons built with the yield of stolen and destroyed lives of the children of defenceless poor people (African ancestors of Meghan Markle and her white children) - Habakkuk.

OYINBO OLE: THIEVES – HABAKKUK

CREEPING DPRK.

BEDFORD, ENGLAND: District Judge Paul Ayers, the Senior Vice President of the Association of Her Majesty's District Judges, which part of Bedford County Court, 3, St Paul's Square, MK 40 1 SQ, was not STOLEN, or which part of the magnificent building did transparent virtue yield, or which part of it did the people of BEDFORD buy, or which part of it preceded SLAVERY: The building or its chattels?

Ignorance is bliss.

Before SLAVERY, what?

"Those who know the least obey the best." George Farquhar

Our Empire did not evolve from NOTHING; then, almost everything was actively and deliberately stolen with GUNS - Habakkuk.

He didn't like them, so He gave them the irrefutably superior skin colour, and in protest, they used extreme violence to steal almost everything He gave to others: Movable and immovable.

Facts are sacred; they can't be overstated.

"I know of no evil that has ever existed, nor can imagine any evil to exist, worse than the tearing of eighty thousand persons annually from their native land, by a combination of the most civilised nations inhabiting the most enlightened part of the globe, but more especially under the sanction of the laws of that Nation which calls herself the most free and the most happy of them all." Prime Minister William Pitt the Younger

Christ did not place Africans in the back row, white men did. The white man was the devil. The white man was the thief.

Closeted white supremacists and deluded Defenders of Faiths (Freemasons): Dissenters of John 14:6.

"Many Scots masters were considered among the most brutal, with life expectancy on their plantations averaging a mere four years. We worked them to death then simply imported more to keep the sugar and thus the money flowing. Unlike centuries of grief and murder, an apology cost nothing. So, what does Scotland have to say?" Herald Scotland: Ian Bell, Columnist, Sunday 28 April 2013

OYINBO OLE: THIEVES - HABAKKUK

Christ did not place Africans in the back row, white men did. The white man was the devil. The white was the thief.

GDC: Kevin Atkinson (NHS) lied under oath

GDC: Jonathan Martin lied on record

GDC: Helen Falcon (MBE) lied on record

GDC: George Rothnie (NHS) lied on record

GDC: Stephanie Twidale lied under oath

GDC: Sue Gregory (OBE) lied on record

GDC: Rachael Bishop lied under oath

GDC: Geraint Evans (NHS) lied on record

GDC: Richard Hill fabricated reports and lied under oath.

Facts are sacred, they cannot be overstated.

Closeted racist white bastards do not believe in His exceptionalism (John 14:6), so they are not deterred by His transparent Justice.

A bastardised, indiscreetly dishonest, unashamedly mediocre, vindictive, potently weaponised, and institutionally racist legal system that is overseen by the FREEMASONS (Mediocre Mafia/New Pharisees) – Habakkuk

A properly organised racist crime syndicate that is overseen by the FREEMASONS (Mediocre Mafia/New Pharisees) – impersonates colour-blind and impartial administrators of the law.

"Rightful liberty is unobstructed action according to our will within limits drawn around us by the equal rights of others. I do not add 'within the limits of the law' because law is often but the tyrant's will, and always so when it violates the rights of the individual." Thomas Jefferson

Then, there, it was a lie only if the FREEMASONS did not prior authorise it, and it was a crime only if the FREEMASONS did not prior authorise it.

They were all white, including their Judges, and they were all incompetent racist liars – Habakkuk 1:4; John 8:44; John 10:10.

OYINBO OLE: THIEVES – HABAKKUK.

Christ does not place Africans in the back row, white men do.

GOOGLE: THE WHITE JUDGE LIED.

GOOGLE: INCOMPETENT LIARS: SOME LAWYERS.

Properly rehearsed ultra-righteousness and deceptively school civilised decorum were preceded by several centuries of merciless racist evil: The greediest economic cannibalism and the nastiest racist terrorism, worse than the worst Jihad, the world will ever know - Habakkuk.

"England is like a prostitute who, having sold her body all her life, decides to quit and close her, and then tells everybody that she wants to be chaste and protect her flesh as if it were jade." He Manzi, Chinese Politician

Facts are sacred.

A properly proofed and approved Judgement by a properly educated Judge should pass through at least four separate filters: The Transcript Writers, The Proof-readers, The Court Clerks, and the Judge.

Based on available evidence, the legal transcript of July 1, 2013, that was approved by our Senior District Judge, albeit England's Class, seemed to have been SEXED-UP.

Based on available evidence, SEXED UP LEGAL TRANSCRIPTS are not uncommon in the administration of English Law.

GDC: A white man, George Rothnie, Postgraduate Dean, Oxford, unrelentingly lied under implied oath

A WHITE MAN. A DISHONEST RACIST BASTARD.

GDC: A white man, Kevin Atkinson, Postgraduate Tutor, Oxford, unrelentingly lied under oath

A WHITE MAN. A DISHONEST RACIST BASTARD.

Christ does not place Africans in the back rows, white men do.

The white man is the devil: The white man is the thief.

"Find the truth and tell it." Harold Pinter

CHAPTER FIVE:

Boris Johnson: Why is England not a Racist Scam?

"Understand, my dear boy, colour prejudice is something I find utterly foreign .... But of course, come in, Sir, there is no colour prejudice among us .... Quite, the Negro is a man like ourselves ..... It is not because he is black that he is less intelligent than we are ......" Frantz Fanon.

Boris Johnson, our religious belief is absolutely incompatible with the belief of Defenders of FAITHS (John 14:6 Dissenters): The Vulgarly Charitable Antichrist Racist Freemasonry Quasi-Religion (Mediocre Mafia/New Pharisees) – Habakkuk 1:4; John 8:44; John 10:10.

BEDFORD, ENGLAND: Based on available evidence, GDC-Witness, Freemason, Brother, Richard William Hill fabricated reports and unrelentingly lied under oath.

A CROOKED WHITE MAN. A DISHONEST RACIST BASTARD.

The crooked and racist white bastard do not believe in the exceptionalism of Christ (John 14:6), so he was not deterred by transparent Justice.

Their people are stupid, and since they oversee the administration of their law, they use incompetent mendacity to conceal incompetent mendacity and hereditary intellectual impotence.

When their people commit racist crimes against ours, closeted racist bastards who oversee the administration of their law criminally bury racial hatred.

Crooked closeted racist bastards are so greedy, they want a world where only they and their children thrive. Their ancestors were so greedy, they wanted a world where only they and their children thrived. They were greedier than the grave and like death, they were never satisfied – Habakkuk 2:5.

In 1892, closeted racist bastards accurately foresaw that incompetently mendacious and functional semi-illiterate closeted racist bastards will become Deputy Postgraduate Deans, Senior District Judges, and Postgraduate Tutors in England, so after several centuries of the greediest economic cannibalism and the evilest racist terrorism the world will ever know, worse than the worst Jihad, armed white Britons, and those they armed, returned to our tribe in the African bush, only a walking distance from the Atlantic Ocean, without invitation, passports or visas, and the sadistic closeted racist bastards used very heavy guns, on wheels, to mercilessly slaughter almost everybody in our tribe, in a dispute over our own money: Natural resources, raw materials, and centuries-old passage taxes. Closeted racist bastards displaced our King (Awujale), evicted him from his Palace, and looted it, and they converted Afin Awujale (Our King's Palace) into their Garrison. In 1893, very many Ijebu girls gave birth to Mulattos. The closeted racist white bastards were Christian sex-machines.

Facts are sacred.

"The truth allows no choice." Dr Samuel Johnson

GOOGLE: IMAGBON 1892.

They wrote their history and ours, and expectedly, both were kind to them.

"History will be kind to me, for I intend to write it." Churchill

So, the Negro, a native of Ijebu, is, like Obama's children, a direct descendant of a Mulatto, and he could be genetically related to incontrovertibly functional semi-illiterate District Judge Paul Ayers of Bedford County Court, 3, St Paul's Square, Bedford MK40 1SQ, the Senior Vice President of the Association of Her Majesty's District Judges.

-----Original Message-----
From: George Rothnie <georgerothnie@hotmail.com>
To: adeolacole@aol.com
Sent: Mon, 8 Mar 2010 20:19
Subject: Re Meeting 9th March

Hi Ola,

We are scheduled to meet tomorrow evening at my surgery about 5.30ish.

Unfortunately something has cropped up which necessytates me having to
postpone the meeting. I'm really sorry it's such short notice.
I will contact you in the week to arrange another date.
 Once agaim my apologies.
 George

OYINBO ODE.

AN IMBECILE: AN ADULT WITH THE BASIC SKILLS OF A CHILD.

George Rothnie: Deputy Postgraduate Dean, Oxford.

"It is incumbent upon the court and all those professionals involved to conclude court proceedings as quickly as possible. This hopefully ensures that a child has stability, love and affection and the parents working together to ensure that he has the best opportunity of developing academically and emotional." District Judge Paul Ayers, Senior Vice President of the Association of Her Majesty's District Judges – proofed and approved Judgement

AN IMBECILE: AN ADULT WITH THE BASIC SKILLS OF A CHILD.

Our semi-illiterate closeted racist waste of money Freemason District Judge of our Empire of Stolen Affluence - Habakkuk.

181

PERCEPTION IS GRANDER THAN REALITY: BEFORE SLAVERY, WHAT?

Irrefutably superior skin colour concealed dark black brain.

A CLOSETED RACIST WHITE FOOL'S APPROVAL!

"Yes, Sir, it does *her* honour, but it would do nobody else honour. I have indeed, not read it all. But when I take up the end of a web, and find it packthread, I do not expect, by looking further, to find embroidery." Dr Samuel Johnson

PURIFIED ROT!

"Gentlemen, you are now about to embark on a course of studies which will occupy you for two years. Together, they form a noble adventure. But I would like to remind you of an important point. Nothing that you will learn in the course of your studies will be of the slightest possible use to you in after life, save only this, that if you work hard and intelligently you should be able to detect when a man is talking rot, and that, in my view, is the main, if not the sole, purpose of education." John Alexander Smith, Oxford University Professor of MORAL PHILOSOPHY.

Then, there, functional semi-illiterate white Judges, nearly all, were FREEMASONS, and some of them were THICKER than a gross of planks.

They see a Senior District Judge, but the Negro sees a closeted racist impostor, an expert of deception, a Freemason, and a white imbecile (an adult with the basic skills of a child; if they are not excessively stupid, the Negro must be mad.

No brain.

Poor in natural resources.

Several centuries of THIEVERY/SLAVERY preceded the stolen trust fund.

Only the skin colour is irrefutably superior; the wearer neither made nor chose it.

They are not the only creation of Almighty God, and they are not immortal, and the irrefutably superior skin colour that they neither made nor chose is not the only wonder of our world.

The report, by the OECD, warns that the UK needs to take significant action to boost the basic skills of the nation's young people. The 460-page study is based on the first-ever survey of the literacy, numeracy and problem-solving at work skills of 16 to 65-year-olds in 24 countries, with almost 9,000 people taking part in England and Northern Ireland to make up the UK results. The findings showed that England and Northern Ireland have some of the highest proportions of adults scoring no higher than Level 1 in literacy and numeracy - the lowest level on the

OECD's scale. This suggests that their skills in the basics are no better than that of a 10-year-old.

AN IMBECILE: AN ADULT WITH THE BASIC SKILLS OF A CHILD.

BORIS JOHNSON: Let me tell you, then, privileged dullards who believed that daily dialogues with IMBECILES (adults with the basic skills of a child) was a worthwhile, 'meaty', and manly job – were SCAMMERS, and Judges who demanded and accepted very valuable consideration in exchange for daily dialogues with IMBECILES (adults with the basic skills of a child) are RACKETEERS (Thieves).

BEDFORD, ENGLAND: District Judge Paul Ayers of Bedford County Court, 3, St Paul's Square, MK40 1SQ, the Senior Vice President of the Association of Her Majesty District Judges: A closeted racist Freemason; a functional semi-illiterate District Judge of imbeciles (adults with the basic skills of a child).

Apart from creating very cushy salaried jobs for incontrovertibly functional semi-illiterate Freemason Judges (imbeciles or adults with the basic skills of a child), who foreseeably FAILED in the very competitive law practice, what do imbeciles need very, very expensive administration of the law for?

OYINBO OLE: THIEVES HABAKKUK.

"Sometimes people don't want to hear the truth because they don't want their illusions

Sheep unnaturally shepherd sheep.

"Mediocrity weighing mediocrity in the balance, and incompetence applauding its brother….." Wilde.

Shepherds know that sheep are imbeciles.

Sheep do not know that shepherds are imbeciles too.

C of E raises serious concerns about Christian Freemasons
https://www.theguardian.com › uk-news › feb › c-of-e-
8 Feb 2018 — Church of England warning that secret society may not be compatible with Christianity echoes concerns from 1987.

Then, the Archbishop of Canterbury, Dr Rowan Williams believed Christianity and Freemasonry were "incompatible" and refused to appoint Freemason clergymen to senior posts. Dr Williams' comments renewed controversy about the Charitable Antichrist Racist Freemasonry Religion (Mediocre Mafia/New Pharisees) – Habakkuk 1:4; John 8:44: John 10:10

For over half of a century, some of the most senior members of the Charitable Antichrist Racist Freemasonry Religion (Mediocre Mafia/New Pharisees) have been in the Church's higher echelons, and very many Judges were members of the Charitable Antichrist Racist Freemasonry Religion (Mediocre Mafia/New Pharisees).

The link between the Church of England, the Judiciary, and Freemasonry Fraternity is centuries old.

The Grand Masonic Temple to Baal, 60 Great Queen St, London WC2B 5AZ, was built in the early 18th century at a height of the barbarously racist traffic in millions of stolen children of defenceless poor people (The black African ancestors of Meghan Markle and her white children) – Habakkuk.

Tens of thousands of leading clergymen and churchgoers are among its almost 500,000 British members the Charitable Antichrist Racist Freemasonry Quasi-Religion: Defenders of Faiths and Dissenters of John 14:6.
Then, the Rev Gregory Cameron, chaplain to Dr Williams, said: "He questions whether it's appropriate for Christian ministers to belong to secret organisations. He also has some anxiety about the spiritual content of Masonry.

Dr Williams, whose father was a Freemason, must have changed his mind as he later appointed a Freemason as Bishop.

A spokesman for the Archbishop said he was "worried about the ritual elements in Freemasonry - which some have seen as possibly Satanically inspired - and how that sits uneasily with Christian belief". He continued: "The other idea is that because they are a society, there could be a network that involves mutual back-scratching, which is something he would be greatly opposed to."

A spokesman for the Freemasons in England said: "As far as we are concerned, there is no incompatibility between Christianity and our organisation whatsoever."

Of course, there is: The closeted racist bastards who use very expensive aprons, with very vulgar embroideries, to decorate the temples of their powerless and useless fertility tools are dissenters of John 14:6 and defenders of FAITHS.

GDC: Richard Hill fabricated reports and unrelentingly lied under oath. A white man. A dishonest racist.

GDC: Kevin Atkinson (NHS) unrelentingly lied under oath. A white man. A dishonest racist.

GDC: Jonathan Martin unrelentingly lied on record. A white man. A dishonest racist.

GDC: Helen Falcon (MBE) unrelentingly lied on record. A white woman. A dishonest racist.

GDC: George Rothnie (NHS) unrelentingly lied on record. A white man. A dishonest racist.

GDC: Stephanie Twiddle, TD, (NHS), unrelentingly lied under oath. A white woman. A dishonest racist.

GDC: Sue Gregory (OBE) unrelentingly lied on record. A white woman. A dishonest racist.

GDC: Rachael Bishop (NHS) unrelentingly lied under oath. A white woman. A dishonest racist.

GDC: Geraint Evans (NHS) unrelentingly lied on record. A white man. A dishonest racist.

Then, there, it was a crime only if the Freemasons did not prior authorise.

BORIS JOHNSON: Freemasons are closeted racist thugs who wear vulgar Pharisees Charitable works as cloaks of deceit. The real question is where do they get the money from, and what do Freemasons' benefactors get in return for their money? If one is happy to accept Saudi's millions, one can't be the Defender of the Faith.

Ultra-righteousness without equitable reparation is continuing racist fraud.

Which part of Bedfordshire Masonic Temple to Baal, the Keep, Bedford Road, Kempston, MK 42, was not stolen, or which part of the Grand Building did transparent virtue yield, or which part of it preceded slavery: The building or its chattels?

OYINBO OLE: THIEVES – HABAKKUK.

Ignorance is bliss.

Based on available evidence, The Grand Masonic Temple to Baal, 60 Great Queen St, London WC2B 5AZ, was built in the early 18th century, at a height of extremely greedy economic cannibalism, and very, very nasty racist terrorism: The barbarously racist traffic in millions of stolen poor children of defenceless poor Africans (the African ancestors of Meghan Markle and her white children) – Habakkuk

Matthew 19:21: He ordered the rich Jew to sell the yield of transparent virtue, give the proceeds to the poor, and follow Him. He orders Freemasons to return stolen affluence to the descendants of the robbed and follow Him.

"The Good Samaritan had money." Mrs Margaret Thatcher (1925 – 2013).

The Iron Lady implied that God Samaritan did charitable works with the yield of transparent virtue.

Richard Oswald, a Freemason, a Christian, and a very, very generous Scotchman, like thousands of Freemasons, did charitable works with the yields of merciless racist evil.

OYINBO OLE: THIEVES – HABAKKUK.

"Time for Scots to say sorry for slavery
Herald Scotland:
Ian Bell, Columnist / Sunday 28 April 2013 / Opinion
Sunday 28 April 2013
According to the American founding father, the son of a Caithness Kirk minister had about him "an air of great simplicity and honesty'". The likes of James Boswell and Laurence Sterne also enjoyed the merchant's company. To his contemporaries, he was, as the author Adam Hochschild has written, '"a wise, thoughtful man who embodied the Scottish virtues of frugality, sobriety, and hard work'". Oswald was a scholar of theology, philosophy, and history. He collected art, particularly Rubens and Rembrandt, and gave handsomely to charity. Oswald, who learned his trade in Glasgow, also represented Britain in negotiations with the Americans after their war of liberation. He was the cosmopolitan epitome of Enlightenment success. But when he wasn't busy with good works, Oswald waded in blood. The precise number of deaths that can be laid at his door is impossible to calculate. As the leading figure in Grant, Oswald & Co, he had investments in each corner of the "'triangular trade'". In his own name, Oswald trafficked at least 13,000 Africans, although he never set foot on their

continent. By the time he bought Auchincruive House and 100,000 acres in Ayrshire in 1764, he was worth £500,000. Writing in 2005, Hochschild thought this was ""roughly equivalent"" to $68 million (about £44m). This is conservative.

Oswald was remarkable, but not unique. Where Glasgow and its merchants in sugar, tobacco, and human life are concerned, there are plenty of names and no shortage of monuments: Dennistoun, Campbell, Glassford, Cochrane, Buchanan, Hamilton, Bogle, Ewing, Donald, Speirs, Dunlop. One way to understand what they wrought is simple: take pleasure in the city''s architecture today and you are likely to be admiring the fruits of slavery.

Glasgow is not alone in that. London, Liverpool and Bristol also have their stories to tell. Edinburgh's once-great banks grew from foundations built on bones. The first Scottish venture into slavery set out from the capital in 1695. Montrose, Dumfries, Greenock and Port Glasgow each tried their hands. In

the language of the present age, they were all in it together. When commerce was coursing around the triangle, most of polite Scotland was implicated. The nobility (and country) rendered bankrupt in 1700 in the aftermath of the Darien Venture was by the mid-1760s contemplating big elegant townhouses and 100,000-acre estates. You could call that a reversal of fortune. Contrary to self-serving myth, it did not happen because of ""frugality, sobriety, and hard work".

Certain things need to be remembered about Scotland and slavery. One is that the mercantile class got stinking rich twice over: despite fortunes made from stolen lives, they were quick to demand compensation when slavery was ended in 1833. Britain's government decided that £20m, a staggering sum, could be raised. In his 2010 book, The Price of Emancipation, Nicholas Draper reckons Glasgow's mob got £400,000 – in modern terms, hundreds of millions. Compensation cases also demonstrated that Scots were not merely following an English lead. According to Draper, a country with 10% of the British population accounted for at least 15% of absentee slavers. By another estimate, 30% of Jamaican plantations were run by Scots. For all the pride taken in the abolitionist societies of Glasgow and Edinburgh, the slave-holders did not suffer because of abolition. They were '"compensated"'.

And that wasn't the worst of it. Thanks to Hollywood movies, the slave economy of the American South is still taken as barbarism's benchmark. Few realise that the behaviour of Scots busy getting rich in the slave-holders" empire was actually worse – routinely worse – than the worst of the cottonocracy. You need only count the corpses................."

Facts are sacred.

OYINBO OLE: THIEVES – HABAKKUK.

Then, the white man was the devil.

'The white man is the devil' – what the Nation of Islam taught ...
https://www.independent.co.uk › World

5 Jun 2016 — In 1974, Muhammad Ali told Michael Parkinson and a stunned chat show audience that the white man of America was "the blue-eyed, blond-headed ...

They were all white, including the Judges, and they were all RACISTS, and incompetent liars — Habakkuk

Ignorant white fools. Racist descendant of white thieves.

"Those who have the power to do wrong with impunity seldom wait long for the will." Dr Samuel Johnson.

Then, there, white Judges, nearly all, were Freemasons; some of them were thicker than a gross of planks.

They did not believe in the exceptionalism of Christ (John 14:6), so they were not deterred by His transparent Justice (John 5:22).

They secretly hate us, and we know.

They fear untamed mind of the self-educated African more than Putin's poisons.

"The colour bar is crude and cruel. The reasoning bar is spineless cowardice.

A bastardised, indiscreetly dishonest, unashamedly mediocre, vindictive, potently weaponised, and institutionally RACIST legal system that is overseen by the FREEMASONS (Mediocre Mafia/New Pharisees) — Habakkuk

"To deny or belittle this good is, in this dangerous century when the resources and pretensions of power continue to enlarge, a desperate error of intellectual abstraction. More than this, it is a self-fulfilling error, which encourages us to give up the struggle against bad laws and class bound procedures and to disarm ourselves before power. It is to throw away a whole inheritance of struggle about the law and within the forms of law, whose continuity can never be fractured without bringing men and women into immediate danger." — E. P Thompson.

CHAPTER SIX:

Boris Johnson: Why is England not a scam?

The Most Reverend and Rt. Hon. Archbishop of
Canterbury
Lambeth Palace
London
SE1 7JU

2 December 2002

Dear Archbishop

I write in response to the reports in The Independent
newspaper of your views on Freemasonry.

According to the reports:

a) you have doubts on the compatibility of Freemasonry
with Christianity and believe that elements of the ritual
may have a Satanic basis

b) you believe Freemasonry to be both a secret society and
a self-serving network

c) you have in the past not appointed to sensitive senior posts candidates who are Freemasons and intend to continue that practice.

For nearly 300 years Freemasonry has existed in an organised way in England and Wales. During that period hundreds of thousands of committed Christians (clergy and laity) have found no incompatibility between their Christian faith and the principles and practices of Freemasonry. Indeed, many have testified that their membership of Freemasonry has strengthened their faith and, in some cases, brought them back into active church membership.

The prime and inalienable qualification for admission into Freemasonry is a belief in God. An individual's religion is a matter for his conscience, and Freemasonry will not interfere in or in any way comment on religious matters. As a result our membership encompasses Christians of all denominations, Jews, Muslims, Hindus, Sikhs, etc., who meet together in harmony, knowing that their religions differ but not allowing those differences to come between them on Masonic occasions.

The suggestion that Freemasonry is "Satanically inspired" in its rituals would be risible were it not for the fact that it questions the basis of the faiths of over 300,000 Freemasons under the United Grand Lodge of England, whatever their religion may be. Even a small amount of elementary research would have shown how nonsensical this dreadful assertion is, and would have enabled you to avoid giving deep and gratuitous offence to so many who are encouraged in every form of Freemasonry to be true to their God above all other considerations.

As for the claim that Freemasonry is a "secret organisation", it must surely be a very peculiar "secret" society which makes its rules and aims available to the public; publishes annual lists of its national and local leaders together with the dates and places of meeting of all of its units; opens its national headquarters to the general public on a daily basis; maintains national and local web sites on the Internet; gives regular briefings to the media; and provides spokesmen to speak anywhere about its nature and activities. Each Freemason is at perfect liberty to tell whomsoever he pleases that he is a Freemason. Indeed, Freemasonry is one of the few organisations to have been specifically declared not to be a secret society. In July 2001 the European Court of Human Rights ruled that (a) Freemasonry was neither a secret, criminal nor an illegal organisation, and (b) that in making appointments or promotions it is illegal to discriminate against a candidate simply because he is a Freemason.

Rather than being a self-serving network, the opposite is true. On at least six occasions during the process of becoming a Freemason the new member is told that it is contrary to our principles and rules to use his membership to gain any form of advantage for himself or anyone else. Any attempt to do so will result in disciplinary proceedings, with sanctions running from admonition to irrevocable expulsion.

I have enclosed two booklets and some leaflets which explain the background to Freemasonry and how it relates to society in general. The booklet "Your Questions Answered" deals in particular with the myths which surround Freemasonry.

I also extend to you an invitation to meet privately with some senior Freemasons to discuss at the true source any doubts you may have, in preference to simply putting your faith in secondary and unreliable information. Your three immediate predecessors each came here for lunch and found it an interesting, stimulating and enjoyable experience. I realise that you have much to consider at the present, and that it may not be convenient to accept this invitation immediately. I trust that you will permit me to write to you again after your Enthronement to reaffirm our wish to welcome you here and show that your doubts about Freemasonry have no justification in fact.

Yours sincerely

R A H Morrow
Grand Secretary

****

R. A. H. Morrow
Grand Secretary, United Grand Lodge of England
Freemason's Hall
Great Queen Street

London
WC2B 5AZ

23 January 2003

Dear Mr Morrow

I have been sorry to learn of the distress of a considerable
number of Freemasons. It is true that a great deal of upset
and hurt has been caused by the newspaper reports about
my purported views on freemasonry. In replying to private
correspondence, I had no intention of starting a public
debate nor of questioning the good faith and generosity of
individual freemasons and I regret the tone and content of
the media coverage.

Much of the distress has been due to what amounts to a
serious misrepresentation of views I am supposed to hold.
The quoted statements about the "satanic" character of
masonic ceremonies and other matters did not come from
me and do not represent my judgement. Since my late
father was a member of the Craft for many years, I have
had every opportunity of observing the probity of
individual members.

Where anxieties exist, however, they are in relation not to
Freemasonry but to Christian ministry, and. my letter
simply reflected a personal unease about Christian
ministers subscribing to what could be and often is
understood (or misunderstood) as a private system of

profession and initiation, involving the taking of oaths of loyalty. Concerns like these have led to a number of debates within the church in recent years and it is clear that there are still widely differing views ? held with sincerity and honesty ? about the compatibility of certain aspects of Freemasonry with Christian belief, ministry and, service.

My statement about resisting the appointment of freemasons to certain posts in Wales needs to be understood against the background of the belief that I and the church had deliberately advanced the cause of Freemasons. In saying that I had resisted the appointment of Freemasons to certain posts I was not suggesting that people had been blackballed, but asserting that I was satisfied that membership of the Craft was neither a disqualifier nor an advantage.

I welcome the manner in which Freemasons have engaged in debate and especially the increasing openness of recent years. Their commitment to charitable causes and the welfare of the wider community is beyond question.

Yours sincerely,

Rowan Williams

Archbishop of Canterbury

****

The response by the Archbishop did not have any spiritual input, had it, the Archbishop would have realised that the principal, if not the sole, argument against the Charitable Antichrist Closeted Racist Freemasonry Religion (Mediocre Mafia/New Pharisees) is that members of the broad church quasi-cult, do not believe in the exceptionalism Christ (John 14:6).

John 14:6 is the cornerstone of Christian belief; it is absolutely incompatible with 'FAITHS'; it is depicted only by 'THE FAITH'.

Freemasons believe in FAITHS, and FAITHS is the byword of the dissenters of the exceptionalism of Christ – John 14:6.

"The prime and inalienable qualification for admission into Freemasonry is a belief in God. An individual's religion is a matter for his conscience, and Freemasonry will not interfere in or in any way comment on religious matters. As a result, our membership encompasses Christians of all denominations, Jews, Muslims, Hindus, Sikhs, etc., who meet together in harmony, knowing that their religions differ but not allowing those differences to come between them on Masonic occasions." R. A. H. Morrow, Grand Secretary, United Grand Lodge of England, Freemason's Hall, Great Queen Street, London, WC2B 5AZ

Members of the Charitable Antichrist Racist Freemasonry Quasi-Religion (Mediocre Mafia/New Pharisees) are free to decorate the temples of their powerless and useless fertility tools with whatever they like, and they are Free to admit motley assemblies of John 14:6 dissenters (Believers in Faiths) to their voodoo like Fraternity. The concern of we, their absolutely irreconcilable Religious Enemies is that FREEMASONS oversee the administration of English Law, and there is an imbalance, and gross unfairness, and conflict interest, as the closeted white supremacist thugs adjudicate in disputes concerning, we, their absolutely irreconcilable RELIGIOUS ENEMIES.

Then, He was lynched like Gadhafi and crucified only because He spoke, He disclosed pictures His unbounded mind painted; He was not punished for speaking, He was prevented from speaking

We do not believe in FAITHS, and we do like those who do, but we want to live in harmony with our absolutely irreconcilable RELIGIOUS ENEMIES, and our desire for harmonious relationship with our irreconcilable RELIGIOUS ENEMIES is only possible under a transparent, colour-blind, and exact administration of English Law.

English Law is equal; its administration is not.

The administration of English Law is overseen by members of the Charitable Antichrist Racist Freemasons (New

Pharisees/ Mediocre Mafia): A gross unbalanced and unfair religiously very sensitive arrangement.

Charitable Antichrist Racist Freemasons are believers of 'FAITHS', dissenters of THE FAITH (John 14:6), and their people are everywhere, and they control almost everything, including the Judiciary and the Police Force.

They find a very, very dull Indian, a believer of 'FAITHS', and a Dissenter of John 14:6, and they adorn him with very high titles, and he becomes Freemasons' Zombie private soldier (IRA of Sinn Fein).

"I think I will ask our legal adviser for any advice he may have. My view is that there are six or seven of us here who had the admission down, but we cannot find it in the transcript and there is wordings that imply that there was, but it is not in black and white….." Dr Shiv Pabary, Member of the Most Excellent Order of our Empire (MBE), Justice of Peace (JP), and the archetypal GDC Committee Chairman

AN IMBECILE: AN ADULT WITH THE BASIC SKILLS OF A CHILD.

Dr Shiv Pabary: Mediocre Member of the Most Excellent Order of our Empire (MMBE), Justice of Incompetent Racist Lies (JIRL)

They use incompetent racist mendacity to compensate hereditary intellectual impotence.

"Those who have the power to do wrong with impunity seldom wait long for the will." Dr Samuel Johnson

BORIS JOHNSON: Give us the legal tools, and we will defend ourselves against the closeted racist bastards who use very expensive aprons to decorate the temples of their powerless and useless fertility tools, and who lie that they don't lie – Psalm 144.

BORIS JOHNSON: Without measurable objectivity, Freemasons awarded themselves the supreme knowledge, but the shallow closeted racist bastards see only molecules, give us the legal tools, and we will show the narrow and shallow fools – atoms.

"The supreme vice is shallowness." Wilde

Like the closeted white supremacist atheist, Dr Clinton Richard Dawkins, they believe that He does not exist because He does not disclose Himself to them, and the shallow closeted racist bastards believe that what they cannot see does not exist, and those who say He revealed Himself to them must be lunatics and/or liars.

"There is no sin except stupidity." Wilde

Deluded closeted racist bastards accept the money of the Antichrist, and in order to avoid being called hypocrites, they say that all gods are God, and they attract more people to their Satanic Cult, and earn more money, and do, 'selflessly', for their vulgar Pharisees' Charitable works.

Freemasonry is a good business, and God is a very good business.

OYINBO OLE: THIEVES – HABAKKUK.

Those they need to spin are among the dullest adults in the industrialised world (the least literate and the least numerate) - OECD.

The report, by the OECD, warns that the UK needs to take significant action to boost the basic skills of the nation's young people. The 460-page study is based on the first-ever survey of the literacy, numeracy and problem-solving at work skills of 16 to 65-year-olds in 24 countries, with almost 9,000 people taking part in England and Northern Ireland to make up the UK results. The findings showed that England and Northern Ireland have some of the highest proportions of adults scoring no higher than Level 1 in literacy and numeracy - the lowest level on the OECD's scale. This suggests that their skills in the basics are no better than that of a 10-year-old.

AN IMBECILE: AN ADULT WITH THE BASIC SKILLS OF A CHILD.

BORIS JOHNSON: Let me tell you, then, there, white Judges (disproportionately predominant) who believed that daily dialogues with IMBECILES was a worthwhile, 'meaty', and manly job, were SCAMMERS, and those who demanded and accepted very valuable consideration in exchange for daily dialogues with imbeciles were RACKETEERS (Thieves).

Facts are sacred; they cannot be overstated.

Adults with the basic skills of a foetus will succeed adults with the basic skills of a child, and the former will need only food and shelter, not very, very expensive administration of English Law.

Based on very proximate observations and direct experiences, white Judges, predominantly, who expended their professional life on daily dialogues with imbeciles (adults with the basic skills of a child) were foreseeably affected by their regular encounters.

"It is incumbent upon the court and all those professionals involved to conclude court proceedings as quickly as possible. This hopefully ensures that a child has stability, love and affection and the parents working together to ensure that he has the best opportunity of developing academically and emotional." District Judge Paul Ayers, the Senior Vice President of the Association of Her Majesty's District Judges – proofed and approved Judgement

A CLOSETED RACIST FOOL'S APPROVAL!

AN IMBECILE: AN ADULT WITH THE BASIC
SKILLS OF A CHILD.

"Yes, Sir, it does *her* honour, but it would do nobody else
honour. I have indeed, not read it all. But when I take up
the end of a web, and find it packthread, I do not expect, by
looking further, to find embroidery." Dr Samuel Johnson

Then, there, white Judges (predominantly) were members
of the Charitable Antichrist Racist Freemasonry Quasi-
Religion (New Pharisees/Mediocre Mafia); some of them
were THICKER than a gross of planks – Habakkuk

Members of the Charitable Antichrist Racist Freemasonry
Quasi-Religion (New Pharisees/Mediocre Mafia) taught
members secret handshakes, not grammar, and the former
was considerably easier to master.

Like his mentally very, very gentle white children,
imbeciles (adults with the basic skills of a child) who sit
before him think he is a genius, they don't know that his
nomination and constructive appointment by some
dementing and demented white Lords was not based on
progressive, colour-blind, and measurable objectivity, and
they do not know that the last time he passed through the
filter of progressive, colour-blind, and measurable
objectivity was when he studied 5th rate law at Poly, and it
shows.

LORDS: "This man I thought had been a Lord of wits, but,
I find, he is only a wit among Lords." Dr Samuel Johnson

LORDS: "500 men, 500 ordinary men, chosen accidentally from among the unemployed." David Lloyd George.

"Those who know the least obey the best." George Farquhar.

BASED ON VERY PROXIMATE OBSERVATIONS AND DIRECT EXPERIENCES, PERCEPTION IS GRANDER THAN REALITY.

NIGERIA: SHELL'S DOCILE CASH COW.
The very highly luxuriant soil of Norwich yields only food. There are no oil wells or gas fields in Bishop's Stortford.

Briton, Cecil Rhodes, 1853 – 1902, was a white supremacist thug, and a thief.

"We shall deal with the racist bastards when we get out of prison." Comrade Robert Mugabe (1924 - 2019).
Then, racist bastards carried and sold millions of stolen children of defenceless poor people (the African ancestors of Meghan Markle and her white children), now, they carry natural resources.

SUBSTITUTION IS FRAUDULENT EMANCIPATION.

"Moderation is a virtue only among those who are thought to have found alternatives." Henry Kissinger

OYINBO OLE: THIEVES – HABAKKUK.

******

"The prime and inalienable qualification for admission into Freemasonry is a belief in God. An individual's religion is a matter for his conscience, and Freemasonry will not interfere in or in any way comment on religious matters. As a result our membership encompasses Christians of all denominations, Jews, Muslims, Hindus, Sikhs, etc., who meet together in harmony, knowing that their religions differ but not allowing those differences to come between them on Masonic occasions.
R. A. H. Morrow
Grand Secretary, United Grand Lodge of England
Freemason's Hall
Great Queen Street
London
WC2B 5AZ

BRAINLESS CLOSETED WHITE SUPREMACISTS'
NONSENSICAL REASONING!

"The supreme vice is shallowness." Wilde

The white man is a dunce; an ignorant descendant of very hardened PROFESSIONAL THIEVES and owners of stolen children of defenceless poor people (the African ancestors of Meghan Markle and her white children) - Habakkuk.

"We have the power to turn against our creators." Dr Richard Dawkins

Which one of their creators?

If as implied by R. A. H. Morrow, Grand Secretary, United Grand Lodge of England, all gods are God, and if as he stated the prime and inalienable qualification for admission into Freemasonry Fraternity is a belief in God, and religion of members of their very charitable Satanic Cult is a matter for the conscience of members of their Antichrist Fraternity, and Freemasonry will not interfere in or in any way comment on religious matters, and membership of their closeted white supremacists' cult encompasses Christians of all denominations, Jews, Muslims, Hindus, Sikhs, etc., who meet together in harmony, knowing that their religions differ but not allowing those differences to come between them on Masonic occasions, have the gods of their different religions ceded power to Judge to Christ – John 5:22; Matthew 25: 31- 46?

Etcetera is a very, very wide, and wild world.

What binds them together, in harmony, is money. It would be world class hypocrisy if those who demand and accept millions from Antichrist disbelieve the gods of their very, very generous benefactors.

Freemasons are Dissenters of John 14:6 and believers in FAITHS only because money matters.

"Money is the most important thing in the world. It represents health, strength, honour, generosity, and beauty as conspicuously as the want of it represents illness, weakness, disgrace, meanness, and ugliness." George Bernard Shaw

BORIS JOHNSON: Slimily vulgar Pharisees' charitable works of Freemasons is not a good deal. Vulgar Pharisees charitable in exchange for what? Believe me, theirs is not a good deal. Then, He rejected the grandest bribe of their ruler – Matthew 4:9.

Christians of all denominations who are not aligned to John 14:6 are auxiliary members of branches of Masonic Temples to Baal; they merely impersonate Christians, and their Masonic Temples impersonate Churches, they are SCAMMERS.

Close to 500,000 Britons are members of the Charitable Antichrist Racist Freemasonry Religion (Mediocre Mafia/New Pharisees), and for centuries, some of the most senior members of the Charitable Antichrist Racist Freemasonry Religion (Mediocre Mafia/New Pharisees) have been in the Church's higher echelons, and very many Judges and Policemen are members of the Charitable Antichrist Racist Freemasonry Religion (Mediocre Mafia/New Pharisees).

FAITHS: The byword for the Charitable Antichrist Racist Freemasonry Religion (Mediocre Mafia/New Pharisees), the dissenters of John 14:6 who do not believe in His exceptionalism and are not deterred by His Justice (John 5:22).

BORIS JOHNSON: "Give us the tools, and we will finish the job." Churchill

NEW HEROD, MATTHEW 2:16: Closeted racist bastards deceive their mentally very gentle children that they are geniuses, and they kill all those who know that they are excessively stupid.

https://www.youtube.com/watch?v=BlpH4hG7m1A&feature=youtu.be

"They may not have been well written from a grammatical point of view but I am confident I had not forgotten any of the facts." Dr Geraint Evans, Postgraduate Tutor, Oxford

AN IMBECILE: AN ADULT WITH THE BASIC SKILLS OF A CHILD.

https://youtu.be/rayVcfyu9Tw

"Why, Sir, Sherry is dull, naturally dull; but it must have taken him a great deal of pains to become what we now see him. Such an excess of stupidity, Sir, is not in Nature." DR SAMUEL JOHNSON

Ignorant descendants of ultra-righteous white thieves, white murderers, white racists, white drug dealers (opium merchants), and white owners of stolen black children of very poor people (African ancestors of Meghan Markle's ancestors and her white children) – Habakkuk

OYINBO OLE: THIEVES – HABAKKUK.

"Sometimes people don't want to hear the truth because they don't want their illusions destroyed." Friedrich Nietzsche

Based on very proximate observations and direct experiences, only their irrefutably superior skin colour is truly good, and without it, the closeted racist bastards will be considerably diminished as human beings.

They want the superiority that is brainlessly and baselessly attached to their irrefutably superior skin colour, but they don't want Freedom of Expression because they don't want their mentally very gentle children to know that their white ancestors were, for several centuries, PROFESSIONAL THIEVES, and they don't want their children to know that properly rehearsed ultra-righteousness and deceptively schooled civilised decorum were preceded by hundreds of years of the greediest economic cannibalism, and the evilest racist terrorism, the world will ever know, and they don't want their children to know that they are brainless closeted racist bastards - Habakkuk.

Like Herod, Putin, MBS, Saddam Hussein, Kim, and babies, closeted racist bastards expect everyone to love them unconditionally, and/or say, and/or print, only what they want to hear, not what their irreconcilable secret enemies truly feel, and secretly say behind their backs - Habakkuk.

Properly rehearsed ultra-righteousness and deceptively schooled civilised decorum were preceded by several continuous centuries of the greediest economic cannibalism and the evilest racist terrorism the world will ever know – Habakkuk

OYINBO OLE: RIGHTEOUS DESCENDANTS OF ULTRA-RIGHTEOUS THIEVES – HABAKKUK.

"England is like a prostitute who, having sold her body all her life, decides to quit and close her business, and then tells everyone that she wants to be chaste and protect her flesh as if it were jade." He Manzi, Chinese Politician.

Then, in the African bush, during the Carrying-Trade, had the very dull and incontrovertibly functional semi-illiterate white men, George Rothnie, Deputy Postgraduate Tutor, Oxford, District Judge Paul Ayers, and Geraint Evans, Postgraduate Tutor, Oxford, been black and young (<25), the closeted racist bastards would have been rejected by the Christian carriers and sellers of stolen children of defenceless very poor people (Meghan Markle's ancestors) – Habakkuk

Humphry Morice (1671 – 16 November 1731) was a British merchant of stolen children of defenceless poor people (African ancestors of Meghan Markle and her white children) - Habakkuk. Rich man's son, Humphry Morice

was a Member of Parliament, and the Governor of the
Bank of England who, like his father before him, was a
leading merchant of stolen lives.

OYINBO OLE: THIEVES – HABAKKUK.

Then, the white man was the devil.

'The white man is the devil' – what the Nation of Islam
taught ...
https://www.independent.co.uk › World

5 Jun 2016 — In 1974, Muhammad Ali told Michael
Parkinson and a stunned chat show audience that the white
man of America was "the blue-eyed, blond-headed ...

Humphry Morice (1671 – 16 November 1731) a British
merchant of stolen children of defenceless poor people
(African ancestors of Meghan Markle and her white
children) – Habakkuk, a very rich man's son, a Member of
the British Parliament, and the Governor of the Bank of
England was leading and engaged merchant of stolen lives
and ship owner:

"He made it his business to learn the details of trade, which
he expressed in careful instructions to his team of captains.
He explained how trading practices varied from one
African port to the next. He knew that staying on the coast
too long gathering cargo risked higher mortality, so he
worked out cooperative practices among his ships to

215

evacuate the slaves quickly. He instructed his captain to buy slaves between the ages of twelve to twenty-five, two males to a female, good and healthy, and not blind, lame, or blemished. He no doubt followed the advice of his Jamaican factors about the defects to be carefully avoided.
Dwarfish, or Gigantick Size wch are all equally disagreeable.
Ugly faces.
Long tripeish breasts wch ye Spaniards mortally hate.
Yellowish skin.
Livid spot in ye skin wch turns to an incurable evil.
Films in ye eyes.
Loss of fingers, toes, or teeth.
Navells sticking out.
Ruptures wch ye Gambian slaves are subject to.
Bandy legs.
Sharp shins.
Lunaticks.
Idiots.
Lethargicks......." Markus Rediker, The Slave Ship. A Human History.

"Mr Bamgbelu clearly has very, very strong views about education and I understand those views are based upon the fact that he is a successful dentist here in Bedford which he attributes to the fact that his parents cared for him and his education when he was young. They ensured that he had a proper fee paying education ...." District Judge Paul Ayers of Bedford County Court, 3, St Paul's Square, MK40 1 SQ, the Senior Vice President of the Association

216

of Her Majesty's District Judges – proofed and approved Judgement.

Financial disclosure in a divorce: 'How can a mere Negro have what I do not have?'

OYINBO OLE: A RIGHTEOUS DESCENDANT OF ULTRA-RIGHTEOUS WHITE THIEVES AND OWNERS OF STOLEN CHILDREN DEFENCELESS POOR PEOPLE (AFRICAN ANCESTORS OF MEGHAN MARKLE AND HER WHITE CHILDREN) - HABAKKUK.

When hereditary RACIAL HATRED (familial) copulates with indiscreet envy, insanity is their offspring.

Indiscreet envy.

Envy is a thief.

"Envy is weak." Yul Brynner.

Brainless elementary sarcasm: His spinal cord seemed to highest centre. Then, at Anglican boys, grammar school, the white man, would be robustly floored for the brainless sarcasm, and whether he got up would have depended on how he landed and/or what he landed on.

Then, the white father and mother of District Judge Paul Ayers of Bedford County Court, the Senior Vice President of the Association of Her Majesty's District

Judges couldn't have had very, very strong views about education, and it is plainly deductible that they did not care, had they, their functional semi-illiterate white son would not have approved and immortalised excessive stupidity at 16, and he would be a properly educated lawyer, privately educated Anthony Julius, Anthony Blair, Geoff Hoon, and Rabinder Singh's Class, and he might practice proper law in STRAND.

An ignorant racist leech; a righteous descendant of ultra-righteous industrial-scale PROFESSIONAL WHITE THIEVES and owners of stolen children of defenceless poor people (African ancestors of Meghan Markle and her white children) - Habakkuk.

Which part of Bedford County Court, 3, St Paul's Square, MK 40 1SQ, was not stolen, or which part of it did transparent virtue yield, or which part of it did the people of Bedford buy, or which preceded the barbarously racist traffic in millions of stolen children of defenceless poor people (African ancestors of Meghan Markle and her white children): The building or its chattels?

OYINBO OLE: THIEVES: HABAKKUK.

Ignorance is bliss?

An ignorant descendant of economic migrants, from Eastern Europe, with camouflage English names, whose white ancestors crossed the English Channels, in dinghy boats, not that long ago, without luggage or decent shoes, and a very hardened racist leech: A righteous descendant of THIEVES and owners of stolen children of defenceless poor people - Habakkuk.

Facts are sacred.

"The truth allows no choice." Dr Samuel Johnson

Before SLAVERY, what?

Then, there, closeted racist white bastards weaponised their mediocre legal system, and used it to persecute Africans who disagree with their Satanic Mumbo Jumbo Quasi-Religion – Habakkuk 1:4; John 8:44: John 10:10.

OXFORD, ENGLAND: British Soldier – Territorial Defence, Stephanie Twidale (TD), unrelentingly lied under oath. Her white ancestors were incompetent racist liars too, they were WHITE THIEVES and owners of stolen children of very, very poor people (Meghan Markle's ancestors) - Habakkuk

A CROOKED WHITE WOMAN. A DISHONEST RACIST COUGAR.

Then, He didn't like theirs, so theirs used extreme violence to CANCEL lives of ours, and the closeted racist white bastards used guns to steal what He gave to our ancestors: Movable and immovable.

Now, He doesn't like them, so they use incompetent racist lies to steal the yield of our Christ granted talent. They were wickeder than the devil, greedier than the grave, and like death, they were never satisfied – Habakkuk 2:5.

The greedy racist bastards are not immortal, and they are not the only creation of Almighty God, and the irrefutably superior skin colour that they neither made nor chose is not the only wonder of our world.

GOOGLE: THE WHITE JUDGE LIED

GOOGLE: JUDGE AYERS BEDFORD.

GOOGLE: INCOMPETENT LIARS SOME LAWYERS

When their people commit racist crimes against ours, closeted racist bastards who oversee the administration of their law (FREEMASONS) criminally bury racial hatred.

Only stupid Africans do not know that Whites measure whites with a very different yardstick, and only stupider Africans expect demons to cast out demons – Matthew 12:27

GDC: Richard Hill fabricated reports and unrelentingly lied under oath

GDC: Kevin Atkinson (NHS) unrelentingly lied under oath

GDC: Helen Falcon (MBE) unrelentingly lied on record

GDC: George Rothnie (NHS) unrelentingly lied on record

GDC: Stephanie Twiddle (NHS) unrelentingly lied under oath

GDC: Sue Gregory (OBE) unrelentingly lied on record

GDC: Rachael Bishop (NHS) unrelentingly lied under oath

GDC: Geraint Evans (NHS) unrelentingly lied on record

Facts are sacred; they can't be overstated.

They were all white, including the Judges, and they were all incompetent racist liars. The closeted racist bastards were not deterred by His Justice because the Freemasons did not believe in His exceptionalism.

They have invented the legal way of killing their RELIGIOUS ENEMIES, albeit hands-off.

GOOGLE: Dr Anand Kamath, dentist.

GOOGLE: Dr Richard Bamgboye, GP.

Based on very, very proximate observations and direct experiences, the white man is the devil.

'The white man is the devil' – what the Nation of Islam taught ...
https://www.independent.co.uk › World

5 Jun 2016 — In 1974, Muhammad Ali told Michael Parkinson and a stunned chat show audience that the white man of America was "the blue-eyed, blond-headed ...

"You will bow. You can't beat the system." Kemi Daramola

Imported devil has bowed to Baal in the Masonic Temple in Brickhill Bedford. She pays tithe (over £100, 000/quasi protection money), since she was imported from Lagos, and prays to Christ in Brickhill Bedford and members of the Charitable Antichrist Racist Freemasons on Bedford Road, in Kempston, answer her prayers.

I shan't. I know who will – Romans 11; 1 John 4:4.

Re:

Fri, 11 Apr 2014 9:28
resh diu (rdiu@me.com)To:you Details

It's sad Ola
I kept telling you to play the game of chess rather than fight it
You take care
If you wish to dispose of 24 park road let me know
Regards

Resh
Dr Resh Diu BDS
www.oradi.co.uk

We must bow to closeted white supremacist thugs who use expensive aprons to decorate the temples of their powerless and useless fertility tools, and we must play the closeted racist bastards like chess, and we must teach our children to bow to descendants of undocumented refugees (genetic aliens) from Eastern Europe, with camouflage English names, and teach them to play shallow closeted racist bastards like chess.

A bastardised, indiscreetly dishonest, unashamedly mediocre, vindictive, potently weaponised, and institutionally racist legal system that is overseen by white Freemason Judges (New Pharisees/Mediocre Mafia) – Habakkuk.

"To deny or belittle this good is, in this dangerous century when the resources and pretensions of power continue to enlarge, a desperate error of intellectual abstraction. More than this, it is a self-fulfilling error, which encourages us to give up the struggle against bad laws and class bound procedures and to disarm ourselves before power. It is to throw away a whole inheritance of struggle about the law and within the forms of law, whose continuity can never be fractured without bringing men and women into immediate danger." - E. P Thompson.

Then, there, white Judges, and white Policemen, nearly all, were FREEMASONS, and some of them were THICKER than a gross of planks - Habakkuk

"All sections of the UK Society are institutionally RACIST." Sir Bernard Hogan-Howe

Bedfordshire Police is part of the UK Society.

Only stupid Negroes believe that they are no longer inferior to whites, under whites' law, after the 1807 Act, and only stupider Negroes do not know that the fellow told the truth when He stated that demons can't cast out demons – Matthew 12:27.

They want skin colour superiority, their brainless and baseless birth right, but they don't want Freedom of Expression because they don't want their mentally gentle children to know that they are excessively stupid.

They are not the only creation of Almighty God, and they are not immortal, and the irrefutably superior skin colour that they neither made nor chose is not the only wonder of our world.

Based on very, very proximate contacts, about 15 years ago, on February 22, 2007, Stephanie Twiddle (TD), who was in the later stages of her seventh decade – stank; the white old-bat had a very distinct body odour. The cougar, an old bat, seemed to fancy me. The libido killer looked like someone who regularly visited THE GAMBIA to see on black rocks – Asewo.

"The truth allows no choice." Dr Samuel Johnson

Facts are sacred.

"Britons stank." W.S

He should know, then, in the swinging 60's, at least, one of his wives was a Briton; all his concubines were Britons.

W.S – Wole Soyinka, not William Shakespeare.

GDC- Expert: Helen Falcon, Member of the Most Excellent Order of our Empire (MBE), unrelentingly lied under implied oath. The ugly cougar, built like a very heavy barn door, with wonky asymmetrical muscular ass (organ grinder) like those of an Olympic Javelin thrower (Fatima Whitbread), looked like someone who had sat on black rocks in THE GAMBIA: Mumsy Asewo.

A CROOKED WHITE WOMAN. A DISHONEST RACIST COUGAR.

OYINBO OLE: THIEVES – HABAKKUK.

Based on available evidence, those who went to Poly could become Judges in Great Britain. What's great about that.

Then, there, white Judges, nearly all, were members of the vulgarly Charitable Antichrist Racist Freemasonry Quasi-Religion (Mediocre Mafia/New Pharisees), some of them were thicker than a gross of planks – Habakkuk 1:4; John 8:44; John 10:10.

"Someone must be trusted. Let it be the Judges." Lord Denning (1899 – 1999)

Based on detailed study, Lord Denning was a Closeted White Supremacist descendant of owners of stolen children of very poor people (Meghan Markle's ancestors) – Habakkuk.

Judges are human beings. Some human beings are racists.

The closeted white supremacist quasi-voodoo-men who use very, very expensive aprons, with vulgar embroideries, to decorate the temples of their powerless and useless fertility tools, do not believe in the exceptionalism of Christ (John 14:6), the deluded closeted racist bastards believe in FAITHS, so they are not deterred by the transparent Justice of the only Good Shepherd – Proverbs 15:3; they tell incompetent racist lies, all the time, indiscreetly, and with impunity, and they lie that they don't lie – Psalm 144.

"Lies are told all the time." Sir Michael Havers (1923 - 1992).

GDC- Expert: Sue Gregory (OBE) Officer of the Most Excellent Order of our Empire, unrelentingly lied under implied oath. Her white ancestors were incompetent racist liars too; they were WHITE THIEVES and owners of stolen children of defenceless poor people (Meghan Markle's ancestors) – Habakkuk

A CROOKED WHITE WOMAN. A DISHONEST RACIST COUGAR.

Our Empire did not evolve; then, almost everything was actively and deliberately stolen with GUNS – Habakkuk.

Before SLAVERY, what?

OYINBO OLE: THIEVES – HABAKKUK

"Those who have the power to do wrong with impunity seldom wait long for the will." Dr Samuel Johnson

Members of the Vulgarly Charitable Antichrist Racist Freemasonry Quasi-Religion (Mediocre Mafia/New Pharisees) should be free to decorate temples of their powerless and useless fertility tools with whatever they want, but we, their irreconcilable RELIGIOUS ENEMIES, do not give a 'FORK' about froth; we need only transparent, colour blind, and exact laws, and Freedom to disclose pictures painted by our minds.

They find a very, very dull Indian, a believer of Faiths, and a dissenter of THE FAITH or John 14:6, and they adorn him with very, very high titles, and unwittingly, he becomes a Freemasons' zombie soldier (IRA of Sinn Fein).

"I think I will ask our legal adviser for any advice he may have. My view is that there are six or seven of us here who had the admission down, but we cannot find it in the transcript and there is wordings that imply that there was, but it is not in black and white ….." Shiv Pabary, Member of the Most Excellent Order of our Empire (MBE), the archetypal GDC Committee Chairman, Justice of Peace (JP), and the archetypal GDC Committee Chairman.

AN IMBECILE: AN ADULT WITH THE BASIC SKILLS OF A CHILD.

"Yes, Sir, it does *her* honour, but it would do nobody else honour. I have indeed, not read it all. But when I take up the end of a web, and find it packthread, I do not expect, by looking further, to find embroidery." Dr Samuel Johnson

Mediocre Member of our Empire (MMBE) and Justice of Incompetent Racist Lies (JIRL) – Habakkuk 1:4; John 8:44; John 10:10.

Shiv Pabary's brother is irreversibly wonky: Based on available evidence, Shiv Pabary seemed wonky too; their mother and father could be related: Siblings or cousins. Charles Darwin married his first cousin, and expectedly, their white children, not all, were physically and/or mentally wonky.

*****

"This statement is about a series of letters and emails I have been recieving. I am the above named person. I live at an address provided to police. In this statement I will also mention XXXXXXXXXXXXXXXXXXXXXXXXXXXX a leaseholder for a property I manage at my place work. I am the company director of DOBERN properties based in Ilford. These emails have been sent to my company email address of mail@debern.co.uk, and also letters have been sent to myself at our company ADDress of P.O BOX 1289, ILFORD, IG2 7XZ over the last Two and a half years, I have recieving a series of letters and emails from DR BAMGeLu. DR BAMGBELU is a leasholder for a property I manage at my place of work. Over the period of his leaseholding, DR BAmGelu has continually failed to pay arrears for the property. In march 2016 my company took DR to court and he was ordered to pay outstanding costs of around £20000 since that time and lead up to the case, DR BaMGBelu has been emailing me and posting me letters that are lengthy and accuses me repeatedly of being a racist in emails and letters tact are regularly Ten to twelve pages long, DR BAMGBELU. lists numerous quots from google searches all refrencing ham I am a bigot and a racist. The most recent letter I received from DR BAMGBELU opens with you are jealous and racist Evil combination you hate us we know it" he goes on to say "I would not have knowingly had anything to do with white supremicists." In the last email I recieved from him on 02/09/2016 DR BaMGBELU stated "you are restricted by poor Education within one of the least literate countries in the world". I would be perfectly happy for DR BAMGBElu to contact myself or my company if he has relevant enquiries to his lease holding, however these continuous letters and emails are causing me distress and I feel intimidated. I am not a racist and these accusatios make uncomfortable. All I want is to conduct between us in a normal manner. I want BambGlu to stop emailing me and sending me letters accusing me of being racist and harassing me." ROBERT KINGSTON, SOLICITOR, ACCOUNTANT, AND COMPANY DIRECTOR, ALBEIT ENGLAND'S CLASS.

A scatter-head white man.

AN IMBECILE: AN ADULT WITH THE BASIC SKILLS OF A CHILD.

"Jews are very good with money." President Donald Trump.

Whose money?

Judas Iscariot, Ghislaine Maxwell father, Ján Ludvík Hyman Binyamin Hoch, and Bernard Madoff were Jews.

"The prime and inalienable qualification for admission into Freemasonry is a belief in God. An individual's religion is a matter for his conscience, and Freemasonry will not interfere in or in any way comment on religious matters.

As a result, our membership encompasses Christians of all denominations, Jews, Muslims, Hindus, Sikhs, etc., who meet together in harmony, knowing that their religions differ but not allowing those differences to come between them on Masonic occasions." R. A. H. Morrow, Grand Secretary, United Grand Lodge of England, Freemason's Hall, Great Queen Street, London, WC2B 5AZ

Which one of the Gods (creators) of India will Lala's lunatic (Psalm 53) turn against?

"We have the power to turn against our creators." Dr Richard Dawkins.

"An individual's religion is a matter for his conscience, and Freemasonry will not interfere in or in any way comment on religious matters." R. A. H. Morrow, Grand Secretary, United Grand Lodge of England, Freemason's Hall, Great Queen Street, London, WC2B 5AZ

John 14:6 is about FAITH, not conscience.

Racist bastards who shipped millions of made in Birmingham guns to Africa, about 200, 000, annually, during several centuries of the evilest racist terrorism and the evilest economic cannibalism the world will ever know, did not have any conscience, and they were neither civilised nor enlightened, and they were not Christians.

"I know of no evil that has ever existed, nor can imagine any evil to exist, worse than the tearing of eighty thousand persons annually from their native land, by a combination of the most civilised nations inhabiting the most enlightened part of the globe, but more especially under the sanction of the laws of that Nation which calls herself the most free and the most happy of them all." Prime Minister William Pitt the Younger

William Pitt the Younger: A closeted white supremacist white man and an incompetent liar.

"The white man was the devil." Mohammed Ali

Then, Britons were wickeder than the devil, greedier than the grave, and like death, racist bastards were never satisfied – Habakkuk 2:5.

OYINBO OLE: THIEVES – HABAKKUK.

"As a result, our membership encompasses Christians of all denominations, Jews, Muslims, Hindus, Sikhs, etc., who meet together in harmony, knowing that their religions differ but not allowing those differences to come between them on Masonic occasions." R. A. H. Morrow, Grand Secretary, United Grand Lodge of England, Freemason's Hall, Great Queen Street, London, WC2B 5AZ

John 14:6 is Sacrosanct, and it is incompatible with everything except itself.

John 14:6 is absolutely incompatible with Islam, Judaism. Hinduism, Sikhism, and etcetera, which is a very, very wide world.

If Lala's husband, the deluded Antichrist closeted white supremacist Briton, the mere Science Journalist (Dr Edward Osborne Wilson), a dissenter of John 14:6, and the creator of the Blind watchmaker, Dr Clinton Richard Dawkins, and all the 33rd Degree Freemasons at the Grand Masonic Temple to Baal, 60 Great Queen St, London WC2B 5AZ, and all 33rd Degree Master Builders, at the Bedfordshire Masonic Temple to Baal, the Keep, Bedford Road, Kempston, MK42, and His Excellency Prime Minister Modi, and His Excellency Prime Minister Naftali Bennett, and Cambridge University Educated rich man's son, Sir, Mr Justice Haddon – Cave, QC, KBE, could prove that GDC-Witness, Freemason, Brother, Richard William Hill did not fabricate reports and unrelentingly told lies under oath, and they could prove that GDC-Witness: Kevin Atkinson (NHS) did not unrelentingly tell lies under oath, and if they could prove that GDC - Expert: Helen Falcon (MBE) did not unrelentingly tell lies on record, and they could prove that GDC -Witness: George Rothnie (NHS) did not unrelentingly tell lies on record, and if they could prove that GDC- Witness: Stephanie Twiddle (NHS) did not unrelentingly tell lies under oath, and if they could prove that GDC- Expert: Sue Gregory (OBE) did not unrelentingly tell lies on record, and if they could prove that GDC: Rachael Bishop (Senior NHS Nurse) did not unrelentingly tell lies under oath, and if they could prove that GDC-Witness: Geraint Evans (NHS) did not unrelentingly tell lies on record, they will confirm the belief of billions of people in our world, which is that Antichrist Vulgarly Charitable Antichrist Freemasonry Quasi-Religion (Mediocre Mafia/ New Pharisees), Antichrist Islam, Antichrist Judaism, and all other motley assemblies of exotic religions and FAITHS, under the common umbrella of the Governor of the Church of England and The Defender of The Faith (the faith, not faiths) are not intellectual flawed Satanic Mumbo Jumbo, and it will also confirm that reasoning and vision have finite boundaries. If reasoning and vision have finite boundaries, our own Messiah must have lied when He disclosed pictures His unbounded mind painted, in the Council, before Jews, and He must have also lied when He audaciously stated that He was exceptional – John 14:6.

"The first quality that is needed is audacity." Churchill

If the fellow told Jews the truth, in the Council, everything that is not aligned to John 14:6 is travelling in the wrong direction and heading straight for the rocks.

"It does no harm to throw the occasional man overboard, but it does not do much good if you are steering full speed ahead for the rocks." Sir Ian Gilmour (1926 – 2007).

CHAPTER SEVEN:

Boris Johnson: Why is England not a scam?

Boris Johnson: Based on available evidence, our irreconcilable religious enemies (FREEMASONS) oversee the administration of English law: A grossly unfair and unbalanced arrangement.

'FAITHS' is the principal byword for Antichrist Racist Freemasonry Religion (Mediocre Mafia/New Pharisees) and it is absolutely incompatible with the exceptionalism of Christ and Christian belief.

Dissenters of John 14:6 are believers of 'FAITHS'. The closeted racist bastards who use very expensive aprons to decorate the temples of their powerless and useless fertility tools are not deterred by His Justice (John 5:22) because they do not believe in His exceptionalism (John 14:6).

Based on very proximate observations and direct experiences, only the irrefutably superior skin colour that they neither made nor chose is truly, and without it, they will be considerably diminished as human beings.

Then, their ancestors fed their people with the yield of the greediest economic cannibalism and the evilest racist terrorism the world will ever know.

Now, they know how to steal for their people; they don't how to repair their scatter-heads.

"This statement is about a series of letters and emails I have been recieving. I am the above named person. I live at an address provided to police. In this statement I will also mention XXXXXXXXXXXXXXXXXXXXXXXXXXX a leaseholder for a property I manage at my place work. I am the company director of DOBERN properties based in Ilford. These emails have been sent to my company email address of mail@debern.co.uk, and also letters have been sent to myself at our company ADDress of P.O BOX 1289, ILFORD, IG2 7XZ over the last Two and a half years, I have recieving a series of letters and emails from DR BAMGeLu. DR BAMGBELU is a leasholder for a property I manage at my place of work. Over the period of his leaseholding, DR BAmGelu has continually failed to pay arrears for the property. In march 2016 my company took DR to court and he was ordered to pay outstanding costs of around £20000 since that time and lead up to the case, DR BaMGBelu has been emailing me and posting me letters that are lengthy and accuses me repeatedly of being a racist in emails and letters tact are regularly Ten to twelve pages long, DR BAMGBELU. lists numerous quots from google searches all refrencing ham I am a bigot and a racist. The most recent letter I received from DR BAMGBELU opens with you are jealous and racist Evil combination you hate us we know it" he goes on to say "I would not have knowingly had anything to do with white supremicists." In the last email I recieved from him on 02/09/2016 DR BaMGBELU stated "you are restricted by poor Education within one of the least literate countries in the world". I would be perfectly happy for DR BAMGBElu to contact myself or my company if he has relevant enquiries to his lease holding, however these continuous letters and emails are causing me distress and I feel intimidated. I am not a racist and these accusatios make uncomfortable. All I want is to conduct between us in a normal manner. I want BambGlu to stop emailing me and sending me letters accusing me of being racist and harassing me." MR ROBERT KINGSTON, SOLICITOR, ACCOUNTANT, AND COMPANY DIRECTOR.

AN IMBECILE: AN ADULT WITH THE BASIC SKILLS OF A CHILD.

A scatter-head white man: Intellectually disorientated and mentally imbalanced. Only the irrefutably superior skin colour that he neither made nor chose is truly good, and without it, he is PURIFIED NOTHING.

A very special tailless white monkey seemed to have the intellect of black monkeys with tails.

OYINBO OLE: THIEVES - HABAKKUK.

"We are just an advanced breed of monkeys on a minor planet of a very average star. But we can understand the Universe. That makes us something very special." Dr Stephen Hawking

They don't like us; we know.

Closeted racist bastards love Africa, but they don't love Africans. The only part of AFRICA they truly love is MONEY; everything else is a lie.

Then, extremely greedy racist bastards, and vicious economic cannibals, carried and sold millions of stolen children of defenceless poor people, only those who did not die while buried alive in the bellies of ships, by extremely nasty racist bastards; those who died became fish food in the Atlantic.

Then, the closeted racist bastards were greedier than the grave and like death, they were never satisfied – Habakkuk 2:5

In some parts of the world, white supremacist Judges are complicit in RACIST FRAUD.

"DR BAMGBELU. lists numerous quots from google searches all refrencing ham I am a bigot and a racist." MR ROBERT KINGSTON, SOLICITOR, ACCOUNTANT, AND COMPANY DIRECTOR.

How did the white cretin know that numerous quots were from google searches?

"By definition therefore there needs to be a contact order for Mr B so that he knows when he is going to see his son. It is absolutely essential that this occurs and mother agrees with that. She said so several times in her evidence. Mrs

Waller agreed that not only should a child have the opportunity of developing relationship with both parents, any sibling should also be there so that inter- sibling relationship could be fostered and nurtured. Obviously in this particular case the children reside in different places. That immediately puts a strain on the children having limited contact with each other. F's sister is very much older than him and she will be further advanced into her adult life. Thus it is not a matter that that sibling relationship can only be fostered by the children being together. Indeed as we all know absence sometimes makes the heart grow fonder. F should have an opportunity of seeing his sister. Wherever he does that it should be done in a friendly and loving environment. If the time comes that his sister goes to university of course his contact with her will be restricted to the time that she is home from university. In years to come when they have both grown up, with their own family they will see less of each other. But it doesn't mean that they don't still love and adore each other as much as they would if they saw each other every day." District Judge Paul Ayers of Bedford County Court, 3, St Paul's Square, Bedford, Mk40 1SQ, the Senior Vice President of the Association of Her Majesty's District Judges – proofed and approved Judgement.

A CLOSETED RACIST FOOL'S APPROVAL.

AN IMBECILE: AN ADULT WITH THE BASIC SKILLS OF A CHILD.

"Yes, Sir, it does *her* honour, but it would do nobody else honour. I have indeed, not read it all. But when I take up the end of a web, and find it packthread, I do not expect, by looking further, to find embroidery." Dr Samuel Johnson.

District Judge Paul Ayers of Bedford County Court, 3, St Paul's Square, Bedford, Mk40 1SQ, the Senior Vice President of the Association of Her Majesty's District Judges implied that like his own white mother and father, the white mothers and fathers of George Rothnie (Scottish George), the Deputy Postgraduate Dean, Oxford, and Geraint Evans, Postgraduate Dean, Oxford, and Robert Kingston, Director Dobern Property Limited, did not have very, very strong views about education.

Why should one's white mother and father have very, very strong views about education if there is irrefutable evidence that one's white ancestors were THIEVES and owners of stolen children of defenceless poor people (Black African ancestors of Meghan Markle and her white children) – Habakkuk?

"Mr Bamgbelu clearly has very, very strong views about education and I understand those views are based upon the fact that he is a successful dentist here in Bedford which he attributes to the fact that his parents cared for him and his education when he was young. They ensured that he had a proper fee paying education…….." District Judge Paul Ayers of Bedford County Court, 3, St Paul's Square, Bedford, Mk40 1SQ, the Senior Vice President of the

Association of Her Majesty's District Judges – proofed and approved Judgement.

Indiscreet envy.

Envy is a thief.

Brainless sarcasm.

It is plainly deductible that the white father and mother of District Judge Paul Ayers of Bedford County Court, 3, St Paul's Square, Bedford, Mk40 1SQ, the Senior Vice President of the Association of Her Majesty's District Judges did not have very, very strong views about education, had they, their functional semi-illiterate white son would not have approved and immortalised excessive stupidity at 16, and he would be a properly educated lawyer, privately educated Anthony Julius, Anthony Blair, Geoff Hoon, and Rabinder Singh's Class, and he might practice proper law in STRAND.

"Envy is weak." Yul Brynner.

When envy and racial hatred copulate, insanity is their offspring.

NIGERIA (oil/gas) is by far more relevant to the economic survival of their white fathers and mothers than Bishop's Stortford. The highly luxuriant soil of Bishop's Stortford yields only food. Then, the white ancestors of the white fathers and mothers were fed like battery hens with the yield of stolen children of defenceless poor people (Black African ancestors of Meghan Markle and her white children) -Habakkuk.

After several centuries of racial hatred, sadism, and savagery, they became ultra-righteous, very enlightened, highly civilised, and charitable. They did charitable works with the yield of the greediest economic cannibalism and the evilest terrorism the world will ever know – Habakkuk 2:5.

Ignorant racist leeches; ultra-righteous descendant of THIEVES and owners of stolen children of defenceless poor people (Black African ancestors of Meghan Markle and her white children) - Habakkuk.

NIGERIA: SHELL'S DOCILE CASH COW.

The highly luxuriant soil of Norwich yields only food.

Nigeria: Babies with huge oil wells and gas fields near their huts eat only 1.5/day; a closeted racist, functional semi-illiterate former debt-collector Solicitor in Norwich whose white father and mother have never seen crude oil, and whose white ancestors were fed like battery hens with yield of stolen children of defenceless poor people (Black African ancestors of Meghan Markle and her white children) is our District Judge in BEDFORD.

OYINBO OLE: THIEVES – HABAKKUK.

Then, closeted racist bastards carried and sold millions of stolen children of defenceless poor people (Black African ancestors of Meghan Markle and her white children); now, they carry natural resources.

SUBSTITUTION: FRAUDULENT EMANCIPATION.

If for several continuous centuries one's ancestors were racist murderers, THIEVES, and owners of stolen children of defenceless poor people, what does one need very, very strong views about education for?

"Moderation is a virtue only among those who are thought to have found alternatives." Henry Kissinger.

"It was our arms in the river of Cameroon, put into the hands of the trader, that furnished him with the means of pushing his trade; and I have no more doubt that they are British arms, put into the hands of Africans, which promote universal war and desolation that I can doubt their having done so in that individual instance. I have shown how great is the enormity of this evil, even on the supposition that we take only convicts and prisoners of war. But take the subject in another way, and how does it stand? Think of 80,000 persons carried out of their native country by we know not what means! For crimes imputed! For light or inconsiderable faults! For debts perhaps! For crime of witchcraft! Or a thousand other weak or scandalous pretexts! Reflect on 80,000 persons annually taken off!

There is something in the horror of it that surpasses all bounds of imagination." – Prime Minister William Pitt the Younger

"The white man was the devil." Mohammed Ali

Christ did not place Africans in the back rows, white men did. The white man was the devil. The white man was the thief.

OXFORD, ENGLAND: Based on available evidence, GDC-Witness, Rachael Bishop (Senior NHS Nurse) unrelentingly lied under oath – Habakkuk 1:4; John 8:44; John 10:10.

A CROOKED WHITE WOMAN. A CLOSETED RACIST COUGAR.

Facts are sacred, they cannot be overstated.

INCOMPETENT RACIST LIES GUARDED BY WHITE SUPREMACISTS' ILLEGAL PARALLEL POWER OF THE FREEMASONS IS THEIR CHIEF OF RACIST TOOLS

OYINBO OLE: THIEVES – HABAKKUK

A bastardised, indiscreetly dishonest, unashamedly mediocre, vindictive, potently weaponised, and institutionally racist legal system that is overseen by white Freemason Judges for the benefit of whites – Habakkuk

"To deny or belittle this good is, in this dangerous century when the resources and pretensions of power continue to enlarge, a desperate error of intellectual abstraction. More than this, it is a self-fulfilling error, which encourages us to give up the struggle against bad laws and class bound procedures and to disarm ourselves before power. It is to throw away a whole inheritance of struggle about the law and within the forms of law, whose continuity can never be fractured without bringing men and women into immediate danger." - E. P Thompson.

Closeted Racist Defenders of Faiths do not believe in the exceptionalism of Christ, so they are not deterred by the transparent Justice of the only Good Shepherd – Proverbs 15:3; John 5:22; Matthew 25: 31 – 46; John 14:6.

The extremely intolerant lunatic Jew (King Herod) removed John's head only because he spoke – Matthew 14.

Members of the Charitable Antichrist Racist Freemasonry Religion fear the untamed mind of the self-educated Negro more than Putin's poison.

John was not punished (decapitated) for speaking; he was permanently prevented from speaking – Matthew 14.

Then, like the Jew, King Herod, MBS, and Kim, intolerant, power drunk, sadistic lunatics used to barbarously butcher those who stated and/or printed truths they didn't want their mentally very gentle children to know about. The last decapitation of living human being in England, with an axe, was in 1817, and beheading was removed from the Statute book, in 1973. In 1973, Kenneth Baker banned flogging. Why remove the heads of those who stated and/or printed what you don't want your mentally very gentle children to know about if it were illegal to flog them?

"There is now less flogging in our great schools than formerly, but then less is learned there; so that what the boys get at one end, they lose at the other." Dr Samuel Johnson

Jews and others lynched him like Gadhafi, and He was crucified only because He spoke: He disclosed pictures His unbounded mind (infinite) painted.

Boris Johnson: Reasoning and vision are unbounded (infinite); the fellow told the truth when He disclosed pictures His unbounded mind painted.

Boris Johnson: Based on available evidence, it is not the truth that Africans are no longer inferior under English Law.

GDC-Witnesses: Two, too many Racist Scotchmen, Kevin Atkinson (Postgraduate Tutor, albeit England's Class) and George Rothnie (Deputy Postgraduate Dean) unrelentingly lied under oath and/or on record. Their Scottish ancestors were incompetent racist liars too: They were industrial-scale professional thieves, extremely nasty racist murderers, drug dealers (opium merchants), indiscriminate murderers, and owners of stolen children of defenceless poor people (Meghan Markle's ancestors) – Habakkuk

TWO CROOKED WHITE SCOTSMEN. DISHONEST RACIST SCOTTISH BASTARDS.

"The white man is the devil." Mohammed Ali

When their people commit racist crimes against ours, closeted racist bastards who oversee the administration of their law criminally bury racial hatred.

Only stupid Negroes expect whites to measure them with the yardstick they use to measure whites, and only stupider Negroes do not know that demons cannot cast out demons – Matthew 12:27.

Defenders of FAITHS do not believe in the exceptionalism of Christ, so they are not deterred by His transparent Justice – Proverbs 15:3; John 5:22; Matthew 25: 31-46; John 14:6.

Christ did not place Africans in the back rows, white men did.

They want skin colour superiority, their brainless and baseless birth right, but they don't want Freedom of Expression because they don't want their mentally gentle children to know that they are excessively stupid, and that their white ancestors were THIEVES and owners of stolen children of very poor people (Meghan Markle's ancestors) – Habakkuk

Then, closeted racist bastards carried and sold millions of stolen children. Now, closeted racist bastards care about climate; then, their ancestors, extremely nasty racists, and economic cannibals, carried and sold millions of children of defenceless Africans (Meghan Markle's ancestors) – Habakkuk. Defenders of FAITHS, closeted racist bastards, did not believe in the exceptionalism of Christ, so they were not deterred by His transparent Justice – Proverbs 15:3; John 5:22; Matthew 25: 31-46; John 14:6.

Like babies, Herod, Putin, Kim, Saddam Hussein, and MBS, closeted racist bastards expect everyone to love them, unconditionally, and say, and/or print only what they want to hear.

Spineless cowards (worms) want superiority, but not Freedom of Expression. Extremely greedy closeted racist bastards eat all their cakes, eat all ours, and they want everything.

"He is arrogant and never at rest. Because he is as greedy as the grave and like death is never satisfied ……" Habakkuk 2:5.

The nemesis is not extinct, and the fact that it tarries isn't proof that it will never come – Habakkuk.

Time will inevitably unfold the truth.

"Indeed, I tremble for my country when reflect that God is just: that his justice cannot sleep for ever: that considering numbers, nature and natural means only, a revolution of the wheel of fortune, an exchange of situation, is among possible events: that it may become probable by supernatural interference!" President Thomas Jefferson

Then, closeted racist white bastards accurately foresaw that a Scottish imbecile, George Rothnie (an adult with the basic skills of a child) will become a Deputy Postgraduate Dean, albeit England's class, they used guns to loot Africa – Habakkuk: Whenever the closeted racist bastards mercilessly slaughtered, they dispossessed, and wherever they robbed, they took possession. They were liars and THIEVES - Habakkuk.

OYINBO OLE: THIEVES – HABAKKUK.

"Those who have robbed have also lied." Dr Samuel Johnson

"Michael Jackson would have been found guilty if he'd been black." Jo Brand

Not all liars are racists, but all racists are malicious liars.

They are more intolerant than lunatic Jihadists, and they kill all those who know facts about them they don't want their mentally gentle children to know about, albeit hands-off. So, the Negro is 'a dead man walking' – Claudio Ranieri

DELUDED FREEMASONS (Mediocre Mafia/New Pharisees): They baselessly and brainlessly awarded themselves the supreme knowledge, but they see only molecules, and they kill all those who see atoms, especially if they were mere Negroes – Matthew 2:16.

New Herod, Matthew 2:16: They deceive their mentally gentle children that they are geniuses, and they kill, albeit hands-off, all those who know that they are brainless racist bastards.

Facts are sacred; they cannot be overstated.

Only foolish Negroes think that they are no longer inferior under English Law. The 1807 Act removed the visible chains, closeted racist bastards will never remove the true chains, substitution is likelier.

Substitution is Fraudulent emancipation.

"Change occurs slowly. Very often a legal change might take place, but the cultural shift required to really accept its spirit lingers in the wings for decades." Sara Sheridan

"Rightful liberty is unobstructed action according to our will within limits drawn around us by the equal rights of others. I do not add 'within the limits of the law' because law is often but the tyrant's will, and always so when it violates the rights of the individual." President Thomas Jefferson

Some dementing or demented white Lords (Alzheimer's disease is considerably more common than ordinarily realised), nominated, and constructively appointed our incontrovertibly functional semi-illiterate former debt-collector Solicitor in Norwich as our District Judge in Bedford.

PERCEPTION IS GRANDER THAN REALITY.

Then, there, some white Lords were members of the vulgarly charitable Antichrist Racist Freemasonry Quasi-Religion (New Pharisees/Mediocre Mafia) – Habakkuk; some of them were THICKER than a gross of planks.

"FAILING SCHOOLS AND A BATTLE FOR BRITAIN: This was the day the British education establishment's 50-year betrayal of the Nation's children lay starkly exposed in all its ignominy. After testing 166,000 people in 24 education systems, the Organisation for Economic Cooperation and Development (OECD) finds that England young adults are amongst the least literate and numerate in the industrialised world." Daily Mail, 09.01.2013

Sheep unnaturally shepherd sheep.

Shepherds know that sheep are stupid; sheep do not know that shepherds are stupider.

"Mediocrity weighing mediocrity in the balance, and incompetence applauding its brother ......" Wilde

LORDS of imbeciles (adults with the basic skills of a child) are likelier to be imbeciles too.

"This man I thought had been a Lord of wits, but, I find, he is only a wit among Lords." Dr Samuel Johnson

"500 men, 500 ordinary men, chosen accidentally from among the unemployed." David Lloyd George.

OYINBO OLE: STRAIGHT-FACED DESCENDANTS OF ULTRA-RIGHTEOUS THIEVES AND OWNERS OF STOLEN CHILDREN OF VERY, VERY POOR PEOPLE (MEGHAN MARKLE'S ANCESTORS) - HABAKKUK

Descendants of Alphonse Gabriel fool the foolish that they are Archangel Gabriel.

Defenders of Faiths (Dissenters of John 14:6): They do not believe in the exceptionalism of Christ (John 14:6), so they are more tolerant to unashamed, and immortal mediocrity,

250

mendacity, and confusion because they are not deterred by His Judgement – John 5:22; John 8:44; John 10:10

If the highly luxuriant soil of Bedford yields only food, and a very Senior District Judge is, incontrovertibly, a functional Semi-illiterate, it's plainly deducible that the white ancestors of his white mother and father were THIEVES and owners of stolen children of Defenceless poor people (Black African ancestor of Meghan Markle and her white children) - Habakkuk.

OYINBO OLE: THIEVES – HABAKKUK.

Then, there, based on observations and direct experiences, functional semi-illiterate white Judges (predominantly), nearly all, were closeted racist bastards - Habakkuk.

"Someone must be trusted. Let it be the Judges." Lord Denning (1899 – 1999)

Judges are human beings. Some human beings are closeted racists.

"All sections of the UK Society are institutionally racist." Sir Bernard Hogan-Howe

The Judiciary is part of the UK Society.

Bedfordshire Police is part of the UK Society.

"Freedom of Expression is the cornerstone of our democracy."

GDC- Expert, Mrs Helen Falcon, Oxford's Postgraduate Dean, and Member of the Most Excellent Order of our Empire (MBE), unrelentingly lied under implied oath.

A WHITE WOMAN. A DISHONEST RACIST COUGAR.

The closeted racist white cougar did not believe in His exceptionalism (John 14:6), so she was not deterred by His Judgement (John 5:22).

Mrs Helen Falcon, MBE: A closeted racist descendant of ultra-righteous THIEVES and owners of stolen children of defenceless poor people (Meghan Markle's ancestors) - Habakkuk

OYINBO OLE: THIEVES – HABAKKUK

Closeted racist bastards want the superiority that is associated with the irrefutably superior skin colour that they neither made nor chose, their brainless and baseless birth right, but they don't want Freedom of Expression because they don't want their mentally gentle children to know that they are excessively stupid.

CREEPING DPRK.

The white man is the devil: The white man is the thief.

Christ does not place Africans in the back rows, white men do.

Christ did not place Africans in the back rows, white men did.

"A typical English man, usually violent and always dull." Wilde

When their people commit racist crimes against ours, closeted racist bastards who oversee the administration of their law criminally bury racial hatred. Whites measure whites with a very different yardstick – Matthew 12:27

Facts are sacred; they can't be overstated.

BEDFORD, ENGLAND: District Judge Paul Ayers, the Senior Vice President of the Association of Her Majesty's District Judges, which part of our County Court, 3, St Paul's Square Bedford, MK40 1SQ, wasn't STOLEN, or which part of it preceded SLAVERY, or which part of it did transparent virtue yield, or which part of it did the people of BEDFORD buy: The building or its chattels?

Ignorance is bliss.

OYINBO OLE: THIEVES – HABAKKUK.

"Those who know the least obey the best." George Farquhar

District Judge Paul Ayers, the Senior Vice President of the Association of Her Majesty's District Judges, you are relevant only because England is rich and your skin colour is irrefutably superior, apart from those, you are PURIFIED NOTHING. It is absolutely impossible for your talent and the yield of your land to sustain your standard of living. You are a LEECH, and your white ancestors were THIEVES, and owners of stolen children (African ancestors of Meghan Markle and her white children) - Habakkuk.

OYINBO OLE: A CLOSETED RACIST DESCENDANT OF ULTRA-RIGHTEOUS WHITE THIEVES - HABAKKUK

District Judge Paul Ayers, the Senior Vice President of the Association of Her Majesty's District Judges, it is absolutely impossible for your talent and the yield of your land to sustain your standard of living. The yield of the talent of your white ancestors and the yield of their land did not sustain their standard of living; they were THIEVES and owners of stolen children of poor people (Meghan Markle's ancestors) – Habakkuk. Facts are sacred; they can't be overstated.

"Time for Scots to say sorry for slavery
Herald Scotland:
Ian Bell, Columnist / Sunday 28 April 2013 / Opinion
Sunday 28 April 2013
According to the American founding father, the son of a Caithness Kirk minister had about him "an air of great simplicity and honesty'". The likes of James Boswell and Laurence Sterne also enjoyed the merchant's company.

To his contemporaries, he was, as the author Adam Hochschild has written, '"a wise, thoughtful man who embodied the Scottish virtues of frugality, sobriety, and hard work'". Oswald was a scholar of theology, philosophy, and history. He collected art, particularly Rubens and Rembrandt, and gave handsomely to charity. Oswald, who learned his trade in Glasgow, also represented Britain in negotiations with the Americans after their war of liberation. He was the cosmopolitan epitome of Enlightenment success. But when he wasn't busy with good works, Oswald waded in blood. The precise number of deaths that can be laid at his door is impossible to calculate. As the leading figure in Grant, Oswald & Co, he had investments in each corner of the "'triangular trade'". In his own name, Oswald trafficked at least 13,000 Africans, although he never set foot on their continent. By the time he bought Auchincruive House and 100,000 acres in Ayrshire in 1764, he was worth £500,000. Writing in 2005, Hochschild thought this was "'"roughly equivalent"'" to $68 million (about £44m). This is conservative.

Oswald was remarkable, but not unique. Where Glasgow and its merchants in sugar, tobacco, and human life are concerned, there are plenty of names and no shortage of monuments: Dennistoun, Campbell, Glassford, Cochrane, Buchanan, Hamilton, Bogle, Ewing, Donald, Speirs, Dunlop. One way to understand what they wrought is simple: take pleasure in the city"'s architecture today and you are likely to be admiring the fruits of slavery. Glasgow is not alone in that. London, Liverpool and Bristol also have their stories to tell. Edinburgh's once-great banks grew from foundations built on bones. The first Scottish venture into slavery set out from the capital in 1695. Montrose, Dumfries, Greenock and Port Glasgow each tried their hands. In the language of the present age, they were all in it together.

When commerce was coursing around the triangle, most of polite Scotland was implicated. The nobility (and country) rendered bankrupt in 1700 in the aftermath of the Darien Venture was by the mid-1760s contemplating big elegant townhouses and 100,000-acre estates. You could call that a reversal of fortune. Contrary to self-serving myth, it did not happen because of "'frugality, sobriety, and hard work". Certain things need to be remembered about Scotland and slavery. One is that the mercantile class got stinking rich twice over: despite fortunes made from stolen lives, they were quick to demand compensation when slavery was ended in 1833. Britain's government decided that £20m, a staggering sum, could be raised. In his 2010 book, The Price of Emancipation, Nicholas Draper reckons Glasgow's mob got £400,000 – in modern terms, hundreds of millions. Compensation cases also demonstrated that Scots were not merely following an English lead. According to Draper, a country with 10% of the British population accounted for at least 15% of absentee slavers. By another estimate, 30% of Jamaican plantations were run by Scots. For all the pride taken in the abolitionist societies of Glasgow and Edinburgh, the slave-holders did not suffer because of abolition. They were '"compensated"'.

And that wasn't the worst of it. Thanks to Hollywood movies, the slave economy of the American South is still taken as barbarism's benchmark. Few realise that the behaviour of Scots busy getting rich in the slave-holders" empire was actually worse – routinely worse – than the worst of the cottonocracy. You need only count the corpses…………….."

OYINBO OLE: THIEVES – HABAKKUK.

Christ did not place Africans in the back rows, white men did.

The white man is the devil - Columbia University
https://ccnmtl.columbia.edu › mmt › mxp › concepts

Referring to Whites as "devils" originates with the teachings of Master W.D. Fard and the legend of Yakub. Fard taught Elijah Muhammad who preached the ...

BEDFORD, ENGLAND: GDC: Richard Hill fabricated reports and unrelentingly lied under oath – Habakkuk.

A WHIITE MAN. A DISHONEST RACIST.

The white man is the devil: The white man is the thief.

Christ does not place Africans in the back rows, white men do.

Our Empire did not evolve from NOTHING: Then, almost everything was actively and deliberately stolen with GUNS - Habakkuk.

"Affluence is not a birth right." David Cameron

The closeted racist greedy bastards were not the only creation of Almighty God, and they were not immortal, and their irrefutably superior skin colour was not the only wonder of our world. They were greedier than the grave and like death, the racist bastards were never satisfied – Habakkuk 2:5.

Ignorance is bliss.

"I do not approve of anything that tampers with natural ignorance. Ignorance is like a delicate exotic fruit; touch it and the bloom is gone. The whole theory of modern education is radically unsound. Fortunately, in England, at any rate, education produces no effect whatsoever. If it did, it would prove a serious danger to the upper classes, and probably lead to acts of violence in Grosvenor Square." Wilde

CHAPTER EIGHT:

Boris Johnson: Why is England not a scam.

"Racism is rife throughout most organisations across Britain." The Mayor of London.

"All sections of the UK Society are institutionally RACIST." Sir Bernard Hogan-Howe

Bedfordshire Police is part of the UK Society.

The Judiciary is part of the UK Society.

GOOGLE: JUDGE AYERS BEDFORD

GOOGLE: INCOMPETENT LIARS: SOME LAWYERS.

"The Court System And Freemasonry Choosing Ctmin
http://www1.tu.no › file › reading

District Judge Ayers, Bedford. Freemasons teach members ... Antichrist Racist Freemasons (Mediocre Mafia): Which part of Bedfordshire Masonic Centre,"

Half-educated school dropout closeted racist bastards in camouflage uniform. Freemasons' Zombie Private Soldiers. IRA of Sinn Fein.

Half-educated school dropout closeted white supremacist thugs in camouflage uniform are white supremacist thugs.

"OJ Simpson in a knit cap is OJ Simpson." Johnnie Cochran (1937 – 2005).

They love the superiority that is automatically attached to the irrefutably superior skin colour that they neither made nor chose, their baseless and brainless birth right; the closeted racist bastards do not want Freedom of Expression because they do want their mentally gentle children to know that they are excessively stupid.

"There is no sin except stupidity." Wilde

OYINBO OLE: RACIST DESCENDANTS OF ULTRA-RIGHTEOUS THIEVES – HABAKKUK

A Closeted Racist White Supremacist Thug, Mark Fuhrman, crossed examined by Francis Lee Bailey Jr (1933 – 2021).

Francis Lee Bailey Jr: Do you use the word Nigger to describe people?

Police Inspector, Mark Fuhrman: No Sir.

Francis Lee Bailey Jr: Have you used the word Nigger to describe people?

Police Inspector, Mark Fuhrman: No Sir.

Francis Lee Bailey Jr: Have you used the word in the last 10 years?

Police Inspector, Mark Fuhrman: Not that I can recall.

Francis Lee Bailey Jr: You mean if you called someone a Nigger you've forgotten it?

Police Inspector, Mark Fuhrman: I am not sure I can answer that question the way you've phrased it sir.

Francis Lee Bailey Jr: You have difficulty in understanding the question. I will rephrase it.

Police Inspector, Mark Fuhrman:

Francis Lee Bailey Jr: Let's assume that sometimes in 1985 or 1986 you referred to a member of the African race as a Nigger is it possible that you have forgotten that act on your part?

Police Inspector, Mark Fuhrman: No Sir, it is not possible.

Francis Lee Bailey Jr: Are you now saying that you've not used that word in the last 10 years, inspector Fuhrman?

Police Inspector, Mark Fuhrman: That is what I am saying.

Francis Lee Bailey Jr: Are you saying on your oath that you have not addressed a black person as a Nigger or spoken about black people as Niggers in the last 10 years, inspector Fuhrman?

Police Inspector, Mark Fuhrman: That is what I am saying Sir.

Francis Lee Bailey Jr: So that anyone who comes to Court and quotes you as using that word in dealing with African American will be a liar, all of them.

Police Inspector, Mark Fuhrman: Yes, they would.

Francis Lee Bailey Jr: All of them.

Police Inspector, Mark Fuhrman: All of them.

******

"The white man is the devil." Mohammed Ali

"A typical English man, usually violent and always dull."
Wilde

When their people commit racist crimes against ours,
closeted racist bastards who oversee the administration of
their law criminally bury racial hatred.

OYINBO OLE: WHITE THIEVES – HABAKKUK.

"By definition therefore there needs to be a contact order
for Mr B so that he knows when he is going to see his son.
It is absolutely essential that this occurs and mother agrees
with that. She said so several times in her evidence. Mrs
Waller agreed that not only should a child have the
opportunity of developing relationship with both parents,
any sibling should also be there so that inter- sibling
relationship could be fostered and nurtured. Obviously in
this particular case the children reside in different places.
That immediately puts a strain on the children having
limited contact with each other. F's sister is very much
older than him and she will be further advanced into her
adult life. Thus it is not a matter that that sibling
relationship can only be fostered by the children being
together. Indeed as we all know absence sometimes makes
the heart grow fonder. F should have an opportunity of

seeing his sister. Wherever he does that it should be done in a friendly and loving environment. If the time comes that his sister goes to university of course his contact with her will be restricted to the time that she is home from university. In years to come when they have both grown up, with their own family they will see less of each other. But it doesn't mean that they don't still love and adore each other as much as they would if they saw each other every day." The Senior Vice President of the Association of Her Majesty's District Judges — proofed and approved Judgement.

OYINBO ODE: A CLOSETED RACIST WHITE FOOL'S APPROVAL.

AN IMBECILE: AN ADULT WITH THE BASIC SKILLS OF A CHILD.

"Yes, Sir, it does *her* honour, but it would do nobody else honour. I have indeed, not read it all. But when I take up the end of a web, and find it packthread, I do not expect, by looking further, to find embroidery." Dr Samuel Johnson.

The functional semi-illiterate white man with power is the real devil.

Then, there, functional semi-illiterate white Judges, nearly all, were FREEMASONS, and nearly all of them were THICKER than a gross of planks.

C of E raises serious concerns about Christian Freemasons
https://www.theguardian.com › uk-news › feb › c-of-e-...

8 Feb 2018 — Church of England warning that secret society may not be compatible with Christianity echoes concerns from 1987.

The closeted racist bastards who use very expensive aprons to decorate the temples of their powerless and useless fertility tools teach their members secret handshakes, not grammar, and the former is considerably easier to master.

Based on available evidence, in England, it is a crime not to be Antichrist: Believer of 'FAITHS' and dissenter of John14:6.

GOOGLE: FREEMASONRY INTELLECTUALLY FLAWED.

https://www.youtube.com/watch?v=rayVcfyu9Tw

"All sections of the UK Society are institutionally racist." Sir Bernard Hogan-Howe

Bedfordshire Police is part of the UK Society.

Facts are sacred; they can't be overstated.

District Judge Paul Ayers of Bedford County Court, 3, St Paul's Square Bedford, MK40 1SQ, the Senior Vice President of the Association of Her Majesty's District

Judges, approved and immortalised (for eternity) the type rot his functional semi-illiterate (deductible) white mother and father used to speak, and the type of tales his white father used to tell when he returned home from Queen Victoria, at odd hours, stoned, and which his poly-educated supervisors in LUTON authorised.

"To survive, you must tell stories ...... I believe that what we become depends on what our fathers teach us at odd moments, when they aren't trying to teach us. We are formed by little scraps of wisdom." Umberto Eco.

His Honour Judge Perusko studied Law at Poly: Lower Class Alternative Education – Proverbs 17:16.

Why should the white mother and father of District Judge Paul Ayers, the Senior Vice President of the Association of Her Majesty's District Judges need very, very strong views about education when there is irrefutable evidence that the white ancestors of his white father and mother were THIEVES and owners of stolen children of defenceless poor people (Black African ancestors of Meghan Markle and her white children): Extremely nasty racist terrorists, and very, very greedy economic cannibals - Habakkuk?

OYINBO OLE: THIEVES – HABAKKUK

"Those who know the least obey the best." George Farquhar

NIGERIA: SHELL'S DOCILE CASH COW.

THE VERY HIGHLY LUXURIANT SOIL OF NORWICH YIELDS ONLY FOOD. THERE ARE NO OIL WELLS OR GAS FIELDS IN NORWICH.

They are not the only creation of Almighty God, and the closeted racist bastards are not immortal, and the irrefutably superior skin colour that they neither made nor chose is not the only wonder of our world.

OYINBO OLE: THIEVES – HABAKKUK.

Children with huge oil wells and gas fields near their huts eat only 1.5/day in Nigeria; a white, bellyful, closeted racist functional semi-illiterate former debt-collector Solicitor in Norwich – whose white father and mother have never seen crude oil, and whose white ancestors were fed like battery hens with the yields of stolen children of defenceless poor people (Black ancestors of Meghan Markle and her white children) – is our District Judge in BEDFORD.

OYINBO OLE: THIEVES - HABAKKUK

https://www.youtube.com/watch?v=BlpH4hG7m1A&feature=youtu.be

"They may not have been well written from a grammatical point of view, but I am confident I had not forgotten any of the facts." Dr Geraint Evans, Postgraduate Tutor, Oxford

AN IMBECILE: AN ADULT WITH THE BASIC
SKILLS OF A CHILD.

The functional semi-illiterate white man is the devil.

https://youtu.be/rayVcfyu9Tw

"Why, Sir, Sherry is dull, naturally dull; but it must have
taken him a great deal of pains to become what we now see
him. Such an excess of stupidity, Sir, is not in Nature." DR
SAMUEL JOHNSON

GDC-Witness, Geraint Evans, England's Class
Postgraduate Tutor, unrelentingly lied under implied oath.

A WHITE MAN. A DISHONEST RACIST WELSH
CROOK.

The white man is the devil.

"A typical English man, usually violent and always dull."
Wilde

When their people commit racist crimes against ours,
closeted racist bastards who oversee the administration of
their law criminally bury racial hatred.

OYINBO OLE: WHITE THIEVES – HABAKKUK

District Judge Paul Ayers of Bedford County Court, 3, St
Paul's Square Bedford, MK40 1SQ, the Senior Vice
President of the Association of Her Majesty's District

Judges implied that like his own white mother and father, the white father and mother of Geraint Evans, England's Class Postgraduate Tutor did not have very, very strong views about education.

message fo Geraint

Fri, 28 May 2010 17:50

GERAINT EVANS (geraint.sueevans@virgin.net)To:you Details
Report details the meeting hel...doc (33 KB)
Dear Ola,

Please find attached the report folloing our meeting last week.
I will be sending a copy to the PCT and have been instructed to do this.

Yours Sincerely,

Geraint

"O.B was given a copy of the notes. He became angry and confrontational on starting to digest them. He accused me of lying, at which point I stood up with the intention of leaving. He retracted this accusation and suggested I was mistaken. Throughout the discussion of the notes he made derogatory comments about the wording and accuracy. He suggested that they were written some time after the visits and that my memory was inaccurate. The notes as stated previously were written within 24 hours of each meeting when fresh in my memory. They may not have been well written from a grammatical point of view but I am confident I had not forgotten any of the facts." Geraint Evans, England's Class Postgraduate Tutor, Oxford (Verbatim).

AN IMBECILE: AN ADULT WITH THE BASIC SKILLS OF A CHILD.

OYINBO OLODO: A CLOSETED RACIST WHITE DUNCE.

A WHITE MAN. AN IMBECILE POSTGRADUATE TUTOR, ALBEIT ENGLAND'S CLASS.

"It is incumbent upon the court and all those professionals involved to conclude court proceedings as quickly as possible. This hopefully ensures that a child has stability, love and affection and the parents working together to ensure that he has the best opportunity of developing academically and emotional." District Judge Paul Ayers, Senior Vice President of the Association of Her Majesty's District Judges – proofed and approved Judgement

IDIOTIC NONSENSE.

AN IMBECILE: AN ADULT WITH THE BASIC SKILLS OF A CHILD.

"I don't want to talk grammar. I want to talk like a lady." George Bernard Shaw

Then, there, white Judges, nearly all, were FREEMASONS; some of them were thicker than a gross of planks.

Then, there, Freemasons teach al their members voodoo handshakes, not grammar, the former is considerably easier to master.

OYINBO OLODO: A CLOSETED RACIST WHITE FOOL'S APPROVAL!

PURIFIED ROT!

"Gentlemen, you are now about to embark on a course of studies which will occupy you for two years. Together, they form a noble adventure. But I would like to remind you of an important point. Nothing that you will learn in the course of your studies will be of the slightest possible use to you in after life, save only this, that if you work hard and intelligently you should be able to detect when a man is talking rot, and that, in my view, is the main, if not the sole, purpose of education." John Alexander Smith, Oxford University Professor of MORAL PHILOSOPHY.

Based on very proximate observations and direct experiences, the functional semi-illiterate white man with power is the devil.

CLOSETED RACIST BASTARDS ATTACH HEREDITARY MEDIOCRITY AND CONFUSION TO

THE SOVEREIGN AND SELL IT TO THE
UNDISCERNING FOR VALUE.

JUDICIAL DIVERSITY: ACCELERATING CHANGE.
"The near absence of women and Black, Asian and
minority ethnic judges in the senior judiciary, is no longer
tolerable. It undermines the democratic legitimacy of our
legal system; it demonstrates a denial of fair and equal
opportunities to members of underrepresented groups, and
the diversity deficit weakens the quality of justice." Sir
Geoffrey Bindman, QC, and Karon Monaghan, QC.

DIVERSE MEDIOCRITY IS AKIN TO RAKING MUCK.

Why should the white mothers and fathers of District Judge
Paul Ayers of Bedford County Court, 3, St Paul's Square
Bedford, MK40 1SQ, the Senior Vice President of the
Association of Her Majesty's District Judges and Geraint
Evans, Postgraduate Tutor, Oxford, need very, very strong
views about education if there is irrefutable evidence that
the white ancestors of their white mothers and fathers were
WHITE THIEVES, racists, murderers, amoral drug dealers
(opium merchants), and owners of stolen children of very
poor people (Meghan Markle's ancestors) – Habakkuk?

OYINBO OLE: THIEVES – HABAKKUK.

"Those who know the least obey the best." George
Farquhar

Ignorance is bliss.

"I do not approve of anything that tampers with natural ignorance. Ignorance is like a delicate exotic fruit; touch it and the bloom is gone. The whole theory of modern education is radically unsound. Fortunately, in England, at any rate, education produces no effect whatsoever. If it did, it would prove a serious danger to the upper classes, and probably lead to acts of violence in Grosvenor Square." Wilde

Facts are sacred, they cannot be overstated.

"We shall deal with the racist bastards when we get out of prison." Comrade Robert Mugabe.

LATENT, BUT VERY POTENT RACE/RELIGIOUS WAR:

Churches, nearly all, are modified franchises of Freemasonry Quasi-Cult.

Anyone, particularly a mere Negro, who refuses to bow to Baal or play the devil, Freemasons' god, like chess, will be killed, albeit hands-off.

"You will bow. You can't beat the system." Kemi Daramola

Imported devil: Esu.

I shan't. I know who will – Romans 11; 1 John 4:4.

Kemi Daramola prays to Christ and pays tithe (about £100, 000 since she joined), quasi protection money, at Brickhill Baptist Church in Bedford, Freemasons in Kempston answer her prayers.

Freemasons are very active in many churches; many churches are mere franchises of the Charitable Antichrist Racist Freemasonry Amalgam of Religions (Mediocre Mafia/New Pharisees) – Habakkuk.

Re:

Fri, 11 Apr 2014 9:28
resh diu (rdiu@me.com)To:you Details
It's sad Ola

I kept telling you to play the game of chess rather than fight it

You take care

If you wish to dispose of 24 park road let me know

Regards

Resh
Dr Resh Diu BDS
www.oradi.co.uk

We must play Freemasons like chess and/or bow to them, and we must teach or children to play closeted racist bastards, members of the Charitable Antichrist Racist Freemasonry Religion, like chess and/or bow to them.

BRAINLESS NONSENSE!

THE INDIAN: A BELIEVER OF FAITHS/ DISSENTER OF JOHN 14:6.

GDC-Witness: Richard Hill fabricated reports and unrelentingly lied under oath. A white man. A dishonest racist. It is a crime only if Freemasons did not prior authorise it.

GDC-Witness: Kevin Atkinson (NHS) unrelentingly lied under oath. A white man. A dishonest racist. It is a crime only if Freemasons did not prior authorise it.

GDC-Expert: Jonathan Martin unrelentingly lied on record. A white man. A dishonest racist. It is a crime only if Freemasons did not prior authorise it.

GDC-Expert: Helen Falcon (MBE) unrelentingly lied on record. A white man. A dishonest racist. It is a crime only if Freemasons did not prior authorise it.

GDC-Witness: George Rothnie (NHS) unrelentingly lied on record. A white man. A dishonest racist. It is a crime only if Freemasons did not prior authorise it.

GDC-Witness: Stephanie Twidale unrelentingly lied under oath. A white man. A dishonest racist. It is a crime only if Freemasons did not prior authorise it.

GDC-Expert: Sue Gregory (OBE) unrelentingly lied on record. A white man. A dishonest racist. It is a crime only if Freemasons did not prior authorise it

GDC-Witness: Rachael Bishop unrelentingly lied under oath. A white man. A dishonest racist. It is a crime only if Freemasons did not prior authorise it.

GDC-Witness: Geraint Evans (NHS) unrelentingly lied on record. A white man. A dishonest racist. It is a crime only if Freemasons did not prior authorise it.

They dishonestly and shamelessly give the false impression that our people (AFRICANS) are no longer inferior under their law.

Only brainless AFRICANS, idealists, utopians, and fantasists expect others to relinquish centuries-old advantageous positions in exchange for NOTHING.

Ignorant racist FOOLS: Righteous descendants of ultra-righteous THIEVES — Habakkuk.

Descendants of Alphonse Gabriel fool the foolish that they are Archangel Gabriel.

They were all white, including the Judges, and they were all RACISTS, and incompetent liars — Habakkuk. Homogeneity in the administration of English Law is the very secure mask of racial hatred.

Closeted racist bastards use incompetent mendacity to conceal familial intellectual impotence, and they were not deterred by His Justice (John 5:22) because they do not believe in His exceptionalism (John 14:6).

"Those who have the power to do wrong with impunity seldom wait long for the will." Dr Samuel Johnson

A thoroughly bastardised, indiscreetly dishonest, unashamedly mediocre, vindictive, potently weaponised, and institutionally RACIST legal system that is overseen by the members of the Charitable Antichrist Racist Freemasonry Quasi-Religion (Mediocre Mafia/New Pharisees) — Habakkuk

"To deny or belittle this good is, in this dangerous century when the resources and pretensions of power continue to enlarge, a desperate error of intellectual abstraction. More than this, it is a self-fulfilling error, which encourages us to give up the struggle against bad laws and class bound procedures and to disarm ourselves before power. It is to throw away a whole inheritance of struggle about the law and within the forms of law, whose continuity can never be fractured without bringing men and women into immediate danger." — E. P Thompson.

LATENT, BUT VERY POTENT TURF WAR:
Descendants of undocumented refugees from Eastern Europe (genetic aliens) with camouflage English names – oppress descendants of the robbed with the yields of the robbery – Habakkuk

They are not the only creation of Almighty God, and they are not immortal, and the irrefutably superior skin colour that they neither made not chose is not the only wonder of our world.

OYINBO OLE: STRAIGHT-FACED DESCENDANTS OF ULTRA-RIGHTEOUS THIEVES AND OWNERS OF STOLEN CHILDREN OF DEFENCELESS POOR PEOPLE (BLACK AFRICAN ANCESTORS OF MEGHAN MARKLE AND HER WHITE CHILDREN) – HABAKKUK.

Closeted racist bastards are greedier than the grave, and like death, the hereditary sadistic savages are never satisfied.

NEW HEROD, MATTHEW 2:16: Like Herod, Saddam Hussein, Putin, Kim, MBS, and babies, closeted racist bastards expect everyone to love them unconditionally, and say and/or print only what they want to hear.

Before SLAVERY, what?

OYINBO OLE: IGNORANT DESCENDANTS OF ULTRA-RIGHTEOUS, INDUSTRIAL-SCALE PROFESSIONAL THIEVES – HABAKKUK.

"Sometimes people don't want to hear the truth because they don't want their illusions destroyed." Friedrich Nietzsche

Closeted racist bastards do not want their mentally very gentle children to know the truth, which is that the centuries-old unspoken myth that intellect is related to the irrefutably superior skin colour that the very fortunate wearer neither made nor chose, is the mother of all racist scams. So, they resorted to Judicial Terrorism to conceal the truth, which is that Africans were, also, properly created by Almighty God, and that several centuries of slavery were imposed with extreme violence and mercilessly sadistic barbarism – Habakkuk.

"I know of no evil that has ever existed, nor can imagine any evil to exist, worse than the tearing of eighty thousand persons annually from their native land, by a combination of the most civilised nations inhabiting the most enlightened part of the globe, but more especially under the

279

sanction of the laws of that Nation which calls herself the most free and the most happy of them all." Prime Minister William Pitt the Younger

The white man is the devil.

The white man is the devil - Columbia University
https://ccnmtl.columbia.edu › mmt › mxp › concepts

Referring to Whites as "devils" originates with the teachings of Master W.D. Fard and the legend of Yakub. Fard taught Elijah Muhammad who preached the ...

Those who shipped millions of made in Birmingham guns to Africa (about 200,000 annually), among those who had no means of treating penetrative gunshot wounds and internal injury, during several centuries of the greediest economic cannibalism, and the evilest racist terrorism the world will ever know, were neither civilised nor enlightened, and they were certainly not Christian.

"A typical English man, usually violent and always dull." Wilde

When their people (whites) commit racist crimes against ours (Africans), closeted racist bastards who oversee the administration of their law criminally bury racial hatred.

OYINBO OLE: THIEVES – HABAKKUK.

"Many Scots masters were considered among the most brutal, with life expectancy on their plantations averaging a mere four years. We worked them to death then simply imported more to keep the sugar and thus the money flowing. Unlike centuries of grief and murder, an apology cost nothing. So, what does Scotland have to say?" Herald Scotland: Ian Bell, Columnist, Sunday 28 April 2013

"The white man is the devil." Mohammed Ali.

Their ancestors used overwhelming extreme violence to CANCEL the lives of millions of our ancestors, and unprovoked.

Closeted racist bastards love Africa, not Africans. The only part of our Africa that closeted racist white bastards truly love is MONEY; everything else is a properly rehearsed mendacity.

Then, closeted racist THIEVES carried and sold millions of stolen children of very poor Africans (Black African ancestors of Meghan Markle and her white children), now, they carry natural resources.

SUBSTITUTION IS FRAUDULENT EMANCIPATION.

"Moderation is a virtue only among those who are thought to have found alternatives." Henry Kissinger.

Extremely greedy racist bastards: They want to eat all their own cakes, and they want to eat all other people's cake, and they want everything – Habakkuk 2:5.

Britain is institutionally Antichrist

"Sometimes people don't want to hear the truth because they don't want their illusions destroyed." Friedrich Nietzsche

Their INSTITUTIONALISED SATANIC SYSTEM is based on incompetent racist lies that guarded and guided by the illegal parallel power of the FREEMASONS.

They use overwhelming incompetent racist lies to cancel our education and livelihood.

They hate us, with merciless sadistic passion, and some of their kindred who oversee the administration of their law are closeted racist white bastards – Habakkuk.

Our people are sandwiched between very highly civilised and ultra-righteous racist white criminals and impartial white supremacist Judges.

"Pardon Him Theodotus: He is a barbarian and thinks the customs of his tribe and Island are the laws of nature." George Bernard Shaw

The most important basis of their oppressive racist power is that their people oversee the administration of their law.

CREEPING DPRK.

"Those who have the power to do wrong with impunity seldom wait long for the will." Dr Samuel Johnson

It is harassment if a mere Negro calls a white criminal a criminal; the blatant crime is not a crime.

A bastardised, indiscreetly dishonest, unashamedly mediocre, vindictive, potently weaponised, and institutionally racist legal system that is overseen by the FREEMASON (Mediocre Mafia/New Pharisees) – Habakkuk.

There, then, white Judges, nearly all, were FREEMASONS; some of them were thicker than a gross of planks – Habakkuk.

The report, by the OECD, warns that the UK needs to take significant action to boost the basic skills of the nation's young people. The 460-page study is based on the first-ever survey of the literacy, numeracy and problem-solving at work skills of 16 to 65-year-olds in 24 countries, with almost 9,000 people taking part in England and Northern Ireland to make up the UK results. The findings showed that England and Northern Ireland have some of the highest proportions of adults scoring no higher than Level 1 in literacy and numeracy - the lowest level on the OECD's scale. This suggests that their skills in the basics are no better than that of a 10-year-old.

AN IMBECILE: AN ADULT WITH THE BASIC SKILLS OF A CHILD.

BORIS JOHNSON: Then, there, functional semi-illiterate white Judges who believed that daily dialogues with IMBECILES was a worthwhile occupation were scammers, and those who demanded and accepted valuable considerations in exchange for daily dialogues with imbeciles were racketeers.

He righteously sat on skulls of stolen children of defenceless poor people (Meghan Markle's ancestors), more skulls than the millions at the doorstep of Comrade Pol Pot: Stolen lives yielded his magnificent court, absolutely inevitable future flats.

NEW HEROD, MATTHEW 2:16: Closeted racist bastards deceive their mentally very, very gentle children that they are geniuses, and they kill all those who know that they are excessively stupid.

KING HEROD: The lunatic Jew removed the head of John only because he spoke: The lunatic Jew did not punish John for speaking, John was permanently prevented from speaking – Matthew 14.

He was lynched like Gadhafi and crucified only because He spoke: He disclosed pictures His unbounded mind painted.

"Natural selection will not remove ignorance from future generations." Dr Richard Dawkins

Adults with the basic skills of a FOETUS will succeed adults with the basic skills of a child (imbeciles), and the former will need only food and shelter.

Now, Boris Johnson uses Nuclear Bombs to guard the continuing propagation of imbeciles. The successors of Boris Johnson will use the mother of Nuclear Bombs to guard the propagation of adults with the basic skills of a foetus, those who natural selection would have natural decommissioned had it not been unnaturally decommissioned.

They should rewrite their law: 'Freedom of expression for imbeciles (adults with the basic skills of a child) should replace 'Freedom of Expression for all'.

"By definition therefore there needs to be a contact order for Mr B so that he knows when he is going to see his son. It is absolutely essential that this occurs and mother agrees with that. She said so several times in her evidence. Mrs Waller agreed that not only should a child have the opportunity of developing relationship with both parents, any sibling should also be there so that inter- sibling relationship could be fostered and nurtured. Obviously in this particular case the children reside in different places. That immediately puts a strain on the children having limited contact with each other. F's sister is very much older than him and she will be further advanced into her adult life. Thus it is not a matter that that sibling relationship can only be fostered by the children being together. Indeed as we all know absence sometimes makes the heart grow fonder. F should have an opportunity of seeing his sister. Wherever he does that it should be done in a friendly and loving environment. If the time comes that his sister goes to university of course his contact with her will be restricted to the time that she is home from university. In years to come when they have both grown up, with their own family they will see less of each other. But it doesn't mean that they don't still love and adore each other as much as they would if they saw each other every day." District Judge Paul Ayers of Bedford County Court, 3, St Paul's Square, MK40 1SQ, the Senior Vice President of the Association of Her Majesty's District Judges – proofed and approved Judgement.

IMMORTAL BRAINLESS NONSENSE: A CLOSETED RACIST SEER

AN IMBECILE: AN ADULT WITH THE BASIC SKILLS OF A CHILD.

"Yes, Sir, it does *her* honour, but it would do nobody else honour. I have indeed, not read it all. But when I take up the end of a web, and find it packthread, I do not expect, by looking further, to find embroidery." Dr Samuel Johnson.

The only evidence of his very, very high IQ is the stolen affluence that his ancestors crossed the English Channels, without luggage or decent shoes, to latch onto.

286

OYINBO OLE: IGNORANT DESCENDANTS OF
THIEVES – HABAKKUK.

LATENT, BUT VERY POTENT TURF WAR:
Descendants of aliens with camouflage English names
oppress descendants of the robbed with the yield of
robbery.

A functional semi-illiterate white man with power is the
devil.

Facts are sacred.

Just as it was in Professor Stephen Hawking's School, then,
at the University of Lagos, the brightest students did
mathematics, physics, and chemistry, and did not attend
lectures at the Faculty of Law.

"In my school, the brightest boys did math and physics, the
less bright did physics and chemistry, and the least bright
did biology. I wanted to do math and physics, but my
father made me do chemistry because he thought there
would be no jobs for mathematicians." Dr Stephen
Hawking.

A grossly overrated, overhyped, overpopulated, and
mediocre trade that is dying slowly and imperceptibly, and
is overseen by the Antichrist Racist Freemasons (Mediocre
Mafia) - Habakkuk 1:4; John 8:44; John 10:10.

"The legal system lies at the heart of any society, protecting rights, imposing duties and establishing a framework for the conduct of almost every social, political, and economic activity. Some argue that the law is in its death throes while others postulate a contrary prognosis that discerns numerous signs of law's enduring strength. Which is it?" Professor Raymond Wacks.

They want brainless and baseless superiority, and they want to be our God, but they don't want Freedom of Expression because they don't want their mentally very gentle children to know that they are crooked, racist, and excessively stupid.

He didn't like them, so He gave them the irrefutably superior skin colour, and in protest, closeted racist white bastards used blatant Judicial Terrorism to steal the yield of the talent He gave to their perceived inferiors (AFRICANS), with inferior skin colour.

Closeted racist bastards, descendants of very, very hardened PROFESSIONAL THIEVES, are not deterred by His Justice (John 5:22), as they do not believe in His exceptionalism – John 14:6.

Facts are sacred. The truth allows no choice.

Closeted racist white bastards persecute our people (AFRICANS) for the dark coat that we neither made nor chose, a

They are not the only creation of Almighty God, and they are not immortal, and the irrefutably superior skin colour that the very fortunate wearer neither made nor chose is not the only wonder of our world.

OYINBO OLE: THIEVES - HABAKKUK

He doesn't like them, so He gave them only the irrefutably superior skin colour, and in protest, they used extreme violence to steal what He gave to others: Movable and immovable.

"All have taken what had other owners and all have had recourse to arms rather than quit the prey on which they were fastened." Dr Samuel Johnson

Very hardened RACIST THIEVES were not deterred by His Justice (John 5:22) because they did not believe in His exceptionalism – John 14:6.

CHAPTER NINE:

Boris Johnson: Why is England not a scam?

Properly rehearsed ultra-righteousness and deceptively schooled civilised decorum were preceded by several centuries of the evilest racist terrorism, and the greediest economic cannibalism the world will ever know – Habakkuk.

"England is like a prostitute who, having sold her body all her life, decides to quit and close her business, and then tells everybody she wants to be chaste an protect her flesh as if it were jade." ... He Manzi, Chinese Politician (Communist Party).

DELUDED PAPER TIGERS: Baseless and brainless superiority is their birth right. Their hairs stand on end when they are challenged by AFRICANS; we and our type are the ones closeted racist bastards will beat up without the support of the YANKS.

"Ethical foreign policy." Robin Cook (1946 – 2005).

If members of the Charitable Antichrist Racist Freemasonry-Religion (Mediocre Mafia/New Pharisees), are as ethical and as brave as they seem to imply, they should use GUNS to evict Putin from Crimea; he stole it with GUNS.

Did Putin poison Bob Dudley; he sits on the largest gas reserve in the world?

Descendants of Alphonse Gabriel fool the foolish that they are Archangel Gabriel.

Facts are sacred, they cannot be overstated.

"The truth allows no choice." Dr Samuel Johnson

OXFORD, ENGLAND: Based on available evidence, GDC-Witness, Stephanie Twidale (TD), British Soldier – Territorial Defence, unrelentingly lied under oath. Her white ancestors were incompetent racist liars too; they were THIEVES and owners of stolen children of defenceless poor people (Meghan Markle's ancestors) – Habakkuk.

A WHITE WOMAN. A DISHONEST RACIST COUGAR.

Closeted racist white bastards do everything legally: Crooked white supremacists' mediocre law.

Had GDC-Witness, Stephanie Twidale (TD), British Soldier – Territorial Defence, been black, she would have been in trouble.

"Michael Jackson would have been found guilty if he'd been black." Jo Brand

Based on available evidence, former Judge, Negress, Constance Briscoe (ugly) is not the only incompetent liar Judge in Great Britain – Habakkuk 1:4; John 8:44; John 10:10.

"Lies are told all the time." Sir Michael Havers (1923 – 1992).

GOOGLE: THE WHITE JUDGE LIED.

Defender of FAITHS (Dissenters of John 14:6): Since the closeted racist bastards do not believe in the exceptionalism of Christ (John 14:6), they are not deterred by the promised transparent Justice by the only Judge – who knows all and sees all – Proverbs 15:3; John 5:22; Matthew 25: 31 – 46

C of E raises serious concerns about Christian Freemasons
https://www.theguardian.com › uk-news › feb › c-of-e-...

8 Feb 2018 — Church of England warning that secret society may not be compatible with Christianity echoes concerns from 1987.

We should teach our children to bow to devils, and we should also teach them to play chess with white demons.

"You will bow. You can't beat the system." Kemi Daramola

I shan't, and I know who will – Romans 11; 1 John 4:4.

I was born here. How much personal money did Eunice have in 1989, and how much of it did she give the Born-Again Christian? She loved what Eunice couldn't afford, and she used her tubes to get it. She pays tithe (protection money) at Brickhill, and the Freemasons, including Freemason Judges answer her prayers.

EKITI OLE: A PARASITE FOUND A HOST.

Our imported Devil: Our Born-Again Christian pays tithe (quasi – protection money) and prays to Christ at Brickhill Baptist Church in Bedford; members of the Charitable Antichrist Racist Freemasonry Religion (Mediocre Mafia/ New Pharisees), in Kempston, answer her prayers.

GDC: Richard Hill fabricated reports and unrelentingly lied under oath.

GDC: Kevin Atkinson (NHS) lied under oath

GDC: Helen Falcon (MBE) lied on record

GDC: George Rothnie (NHS) lied on record

GDC: Stephanie Twidale lied under oath

GDC: Sue Gregory (OBE) lied on record

GDC: Rachael Bishop lied under oath

GDC: Geraint Evans (NHS) lied on record

They were all white, including the Judges, and they were all RACISTS.

OYINBO OLE: THIEVES – HABAKKUK.

Based on very proximate observations and direct experiences, they are innately, and instinctively extremely nasty people.

If, for several continuous centuries, one's white ancestors were extremely vicious racists, indiscriminate murderers, very greedy economic cannibals and THIEVES, drug dealers (opium merchants), and owners of stolen children of defenceless poor people (Black African ancestors Meghan Markle and her white children), it will be naïve not to expect devilish tendencies to be part of one's genetic inheritances.

Based on very proximate observations and direct experiences, the white man is the devil.

"A typical English man, usually violent and always dull." Wilde

When their people commit racist crimes against ours, closeted racist bastards who oversee the administration of their law criminally bury racial hatred.

"Those who have the power to do wrong with impunity seldom wait long for the will." Dr Samuel Johnson

Facts are sacred; they can't be overstated.

-----Original Message-----
From: resh diu <rdiu@me.com>
To: adeolacole <adeolacole@aol.com>
Sent: Fri, 11 Apr 2014 9:28
Subject: Re:

It's sad Ola

I kept telling you to play the game of chess rather than fight it

You take care

If you wish to dispose of 24 park road let me know

Regards

Resh
Dr Resh Diu BDS
www.oradi.co.uk

They stalk those who do not believe in their Satanic Mumbo Jumbo (dissenters of their quasi-voodoo religion) like prey, and they hunt in packs. Their people (believers of Faiths) are everywhere, and they control almost everything.

Then, there, when their people committed racist crimes against Africans, closeted racist bastards who oversee the administration of their law – criminally bury racial hatred.

Only stupid Negroes do not know that whites measure whites with a very, very different yardstick, and only stupider Negroes expect demons to cast out demons – Matthew 12:27.

OYINBO OLE: Ignorant descendants of ultra-righteous THIEVES and owners of stolen children of defenceless poor people (Meghan Markle's ancestors) – Habakkuk.

Facts are sacred; they cannot be overstated.

They are not the only creation of Almighty God, and they are not immortal, and the irrefutably superior skin colour that they neither made nor chose is not the only wonder of our world.

"Freedom to report the truth is a basic right to which the court gives a high level of protection, and the author's right to his story includes the right to tell it as he wishes." Lord Toulson

GDC: Sue Gregory (OBE) Officer of the Most Excellent Order of our Empire unrelentingly lied under implied oath – Habakkuk 1:4; John 8:44; John 10:10.

GOOGLE: SUE GREGORY (OBE) RACIST SATANIC NETWORK

A WHITE WOMAN. A DISHONEST RACIST COUGAR.

A bastardised, indiscreetly dishonest, vindictive, unashamedly mediocre, potently weaponised, and institutionally racist legal system that is overseen by members of the charitable Antichrist Racist Freemasonry Religion (Mediocre Mafia/ New Pharisees) – Habakkuk

OYINBO OLE: THIEVES – HABAKKUK.

"To disagree with three – fourths of the British public on all points is one of the first elements of sanity, one of the deepest consolations in all moments of spiritual doubt." Wilde

"Racism is alive and well and living in Tower Hamlets, in Westminster and, yes, sometimes in the judiciary." Judge Peter Herbert, Officer of the Most Excellent Order of the British Empire (OBE)

OUR JUDICIARY IS NOT A BRANCH OF THE CHARITABLE ANTICHRIST RACIST FREEMASONRY RELIGION (MEDIOCRE MAFIA/NEW PHARISEES).

https://youtu.be/rayVcfyu9Tw

GDC: Helen Falcon (MBE) Member of the Most Excellent Order of our Empire unrelentingly lied under implied oath – Habakkuk 1:4; John 8:44; John 10:10.

GOOGLE: HELEN FALCON, RACIST EMPRESS.

A WHITE WOMAN. A DISHONEST RACIST COUGAR.

Everything is assumed in favour of the irrefutably superior skin colour that the wearer neither made nor chose.

BEDFORD, ENGLAND: District Judge Paul Ayers, which part of Bedford County Court was not stolen, or which part of it did transparent virtue yield, or which part of it did the people of Bedford buy, or which part of it preceded SLAVERY: The building or its chattels?

OYINBO OLE: IGNORANT DESCENDANTS OF ULTRA-RIGHTEOUS THIEVES – HABAKKUK

"Sometimes people don't want to hear the truth because they don't want their illusions destroyed." Friedrich Nietzsche

They want all the advantages automatically attached to the irrefutably superior skin colour that they neither made nor chose, but they don't want Freedom of Expression because they don't want their mentally gentle children to know that they are crooked white supremacist and closeted racist bastards.

The very subjective harassment law is their instrument of threatening, and punishing those who expose hereditary intellectual impotence, racial hatred, and crookedness

BORIS JOHNSON: The fact that A is better than B isn't proof that A and B are not crap.

BORIS JOHNSON: Anything that is not aligned with infinity is intellectually flawed.

BORIS JOHNSON: The fellow told Jews the truth when He disclosed pictures His unbounded mind painted – John 14:6.

BORIS JOHNSON: If the bottom of a whole descends to the basement and the top of that whole simultaneously descends to the bottom from whence the former bottom vacated, there will be change, but there wouldn't be relative change as the distance between the bottom (new basement) and the top (new bottom) will remain unchanged. The former top is oblivious to the notion of relativity; deluded, it refuses to accept that it is the new bottom.

OYINBO OLE: IGNORANT DESCENDANTS OF THIEVES AND OWNERS OF STOLEN CHILDREN OF DEFENCELESS POOR PEOPLE (BLACK AFRICAN ANCESTORS OF MEGHAN MARKLE AND HER WHITE CHILDREN) – HABAKKUK

Helen Falcon, MBE, Member of the Most Excellent Order of our Empire, the Postgraduate Dean, Oxford thinks she is a genius, and since she appointed Geraint Evans, the

Postgraduate Tutor, Oxford, the white Welsh man, thinks that he can't be very stupid.

https://www.youtube.com/watch?v=BlpH4hG7m1A&feature=youtu.be

"They may not have been well written from a grammatical point of view, but I am confident I had not forgotten any of the facts." Dr Geraint Evans, Postgraduate Tutor, Oxford

AN IMBECILE: AN ADULT WITH THE BASIC SKILLS OF A CHILD

A WHITE WELSHMAN. A DISHONEST RACIST FROM THE VALLEYS.

Members of the Charitable Antichrist Racist Freemasonry Religion deliberately used very, very soft education to fry the brains of their people, and they became their zombie private soldiers: IRA of Sinn Fein.

NORTHAMPTON, ENGLAND: Based on available evidence, GDC-Witness, Geraint Evans, Rowtree Dental Care, Northampton, unrelentingly lied under implied oath. His Welsh ancestors were incompetent racist liars too; they were THIEVES and owners of stolen children of defenceless poor people (Meghan Markle's ancestors) – Habakkuk

A WHITE WELSHMAN. A DISHONEST RACIST.

"The earth contains to racist of human beings so totally vile and worthless as the Welsh…." Walter Savage Landor

Defender of FAITHS (Dissenters of John 14:6): Since the very, very powerful closeted racist white bastards do not believe in the exceptionalism of our own Messiah (John 14:6), they are not deterred by the promised transparent Justice by the only Judge – who, alone, knows all and sees all – Proverbs 15:3; John 5:22; Matthew 25: 31 - 46

NIGERIA: SHELL'S DOCILE CASH COW.

OYINBO OLE: THIEVES - HABAKKUK

Ultra-righteousness without equitable reparation is continuing racist fraud.

There are no oil wells or gas fields in the valleys of Wales; England is the natural resources of Wales. If one were to detach Wales from England at the River Severn in Gloucestershire, and in Monmouthshire, she will instantly become poorer than Albania.

https://youtu.be/rayVcfyu9Tw

"Why, Sir, Sherry is dull, naturally dull; but it must have taken him a great deal of pains to become what we now see him. Such an excess of stupidity, Sir, is not in Nature." DR SAMUEL JOHNSON

SHEEP UNNATURALLY SHEPHERD SHEEP.

SHEPHERDS KNOW THAT THEIR SHEEP ARE
MORONS; SHEEP DO NOT KNOW THAT THEIR
SHEPHERDS ARE MORONS TOO.

Andreas Schleicher, the OECD's deputy director for
education and skills, said Japan was good at developing
skills but its "education system works in silos and
productivity growth is so-so. Compare this to the UK and
US, where they are no longer good at developing talent but
very good at extracting value from the best workers.

IT IS HIGHLY UNLIKELY THAT FUNCTIONAL
SEMI-ILLITERATE PRIVILEGED DULLARDS ARE
INCLUDED IN THE BEST WORKERS THAT MR
ANDREAS SCHLEICHER SPOKE ABOUT.

https://www.youtube.com/watch?v=BlpH4hG7m1A&featu
re=youtu.be

FAITHS: The byword for Charitable Antichrist Racist
Freemasonry Religion.

"Prince Charles news: Why Prince Charles would choose
NOT to become Defender of the Faith: Prince Charles will
become the next King of England and is currently the
oldest King in Waiting in history at 71, having spent nearly
his entire life as first-in-line. When he does succeed Queen
Elizabeth II, however, he said he would drop one of the
monarchy's core mottos. The Queen's full title is currently

"Elizabeth the Second, by the Grace of God, of the United Kingdom of Great Britain and Northern Ireland and of Her other Realms and Territories Queen, Head of the Commonwealth, Defender of the Faith". When Prince Charles eventually takes her position, he will inherit those titles, but he has voiced his intention to change the "Defender of the Faith" moniker. Bestowed on King Henry VIII in 1517 by the Pope, it reflects the monarch's position as supreme governor of the Church of England. As such, it relates to their ability to preserve the national faith, which, since Henry VIII's rule is Christianity. However, in the more than 500 years since the title came into being, the UK's religious landscape has markedly diversified. The new interfaith identity of the country has led Prince Charles to voice his preference for the streamlined "Defender of Faith" instead. He revealed his intentions in 2008, in a bid to add a contemporary spin to the monarchy. British monarchs are all known as "Defender of the Faith" University College London's Constitution Unit said the moved showed support for religious freedom. They said: "Charles was making the point that, in a country with many religions now present, the sovereign should be concerned to see all religion defended and not just the Church of England. "Because Latin has no definite article, he offered 'Defender of Faith' as an alternative and viable translation to signify how a sovereign should nowadays understand the contemporary meaning of the title. "In practice, religion is protected by laws made by Parliament or as a result of international agreements like the European Convention on Human Rights." LIAM DOYLE, Thu, Jul 2, 2020.

******

TWEETS:

GDC: Richard Hill (NHS) fabricated reports

THE RACIST WHITE MAN IS THE DEVIL

BEDFORD: District Judge, NIGERIA (oil/gas) is more relevant to the survival of your white spouse and your children, and your father and his spouse than LUTON

AN IGNORANT DESCENDANT OF WHITE THIEVES

GDC: Richard Hill (NHS) lied under oath

THE RACIST WHITE MAN IS THE DEVIL

BEDFORD: District Judge, NIGERIA (oil/gas) is more relevant to the survival of your white spouse and your children, and your father and his spouse than LUTON

AN IGNORANT DESCENDANT OF WHITE THIEVES

GDC: Kevin Atkinson (NHS) lied under oath

THE RACIST WHITE MAN IS THE DEVIL

BEDFORD: District Judge, NIGERIA (oil/gas) is more relevant to the survival of your white spouse and your children, and your father and his spouse than LUTON

AN IGNORANT DESCENDANT OF WHITE THIEVES

GDC: Jonathan Martin lied on record

THE RACIST WHITE MAN IS THE DEVIL

BEDFORD: District Judge, NIGERIA (oil/gas) is more relevant to the survival of your white spouse and your children, and your father and his spouse than LUTON

AN IGNORANT DESCENDANT OF WHITE THIEVES

GDC: Helen Falcon (MBE) lied on record

THE RACIST WHITE WOMAN IS THE DEVIL

BEDFORD: District Judge, NIGERIA (oil/gas) is more relevant to the survival of your white spouse and your children, and your father and his spouse than LUTON

AN IGNORANT DESCENDANT OF WHITE THIEVES

GDC: George Rothnie (NHS) lied on record

THE RACIST WHITE MAN IS THE DEVIL

BEDFORD: District Judge, NIGERIA (oil/gas) is more relevant to the survival of your white spouse and your children, and your father and his spouse than LUTON

AN IGNORANT DESCENDANT OF WHITE THIEVES

GDC: Stephanie Twidale (NHS) lied under oath

THE RACIST WHITE WOMAN IS THE DEVIL

BEDFORD: District Judge, NIGERIA (oil/gas) is more relevant to the survival of your white spouse and your children, and your father and his spouse than LUTON

AN IGNORANT DESCENDANT OF WHITE THIEVES

GDC: Sue Gregory (OBE) lied on record

THE RACIST WHITE WOMAN IS THE DEVIL

BEDFORD: District Judge, NIGERIA (oil/gas) is more relevant to the survival of your white spouse and your children, and your father and his spouse than LUTON

AN IGNORANT DESCENDANT OF WHITE THIEVES

GDC: Rachael Bishop (NHS) lied under oath

THE RACIST WHITE WOMAN IS THE DEVIL

BEDFORD: District Judge, NIGERIA (oil/gas) is more relevant to the survival of your white spouse and your children, and your father and his spouse than LUTON

AN IGNORANT DESCENDANT OF WHITE THIEVES

GDC: Geraint Evans (NHS) lied on record

THE RACIST WHITE MAN IS THE DEVIL

BEDFORD: District Judge, NIGERIA (oil/gas) is more relevant to the survival of your white spouse and your children, and your father and his spouse than LUTON

AN IGNORANT DESCENDANT OF WHITE THIEVES

CHAPTER TEN:

Boris Johnson: Why is England not a scam?

Then, there, the King died, and the Crown Prince, a
Freemason, became the King.

Then, LUCIFER, the ruler of Freemasons ruled our world, and
there was an imbalance of Religious Power, and a conflict of
interest, as in addition to the total control of the administration
of the Law by the Freemasons, the King was a Freemason.

Then, our irreconcilable religious enemies, members of the
Charitable Antichrist Racist Freemasonry Quasi-Religion
(Mediocre Mafia/New Pharisees) imposed their shallow and
intellectually flawed belief on, we, their irreconcilable
Religious Enemies: Fundamentalist, John 14:6 Christians.

Which part of Bedfordshire Masonic Temple to Baal, the
Keep, Bedford Road, Kempston, MK42, was not stolen, or
which part of it was built with the yield of transparent virtue,
or which part of it preceded SLAVERY: The building or its
chattels?

Ignorance is bliss.

"Those who know the least obey the best." George Farquhar

OYINBO OLE: Racist descendants of THIEVES and owners of stolen children of defenceless poor people (Meghan Markle's ancestors) – Habakkuk

The Grand Mason Temple to Baal, the Mother Temple, 60 Great Queen St, London WC2B 5AZ, was built in the early 18th century, at a height of racist economic cannibalism: The barbarously racist traffic in millions of stolen children of defenceless poor people (Meghan Markle's ancestors) – Habakkuk

OYINBO OLE: HABAKKUK

Descendants of Alphonse Gabriel fool the foolish that they are Archangel Gabriel.

BEDFORD, ENGLAND: Based on available evidence, GDC-Witness, Freemason, Brother, Richard William Hill fabricated reports and unrelentingly lied under oath - Habakkuk 1:4; John 8:44; John 10:10. His white ancestors were incompetent racist liars too; they were THIEVES and owners of stolen children of defenceless poor people (Meghan Markle's ancestors) – Habakkuk

A WHITE MAN. A DISHONEST RACIST

Facts are sacred, they can't be overstated.

They tell lies all the time, and they lie that they don't lie – Psalm 144.

"Lies are told all the time." Sir Michael Havers (1923 – 1992).

When the closeted racist bastards 'FORK', which is all the time, genius Jews are their go-to-people.

They didn't foresee that the Corporal would flip, and if they did, they couldn't help themselves when he did.

"Jews are intelligent and creative, Chinese are intelligent but not creative, Indians are servile, and Africans are morons." Professor Watson (DNA) paraphrased.

It is a lie and/or it is a crime only if members of the Charitable Antichrist Racist Freemasonry Quasi-Religion did not prior authorise it.

They were all white: Homogeneity in the administration of English Law is the impregnable secure mask of merciless racist evil.

Boris Johnson: Reasoning and vision are unbounded; the fellow told the truth when He disclosed pictures His unbounded mind painted – John 14:6.

Boris Johnson: Our common genetic pool is getting weaker, and our world is dying slowly and imperceptibly. We are travelling in the wrong direction; only the Good Shepherd has infinite reasoning and vision, and only the fellow knows the way – John 14:6.

Boris Johnson: The bottom has descended to the basement, and since there is harmony, the top must have simultaneously descended to the bottom from whence the basement vacated. There is harmonious change but no relative change as the distance between the basement and the bottom remains unchanged. So, effectively, there is a collective decline.

The former top refuses to accept that it is the new bottom in the harmonious relationship.

BORIS JOHNSON: If the bottom descends to the basement and top stays at the top or ascends higher up, there will be disharmonious fracture, which antagonises the basis of harmonious one-man-one-vote democracy.

Facts are sacred, and they cannot be overstated.

If Her Majesty's appointee, District Judge Paul Ayers of Bedford County Court, the Senior Vice President of the Association of Her Majesty's District Judges, read his Judgement before he approved it, the white man, a mere former debt-collector Solicitor in Norwich, albeit a former Partner at Cole's Solicitors, must have been excessively stupid; if he didn't, he must have been stupider, and lied as he implied that it did – Habakkuk 1:4; John 8:44; John 10:10. His white ancestors were incompetent liars too; they were THIEVES and owners of stolen children of defenceless poor people (Meghan Markle's ancestors) – Habakkuk.

Facts are sacred.

"The truth allows no choice." Dr Samuel Johnson

NORTHAMPTON, ENGLAND: GDC-Witness, Rachael Bishop, Senior NHS Nurse, unrelentingly lied under oath.

A WHITE WOMAN. A DISHONEST RACIST COUGAR

PERCEPTION IS GRANDER THAN REALITY.

Boris Johnson: Your orderliness is confusion; the Negro has evolved in another direction. Believe me, anything that is not aligned to infinity or John 14:6 is intellectually flawed. If you do not believe me, you must prove that your white kindred, Ms Rachael Bishop, Senior NHS Nurse, is not a closeted racist white criminal who unrelentingly lied under oath.

What exactly is the point of a legal system that is overseen by white members of the charitable Antichrist Racist Freemasonry Religion that allows only white people to tell lies under oath (persecutory Negrophobia and Negrophobic perjury) – Habakkuk 1:4; John 8:44; John 10:10.

Almost everything is assumed in favour of the indisputably superior skin colour that the wearer neither made nor chose.

They are not the only creation of Almighty God, and their irrefutably superior skin colour is not the only wonder of our world.

Then, when the Crown Prince, a closeted member of the vulgarly Antichrist Racist Freemasonry-Religion (Mediocre Mafia/New Pharisees) became King, the ruler of their Satanic Mumbo Jumbo Cult became the ruler of the

State, and their leverage over their irreconcilable religious enemies increased, very significantly.

WHITE PRIVILEGE: The centuries-old unspoken myth that intellect is related to the indisputably superior skin colour that the wearer neither made nor chose is the mother of all racist scams.

District Judge Paul Ayers, the Senior Vice President of the Association of Her Majesty's District Judges, which part of Bedford County Court, 3, St Paul's Square was not stolen, or which part of it preceded SLAVERY, or which part of it did the people of BEDFORD buy?

OYINBO OLE: IGNORANT DESCENDANTS OF THIEVES - HABAKKUK

Ignorance is bliss.

"I do not approve of anything that tampers with natural ignorance. Ignorance is like a delicate exotic fruit; touch it and the bloom is gone. The whole theory of modern education is radically unsound. Fortunately, in England, at any rate, education produces no effect whatsoever. If it did, it would prove a serious danger to the upper classes, and probably lead to acts of violence in Grosvenor Square." Wilde

The report, by the OECD, warns that the UK needs to take significant action to boost the basic skills of the nation's young people. The 460-page study is based on the first-ever survey of the literacy, numeracy and problem-solving at work skills of 16 to 65-year-olds in 24 countries, with almost 9,000 people taking part in England and Northern Ireland to make up the UK results. The findings showed that England and Northern Ireland have some of the highest proportions of adults scoring no higher than Level 1 in literacy and numeracy - the lowest level on the OECD's scale. This suggests that their skills in the basics are no better than that of a 10-year-old.

AN IMBECILE: AN ADULT WITH THE BASIC SKILLS OF A CHILD.

Facts are sacred; they cannot be overstated.

Apart from creating very cushy salaried jobs for incontrovertibly functional semi-illiterate white Judges, who foreseeably FAILED in the practice of the grossly overrated mediocre trade (quasi-communism), what do imbeciles (adults with the basic skills of a child) need very, very expensive administration of the Law for?

"Natural selection will not remove ignorance from future generations." Dr Richard Dawkins

It is deductible that adults with the basic skills of a foetus will succeed imbeciles (adults with the basic skills of a child), and the former will need only food shelter.

Now, they use Nuclear Bombs to preserve the propagation of imbeciles (adults with the basic skills of a child), then, the mother of Nuclear Bombs will be used to preserve the continuing propagation of adults with the basic skills of a FOETUS.

They foresaw that some of their descendants will be imbeciles (adults with the basic skills of a child), so they used guns to loot Africa, and they used the yields of several centuries of the evilest racist terrorism and the greediest economic cannibalism the world will ever know to create an Eldorado for millions of white imbeciles (adults with the basic skills of a child), and they decommissioned natural selection, and they reversed evolution, and they used the yield of millions of stolen children of defenceless poor people to, retrogressively, make it possible for millions of imbeciles of all shades to breed irresponsibly.

Boris Johnson: If paying incontrovertibly functional white Judges (predominantly) several scores of thousands of pounds of other people's monies, annually, to have daily dialogues with imbeciles (adults with the basic skills of a child) - is not a scam, paying the successors of irrefutably functional semi-illiterate white Judges (predominantly) – very many scores of thousands of pounds of other people's monies, annually, to have daily dialogues with adults with the basic skills of a FOETUS, will be the mother of all RACKETS.

OYINBO OLE: IGNORANT DESDENDANTS OF THIEVES - HABAKKUK.

"A government that robs Peter to pay Paul can always depend on the support of Paul." George Bernard Shaw

Facts are sacred.

Just as it was in Professor Stephen Hawking's School, then, at the University of Lagos, the brightest students did mathematics, physics, and chemistry, and did not attend lectures at the Faculty of Law.

"In my school, the brightest boys did math and physics, the less bright did physics and chemistry, and the least bright did biology. I wanted to do math and physics, but my father made me do chemistry because he thought there would be no jobs for mathematicians." Dr Stephen Hawking.

A grossly overrated, overhyped, overpopulated, and mediocre trade that is dying slowly and imperceptibly, and is overseen by the Antichrist Racist Freemasons (Mediocre Mafia) - Habakkuk 1:4; John 8:44; John 10:10.

"The legal system lies at the heart of any society, protecting rights, imposing duties, and establishing a framework for the conduct of almost every social, political, and economic activity. Some argue that the law is in its death throes while others postulate a contrary prognosis that discerns numerous signs of law's enduring strength. Which is it?" Professor Raymond Wacks.

Facts are sacred; they can't be overstated.

Accurate seers: The accurately foresaw that a functional semi-illiterate former, mere, debt-collector Solicitor in Norwich (coastal dole) whose white father and mother have never seen crude oil, and whose white ancestors, including self-righteous John Bunyan (1628-1688) were fed like battery-hens with the yield of stolen children of defenceless poor people (Meghan Markle's ancestors),will be our District Judge in BEDFORD, racist bastards and economic cannibals, cowardly embarked on armed robbery, indiscriminate destruction of movable and immovable creations of Almighty God, and dispossession raids of defenceless poor people (Meghan Markle's ancestors), in Africa – Habakkuk.

OYINBO OLE: THIEVES – HABAKKUK

"Those who know the least obey the best." George Farquhar

Then, in 1892, after several centuries of the greediest economic cannibalism and evilest racist terrorism the world will ever know, racist white bastards and those they armed returned to our tribe, in the African bush, Ijebu, only a walking distance from the Great Atlantic Ocean, and they used very heavy guns, on wheels, to slaughter almost everybody, the remainder, those who were not carried during the barbarously racist carrying-trade and their descendants. The racist white bastards, Defenders of Faiths, evicted our King, the Awujale of Ijebu-Land, from his Palace, and looted it, and converted it into their Military

Garrison, and in 1893, very many sensuous Ijebu girls:
Maidens, children, and married women gave birth
Mulattos. The armed racist white bastard Christians were
evidently inter-racial sex-machines.

Like Obama's children some Ijebus are white inside as
they are direct descendants of Mulattos.

Christ did not place Africans in the back rows, white men
did.

The white man was the devil. The white man was the thief.

GOOGLE: IMAGBON 1892.

The armed racist bastard Christians were white racist sex-
machines in the African bush, and they evidently loved,
industrial-scale, non-consensual, inter-racial 'stuff' with
Ijebu girls; they did not, similarly, love inter-racial man-to-
man fist fight.

In 1911, only about a decade later (1892 – 1911), an
indiscreetly white Supremacist thug, the Home Secretary,
banned inter-racial fist fight, for very obvious reasons.
They ate their cakes and had it:
The racist bastards loved inter-racial stuff with sensuous
women in the African bush (inter-racial sex-machine in the
African bush); they did not love inter-racial man-to-man
fist fight.

Then, armed racist bastards, and those they armed, indiscriminately slaughtered Negroes with tools, in the African bush. The bottom line was raw materials and natural resources. They were as greedy as the grave, and like death, the closeted racist bastards were never satisfied – Habakkuk.

Then, they wrote their history and ours, and both favoured them.

"History will be kind to me, for I intend to write it." Churchill.

"Despite Britain's rich history of black boxers, racist attitudes about the mental and physical dispositions of black people permeated the game; full-time British segregationist campaigners such as the evangelical preacher Frederick Brotherton Meyer argued that white athletes did not have the "animal development" of black people and could therefore not compete with their "instinctive passion" for violence. There were also worries over the consequences of emboldening Britain's colonial subjects. For a nervous British establishment, there were far too many negative ramifications for their rule over the Empire if even an innocent sports tournament could even temporarily demonstrate the equality of black and white people. This is why in 1911, Home Secretary Winston Churchill banned interracial boxing matches, and the BBBC followed suit. The BBBC's bar remained in place until the 1940s." Tribune

GDC-Witness: Based on available evidence, Kevin Atkinson (Scottish Kev) unrelentingly lied under oath.

A WHITE SCOTCHMAN. A DISHONEST RACIST.

Intellectually impotent white nonentities, racist descendants of ultra-righteous THIEVES, and owners of stolen children of defenceless poor people (Black African ancestors of Meghan Markle and her white children) – Habakkuk

No brain.
Poor in natural resources.
Several centuries of armed robbery and slavery preceded the huge stolen trust fund.
White Privilege: The skin colour is irrefutably superior; the very, very fortunate wearer neither made nor chose it.

Our incontrovertibly functional semi-illiterate District Judge of our Empire of stolen affluence - Habakkuk.

Everything, absolutely everything is assumed in favour of the irrefutably superior skin colour that the wearer neither made nor chose.

Our Empire did not evolve; then, almost everything was actively and deliberately stolen with guns - Habakkuk.

OYINBO OLE: THIEVES – HABAKKUK.

"Affluence is not a birth right." David Cameron

WHITE PRIVILEGE: The centuries-old unspoken myth that intellect is linked to the irrefutably superior skin colour that the very, very fortunate wearer neither made nor chose is the mother of all racist scams.

TARZAN IN AFRICA: Shepherds did not bring stolen children of defenceless poor people back home (Meghan Markle's ancestors), they took them to the Americas and the West Indies and lied to their moron sheep that they were paragons of wisdom and virtue who, like, Mother Teresa, did only virtuous works in Africa.

GDC-Witness: Stephanie Twiddle, British Soldier – Territorial Defence (TD) unrelentingly lied under oath. Her white ancestors were incompetent racist liars too; they were THIEVES and owners of stolen children of defenceless poor people (Meghan Markle's ancestors) - Habakkuk

A WHITE WOMAN. A DISHONEST RACIST COUGAR.

When their people commit racist crimes against our people, racist bastards, Defenders of Faiths, dissenters of John 14:6, who oversee the administration of their law criminally bury racial hatred; the ultra-righteous closeted white supremacist thugs who use very expensive aprons to decorate the temples of their powerless and useless fertility tools do not believe in the exceptionalism of Christ, so they are not deterred by His transparent Justice – Proverbs 15:3; John 5:22; Matthew 25: 31-46; John 14:6.

WHITE PRIVILEGE/APARTHEID BY STEALTH: They love the superiority that is automatically attached to the irrefutably superior skin colour that they neither made nor chose, their brainless and baseless birth right; they don't love Freedom of Expression because they don't want their mentally gentle children to know that they are excessively stupid.

They love Apartheid by stealth.

OYINBO ODE: A CLOSETED RACIST WHITE DUNCE.

Some Lords nominated and constructively appointed a poly-educated, incontrovertibly functional semi-illiterate, mere, former debt-collector Solicitor, in Norwich (coastal dole), as our District Judge in BEDFORD.

A functional semi-illiterate waste of money fake judge (Proverbs 17:16).

PERCEPTION IS GRANDER THAN REALITY.

WHITE PRIVILEGE: Everything is assumed in favour of the irrefutably superior skin colour that the wearer neither made nor chose.

A closeted racist descendant of RIGHTEOUS WHITE THIEVES and owners of kidnapped children of defenceless poor people (Meghan Markle's ancestors) - Habakkuk.

A properly schooled impostor and an expert of deception.

"There is no sin except stupidity." Wilde

His spinal cord seemed to be his highest centre.

*****

When the FORK, genius Jews are their go-to-people.

Then, they did not foresee that the Corporal would flip, and if they did, they couldn't help themselves when he did.

Gigantic yields of millions of stolen and destroyed lives of the children of defenceless poor people (Meghan Markle's ancestors) during several centuries of the greediest economic cannibalism and the evilest racist terrorism the world ever know, not feudal agriculture, lured Eastern European Jews to Great Britain.

Before SLAVERY, what?

"Sometimes people don't want to hear the truth because they don't want their illusions destroyed." Friedrich Nietzsche

OYINBO OLE: Ignorant descendants of ultra-righteous THIEVES and owners of stolen children of defenceless poor people (Meghan Markle's ancestors) - Habakkuk

Then, they were taught a lesson in Germany, so, now, they allow very poor quality of human beings, certainly mentally, to rise to the top, seemingly in pursuance of avoiding another Holocaust.

Boris Johnson: Your white kindred is a dunce; the intellect that the poly-educated former debt-collector Solicitor inherited from his white father and mother is, evidently, not good.

Boris Johnson: This Negro does not believe that white imbeciles, predominantly, are capable of proper academic law – Habakkuk 1:4.

CHAPTER ELEVEN:

Boris Johnson, why is England not a scam?

"A feeling of inferiority? No, a feeling of nonexistence. Sin is Negro as virtue is white. All those white men in a group, guns in their hands, cannot be wrong. I am guilty. I do not know of what, but I know that I am no good." Frantz Fanon

"It is incumbent upon the court and all those professionals involved to conclude court proceedings as quickly as possible. This hopefully ensures that a child has stability, love and affection and the parents working together to ensure that he has the best opportunity of developing academically and emotional." District Judge Paul Ayers, the Senior Vice President of the Association of Her Majesty's District Judges – proofed and approved Judgement

AN IMBECILE: AN ADULT WITH THE BASIC SKILLS OF A CHILD.

Immortal and unashamed mediocrity and confusion.

"Yes, Sir, it does *her* honour, but it would do nobody else honour. I have indeed, not read it all. But when I take up the end of a web, and find it packthread, I do not expect, by looking further, to find embroidery." Dr Samuel Johnson

The report, by the OECD, warns that the UK needs to take significant action to boost the basic skills of the nation's young people. The 460-page study is based on the first-ever survey of the literacy, numeracy and problem-solving at work skills of 16 to 65-year-olds in 24 countries, with almost 9,000 people taking part in England and Northern Ireland to make up the UK results. The findings showed that England and Northern Ireland have some of the highest proportions of adults scoring no higher than Level 1 in literacy and numeracy - the lowest level on the OECD's scale. This suggests that their skills in the basics are no better than that of a 10-year-old.

AN IMBECILE: AN ADULT WITH THE BASIC SKILLS OF A CHILD.

OUR IMBECILE DISTRICT JUDGE OF OUR EMPIRE OF STOLEN AFFLUENCE: AN ADULT WITH THE BASIC SKILLS OF A CHILD.

Apart from creating very cushy salaried jobs for incontrovertibly functional semi-illiterate white Judges (predominantly), who foreseeably FAILED in the very, very competitive law practice, what do IMBECILES (adults with the basic skills of a child) need very, very expensive administration of the law for?
"The one great principle of the English law is, to make business for itself. There is no other principle distinctly, certainly, and consistently maintained through all its narrow turnings. Viewed by this light it becomes a

coherent scheme, and not the monstrous maze the laity are apt to think it." Charles Dickens

WHITE PRIVILEGE: Based on very, very proximate observations and direct experiences, they love brainless and baseless skin colour superiority, their inviolable birth right, but they don't love Freedom of Expression because they don't want their mentally very gentle children to know that they are excessively stupid, poly-educated white functional semi-illiterates – Proverbs 17:16.

Our irrefutably functional semi-illiterate White Freemason District Judge of our Empire of stolen affluence: OYINBO OLE – Habakkuk.

District Judge Paul Ayers, the Senior Vice President of the Association of Her Majesty's District Judges righteously sat on bones of stolen children of defenceless poor Africans, more bones than the millions of skulls at the doorstep of Comrade of Pol Pot. The incontrovertibly functional semi-illiterate former, mere, debt-collector Solicitor in Norwich (coastal dole) rides a very powerful tiger, deluded, he thinks he is a tiger; dismounted, the closeted racist functional semi-illiterate white man, albeit England's Class Senior Judge, will instantly revert to PURIFIED NOTHING.

PERCEPTION IS GRANDER THAN REALITY.

If they knew what we truly felt, and said behind their backs, the closeted racist bastards would have killed us, albeit hands off. They do, now.

New Herod, Matthew 2:16: They deceive their mentally very gentle children that they are geniuses, and they kill, albeit hands-off all those who know that they are brainless racist bastards.

A CLOSETED RACIST WHITE FOOL'S APPROVAL!

PURIFIED ROT!

"Gentlemen, you are now about to embark on a course of studies which will occupy you for two years. Together, they form a noble adventure. But I would like to remind you of an important point. Nothing that you will learn in the course of your studies will be of the slightest possible use to you in after life, save only this, that if you work hard and intelligently you should be able to detect when a man is talking rot, and that, in my view, is the main, if not the sole, purpose of education." John Alexander Smith, Oxford University Professor of MORAL PHILOSOPHY.

FREEMASONS ATTACH UNSHAMED MEDIOCRITY AND CONFUSION TO DEVOUT CHRISTIAN SOVEREIGNS, AND SELL IT TO THE UNDISCERNING FOR VERY VALUABLE CONSIDERATION.

JUDICIAL DIVERSITY: ACCELERATING CHANGE.
Sir Geoffrey Bindman, QC Karon Monaghan QC "The
near absence of women and Black, Asian and minority
ethnic judges in the senior judiciary, is no longer tolerable.
It undermines the democratic legitimacy of our legal
system; it demonstrates a denial of fair and equal
opportunities to members of underrepresented groups, and
the diversity deficit weakens the quality of justice."

Based on available evidence, their own Money, NIGERIA
(oil/gas) is by far more relevant to the economic survival of
all the white children of District Judge Paul Ayers, the
Senior Vice President of the Association of Her Majesty's
District Judges, than Bedford. Then, the white ancestors of
District Judge Paul Ayers, the Senior Vice President of the
Association of Her Majesty's District Judges, were fed like
battery-hens with the yields of stolen children of
defenceless poor people (Meghan Markle's ancestors) –
Habakkuk

"It was our arms in the river of Cameroon, put into the
hands of the trader, that furnished him with the means of
pushing his trade; and I have no more doubt that they are
British arms, put into the hands of Africans, which promote
universal war and desolation that I can doubt their having
done so in that individual instance. I have shown how great
is the enormity of this evil, even on the supposition that we
take only convicts and prisoners of war. But take the
subject in another way, and how does it stand? Think of
80,000 persons carried out of their native country by we
know not what means! For crimes imputed! For light or

inconsiderable faults! For debts perhaps! For crime of witchcraft! Or a thousand other weak or scandalous pretexts! Reflect on 80,000 persons annually taken off! There is something in the horror of it that surpasses all bounds of imagination." – Prime Minister William Pitt the Younger.

Christ did not place Africans in the back rows, white men did.
The white man was the devil. The white man was the thief.

Properly rehearsed righteousness and deceptively schooled civilised decorum were preceded by several centuries of the greediest economic cannibalism and the evilest racist terrorism the world will ever know.

District Judge Paul Ayers, the Senior Vice President of the Association of Her Majesty's District Judges is a distinguished and very high-ranking member of their overhyped Mediocre Trade; the very broad Church that admits geniuses and imbeciles.

Then, there, in order to conceal the only truth, which is that the top is the new bottom, closeted racist bastards resort to Judicial terrorism that was tacitly guarded by closeted white supremacist Freemason Judges, who oversaw the administration of the Law.

BEDFORD, ENGLAND: GDC-Witness, Freemason, Brother, Richard William Hill fabricated reports and unrelentingly lied under oath – Habakkuk 1:4; John 8:44;

John 10:10. His white ancestors were incompetent racist liars too; they were THIEVES and owners of stolen children of defenceless poor people – Habakkuk.

A WHITE MAN: A DISHONEST RACIST

Brainless defenders of FAITHS (FREEMASONS) do not believe in the exceptionalism of Christ, so they are not deterred by His transparent Justice – Proverbs 15:3; John 5:22; Matthew 25: 31-46; John 14:6.

Which part of Bedfordshire Masonic Temple to Baal, the Keep, Bedford Road, Kempston, MK42, was not STOLEN, or which part of the magnificent building did transparent virtue yield, or which part of it preceded SLAVERY: The building or its chattels?

Ignorance is bliss.

"Those who know the least obey the best." George Farquhar

The Grand Masonic Temple to Baal, 60 Great Queen St, London WC2B 5AZ, was built in the early 18th century, at a height of the economically cannibalistic and barbarous traffic in millions of stolen children of defenceless poor people (Meghan Markle's ancestors) – Habakkuk

C of E raises serious concerns about Christian Freemasons
https://www.theguardian.com › uk-news › feb › c-of-e-...

8 Feb 2018 — Church of England warning that secret society may not be compatible with Christianity echoes concerns from 1987.

Facts are sacred, they can't be overstated.

Our Defenders of Faiths, dissenters of John 14:6: Bywords for the vulgarly charitable, closeted white supremacist, Antichrist Freemasonry Quasi-Religion (New Pharisees).

Then, their ruler's offer was rejected – Matthew 4:9.

GDC: Richard Hill fabricated reports and unrelentingly lied under oath.

GDC: Stephanie Twidale (TD) unrelentingly lied under oath.

GDC: Helen Falcon (MBE) unrelentingly lied under implied oath.

The closeted white supremacist Defenders of Faiths do not believe in His exceptionalism, so they aren't deterred by the transparent Justice of the only Good Shepherd – Proverbs 15:3; John 5:22; Matthew 25: 31 – 46; John 14:6.

GDC: Anthony Kravitz (OBE), BDA's homunculus white man, lied when he implied that he didn't know that his white kindred lied under oath.

GDC: Shiv Pabary (MBE) unrelentingly lied under oath. Our Empire didn't evolve; then, almost everything was actively stolen – Habakkuk. "Affluence isn't a birth right." David Cameron. "The best opportunity of developing academically and emotional." District Judge Ayers, Bedford: A closeted racist white imbecile. Ignorant descendants of thieves; owners of stolen children. "Those who know the least obey the best." Farquhar. Scottish, White, Kevin Atkinson (GDC/NHS) lied under oath: A dishonest racist

Nigeria: Shell's docile cash cow: Nincompoops thrive in Great Britain; what's great about that?

Then, when their people committed racist crimes against Africans, the closeted racist bastards who oversaw the administration of their law – criminally buried racial hatred – Habakkuk 1:4; John 8:44; John 10:10.

Abuse of power is the purest definition of evil.

Based on very proximate observations and direct experiences, the white man is the devil.

Only stupid Africans do not know that whites measure whites with a very, very different yardstick, and only stupider Africans expect demons to cast out demons – Matthew 12:27.

Seemingly with the tacit approval of closeted white supremacist Freemason Judges, racist bastards do racist criminality and call it civilised and impartial administration of the law; closeted racist white bastards do whatever they like.

"A complaint such as Mrs Bishop's could trigger an enquiry." Stephen Henderson, LLM, BDS, Head at MDDUS

A crooked, closeted racist white bastard.

GOOGLE: MDDUS HENDERSON LETTERS

Based on available evidence, GDC-Witness, Ms Rachael Bishop, Senior NHS Nurse, unrelentingly lied under oath – Habakkuk 1:4: John 8:44; John 10:10.

A WHITE WOMAN. A DISHONEST RACIST COUGAR.

OYINBO OLE: IGNORANT DESCENDANTS OF ULTRA-RIGHTEOUS THIEVES - HABAKKUK.

They greedily eat all their cakes, and all the cakes of other people; the closeted racist bastards want everything: The closeted white supremacist Defenders of Faiths do not believe in the exceptionalism of our own Messiah (John 14:6), but resort to Judicial Terrorism to stifle and conceal the display of His infinite reasoning and vision.

"The highest reach of injustice is to be deemed just when you are not." Plato

BORIS JOHNSON: I have decoded the system, it is a scam, and it is controlled by the FREEMASONS.

"You can't beat the system. You will bow." Kemi Daramola

Esu.
Imported devil.

I shan't. I know who will.

She prays and pays tithe (quasi-protection money) to Freemasons at Brickhill Baptist Church, Bedford, and Freemasons in Kempston answers her prayers.

-----Original Message-----
From: resh diu <rdiu@me.com>
To: adeolacole <adeolacole@aol.com>
Sent: Fri, 11 Apr 2014 9:28
Subject: Re:

It's sad Ola

I kept telling you to play the game of chess rather than fight it

You take care

If you wish to dispose of 24 park road let me know

Regards

Resh
Dr Resh Diu BDS
www.oradi.co.uk

To survive in Great Britain, we must bow to Freemasons even if they were thicker than a gross of planks, and we must play closeted white supremacist 'devils' like chess, and we must teach our children to bow to quasi-voodoo men who use very expensive aprons to decorate the temples of their powerless and useless fertility tools, and we must teach them to play closeted racist nincompoops, impostors, and experts of deception like chess.

BRAINLESS NONSENSE!

GDC-Witness: Richard Hill fabricated reports and unrelentingly lied under oath. His white ancestors were incompetent racist liars too, they were THIEVES and owners of stolen children of defenceless poor Africans (Black African ancestors of Meghan Markle and her white children) – Habakkuk. Closeted racist bastards who use very expensive apron to decorate the temples of their powerless and useless fertility tools persecute Christians who do not believe in their brainless Satanic Mumbo Jumbo, and who do not pay quasi-protection money.

GDC: Kevin Atkinson (NHS) unrelentingly lied under oath. His white ancestors were incompetent racist liars too, they were THIEVES and owners of stolen children of defenceless poor Africans (Black African ancestors of Meghan Markle and her white children) – Habakkuk. Closeted racist bastards who use very expensive apron to decorate the temples of their powerless and useless fertility tools persecute Christians who do not believe in their brainless Satanic Mumbo Jumbo, and who do not pay quasi-protection money.

GDC: Jonathan Martin unrelentingly lied on record. His white ancestors were incompetent racist liars too, they were THIEVES and owners of stolen children of defenceless poor Africans (Black African ancestors of Meghan Markle and her white children) – Habakkuk. Closeted racist bastards who use very expensive apron to decorate the temples of their powerless and useless fertility tools persecute Christians who do not believe in their brainless Satanic Mumbo Jumbo, and who do not pay quasi-protection money.

GDC: Helen Falcon (MBE) unrelentingly lied on record. Her white ancestors were incompetent racist liars too, they were THIEVES and owners of stolen children of defenceless poor Africans (Black African ancestors of Meghan Markle and her white children) – Habakkuk. Closeted racist bastards who use very expensive apron to decorate the temples of their powerless and useless fertility tools persecute Christians who do not believe in their brainless Satanic Mumbo Jumbo, and who do not pay quasi-protection money

GDC: George Rothnie (NHS) unrelentingly lied on record. His white ancestors were incompetent racist liars too, they were THIEVES and owners of stolen children of defenceless poor Africans (Black African ancestors of Meghan Markle and her white children) – Habakkuk. Closeted racist bastards who use very expensive apron to decorate the temples of their powerless and useless fertility tools persecute Christians who do not believe in their brainless Satanic Mumbo Jumbo, and who do not pay quasi-protection money.

GDC: Stephanie Twiddle, TD, (NHS) unrelentingly lied under oath. Her white ancestors were incompetent racist liars too, they were THIEVES and owners of stolen children of defenceless poor Africans (Black African ancestors of Meghan Markle and her white children) – Habakkuk. Closeted racist bastards who use very expensive apron to decorate the temples of their powerless and useless fertility tools persecute Christians who do not believe in their brainless Satanic Mumbo Jumbo, and who do not pay quasi-protection money.

GDC: Sue Gregory (OBE) unrelentingly lied on record. Her white ancestors were incompetent racist liars too, they were THIEVES and owners of stolen children of defenceless poor Africans (Black African ancestors of Meghan Markle and her white children) – Habakkuk.

Closeted racist bastards who use very expensive apron to decorate the temples of their powerless and useless fertility tools persecute Christians who do not believe in their brainless Satanic Mumbo Jumbo, and who do not pay quasi-protection money.

GDC: Rachael Bishop (NHS) unrelentingly lied under oath. Her white ancestors were incompetent racist liars too, they were THIEVES and owners of stolen children of defenceless poor Africans (Black African ancestors of Meghan Markle and her white children) – Habakkuk. Closeted racist bastards who use very expensive apron to decorate the temples of their powerless and useless fertility tools persecute Christians who do not believe in their brainless Satanic Mumbo Jumbo, and who do not pay quasi-protection money.

GDC: Geraint Evans (NHS) unrelentingly lied on record. His white ancestors were incompetent racist liars too, they were THIEVES and owners of stolen children of defenceless poor Africans (Black African ancestors of Meghan Markle and her white children) – Habakkuk. Closeted racist bastards who use very expensive apron to decorate the temples of their powerless and useless fertility tools persecute Christians who do not believe in their brainless Satanic Mumbo Jumbo, and who do not pay quasi-protection money.

When closeted racist bastards tell incompetent racist lies in pursuance of the best interests of imbeciles, to save their unashamed face, they unilaterally declare the victim of their uneducated RACIAL HATRED, a lunatic.

Ignorant racist FOOLS.

Racist descendants of ultra-righteous THIEVES — Habakkuk.

They were all white, including the Judges, and they were all RACISTS, and incompetent liars — Habakkuk. Homogeneity in the administration of English Law is the impregnable secure mask of merciless racial hatred.

Closeted racist bastards use incompetent mendacity to conceal hereditary intellectual impotence. Closeted racist bastards are not deterred by his Justice (John 5:22) because they do not believe in his exceptionalism (John 14:6).

OYINBO OLE: STRAIGHT-FACED DESCENDANTS OF ULTRA-RIGHTEOUS THIEVES — HABAKKUK

"Those who have the power to do wrong with impunity seldom wait long for the will." Dr Samuel Johnson.

A bastardised, indiscreetly dishonest, unashamedly mediocre, vindictive, potently weaponised, and institutionally RACIST legal system that is overseen by the FREEMASONS — Habakkuk

"To deny or belittle this good is, in this dangerous century when the resources and pretensions of power continue to enlarge, a desperate error of intellectual abstraction. More than this, it is a self-fulfilling error, which encourages us to give up the struggle against bad laws and class bound procedures and to disarm ourselves before power. It is to throw away a whole inheritance of struggle about the law and within the forms of law, whose continuity can never be fractured without bringing men and women into immediate danger." — E. P Thompson.
*****

Tweets:

GDC: Richard Hill (NHS)fabricated reports.
A WHITE MAN. A DISHONEST RACIST.
If the white man, albeit Bedford's Class District Judge read his judgement, he was a FOOL; if he didn't, he LIED as he implied that he did.
IGNORANT DESCENDANTS OF THIEVES
https://www.youtube.com/watch?v=BlpH4hG7m1A

GDC: Richard Hill lied under oath.
A WHITE MAN. A DISHONEST RACIST. NIGERIA: SHELL'S CASH COW.
Our white District Judge approved what his semi-illiterate father and mother spoke.
A closeted racist Superior skin colour; what else?
Our brainless dunce.
https://www.youtube.com/watch?v=BlpH4hG7m1A

GDC: Richard Hill fabricated reports.
A WHITE MAN. A DISHONEST RACIST. NIGERIA:
SHELL'S CASH COW.
A semi-illiterate former debt-collector Solicitor in
NORWICH whose white mother and father have never
seen crude oil is our District Judge in BEDFORD.
https://www.youtube.com/watch?v=BlpH4hG7m1A

GDC: Richard Hill fabricated reports.
A WHITE MAN. A DISHONEST RACIST.
NIGERIA: SHELL'S CASH COW.
BEDFORD: District Judge, NIGERIA (oil/gas) is by far
more relevant to the survival of your white children than
LUTON; your ancestors were THIEVES.
https://www.youtube.com/watch?v=BlpH4hG7m1A
Boris Johnson: Why is England not a racist scam?

*****

Then, there, closeted racist bastards were very highly
civilised, and they did everything legally, so when they
committed racist crimes against Africans, it was always
with the informal prior permission of closeted white
supremacist Freemason Judges, and it was always
selflessly in pursuance of the best interest of IMBECILES
(adults with the basic skills of child) – Habakkuk 1:4; John
8:44; John 10:10.

The report, by the OECD, warns that the UK needs to take significant action to boost the basic skills of the nation's young people. The 460-page study is based on the first-ever survey of the literacy, numeracy and problem-solving at work skills of 16 to 65-year-olds in 24 countries, with almost 9,000 people taking part in England and Northern Ireland to make up the UK results. The findings showed that England and Northern Ireland have some of the highest proportions of adults scoring no higher than Level 1 in literacy and numeracy - the lowest level on the OECD's scale. This suggests that their skills in the basics are no better than that of a 10-year-old.

AN IMBECILE: AN ADULT WITH THE BASIC SKILLS OF A CHILD.

Adults with the basic skills of a FOETUS will succeed adults with the basic skills of a child, and the former will need only food and shelter.

Then, there, White Judges, predominantly, and nearly all, were members of the Charitable Antichrist Racist Freemasonry Quasi-Religion (Mediocre Mafia/New Pharisees); some of them were thicker than a gross of planks - Habakkuk.

DELUDED PAPER TIGERS: "England will fight to the last American." American saying. Their hairs stand on end when they are challenged by Africans; Africans and their type are the ones racist bastards could beat up without the support of the YANKS.

If members of the Charitable Antichrist Racist Freemasonry Religion (Mediocre Mafia/New Pharisees) are as brave and as ethical as they seem to imply, they should forcibly evict Putin from Crimea; he forcibly stole it.

"Ethical foreign policy." Robin Cook (1946 – 2005).

The closeted racist bastards love the superiority that is 'fraudulently' attached to the irrefutably superior skin colour that they neither made nor chose, their brainless and baseless birth right, but they don't love Freedom of Expression because they don't want their mentally very gentle children to know that they are excessively stupid - Habakkuk. They love Apartheid by stealth: The natural instinct of the privileged dullard is Apartheid by stealth.

OXFORD, ENGLAND: Based on available evidence, British Soldier – Territorial Defence, Stephanie Twiddle (TD) unrelentingly lied under oath. Her white ancestors were incompetent racist liars too; they were THIEVES and owners of stolen children of defenceless poor people (Meghan Markle's ancestors) – Habakkuk.

A WHITE WOMAN. A DISHONEST RACIST COUGAR.

Based on very proximate observations, the white old bat looked like one of the dirty British cougars who regularly visited the Gambia to sit on black hard rocks.

Then, closeted white Supremacist Defenders of Faiths (Freemasons) investigated the racist crimes of their people against Africans, and when they found they were based on truths, as they did not believe in the exceptionalism of Christ, and they were not deterred by the transparent Justice of what they did not believe in (John 14:6; John 5:22; Matthew 25: 31-46; Proverbs 15:3), racist bastards criminally buried RACIAL HATRED.

BEDFORD, ENGLAND: District Judge Paul Ayers, the Senior Vice President of the Association of Her Majesty's District Judges, which part of Bedford County Court, 3, St Paul's Square Bedford, MK40, 1 SQ, was not stolen, or which part of it preceded SLAVERY, or which part of it did the people of Bedford buy, or which part of it did transparent virtue yield: The building or its chattels - Habakkuk?

Ignorance is bliss.

OYINBO OLE: Racist descendants of ultra-righteous THIEVES and owners of stolen children of defenceless poor people (Meghan Markle's ancestors) – Habakkuk.

Only stupid Negroes expect demons to cast out demons, and only stupider Negroes do not know that whites measure whites with a very, very different yardstick - Habakkuk 1:4; John 8:44; John 10:10.

"Mama, look, a Negro." Frantz Fanon

The report, by the OECD, warns that the UK needs to take significant action to boost the basic skills of the nation's young people. The 460-page study is based on the first-ever survey of the literacy, numeracy and problem-solving at work skills of 16 to 65-year-olds in 24 countries, with almost 9,000 people taking part in England and Northern Ireland to make up the UK results. The findings showed that England and Northern Ireland have some of the highest proportions of adults scoring no higher than Level 1 in literacy and numeracy - the lowest level on the OECD's scale. This suggests that their skills in the basics are no better than that of a 10-year-old.

AN IMBECILE: AN ADULT WITH THE BASIC SKILLS OF A CHILD.

Boris Johnson: Why is England not a scam?

BORIS JOHNSON: Then, there, White Judges (predominantly) who believed that daily dialogues with imbeciles was a worthy and proper occupation, were SCAMMERS, and Freemason Judges who demanded and accepted very valuable consideration for daily dialogues with imbeciles were RACKETEERS (Thieves).

https://www.youtube.com/watch?v=BlpH4hG7m1A&feature=youtu.be

"They may not have been well written from a grammatical point of view but I am confident I had not forgotten any of the facts." Dr Geraint Evans, Postgraduate Tutor, Oxford

https://youtu.be/rayVcfyu9Tw

"Why, Sir, Sherry is dull, naturally dull; but it must have taken him a great deal of pains to become what we now see him. Such an excess of stupidity, Sir, is not in Nature." DR SAMUEL JOHNSON

Based on available evidence, Dr Geraint Evans, Postgraduate Tutor, Oxford, a white man, unrelentingly lied under implied oath; a dishonest racist.

Based on very proximate observations and direct experiences, the white man is the devil.

-----Original Message-----
From: George Rothnie <georgerothnie@hotmail.com>
To: adeolacole@aol.com
Sent: Mon, 8 Mar 2010 20:19
Subject: Re Meeting 9th March

Hi Ola,

We are scheduled to meet tomorrow evening at my surgery about 5.30ish.
Unfortunately something has cropped up which necessytates me having to
postpone the meeting. I'm really sorry it's such short notice.

I will contact you in the week to arrange another date.

Once agaim my apologies.

George

Based on available evidence, Dr George Rothnie, a white man, and the Deputy Postgraduate Dean, Oxford, unrelentingly lied under implied oath.

The white man is the devil - Columbia University
https://ccnmtl.columbia.edu › mmt › mxp › concepts

Referring to Whites as "devils" originates with the teachings of Master W.D. Fard and the legend of Yakub. Fard taught Elijah Muhammad who preached the ...

BORIS JOHNSON. Apart from creating very cushy salaried jobs for incontrovertibly functional semi-illiterate white Judges (predominantly) who foreseeably FAILED in the practice of their grossly overrated, overhyped, and mediocre trade that admits geniuses and imbeciles alike, what do imbeciles (adults with the basic skills of a child) need very expensive administration of the law for?

Boris Johnson: Why is paying incontrovertibly functional semi-illiterate white Judges (predominantly) who foreseeably FAILED in the very competitive law practice, several scores of thousands of pounds of other people's money, annually, for having daily dialogues with imbeciles of all shades (adults with the basic skills of a child), not a bloody waste of money?

"Natural selection will not remove ignorance from future generations." Dr Richard Dawkins

Adults with the basic skills of a FOETUS will succeed adults with the basic skills of a child, and the former will need only food and shelter.

"Sometimes people don't want to hear the truth because they don't want their illusions destroyed." Friedrich Nietzsche.

They accurately foresaw that some of their descendants will be IMBECILES (adults with the basic skills of a child), so they used guns, made in Birmingham, to loot Africa, and they used the yield of several centuries of the greediest economic cannibalism and the evilest racist terrorism the world will ever know to create an ELDORADO for millions of white IMBECILES (adults with the basic skills of a child), and they decommissioned natural selection, and they reversed evolution, and they retrogressively weakened the common genetic pool, and they made it possible for millions of imbeciles, of all shades, to breed.

Ignorance is bliss.

"The English think incompetence is the same thing as sincerity." Quentin Crisp.

Almost everything is based on mediocrity, style, and lies, and dressed up as truth and substance, and all guarded by illegal (unelected) parallel power of members of the Charitable Antichrist Racist Freemasonry Religion (Mediocre Mafia/New Pharisees) – who use very expensive aprons, with vulgarly embroideries, to decorate the temples of their powerless and useless fertility tools; the closeted white supremacist thuggish bastards lie that they don't lie – Psalm 144.

Based on available evidence, the administration of English Law is incompetent art that incompetently imitates life – Habakkuk 1:4.

"In all unimportant matters, style, not sincerity, is the essential. In all important matters, style, not sincerity, is the essential." Wilde

JUDICIAL DIVERSITY: ACCELERATING CHANGE
"The near absence of women and Black, Asian and minority ethnic judges in the senior judiciary, is no longer tolerable. It undermines the democratic legitimacy of our legal system; it demonstrates a denial of fair and equal opportunities to members of underrepresented groups, and the diversity deficit weakens the quality of justice." Sir Geoffrey Bindman, QC, and Karon Monaghan, QC.

"All sections of the UK Society are institutionally racist." Sir Bernard Hogan-Howe

The Judiciary is part of the UK Society.

We do not trust semi-illiterate white Judges (disproportionately, Judges are white).

"Someone must be trusted. Let it be the Judges." Lord Denning (1899 – 1999), a closeted white supremacist Briton, and a Defender of FAITHS.

Lord Brittan (1939 – 2015): "A German Jew." Lord Denning

Lord Brittan's dad was a Jew, but he was an economic migrant from Lithuania.

Saxe-Coburg and Gotha family crossed the English Channels.

Mustafa Mehmet is Turkish; Boris Johnson isn't.

Deluded Richard Dawkins, a mere Science Journalist (Edward Wilson), a closeted White Supremacist Antichrist Briton, and Lala's husband, what is the real name of your white father's father, and where did he come from? Or did the white ancestors of your white father's father blindly (the blind watch maker) evolve from white monkeys with tails to tailless white monkeys, in the, then, vast jungles of Cambridgeshire?

"We are just an advanced breed of monkeys on a minor planet of a very average star. But we can understand the Universe. That makes us something very special." Dr Stephen Hawkins

Ignorance is bliss: Defenders of Faiths.

Defenders of Faith oversee the administration of English Law.

"I do not approve of anything that tampers with natural ignorance. Ignorance is like a delicate exotic fruit; touch it and the bloom is gone. The whole theory of modern education is radically unsound. Fortunately, in England, at any rate, education produces no effect whatsoever. If it did, it would prove a serious danger to the upper classes, and probably lead to acts of violence in Grosvenor Square." Wilde

'Oya jeun Edumare yo tan, o si wipe ki aja ode ki o ma ka lo.'

Gigantic yields of millions of stolen and destroyed lives seemed to have distorted the realities of descendants of aliens with camouflage English names.

The real name of Nigella Lawson's great grandfather was Gustav Liebson; he came from Latvia in the 1890s to latch on to the yields of millions of stolen children of defenceless poor people (Meghan Markle's ancestors) – Habakkuk.

"Agriculture, not only gives riches to a nation, but the only one she can call her own." Dr Samuel Johnson

Gigantic yields of millions of stolen children of defenceless poor Africans (Meghan Markle's ancestors), not feudal agriculture, lured Eastern European Jews to Britain.

Before SLAVERY, what?

The victims of Nazi Holocaust became the beneficiaries of the mother of all Holocausts, the Black Holocaust.

TURF WAR: Descendants of mere undocumented refugees from Eastern Europe and other places (genetic aliens), with camouflage English names, whose white ancestors arrived, not that long ago, without luggage or decent shoes, and blended with the yields of millions of stolen and destroyed children of defenceless poor people (Meghan Markle's ancestors), oppress the descendants of the robbed with the yields of the robbery – Habakkuk.

The real of Ghislaine Maxwell father was Ján Ludvík Hyman Binyamin Hoch; he was a very, very crooked Jew from Czechoslovakia who believed that THIEVERY was the byword for CAPITALISM.

District Judge Paul Ayers, Senior Vice President of the Association of Her Majesty's District Judges what is the real name of your white father's father, and when did he cross the English Channels, and where did he come from?

Saxe-Coburg and Gotha family crossed the English Channels.

A closeted racist descendant of undocumented refugees from Eastern Europe, a genetic alien, with camouflage English names, sat on bones of stolen and destroyed children of other people (Meghan Markle's ancestors), more bones than the millions of the skulls at the doorstep of Comrade Pol Pot.

Ignorance is bliss.

"Those who know the least obey the best." George Farquhar

Facts are sacred; they can't be overstated.

Then, at the University of Lagos, one would look at a functional semi-illiterate white man, with a great snout, but wouldn't talk to him; talk to trash about what?

"I am very fond of my pigs, but it doesn't stop me from eating them." Archbishop Runcie (1921 – 2000).

If one bred thousands of white pigs with great snouts – for bacon, the stupidest of the white pigs with great snouts deserves to be slaughtered and eaten first.

CHAPTER TWELVE:

Boris Johnson: Why is England not a scam?

If District Judge Paul Ayers of Bedford County Court, 3, St Paul's Square, MK40 1SQ, Her Majesty's appointee, read his approved Judgement before he published it, he was excessively stupid; if the white man did not read his approved judgement before he, immortally, published it, he must have lied, as he implied that he did. His white ancestors were incompetent racist liars too; they were industrial-scale PROFESSIONAL THIEVES and owners of stolen children of defenceless poor people (Meghan Markle's ancestors) – Habakkuk

Prior to Covid-19, what was in Norwich for functional semi-illiterate white Solicitors (predominantly) to do?

"The truth allows no choice." Dr Samuel Johnson

Facts are sacred.

"Sometimes people don't want to hear the truth because they don't want their illusions destroyed." Friedrich Nietzsche

Then, in our tribe in the African bush, we will stand before brainless opportunist racist thugs, eyeball to eyeball, and tell them to FACK OFF; if they dared make any wrong move, they shall summarily get 'it'.

"We shall deal with the racist bastards when the get out of prison." Comrade Robert Mugabe

OYINBO OLE: Straight-faced descendants of ultra-righteous THIEVES and owners of stolen children of defenceless poor people (Meghan Markle's ancestors) – Habakkuk

They are not the only creation of Almighty God, and they are not immortal, and their irrefutably superior skin colour is not the only wonder of our world, and their apparent righteousness, enlightenment and civilisation were preceded by several centuries of the greediest economic cannibalism and evilest racist terrorism the world will ever know - Habakkuk.

Before SLAVERY, what?

"The fact is, that civilisation requires slaves. The Greeks were quite right there. Unless there are slaves to do the ugly, horrible, uninteresting work, culture and contemplation become almost impossible. Human slavery is wrong, insecure, and demoralising...." Wilde

It took merciless racist bastards several centuries of the greediest economic cannibalism and the evilest racist terrorism to realise that their guns fuelled racist sadism was evil and wrong. They were merciless, and they were greedier than the grave, and like death, they were never satisfied – Habakkuk 2:5.

"It was our arms in the river of Cameroon, put into the hands of the trader, that furnished him with the means of pushing his trade; and I have no more doubt that they are British arms, put into the hands of Africans, which promote universal war and desolation that I can doubt their having done so in that individual instance. I have shown how great is the enormity of this evil, even on the supposition that we take only convicts and prisoners of war. But take the subject in another way, and how does it stand? Think of 80,000 persons carried out of their native country by we know not what means! For crimes imputed! For light or inconsiderable faults! For debts perhaps! For crime of witchcraft! Or a thousand other weak or scandalous pretexts! Reflect on 80,000 persons annually taken off! There is something in the horror of it that surpasses all bounds of imagination." – Prime Minister William Pitt the Younger

Christ did not place Africans in the back row, white men did.

Descendants of Alphonse Gabriel fool the foolish that they are Archangel Gabriel.

"There is no sin except stupidity." Wilde

African bush saying: 'Omo ale ti ko gbo ede baba re: A bastard has not met her biological father and hasn't fully acquired the consistent capacity to employ his language.

OYINBO OLE: The only evidence of the purportedly higher IQ of the poly-educated former, mere, debt-collector Solicitor, in Norwich, albeit a former Partner at Cole's Solicitors - is the stolen affluence that his white ancestors, mere white peasants, and very hardy white agricultural labourers, crossed the English Channels, in dinghy boats, without luggage or decent shoes, to latch onto.

"Those who know the least obey the best." George Farquhar.

Gigantic yields of millions of stolen children of defenceless poor people (Meghan Markle's ancestors) immeasurably transformed the standard of living of the descendants of barbarians and rabbit hunters, who used to live off the land, but their intellects seem untouched - Habakkuk.

"Pardon him Theodotus: He is a barbarian and thinks that the customs of his tribe and Island are the laws of nature." George Bernard Shaw.

Based on very, very proximate observations and direct experiences, not all white people are openly racist, but nearly all white people are white Supremacists, and all incontrovertibly functional semi-illiterate white Judges (disproportionately, Judges are white) are white supremacists.

"Sometimes people don't want to hear the truth because they don't want their illusions destroyed." Friedrich Nietzsche

The only BLACK racist bastards truly love is our money; everything else is a lie - Habakkuk.

"Those who have robbed have also lied." Dr Samuel Johnson.

Then, white Judges, nearly all, were members of the Charitable Antichrist Racist Freemasonry Religion (Mediocre Mafia/New Pharisees); some of them were THICKER than a gross of planks - Habakkuk.

Charitable Antichrist Racist Freemasonry Quasi-Religion (Mediocre Mafia/New Pharisees) teaches members, including some white Judges, secret handshakes, not grammar, and the former is considerably easier to master.

NIGERIA: SHELL'S DOCILE CASH COW.

Based on available evidence, their own Money, Nigeria (oil/gas) is by very far more relevant to the economic survival of the white mother and father, and the white spouse, and all the white children of White District Judge Paul Ayers of Bedford County Court, 3, Paul's Square, Bedford, MK40 1SQ, than the yields of the very, very highly luxuriant soil of NORWICH. OYINBO OLE: Straight-faced descendants of Antichrist industrial-scale professional THIEVES, drug dealers (opium merchants), murderers, very hardened racist thugs, and owners of stolen children of defenceless poor people (Black African ancestors of Meghan Markle's ancestors and her white children) – Habakkuk

If one were to ask White District Judge Paul Ayers of Bedford County Court, 3, St Paul's Square Bedford, MK40 1SQ, the Senior Vice President of the Association of Her Majesty's District Judges, and a mere former debt-collector Solicitor in Norwich, albeit a former Partner at Cole's Solicitor, to show one all his white children and white grandchildren, if he agrees, one should ask all his white children and white grandchildren to handwrite short essays, if they agree, and if they could write legibly, Dr Richard Dawkins and OECD implied that they should be duller than their incontrovertibly functional semi-illiterate, closeted white supremacist white father.

OYINBO OLE: RIGHTEOUS DESCENDANTS OF ULTRA-RIGHTEOUS WHITE THIEVES– HABAKKUK.

Facts are sacred, they can't be overstated.

"Natural selection will not remove ignorance from future generations." Dr Richard Dawkins

England's young people are near the bottom of the global league table for basic skills. OECD finds 16- to 24-year-olds have literacy and numeracy levels no better than those of their grandparents' generation

England is the only country in the developed world where the generation approaching retirement is more literate and numerate than the youngest adults, according to the first skills survey by the Organisation for Economic Co-operation and Development.

In a stark assessment of the success and failure of the 720-million-strong adult workforce across the wealthier economies, the economic thinktank warns that in England, adults aged 55 to 65 perform better than 16- to 24-year-olds at foundation levels of literacy and numeracy. The survey did not include people from Scotland or Wales.

The OECD study also finds that a quarter of adults in England have the maths skills of a 10-year-old. About 8.5 million adults, 24.1% of the population, have such basic levels of numeracy that they can manage only one-step tasks in arithmetic, sorting numbers or reading graphs. This is worse than the average in the developed world, where an average of 19% of people were found to have a similarly poor skill base.

Closeted racist white bastards disembarked in the 15th century, uninvited, and they remain in Africa, and expectedly, things did not turn out well for Africans and Africa.

"If aliens visit us, the outcome would be much as when Columbus landed in America, which didn't turn out well for the Native Americans." Dr Stephen Hawking.

Then, racist bastards carried and sold millions of stolen children of defenceless poor people (Meghan Markle's ancestors); now, they carry natural resources. Substitution is Fraudulent Emancipation.

OYINBO OLE: THIEVES – HABAKKUK.

"Moderation is a virtue only among those who are thought to have found alternatives." Henry Kissinger.

Children with huge oil wells near their huts eat only 1.5/day in NIGERIA; a closeted white supremacist former debt-collector Solicitor in Norwich whose white mother and father have never seen crude oil, and whose white ancestors, including John Bunyan (1628 – 1688) were fed like battery hens with the yields of stolen children of defenceless poor people (Meghan Markle's ancestors) – is our Senior District Judge, in Bedford, Great Britain. Which part of STOLEN 5HYT is great?

Our Empire did not evolve; then, almost everything was actively and deliberately stolen with GUNS – Habakkuk

"Affluence is not a birth right." David Cameron

Before SLAVERY, what?

Based on available evidence, it is not the truth that Negress, former Judge, Constance Briscoe is the only incompetent liar, in high position, in Great Britain.

362

"Lies are told all the time." Sir Michael Havers (1923 – 1992).

OXFORD, ENGLAND: Based on available evidence, GDC-Witness, Stephanie Twiddle (TD), British Soldier - Territorial Defence, unrelentingly lied under oath – Habakkuk 1:4; John 8:44; John 10:10. Her white ancestors were incompetent racist liars too; they were THIEVES and owners of stolen children of defenceless poor people (Meghan Markle's ancestors).

A WHITE WOMAN. A DISHONEST RACIST COUGAR.

The leverage of Defenders of FAITHS (dissenters of John 14:6) is incompetent mendacity guarded by unchecked, unbounded, and the illegal power of Antichrist Freemasons, the defenders of faiths, and the dissenters of John 14:6.

Closeted White Supremacist Defenders of FAITHS do not believe in the exceptionalism of Christ (John 14:6), so they are not deterred by His transparent Justice – Matthew 25: 31 – 46; John 5:22; Proverbs 15:3. Closeted white supremacist bastards who use very expensive aprons to decorate the temples of their powerless and useless fertility tools eat their cakes and have them: They do not believe in the exceptionalism of Christ, but use Judicial Terrorism to stifle and/or conceal the display of His power.

BEDFORD, ENGLAND: Based on available evidence, GDC-Witness, Brother, Richard William Hill (NHS), postgraduate tutor, albeit England's Class, unrelentingly lied under oath, and unrelentingly fabricated reports – Habakkuk 1:4; John 8:44; John 10:10. His white ancestors were incompetent racist liars too; they were THIEVES and owners of stolen children of defenceless poor people (Meghan Markle's ancestors).

A WHITE MAN. A DISHONEST RACIST DEFENDER OF FAITHS.

"Of black men, the numbers are too great who are now repining under English cruelty." Dr Samuel Johnson

Based on very proximate observations and direct experiences, the white man is the devil.
When they 'FORK', which is often, genius Jews are their go-to-people. They didn't foresee that the Corporal would flip, and if they did, they didn't help themselves when he did.

The incontrovertibly functional semi-illiterate white District Judge, the Senior Vice President of the Association of Her Majesty's District Judges, and some of those who sit before him seemed worthless, certainly, intellectually: A bloody waste of money – Proverbs 17:16.

Then, they were taught a lesson by the Corporal. Now, solely, in pursuance of preventing another Holocaust, they allow the mentally subhuman closeted white supremacists to become postgraduate tutors. Our Prime Minister invite foreign students to buy 5HYT from 5HYT. Why is our Prime Minister not a Yahoo Boy (fraudulent misrepresentation)?

Based on available evidence, GDC-Witness, Geraint Evans, Dentist, of Rowtree Dental Care, Northampton, unrelentingly lied under implied oath. His Welsh ancestors were crooked too; they THIEVES and owners of stolen children of defenceless poor people (Meghan Markle's ancestors) - Habakkuk

A WHITE MAN. A DISHONEST RACIST.

OYINBO OLE: AN IGNORANT DESCENDANT OF ULTRA-RIGHTEOUS WHITE THIEVES – HABAKKUK.

"The earth contains to race of human beings so totally vile and worthless as the Welsh ...." Walter Savage Landor

Based on available evidence, England is the natural resources of Wales. If Wales were to be detached from England at River Severn, and in Monmouthshire, she will instantly become poorer than Albania.

Based on very proximate observations and direct experiences, then, in the Valleys of Wales, there were many thousands of white sheep and people; and all the white sheep, but not all the people were incestuously conceived, and all white sheep, but not all the people were excessively stupid.

If Deluded, Antichrist, and Closeted White Supremacist
Clinton Richard Dawkins, a vociferous mere Science
Journalist (Edward Wilson), and Lala's husband, could
prove that White GDC-Witness, Geraint Evans, Dentist, of
Rowtree Dental Care, Northampton, did not unrelentingly
tell lies under implied oath, and if he could prove that
White District Judge Paul Ayers of Bedford County Court,
the Senior Vice President of the Association of Her
Majesty's District Judges, is not a functional semi-illiterate
and an incompetent liar, and if he could prove that GDC-
Witness, Freemason, Brother, Richard William Hill did not
fabricate reports and unrelentingly told lies under oath, he
will confirm the belief of millions of people in our world,
which is that all atheists are not supremely shallow lunatics
(Psalm 53), and he will also confirm the belief of billions
of people in this finite mysterious place, which is that
Antichrist Freemasonry Quasi-Religion, Antichrist Islam,
Antichrist Judaism, and all other motley assemblies of
exotic religions and faiths under the Common Umbrella of
the Governor of the Church of England and the Defender
of the FAITH - are not intellectually flawed Satanic
Mumbo Jumbo, and it will also confirm that reasoning and
vision have boundaries, if reasoning and vision have finite
boundaries, He must have lied when, before the Jews, in
the Council, He disclosed pictures His unbounded mind
painted, and He must have also lied, when He audaciously
stated: "I am the way and the truth and the life. No one
comes to the Father except through me" (**John 14:6**). If the
fellow told the truth before Jews, in the Council,
everything that is not aligned to John 14:6 is traveling in

the wrong direction and heading straight for very hard rocks.

Ignorance is bliss.

"It does no harm to throw the occasional man overboard, but it does not do much good if you are steering full speed ahead for the rocks." Sir Ian Gilmour, KBE (1926 – 2007).

****

TWEETS:
GDC: Kevin Atkinson (NHS) lied under oath
A DISHONEST RACIST
BEDFORD: District Judge, the talents of your white ancestors and the yield of their land did not sustain their standard of living: they were THIEVES- Habakkuk
NIGERIA: SHELL'S DOCILE CASH COW
https://www.youtube.com/watch?v=BlpH4hG7m1A
GDC: George Rothnie (NHS) lied on record
A DISHONEST RACIST
BEDFORD: District Judge, the talents of your white ancestors and the yield of their land did not sustain their standard of living: they were THIEVES- Habakkuk
NIGERIA: SHELL'S DOCILE CASH COW
https://www.youtube.com/watch?v=BlpH4hG7m1A

GDC: Stephanie Twidale lied under oath
A DISHONEST RACIST
BEDFORD: District Judge, the talents of your white ancestors and the yield of their land did not sustain their standard of living: they were THIEVES- Habakkuk

NIGERIA: SHELL'S DOCILE CASH COW
https://www.youtube.com/watch?v=BlpH4hG7m1A

GDC: Sue Gregory (OBE) lied on record
A DISHONEST RACIST
BEDFORD: District Judge, the talents of your white
ancestors and the yield of their land did not sustain their
standard of living: they were THIEVES- Habakkuk
NIGERIA: SHELL'S DOCILE CASH COW
https://www.youtube.com/watch?v=BlpH4hG7m1A

GDC: Rachael Bishop lied under oath
A DISHONEST RACIST
BEDFORD: District Judge, the talents of your white
ancestors and the yield of their land did not sustain their
standard of living: they were THIEVES- Habakkuk
NIGERIA: SHELL'S DOCILE CASH COW
https://www.youtube.com/watch?v=BlpH4hG7m1A

GDC: Geraint Evans (NHS) lied on record
A DISHONEST RACIST
BEDFORD: District Judge, the talents of your white
ancestors and the yield of their land did not sustain their
standard of living: they were THIEVES- Habakkuk
NIGERIA: SHELL'S DOCILE CASH COW
https://www.youtube.com/watch?v=BlpH4hG7m1A

GDC: Richard Hill lied under oath
A DISHONEST RACIST

BEDFORD: District Judge, the talents of your white ancestors and the yield of their land did not sustain their standard of living: they were THIEVES- Habakkuk
NIGERIA: SHELL'S DOCILE CASH COW
https://www.youtube.com/watch?v=BlpH4hG7m1A

GDC: Richard Hill fabricated reports
A DISHONEST RACIST
BEDFORD: District Judge, the talents of your white ancestors and the yield of their land did not sustain their standard of living: they were THIEVES- Habakkuk
NIGERIA: SHELL'S DOCILE CASH COW
https://www.youtube.com/watch?v=BlpH4hG7m1A

CHAPTER THIRTEEN:

Boris Johnson: Why is England not a scam?

Herod was a Jew.

Herod removed John's head only because he spoke. John was not punished for speaking; he was permanently prevented from speaking.

The lunatic mob lynched Him like Gadhafi, and He was crucified only because He disclosed pictures His unbounded mind painted; He was prevented from speaking.

Boris Johnson: How should we defend ourselves against confused administration of English Law and those who are above English Law (Defenders of FAITHS/Freemasons)?

BORIS JOHNSON: Why is England not a scam?

They must get whatever they want, and incompetent mendacity guarded by unbounded illegal power – is the tool of the Defenders of FAITHS. They are not deterred by His Justice (John 5:22; Matthew 25: 31-46) because closeted racist bastards do not believe in His exceptionalism (John 14:6).

BEDFORD, ENGLAND: GDC-Expert, Sue Gregory (OBE), Officer of the Most Excellent Order of our Empire, unrelentingly lied under implied oath.

A WHITE WOMAN. A DISHONEST RACIST COUGAR.

NEW HEROD, MATTHEW 2:16: They deceive their mentally very, very children that they are geniuses, and they kill all those who know that they are brainless, closeted racist bastards. If we are not very smart, why are we very rich? Shepherds did not bring stolen Africans back home (Black African ancestors of Meghan Markle and her white children), they lied to their mentally very gentle children that the were paragons of wisdom and virtue who, like Mother Teresa, did only virtuous works in Africa.

FAITHS: The emblem of the dissenters of John 14:6, and the most important Hall Mark of the Charitable Antichrist Racist Freemasonry Religion (Mediocre Mafia/New Pharisees).

They are greedier than the grave and like death, the closeted racist bastards are never satisfied – Habakkuk 2:5. They are not the only creation of Almighty God, they are not immortal, and the irrefutably superior skin colour that they neither made nor chose, their brainless and baseless birth right, is not the only wonder of our world - Habakkuk.

GDC: Richard Hill (NHS), a white man, unrelentingly lied under oath

GDC: Kevin Atkinson (NHS), a white man, unrelentingly lied under oath

GDC: Jonathan Martin, a white man, unrelentingly lied on record

GDC: Helen Falcon (MBE) a white man, unrelentingly lied on record

GDC: George Rothnie (NHS) a white man, unrelentingly lied on record

GDC: Stephanie Twidale (NHS), a white woman, unrelentingly lied under oath

GDC: Sue Gregory (OBE), a white woman, unrelentingly lied on record

GDC: Rachael Bishop (NHS), a white woman, unrelentingly lied under oath

GDC: Geraint Evans (NHS), a white man, unrelentingly lied on record.

They were all white, including the Judges, and they were all racists, and incompetent liars - Habakkuk.

A thoroughly confused, bastardised, unashamedly mediocre, corrupt, potently weaponised, vindictive, and indiscreetly racist legal system that is overseen by the members of the Charitable Antichrist Racist Freemasonry

Religion (Mediocre Mafia/New Pharisees) – Habakkuk 1:4; John 8:44; John 10:10.

BORIS JOHNSON: Because, we are aligned to infinite reasoning and vision, our minds are finer.

BORIS JOHNSON: Genetic mix is the Holy Grail. Education, formal and informal, will polish only what genetic mix presents to it.

Then, there, verdicts always preceded hearings; in the hearings, incompetent art incompetently imitated life, and closeted racist bastards used incompetent mendacity guarded by illegal power (unelected) to, seamlessly, criminally fit hearings to prior agreed verdicts.

They tell incompetent lies all the time, and they lie that they don't lie – Psalm 144. Antichrist racist bastards have created a new order where incompetent mendacity and innate intellectual impotence guided and guarded by unbounded and unchecked illegal power (unelected) reigns.

"Lies are told all the time." Sir Michael Havers

BEDFORD, ENGLAND: District Judge Paul Ayers of our County Court, 3, St Paul's Square, MK40 1SQ, based on available evidence, it is absolutely impossible for your talent and the yield of your land to sustain your standard of living; your white ancestors were THIEVES and owners of stolen children of defenceless poor people (Black African ancestors of Meghan Markle and her white children) – HABAKKUK

Facts are sacred; they can't be overstated.

"Sometimes people don't want to hear the truth because they do not want their illusions destroyed." Friedrich Nietzsche

The report, by the OECD, warns that the UK needs to take significant action to boost the basic skills of the nation's young people. The 460-page study is based on the first-ever survey of the literacy, numeracy and problem-solving at work skills of 16 to 65-year-olds in 24 countries, with almost 9,000 people taking part in England and Northern Ireland to make up the UK results. The findings showed that England and Northern Ireland have some of the highest proportions of adults scoring no higher than Level 1 in literacy and numeracy - the lowest level on the OECD's scale. This suggests that their skills in the basics are no better than that of a 10-year-old.

AN IMBECILE: AN ADULT WITH THE BASIC SKILLS OF A CHILD.

Creeping DPRK: They want us to say only what they want to hear, not what we truly feel, and say behind the backs of descendants of undocumented refugees from Eastern Europe, genetic aliens, with camouflage English names.

BORIS JOHNSON: Then, there, white Judges (predominantly) who believed that daily dialogues with imbeciles – was a proper job – were SCAMMERS, and white Judges (predominantly) who demanded and accepted very valuable consideration in exchange for daily dialogues with imbeciles – were RACKETEERS (Thieves).

LATENT, BUT VERY POTENT TURF WAR: Closeted racist descendants of undocumented refugees, genetic aliens, with camouflage English names oppress the descendants of the robbed with the yields of the robbery - Habakkuk.

BORIS JOHNSON: Apart from creating very cushy salaried jobs for incontrovertibly functional semi-illiterate white Judges (disproportionately, Judges are white), who foreseeably FAILED in the practice of their grossly overrated and mediocre trade, what do imbeciles (adults with the basic skills of a child) need very, very need very expensive administration of the law for – quasi-communism – Proverbs 17:16?

"By definition therefore there needs to be a contact order for Mr B so that he knows when he is going to see his son. It is absolutely essential that this occurs and mother agrees with that. She said so several times in her evidence. Mrs Waller agreed that not only should a child have the opportunity of developing relationship with both parents, any sibling should also be there so that inter- sibling relationship could be fostered and nurtured. Obviously in this particular case the children reside in different places. That immediately puts a strain on the children having limited contact with each other. F's sister is very much older than him and she will be further advanced into her adult life. Thus it is not a matter that that sibling relationship can only be fostered by the children being together. Indeed as we all know absence sometimes makes

the heart grow fonder. F should have an opportunity of seeing his sister. Wherever he does that it should be done in a friendly and loving environment. If the time comes that his sister goes to university of course his contact with her will be restricted to the time that she is home from university. In years to come when they have both grown up, with their own family they will see less of each other. But it doesn't mean that they don't still love and adore each other as much as they would if they saw each other every day." District Judge Paul Ayers of Bedford County Court, 3, St Paul's Square, MK40 1SQ, the Senior Vice President of the Association of Her Majesty's District Judges – proofed and approved Judgement.

Idiotic nonsense.

AN IMBECILE: AN ADULT WITH THE BASIC SKILLS OF A CHILD.

Our incontrovertibly functional semi-illiterate overpromoted Freemason Judge of our Empire of STOLEN AFFLUENCE – Habakkuk.

A CLOSETED RACIST FOOL'S APPROVAL!

"Yes, Sir, it does *her* honour, but it would do nobody else honour. I have indeed, not read it all. But when I take up the end of a web, and find it packthread, I do not expect, by looking further, to find embroidery." Dr Samuel Johnson

PERCEPTION IS GRANDER THAN REALITY.

Like his white children, imbeciles (adults with the basic skills of a child) who sit before him do not know that his nomination, and constructive appointment, by some demented or dementing white Lords – was not based on colour-blind, and progressive measurable objectivity.

The last time the closeted white supremacist former debt-collector Solicitor, in Norwich (coastal dole) passed through the filter of objectivity was when he studied 5th Rate Law at Poly, and it shows, and glaringly.

They want baseless and brainless skin colour superiority, their birth right, but they don't want Freedom of Expression because they don't want their mentally very gentle children to know that they are excessively stupid.

NIGERIA: SHELL'S DOCILE CASH COW. THERE ARE NO OIL WELLS OR GAS FIELDS IN NORWICH. THE HIGHLY LUXURIANT SOIL OF BISHOP'S STORTFORD YIELDS ONLY FOOD.

Cecil Rhodes (1853 - 1902) was an armed robber.

"We shall deal with the racist bastards when we get out of prison." Robert Mugabe (1924 – 2019).

Nigerian children with huge oil wells and gas fields near their huts eat only 1.5/day; a closeted racist functional semi-illiterate white man, a mere former debt collector Solicitor in Norwich (coastal dole) whose white mother and father have never seen crude oil, and whose white ancestors, including John Bunyan (1628 – 1688), were fed like battery hens with yields of stolen children of defenceless poor people (Black African ancestors of Meghan Markle and her white children) – Habakkuk

OYINBO OLE: RIGHTEOUS DESCENDANTS OF ULTRA-RIGHTEOUS THIEVES - HABAKKUK

Then, there, when whites commit racist crimes against blacks, racist white bastards (FREEMASONS) who oversee the administration of their law criminally bury RACIAL HATRED. Only stupid Negroes do not know that whites measure whites with a very different yardstick, and only stupider Negroes expect demons to cast out demons – Matthew 12:27.

Based on very proximate observations and direct experiences, the white man is the devil.

The white man is the devil - Columbia University
https://ccnmtl.columbia.edu › mmt › mxp › concepts

Referring to Whites as "devils" originates with the teachings of Master W.D. Fard and the legend of Yakub. Fard taught Elijah Muhammad who preached the.

OYINBO OLE: STRAIGHT-FACED DESCENDANTS OF THIEVES – HABAKKUK.

District Judge Paul Ayers, the Senior Vice President of the Association of Her Majesty's District Judges approved and immortalised what his functional semi-illiterate white mother and father spoke (deductible), the type of stories his white father used to tell when he returned home from Queen Victoria, at odd hours, STONED, and which is poly-educated white supervisors in LUTON authorised.

"To survive, you must tell stories. …. I believe that what we become depends on what our fathers teach us at odd moments, when they aren't trying to teach us. We are formed by little scraps of wisdom. " — Umberto Eco

Based on available evidence, His Honour Judge Perusko studied law at Poly (Lower-class alternative education) – Proverbs 17:16.

Why should the white mother and father of His Honour Judge Perusko need very, very strong views about education if the talent of their white son is only good enough for Second Rate Alternative Poly Education, and why is very, very expensive private education that leads to Poly or Polytechnic University (not Russell Group), not a bloody waste of money – Proverbs 17:16?

Why should the white father and mother of District Judge Paul Ayers of Bedford County Court, 3, St Paul's Square, MK40 1SQ, the Senior Vice President of the Association of Her Majesty's District Judges, need very, very strong views about education if there is irrefutable evidence that the white ancestors of white father and mother were extremely nasty racist murderers (nastier than the Talibans), professional thieves, drug dealers (opium merchants), and owners of stolen children of defenceless poor people (Meghan Markle's ancestors) – Habakkuk, and why is very, very expensive private education that leads to unashamed functional semi-illiteracy, and daily dialogues with imbeciles (adults with the basic skills of a child, in a District Court, not a bloody waste of money – Proverbs 17:16?

If the highly luxuriant soil of Bedfordshire yields only food, and our District Judge is incontrovertibly a functional semi-illiterate, it's plainly deductible that his white ancestors were THIEVES and owners of stolen children of defenceless poor people (Meghan Markle's ancestors) – Habakkuk

OYINBO OLE: An ignorant descendant of ultra-righteous WHITE THIEVES and owners of stolen children of defenceless poor people (Meghan Markle's ancestors) – Habakkuk.

Based on available evidence, it is absolutely impossible for the Christ granted talent, the yield of the land, and the yield of transparently virtuous works of District Judge Paul Ayers, the Senior Vice President of the Association of Her Majesty's District Judges, to sustain his standard of living; based on very proximate observations and direct experiences, the white man is a leech, and his white ancestors were industrial-scale professional WHITE

THIEVES and owners of stolen children of defenceless poor people (Meghan Markle's ancestors) - Habakkuk

Ignorance is bliss.

Facts are sacred.

They want skin colour superiority, their baseless and brainless birth right, but they don't want Freedom of Expression because they don't want their mentally very gentle children to know that they are excessively stupid closeted racist bastards – Habakkuk.

"Those who know the least obey the best." George Farquhar

OYINBO OLE: The only evidence of his purportedly higher IQ is the stolen affluence that his white ancestors crossed the English Channels, without luggage or decent shoes, to latch onto.

DELUDED PAPER TIGERS: "England will fight to the last American." American saying

Their hairs stand on end when they are challenged by Africans; we and our type are the ones racist bastards will beat up without the support of the YANKS – Habakkuk.

If members of the Charitable Antichrist Racist Freemasonry Quasi-Religion (Mediocre Mafia/New Pharisees) are as ethical and as brave as they imply, they should forcibly evict Putin from Crimea; he forcibly stole it.

Putin sits on the largest gas reserve in the world; did he poison Bob Dudley?

"Ethical foreign policy." Robin Cook.

They love the superiority that is automatically attached to the irrefutably superior skin colour that they neither made nor chose, their brainless and baseless birth right; they don't love Freedom of Expression because they don't want their mentally gentler children to know that they are excessively stupid.

Facts are sacred; they cannot be overstated.
"The truth allows no choice." Dr Samuel Johnson

Closeted racist bastards love only Apartheid by stealth.

New Herod, Matthew 2:16: They deceive their mentally gentle children that they are geniuses, and they kill all those who know that they are brainless racist bastards.

Based on available evidence, a white High Court Judge lied on record; his white ancestors were incompetent racist liars too, they were THIEVES and owners of stolen children of defenceless poor people (Meghan Markle's ancestors) - Habakkuk.

DEFENDER OF FAITHS: They do not believe in exceptionalism of Christ (John 14:6), so they are not deterred by his transparent Justice (John 5:22).

WHITE PRIVILEGE: Their skin colour is irrefutably superior; ours is inferior, and a curse. Our deeper asset (deeper than skin colour) is useless without Freedom of Expression. Closeted racist white bastards stifle Freedom of Expression and create an imbalance: Conflict of interest.

The indiscreetly weaponised administration of their law is the poisoned arrowhead of hereditary RACIAL HATRED – Habakkuk 1:4; John 8:44; John 10:10.

GDC- Expert: Poly-educated Jonathan Martin, Senior Executive at the GDC, a white man, and a dishonest racist, unrelentingly lied under implied oath - Habakkuk 1:4; John 8:44; John 10:10.

Why should the white mother and father of GDC's Jonathan Martin, need very, very strong views if the natural talent of their white son is only good enough for Lower Class alternative Poly-education – Proverbs 17:16? Based on very proximate observations and direct experiences, only their irrefutably superior skin colour is truly good, and they neither made nor chose it.

OYINBO OLE: THIEVES – HABAKKUK.

"Mr Bamgbelu clearly has very, very strong views about education and I understand those views are based upon the fact that he is a successful dentist here in Bedford which he attributes to the fact that his parents cared for him and his education when he was young. They ensured that he had a proper fee paying education …….. " District Judge Paul Ayers of Bedford County Court, 3, St Paul's Square, MK40 1 SQ, the Senior Vice President of the Association of Her Majesty's District Judges – proofed and approved Judgement.

When hereditary RACIAL HATRED copulates with uncontrollable envy, insanity is their offspring.

Closeted racist bastards are as greedy as the grave, and like death, closeted white supremacist thugs are never satisfied – Habakkuk 2:5.

They are not the only creation of Almighty God, and they are not immortal, and their irrefutably superior skin colour is not the only wonder of our world.

OYINBO: Racist descendants of ultra-righteous THIEVES and owners of stolen children of poor people (Meghan Markle's ancestors: the nastiest racist terrorists, and the greediest economic cannibals the world will ever know.

Financial disclosure in a divorce: 'How can a mere Negro have what I do not have?'

Indiscreet envy.

Envy is a thief.

"Envy is weak." Yul Brynner.

Poly-class brainless sarcasm.

It's plainly deductible that the white father and mother of
District Judge Paul Ayers of Bedford County Court, 3, St
Paul's Square MK40 1SQ, the Senior Vice President of the
Association of Her Majesty's District Judges, did not have
very, very strong views about education, and they did not
care, had they, their incontrovertibly functional semi-
illiterate white son would not have approved and
immortalised excessive stupidity at 16, and he would be a
properly educated lawyer, privately educated Anthony
Julius, Anthony Blair, Geoff Hoon, and Rabinder Singh's
Class, and he might practice proper law in STRAND.

An ignorant racist leech; an ultra-righteous descendant of
righteous PROFESSIONAL THIEVES, industrial-scale
racist murderers, drug dealers (opium merchants), and
owners of stolen children of defenceless poor people
(Black African ancestors of Meghan Markle and her white
children) - Habakkuk.

GDC- Witness: George Rothnie, Deputy Postgraduate
Dean, albeit England's Class (NHS), a white man, and a
dishonest racist, unrelentingly lied under implied oath -
Habakkuk 1:4; John 8:44; John 10:10

GDC- Witness: Kevin Atkinson, Postgraduate Tutor, albeit
England's Class (NHS), a white man, and a dishonest

racist, unrelentingly lied under oath - Habakkuk 1:4; John 8:44; John 10:10

BORIS JOHNSON: Which part of Bedford County Court, 3 St Paul's Square, MK40 1SQ, preceded the barbarously racist traffic in millions of stolen children of defenceless poor people (Black African ancestors of Meghan Markle's ancestors): The building or its chattels?

Ignorance is bliss.

He didn't like them, so He gave them the irrefutably superior skin colour, and in protest, their white ancestors used extreme violence to steal almost everything He gave to others: Movable and immovable.

OYINBO OLE: THIEVES – HABAKKUK.

"Many Scots masters were considered among the most brutal, with life expectancy on their plantations averaging a mere four years. We worked them to death then simply imported more to keep the sugar and thus the money flowing. Unlike centuries of grief and murder, an apology cost nothing. So, what does Scotland have to say?" Herald Scotland: Ian Bell, Columnist, Sunday 28 April 2013

Then, extremely nasty economic cannibals fed their people with yields of the evilest racist terrorism the world will ever know. They were greedier than the grave and like death, they were never satisfied – Habakkuk 2:5.

OYINBO OLE: THIEVES – HABAKKUK.

Based on available evidence, the white man was the devil.

"All have taken what had other owners, and all have had recourse to arms rather than quit they prey on which they were fastened." Dr Samuel Johnson

WHITE PRIVILEGE: The centuries-old unspoken myth that intellect is related to the irrefutably superior skin colour that they neither made nor chose - is the mother of all racist scams – Habakkuk.

Racist bastards stifle Freedom of Expression, and stealthily promote, and guard brainless and baseless skin colour superiority: APARTHEID BY STEALTH.

Based on very proximate observations and direct experiences, the natural instinct of the closeted racist white supremacist privileged dullard – is Apartheid by stealth.

They accurately foresaw that District Judge Paul Ayers of Bedford County Court, 3, St Paul's Square, MK40 1SQ, will become the Senior Vice President of the Association of Her Majesty's District Judges, so they embarked on armed robbery and dispossession raids all over the world – Habakkuk. Whenever racist bastards (Defenders of Faiths/Dissenters of John 14:6) slaughtered fellow human beings (Africans), they dispossessed them, and wherever they robbed, they took possession – Habakkuk.

Defenders of Faiths/Dissenters of John 14:6: Then, racist bastards did not believe in the exceptionalism of Christ (John 14:6), so they were not deterred by His transparent Justice – Proverbs 15:3; John 5:22; Matthew 25: 31 – 46.

They want intellectual superiority, He doesn't like them, so He gave them the irrefutably superior skin colour, and their white ancestors, the dissenters of John 14:6, and the Defenders of Faiths; the evilest racist terrorists, and the greediest economic cannibals the world will ever know, used extreme violence to steal almost everything He gave to others, movable and immovable – James 4; Habakkuk.

"I know of no evil that has ever existed, nor can imagine any evil to exist, worse than the tearing of eighty thousand persons annually from their native land, by a combination of the most civilised nations inhabiting the most enlightened part of the globe, but more especially under the sanction of the laws of that Nation which calls herself the most free and the most happy of them all." Prime Minister William Pitt the Younger

OYINBO OLE: Racist descendants of ultra-righteous THIEVES and owners and stolen children of defenceless poor people (Black African ancestors Meghan Markle's ancestors) – Habakkuk.

Properly rehearsed ultra-righteousness and deceptively schooled civilised decorum were preceded by several centuries of very, very greedy economic cannibalism, and the evilest racist terrorism the world will ever know.

They are as greedy as the grave, and like death, they are never satisfied. The eat all their cakes and eat other people's cakes, and the closeted racist very greedy bastards want everything – Habakkuk 2:5.

"A typical English man, usually violent and always dull." Wilde

"England is like a prostitute who, having sold her body all her life, decides to quit and close her business, and then tells everybody she wants to be chaste and protect her flesh as if it were jade." He Manzi, Chinese Politicians.

BEDFORD, ENGLAND: GDC-Insider, Sue Gregory (OBE), Officer of the Most Excellent Order of our Empire, unrelentingly lied unrelentingly lied under implied oath – Habakkuk 1:4; John 8:44; John 10:10. Her white ancestors were incompetent racist liars too; they were THIEVES and owners of stolen children of defenceless poor people (Meghan Markle's ancestors) – Habakkuk

A WHITE WOMAN. A DISHONEST RACIST COUGAR.

Then, there, some closeted racist white supremacist Judges were complicit in Racial Hatred and Fraud.

Then, there, white Judges, nearly all, were white, Christians, and FREEMASONS, and some of them were thicker than a gross of planks – Habakkuk.

<u>C of E raises serious concerns about Christian Freemasons</u>
https://www.theguardian.com › uk-news › feb › c-of-e-...
8 Feb 2018 — Church of England warning that secret
society may not be compatible with Christianity echoes
concerns from 1987.

Dissenters of John 14:6, Defenders of Faiths: The closeted
racist bastards do not believe in the exceptionalism of our
own Messiah, so resort to criminality (persecutory
Negrophobia and Negrophobic perjury in order to conceal
Christ's infinite reasoning and vision.

In an open dialogue with Justice Ruth Bader Ginsburg
(1933 – 2020), Lady Hale lamented funding. What is the
value of several layers of unashamed mediocrity and
confusion?

A properly proofed and approved Judgement by a properly
educated Senior Judge, in a properly organised legal
system – should pass through at least four separate filters:
The Transcript writers, the proof-readers, the court clerks,
and the Judge.

OXFORD, ENGLAND: GDC-Witness, British Soldier –
Territorial Defence, Stephanie Twidale (TD) unrelentingly
lied under oath – Habakkuk 1:4; John 8:44; John 10:10.

A WHITE WOMAN. A DISHONEST RACIST
COUGAR.

The white woman was incompetent and incapable Negrophobic criminal perjurer; they were professional racist killers, albeit hands-off.

Google: Dr Anand Kamath, dentist.
Google: Dr Richard Bamgboye, GP.

Defenders of Faiths (FREEMASONS): Molecular, shallow, and brainless nonsense; closeted white supremacist racist bastards.

"The supreme vice is shallowness." Wilde

Boris Johnson: The genetic pool is weakening, if you do not reset the clock, and realign this system to the notion of infinite reasoning and vision (John 14:6), society will collapse.

Boris Johnson: Reasoning and vision are unbounded (infinite), and the fellow is who He says He is – John 14:6.

Boris Johnson: The Negro is a 'Foetus'; what he sees is clearer than a vision – Act 2:17.

Boris Johnson: Believe me, I sacrifice myself only; the fellow is who He says He is, and anything that is not aligned to John 14:6 – is intellectually flawed and travelling in the wrong direction.

Members of the Charitable Antichrist Racist Freemasonry Quasi-Religion (Mediocre Mafia/New Pharisees),

Defenders of Faiths, and Dissenters of John 14:6, are free to use whatever they like to decorate the temples of their powerless and useless fertility tools, but the closeted white supremacist bastards should not be above English law, and they should not have the power to award themselves the monopoly of knowledge or impose an artificial ceiling on reasoning and vision.

He was lynched like Gadhafi and crucified by very shallow lunatics only because He spoke: He disclosed pictures His unbounded mind painted. He was not punished for speaking; He was prevented from speaking.

CHAPTER FOURTEEN:

Boris Johnson: Why is England not a scam?

Just as it was in Professor Stephen Hawking's School, then, at the University of Lagos, the brightest students did mathematics, physics, and chemistry, and did not attend lectures at the Faculty of Law.

"In my school, the brightest boys did math and physics, the less bright did physics and chemistry, and the least bright did biology. I wanted to do math and physics, but my father made me do chemistry because he thought there would be no jobs for mathematicians." Dr Stephen Hawking.

A grossly overrated, overhyped, overpopulated, and mediocre trade that is dying slowly and imperceptibly, and is overseen by the Antichrist Racist Freemasons (Mediocre Mafia) - Habakkuk 1:4; John 8:44; John 10:10.

"The legal system lies at the heart of any society, protecting rights, imposing duties, and establishing a framework for the conduct of almost every social, political, and economic activity. Some argue that the law is in its death throes while others postulate a contrary prognosis that discerns numerous signs of law's enduring strength. Which is it?" Professor Raymond Wacks.

Facts are sacred.

"The truth allows no choice." Dr Samuel Johnson

Closeted White Supremacist, Dr Clinton Richard Dawkins, a thoroughly deluded lunatic (Psalm 53), Antichrist, closeted white supremacist Blind Watchmaker's ancestors, were PROFESSIONAL THIEVES and owners of stolen children of defenceless poor people, and the ultra-righteous, and very, very highly civilised racist bastards accurately foresaw that their descendants will be imbeciles (adults with the basic skills of a child), so they used overwhelming violence to loot Africa.

Prior to SLAVERY, his white ancestors were mere agricultural labourers, who worked with forks and spades on the estates of Robber Barons and Landowners.

"All have taken what had other owners, and all have had recourse to arms rather than quit the prey on which they were fastened…" Dr Samuel Johnson

The relatively little man wiggles his ass from side to side when he walks, just like Alan Clark (1928 – 1999). Had Slavery not decommissioned natural selection, reversed evolution, and immeasurably transformed the standard of living of Europeans, Dr Clinton Richard Dawkins would have worked as an agricultural labourer just like his white ancestors - Habakkuk.

"It was our arms in the river of Cameroon, put into the hands of the trader, that furnished him with the means of pushing his trade; and I have no more doubt that they are British arms, put into the hands of Africans, which promote universal war and desolation that I can doubt their having done so in that individual instance. I have shown how great is the enormity of this evil, even on the supposition that we take only convicts and prisoners of war. But take the subject in another way, and how does it stand? Think of 80,000 persons carried out of their native country by we know not what means! For crimes imputed! For light or inconsiderable faults! For debts perhaps! For crime of witchcraft! Or a thousand other weak or scandalous pretexts! Reflect on 80,000 persons annually taken off! There is something in the horror of it that surpasses all bounds of imagination." – Prime Minister William Pitt the Younger.

OYINBO OLE: THIEVES - HABAKKUK

Based on available evidence, the white man was the devil.

"Of black men, the numbers are too great who are now repining under English cruelty." Dr Samuel Johnson.

Christ did not place Africa and Africans in the back row, white men did.

The white man is the devil - Columbia University
https://ccnmtl.columbia.edu › mmt › mxp › concepts

Referring to Whites as "devils" originates with the teachings of Master W.D. Fard and the legend of Yakub. Fard taught Elijah Muhammad who preached the ...

Richard Dawkins, a thoroughly deluded (Psalm 53), Antichrist, closeted white supremacist Blind Watchmaker's kindred use Nuclear Bombs to guard the propagation of imbeciles (adults with the basic skills of a child).

"Natural selection will not remove ignorance from future generations." Dr Richard Dawkins

Adults with the basic skills of a foetus will succeed adults with the basic skills of a child, and the former will need only food and shelter. Then, the kindred of Lala's husband, Richard Dawkins, a thoroughly deluded (Psalm 53) Antichrist, closeted white supremacist Blind Watchmakers' descendant, will use sticks and stones to preserve the continuing propagation of adults with the basic skills of a foetus.

"I know not with what weapons World War III will be fought, but World War IV will be fought with sticks and stones" Albert Einstein

-----Original Message-----

*****

From: George Rothnie <georgerothnie@hotmail.com>
To: adeolacole@aol.com
Sent: Mon, 8 Mar 2010 20:19
Subject: Re Meeting 9th March

Hi Ola,

We are scheduled to meet tomorrow evening at my surgery about 5.30ish.
Unfortunately something has cropped up which necessytates me having to
postpone the meeting. I'm really sorry it's such short notice.

I will contact you in the week to arrange another date.

Once agaim my apologies.

George

*****

Idiotic nonsense.

AN IMBECILE: AN ADULT WITH THE BASIC SKILLS OF A CHILD

Only his irrefutably superior skin colour is truly good; the Scotchman neither made nor chose the invaluable asset.

GDC-Witness, incontrovertibly functional semi-illiterate, George Rothnie (Scottish George), Deputy Postgraduate Dean, Oxford, unrelentingly lied under implied oath; his Scottish ancestors lied too; they were owners of stolen children of defenceless poor people (Meghan Markle's ancestors) – Habakkuk

A WHITE SCOTCHMAN. A DISHONEST RACIST

District Judge Paul Ayers of Bedford County Court, 3, St Paul's Square, MK40 1SQ, implied that like his own white mother and father, the white father and mother of Edinburgh University Educated George Rothnie, the Deputy Postgraduate Dean, Oxford, did not have very, very strong views about education

"It is incumbent upon the court and all those professionals involved to conclude court proceedings as quickly as possible. This hopefully ensures that a child has stability, love and affection and the parents working together to ensure that he has the best opportunity of developing academically and emotional." District Judge Paul Ayers, Senior Vice President of the Association of Her Majesty's District Judges – proofed and approved Judgement

OYINBO ODE: A CLOSETED RACIST FOOL'S APPROVAL!

Based on available evidence, when whites commit racist crimes against our people (AFRICANS), whites who oversee the administration of their law, Dissenters of John 14:6 (Defenders of FAITHS), criminally bury RACIAL HATRED.

Only foolish Africans do not know that Dissenters of John 14:6 (Defenders of FAITHS) are demons, and demons will not cast out demons – Matthew 12:27.

The only Judge is watching them, and the nemesis is not extinct, and the fact that it tarries isn't the proof that it will never some – Proverbs 15:3; John 5:22, Habakkuk; Matthew 25: 31-46.

They are not the only creation of Almighty God, and their irrefutably superior skin colour is not the only wonder of our world.

Since racists, murderers, extremely nasty and insatiably greedy economic cannibals found our ancestors in the African bush, in the 15th century, things have not out well for Africans and Africa – Habakkuk 2:5.

The white man was the devil. The white man is the devil.

"Of black men, the numbers are too great who are now repining under English cruelty." Dr Samuel Johnson

Edinburgh University Educated, Dr George Rothnie, Deputy Postgraduate Tutor, Oxford: An adult with the basic skills of a child (an imbecile).

Our Edinburgh University Educated Prime Minister, the Scholar from Fife, couldn't spell; in the country of the blind, the partially sighted is the shepherd.

Sheep unnaturally shepherd sheep.

Shepherds know that sheep are imbeciles (adults with the basic skills of a child): Sheep do not know that shepherds are imbeciles too.

"Mediocrity weighing mediocrity is the balance, and incompetence applauding its brother….." Dr

"Jews are very good with money." President Donald Trump

Whose money?

When closeted white supremacist dissenters of John 14:6 (Defenders of FAITHS) 'FORK', which is very, very often, genius Jews are their GO-TO-PEOPLE, their 'Jim will fix it'; they didn't foresee that the Corporal would flip, and they couldn't help themselves when he did.

"Jews are very intelligent and creative, Chinese are intelligent but not creative, Indians are servile, and Africans are morons." Dr Watson (DNA) paraphrased

BEDFORD, ENGLAND: District Judge Paul Ayers, the Senior Vice President of the Association of Her Majesty's District Judges, their own Money, NIGERIA (oil/gas) is by far more relevant to the economic survival of your white father and mother, and your white spouse, and all your white children than NORWICH; then, the white ancestors of your white mother and father were fed like battery hens with the yields of stolen children of defenceless poor people (Meghan Markle's ancestors) – Habakkuk. You are a leech; your white ancestors were THIEVES and owners of stolen children of defenceless Africans (Meghan Markle's ancestors) – Habakkuk. Those are parts of what we believe and say about you behind your back.

They kill those they can't spin, albeit hands -off.

NEW HEROD, MATTHEW 2:16: They deceive their mentally very, very gentle children that they are geniuses, and they kill all those who know that they are not, albeit hands-off.

OYINBO OLE: RACIST DESCENDANTS OF ULTRA-RIGHTEOUS THIEVES – HABAKKUK. They are not the only creation of Almighty God, and they are not immortal, and the irrefutably superior skin colour that they neither made nor chose is not the only wonder of our world.

The only evidence of his purportedly higher IQ is the stolen affluence that his ancestors, mere agricultural labourers crossed the English Channels without luggage or decent shoes, to latch onto.

Before SLAVERY, what?

OYINBO OLE: IGNORANT DESCENDANTS OF THIEVES – HABAKKUK.

Why should the white mother and father of District Judge Bedford, the Senior Vice President of the Association of Her Majesty's District Judges, and the white mother and father of George Rothnie, Deputy Postgraduate Dean, Oxford, need very, very strong views about education if there is irrefutable evidence that the white ancestors of their white fathers and mothers were THIEVES and owners of stolen children of defenceless poor people (Meghan Markle's ancestors) — Habakkuk.

Facts are sacred; they cannot be overstated.

"Sometimes people don't want to hear the truth because they don't want their illusions destroyed." Friedrich Nietzsche

BEDFORD, ENGLAND: Sue Gregory (OBE), Officer of the Most Excellent Order of our Empire unrelentingly lied under implied oath – Habakkuk 1:4; John 8:44; John 10:10. Her white ancestors lied too; they were THIEVES and owners of stolen children of defenceless poor people (Meghan Markle's ancestors) – Habakkuk.

A WHITE WOMAN: A DISHONEST RACIST COUGAR.

Facts are sacred; they can't be overstated.

Believers of Faiths/ John 14:6 Dissenters are not deterred by John 5:22 because they do not believe in His exceptionalism (THE FAITH).

Boris Johnson: Reasoning, and vision are unbounded, and the fellow told Jews the truth, in the Council, when He disclosed pictures His unbounded mind painted.

Boris Johnson: If you don't align this system to John 14:6, networks of racist criminals, Freemasons, and mediocrity will thrive, and the system will collapse.

CORBY, ENGLAND: GDC-Witness, Kevin Atkinson (Scottish Kev) unrelentingly lied under oath. His Scottish ancestors (whites) were incompetent racist liars too; they were THIEVES and owners of stolen children of defenceless poor people (Meghan Markle's ancestors) – Habakkuk

A WHITE MAN: A DISHONEST RACIST SCOTCHMAN.

"Of black men, the numbers are too great who are now repining under English cruelty." Dr Samuel Johnson

If Lala's husband, the thoroughly deluded, closeted white supremacist, and Antichrist Briton, Dr Richard Dawkins could prove that District Judge Paul Ayers of Bedford County Court, the Senior Vice President of the Association of Her Majesty's District Judges is not a functional semi-illiterate, closeted white supremacist, and an incompetent liar, and if their genius could prove that GDC-Witness, George Rothnie (Scottish George), a Deputy Postgraduate Dean, Oxford, did not unrelentingly tell lies under implied oath, and if the Science Journalist (Edward Wilson), could prove that GDC-Witness, Kevin Atkinson (Scottish Ken) did not, criminally, unrelentingly tell lies under oath, and if he could prove that GDC-Expert, Sue Gregory, OBE, Officer of the Most Excellent Order of Empire did not unrelentingly tell lies under implied oath, Oxford University Educated Cambridge University Professor will confirm the belief of billions of people in our world, which is that Antichrist Freemasonry Quasi-Religion (Mediocre Mafia/New Pharisees), Antichrist Islam, Antichrist

Judaism, and all other motley assemblies of exotic religions and faiths, under the common umbrella of the Governor of the Church of England, and THE DEFENDER OF THE FAITH ('THE' - BEING THE PRINCIPAL WORD), are not intellectually flawed satanic mumbo jumbo, and it will also confirm that reasoning and vision have finite boundaries. If reasoning and vision have finite boundaries, the fellow must have LIED when He disclosed to Jews, in the Council, pictures His unbounded mind painted, and He, Christ, must have also lied when He audaciously stated: "I am the way and the truth and the life. No one comes to the Father except through me." John 14:6.

"The first quality that is needed is audacity." Churchill

If the fellow told Jews the truth in the Council when He disclosed pictures His unbounded mind painted, everything that is not aligned to John 14:6 - is travelling in the wrong direction and heading straight for very hard rocks.

"It does no harm to throw the occasional man overboard, but it does not do much good if you are steering full speed ahead for the rocks." Sir Ian Gilmour (1926 – 2007).

They were closeted racist bastards who desired to conduct racial hatred legally under their law, and those they needed to convince were exactly like them, closeted racist bastards, too.

NORTHAMPTON, ENGLAND: Based on available evidence, GDC-Witness, Ms Rachael Bishop, Senior NHS Nurse, unrelentingly lied under oath – Habakkuk 1:4; John 8:44; John 10:10.

A WHITE WOMAN. A DISHONEST COUGAR.

Boris Johnson: Your kindred must tell lies; they are intellectually inferior, only their skin colour is irrefutably superior. The most important part of the leverage is that the Judges' skin colour is irrefutably superior too, and they are closeted racists too.

Sincere immodesty is sincerer than insincere modesty.

Boris Johnson, I am a 'foetus'; what I can see is clearer than visions, prophesies, and dreams (Act 2:17): The fellow is who he says He is.

Boris Johnson: Genetic mix - is the Holy Grail. Education (formal and informal) will polish what genetic mix presents to it.
There is no factual and scientific evidence that Richard Dawkins's inherited X and Y chromosomes, and particularly the X chromosome, are the best, and the fact that A is better than B is not proof that A and B are not crap.

Boris Johnson: Any permutation that is not aligned with the notion of infinity is intellectually flawed; akin to doing a simultaneous equation with only one of the available equations.

Boris Johnson: If the bottom of a whole descends to the basement, and the top of the whole simultaneously descends to the bottom from whence the former bottom vacated, they should be harmonious change, but there wouldn't be relative change as the distance between the bottom (former top) and the basement (former bottom) will remain unchanged. The former top is oblivious to the notion of relativity, so it refuses to accept that it is the new bottom.

Boris Johnson: If the bottom of a whole descends to the basement, and if the top of that whole stays at the top or ascends higher up, there will be disharmonious change and would be relative change as the distance between the bottom and top will increase. Disharmonious fracture is more progressive than harmonious change.

Progressive harmonious fracture antagonises one-man-one-vote democracy.

Google: Helen Falcon: Racist Empress of Privileged Dullards.

Based on available evidence, Mrs Helen Falcon, Member of the Most Excellent Order of our Empire unrelentingly lied under implied oath.

A WHITE WOMAN. A DISHONEST RACIST
COUGAR.

Based on evidence, parts of the administration of English
law are irreparably mediocre, indiscreetly racist, and
confused.

Facts are sacred; they can't be overstated.

"The truth allows no choice." Dr Samuel Johnson

Members of the Charitable Antichrist Racist Freemasonry
Quasi-Religion (Mediocre Mafia or New Pharisees): They
control everything except the individual, Christ granted,
intellect. They use Judicial Terrorism to conceal hereditary
intellectual impotence.

Facts are sacred.

Deluded Antichrist Closeted White Supremacist Britons,
the white ancestors of Richard Dawkins' Blind Watch
Maker accurately foresaw that Bedford's District Judge
Paul Ayers, the Senior Vice President of the Association of
Her Majesty's District Judges, an incontrovertibly
functional semi-illiterate former, mere, debt-collector
Solicitor in Norwich (coastal dole), will need to thrive in
Britain, with zero Christ granted talent so, they used, made
in Birmingham, guns to loot Africa – Habakkuk.

The White Supremacist Judge is a very powerful racist
thug.

BEDFORD, ENGLAND: GDC-Witness, Freemason, Brother Richard Hill fabricated reports and unrelentingly lied under oath.

A DISHONEST RACIST: A WHITE MAN.

Boris Johnson: Why is England not a racist scam?

Closeted racist bastards love irrefutably superior skin colour superiority, the baseless and brainless birth right, which they neither made nor chose; they don't love. Freedom of Expression because they don't want their mentally very gentle children to know that they are crooked, racist, and excessively stupid; based on very proximate observations and direct experiences only their irrefutably superior skin colour is truly good.

Deluded Antichrist Closeted White Supremacist Britons, the white ancestors of Richard Dawkins' Blind Watch Maker accurately foresaw that GDC-Witness, Freemason, Brother Richard Hill will fabricate reports and unrelentingly tell lies under oath, they embarked on armed robbery and dispossession raids in Africa.

OYINBO OLE: Racist descendants of THIEVES and owners of stolen children of defenceless poor people (Black African ancestors of Meghan Markle and her white children) - Habakkuk

"Meghan Markle was the subject of explicit and obnoxious racial hatred." John Bercow

"Racism is rife throughout most organisations across Britain." The Mayor of London

"White Supremacy is real, and it needs to be shattered." Dr Cornel West.

"All sections of the UK Society are institutionally RACIST." Sir Bernard Hogan-Howe

The Judiciary is part of the UK Society.

"Racism is alive and well and living in Tower Hamlets, in Westminster and, yes, sometimes in the judiciary." Judge Peter Herbert, Officer of the Most Excellent Order of the British Empire (OBE).

"Of black men, the numbers are too great who are now repining under English cruelty." Dr Samuel Johnson.

THE JUDICIARY IS NOT A BRANCH OF THE CHARITABLE ANTICHRIST RACIST FREEMASONRY COMPOUD-RELIGION (MEDIOCRE MAFIA/NEW PHARISEES).

Then, there, white Judges, nearly all, were White Supremacists, Christians, and Freemasons; some of them were thicker than a gross of planks.

C of E raises serious concerns about Christian Freemasons
https://www.theguardian.com › uk-news › feb › c-of-e-...

8 Feb 2018 — Church of England warning that secret society may not be compatible with Christianity echoes concerns from 1987.

BORIS JOHNSON: The fellow is who He says He is, and He will get what He wants – Proverbs 16:33.

https://www.youtube.com/watch?v=BlpH4hG7m1A&feature=youtu.be

"They may not have been well written from a grammatical point of view but I am confident I had not forgotten any of the facts." Dr Geraint Evans, Postgraduate Tutor, Oxford

AN IMBECILE: AN ADULT WITH THE BASIC SKILLS OF A CHILD - HABAKKUK

https://youtu.be/rayVcfyu9Tw

"Why, Sir, Sherry is dull, naturally dull; but it must have taken him a great deal of pains to become what we now see him. Such an excess of stupidity, Sir, is not in Nature." DR SAMUEL JOHNSON

GDC: Based on available evidence, Geraint Evans, Postgraduate Tutor, Oxford, unrelentingly lied on record. Had he been black, he would have been in trouble.

"Michael Jackson would have been found guilty if he'd been black." Jo Brand

Then, there, it was a crime only if FREEMASONS did not prior authorise it.

-----Original Message-----
From: George Rothnie <georgerothnie@hotmail.com>
To: adeolacole@aol.com
Sent: Mon, 8 Mar 2010 20:19
Subject: Re Meeting 9th March

Hi Ola,

We are scheduled to meet tomorrow evening at my surgery about 5.30ish.
Unfortunately something has cropped up which necessytates me having to
postpone the meeting. I'm really sorry it's such short notice.

I will contact you in the week to arrange another date.

Once agaim my apologies.

George

Dr George Rothnie, Deputy Postgraduate Dean Oxford.

AN IMBECILE: AN ADULT WITH THE BASIC SKILLS OF A CHILD – HABAKKUK

GDC: Based on available evidence, George Rothnie, unrelentingly lied on record.

Facts are sacred.

"The truth allows no choice." Dr Samuel Johnson.

BORIS JOHNSON: Reasoning and vision are unbounded. The fellow is who He says He is.

BORIS JOHNSON: The fact that one can't see a thing isn't proof that a thing is not there.

BORIS JOHNSON: The fact that A is better than B isn't proof that A and B are not crap. Anything that is not aligned to the fellow with infinite reasoning and vision, is retrogressive, and intellectually flawed.

Paying incontrovertibly functional semi-illiterate white Judges, who foreseeably FAILED in the independent practice of their Mediocre Trade, loads of other people money for having daily dialogues with imbeciles (adults with the basic skills of a child) is quasi-fraudulent, a RACKET.

Just as it was in Professor Stephen Hawking's School, then, at the University of Lagos, the brightest students did mathematics, physics, and chemistry, and did not attend lectures at the Faculty of Law.

"In my school, the brightest boys did math and physics, the less bright did physics and chemistry, and the least bright did biology. I wanted to do math and physics, but my father made me do chemistry because he thought there would be no jobs for mathematicians." Dr Stephen Hawking.

A grossly overrated, overhyped, overpopulated, and mediocre trade that is dying slowly and imperceptibly, and is overseen by the Antichrist Racist Freemasons (Mediocre Mafia) — Habakkuk 1:4; John 8:44; John 10:10.

"The legal system lies at the heart of any society, protecting rights, imposing duties, and establishing a framework for the conduct of almost every social, political, and economic activity. Some argue that the law is in its death throes while others postulate a contrary prognosis that discerns numerous signs of law's enduring strength. Which is it?" Professor Raymond Wacks.

Deluded Antichrist Closeted White Supremacist Dawkin's ancestors were very Accurate Watch Makers and Blind Seers accurately foresaw a closeted racist, functional semi-illiterate former debt-collector Solicitor in Norwich, Bedford's District Judge Paul Ayers, the Senior Vice President of the Association of Her Majesty's District Judges, will be a member of their Mediocre Trade, and our District Judge in BEDFORD, they embarked on armed robbery and dispossession raids in AFRICA: Whenever the racist bastards slaughtered our ancestors, they dispossessed them, and wherever they robbed, they took possession - Habakkuk.

413

OYINBO OLE: RIGHTEOUS DESCENDANTS OF ULTRA-RIGHTEOUS THIEVES – HABAKKUK.

Almost everything is assumed in favour of the irrefutably superior skin colour that the very fortunate wearer neither made nor chose.

Closeted racist bastards want everyone to view our world only from, only, their perspective: Creeping DPRK.

They see a Senior Judge, albeit England's Class; a Negro sees a properly schooled impostor and an expert of deception who seemed to have fraudulently sold unashamed mediocrity and confusion to the undiscerning for decades; if they are not excessively stupid, the Negro must be mad.

Bedford's District Judge, the Senior Vice President of the Association of Her Majesty's District Judges, based on available evidence, the yield of the land and the yield of the talents of your white ancestors did not sustain their standard of living; you are leech, and your white ancestors were THIEVES and owners of stolen children of defenceless poor Africans (Meghan Markle's ancestors) – Habakkuk

Facts are sacred; they can't be overstated.

Before SLAVERY (economic cannibalism), what?

Prior to Slavery (economic cannibalism), Great Britain had £Zero; there was only sustenance agriculture.

Then, the yields of stolen children of other people were used to build Magnificent Courts and pay the wages of white Judges who sent white people who stole money to prisons built with the yields of stolen lives - Habakkuk.

NIGERIA: SHELL'S DOCILE CASH COW: Children with huge oil wells and gas fields near the huts eat only 1.5/day in NIGERIA; a bellyful, closeted racist, functional semi-illiterate former debt collector Solicitor in Norwich (coastal dole) whose white mother and father have never seen crude oil, and whose white ancestors were fed like battery hens with the yields of stolen children of defenceless poor people (Meghan Markle's ancestors) is our District Judge in BEDFORD – Habakkuk

OXFORD, ENGLAND: British Soldier – Territorial Defence, Stephanie Twidale (TD), GDC-Witness, unrelentingly lied under oath. Her white ancestors were incompetent racist liars too; they were THIEVES and owners of stolen children of defenceless poor people.

A WHITE WOMAN. A DISHONEST RACIST COUGAR

A bastardised, indiscreetly dishonest, unashamedly mediocre, vindictive, potently weaponised, and institutionally racist legal system that is overseen by the members of the Charitable Antichrist Racist Freemasons Religion for the benefit of imbeciles (adults with the basic skills of a child) – Habakkuk

CHAPTER FIFTEEN:

Boris Johnson: Why is England not a Scam?

"Give me liberty or give me death." Patrick Henry

Boris Johnson, I am aware of the existence of the supernatural, what should I do?

****

In order to conceal the truth, which is that the top is the new bottom, racist privileged-dullards resort to Judicial Terrorism: Incompetent Criminalised Negrophobic Perjury and Persecutory Negrophobia propagates whiteness, and 'violent' white domination.

"A typical English man, usually violent and always dull." Wilde

Then, on the plantations, the brightest of the stolen Africans who were unlawfully imprisoned and forced to work for NOTHING, naturally rebelled against indefinite servitude, as only morons will surrender to indefinite servitude; they were deselected (mercilessly killed or unnatural deselected, through being summarily fed bullets, sadistically flogged to death, or frogmarched to the woods, at gunpoint, and hanged from tall trees, without hoods) by their European Christian owners, and the weak common genetic pool of the kidnapped Africans weakened further.

Then, on the plantations, the placid, but very bright slaves (women and their children), refused to do stuff with the libidinous European Christian bastards (sex machines), as they knew that the owners of the cows owned their calves, and more importantly, they did not want to make their captors richer, and it would have been selfish to make slave babies and leave them on hell on earth, their refusal to voluntarily produce Slave babies, further, weakened the common genetic pool of the stolen AFRICANS.

Very many kidnapped Africans were raped by the European Christians, and they produced thousands Mulatto slave babies: Then, the owners of the cows owned their calves.

Then, white men were devils, as they did not believe in His exceptionalism (John 14:6), so they were not deterred by His Justice (John 5:22; Matthew 25: 31-46).

Then, on the plantations, European Christians selected the prettiest (women and children) among their stolen African possessions – as pleasure slaves, and they became Mulatto baby-slaves' factory. The rest (male and female) were artificially paired up and deliberately bred for labour.

Genetic damage is the most enduring residue of European commerce in millions of stolen children of defenceless poor people (Black African ancestors of Meghan Markle ad her white children) – Habakkuk.

They are scared: The brain is not in the irrefutably superior skin colour that they neither made nor chose, and their children must not know. The centuries-old unspoken myth that intellect is related to their indisputably superior skin colour is the mother of all racist scams.

Thu, 3 Sep 2015 20:00
cqc (NHS SHARED BUSINESS SERVICES LTD (BRISTOL)) (SBS-B.cqc@nhs.net)To:you Details
Hello,

Thank you for your below email

Kindly request you to provide your contact details (telephone number) so we can contact you and explain.

If any query please let me know

Thanks and Regards,
Kanchan Jaisinghani
Collections
Debt Management Team
Shared Business Services
Tel 0303-123-1155

Fax 0117-933-8890
E-mail: sbs-b.cqc@nhs.net
Website: www.sbs.nhs.uk
Government Business Award Winner
Central Government Supplier of the Year 2011.
******

Sir Major was a winner too; he banged the libidinous, adulterous, ugly, Jewish cougar – Egg Winner.

They brainlessly and baselessly believe that they were superiorly created, since it is obvious that they are not superior, in anyway whatsoever, then, they use extreme violence to steal what He gave others. Now, they use blatant Judicial Terrorism to appropriate the yield of the talent He gave to others.

OYINBO OLE: STRAIGHT-FACED DESCENDANTS OF THIEVES – HABAKKUK.

GDC: Richard Hill (NHS) fabricated reports and unrelentingly lied under oath.

GDC: Kevin Atkinson (NHS) unrelentingly lied under oath

GDC: Jonathan Martin unrelentingly lied on record

GDC: Helen Falcon (MBE) unrelentingly lied on record

GDC: George Rothnie (NHS) unrelentingly lied on record

GDC: Stephanie Twiddle (NHS) unrelentingly lied under oath

GDC: Sue Gregory (OBE) unrelentingly lied on record

GDC: Rachael Bishop (NHS) unrelentingly lied under oath

GDC: Geraint Evans (NHS) unrelentingly lied on record.

Christ does not place Africans in the back row, white men do.

The cornerstone of their system is the baseless and brainless believe that they are superiorly created by Almighty God, but as it is very obvious that they are not, mentally and/or physically, their ancestors used extreme violence to steal what He gave ours, and they employ indiscreet and unashamed Judicial Terrorism to steal the yield of our Christ granted talents.

The white man is the devil.

Creeping DPRK.

They were all white, including the Judges, and they were all RACISTS, and incompetent liars.

Homogeneity in the administration of English law is the impregnable secure mask of merciless RACIAL HATRED – Habakkuk 1:4; John 8:44; John 10:10.

The eat all their cakes, and they eat our cakes, and they want everything. Their ancestors used extreme violence to take everything: Movable and immovable. The racist white bastards were the greediest economic cannibals and the nastiest racist terrorists the world will ever know. Whenever they merciless slaughtered poor people, the racist bastards dispossessed the poor, wherever they robbed the took possession.

The poor will always be with you – Matthew 26:11.

The closeted racist white bastards were as greedy as the grave and, like death, they were never satisfied – Habakkuk 2:5.

"Many Scots masters were considered among the most brutal, with life expectancy on their plantations averaging a mere four years. We worked them to death then simply imported more to keep the sugar and thus the money flowing. Unlike centuries of grief and murder, an apology cost nothing. So, what does Scotland have to say?" Herald Scotland: Ian Bell, Columnist, Sunday 28 April 2013

"Of black men, the numbers are too great who are now repining under English cruelty." Dr Samuel Johnson

The white man was the devil.

They were not deterred by His Justice (John 5:22) because they did not believe in exceptionalism (John 14:6).

A bastardised, indiscreetly dishonest, unashamedly mediocre, vindictive, potently weaponised, and institutionally racist legal system that is overseen by FREEMASONS (Mediocre Mafia/New Pharisees) – Habakkuk

"To deny or belittle this good is, in this dangerous century when the resources and pretensions of power continue to enlarge, a desperate error of intellectual abstraction. More than this, it is a self-fulfilling error, which encourages us to give up the struggle against bad laws and class bound procedures and to disarm ourselves before power. It is to throw away a whole inheritance of struggle about the law and within the forms of law, whose continuity can never be fractured without bringing men and women into immediate danger." - E. P Thompson.

"You will bow. You can't beat the system." Kemi Daramola.

Imported devil (Jezebel). She pays tithe (quasi-protection money) and prays to Christ in a Brickhill Church, in Bedford, and Charitable Antichrist Racist FREEMASONS (Mediocre Mafia/New Pharisees), in Kempston, answer her prayers.

I shan't. I know who will - Romans 11; 1 John 4:4.

Princess Kemi Daramola from Aisegba, Ekiti, our imported Born-Again Christian who told lies when she spoke intelligibly and told the mother of all lies when she spoke unintelligibly (in unknown tongues), bowed to Freemasons, and played the closeted white supremacists like chess, and let them loose on her importer, and the father of her children.

"Lies are told all the time." Sir Michael Havers

Born-Again Christians, not all, lie that they don't lie – Psalm 144.

GOOGLE: FREEMASONRY INTELLECTUALLY FLAWED.
https://www.youtube.com/watch?v=rayVcfyu9Tw

C of E raises serious concerns about Christian Freemasons
https://www.theguardian.com › uk-news › feb › c-of-e-...

8 Feb 2018 — Church of England warning that secret society may not be compatible with Christianity echoes concerns from 1987.

Re:

Fri, 11 Apr 2014 9:28

resh diu (rdiu@me.com)To:you Details

It's sad Ola

I kept telling you to play the game of chess rather than fight it

You take care

If you wish to dispose of 24 park road let me know

Regards

Resh

Dr Resh Diu BDS

www.oradi.co.uk

To survive in Great Britain, Africans must bow to genetic aliens, closeted racist descendants of undocumented refugees from Eastern Europe, with camouflage English names, whose ancestors crossed the English Channels, not that long ago, in dinghy boats, without luggage or decent shoes, and Africans must teach their children to bow to FREEMASONS and play quasi-voodoo-men (FREEMASONS) like chess.

LATENT BUT VERY POTENT TURF WAR:
Descendants of aliens with camouflage English names oppress the descendants of the robbed with the yield of the robbery – Habakkuk.

"Those who know the least obey the best." George Farquhar

If thoroughly deluded, Closeted White Supremacist, and Antichrist Richard Dawkins could prove that a white man, District Judge Paul Ayers of Bedford County Court, 3, St Paul Square, Bedford, MK40 1SQ, is not a functional semi-illiterate and an incompetent liar, and if the England's Class Biology Genius could prove British Soldier – Territorial Defence, Stephanie Twidale (TD), GDC-Witness, did not unrelentingly tell lies under oath, and if he could prove that GDC -Witness Richard Hill did not fabricate reports and unrelentingly told lies under oath, and he could prove that GDC-Expert, Sue Gregory (OBE) Officer of the Most Excellent Order of our Empire, did not unrelentingly tell lies under implied oath, and if he could prove that GDC: Kevin Atkinson (NHS) did not unrelentingly tell lies under oath, and if he could prove that GDC: Jonathan Martin did not unrelentingly tell lies on record, and if he could prove that GDC: Helen Falcon (MBE) did not unrelentingly tell lies on record, and if he could prove that GDC: George Rothnie (NHS) did not unrelentingly tell lies on record, and if he could prove that GDC: Rachael Bishop (NHS) did not unrelentingly tell lies under oath, and if he could prove that GDC: Geraint Evans (NHS) did not unrelentingly tell lies on record, he will confirm the belief of billions of people in our world, which is that Antichrist Islam, Antichrist Atheism, Antichrist Judaism, Antichrist Freemasonry Quasi-Religion, and all other exotic Faiths and Religions under the common umbrella of the Governor of the Church of England and the

425

Defender of THE FAITH are not intellectually flawed Satanic Mumbo Jumbo, and he will confirm the belief of scores of millions of people, which is that the administration of English Law is not a weaponised, Satanic Negrophobic charade, and he will, also, confirm that reasoning and vision are bounded. If reasoning and vision have finite boundaries, He must have lied when He disclosed pictures His unbounded mind painted, and He must have also lied when He audaciously stated: "I am the way and the truth and the life. No one comes to the Father except through me." John 14:6.

"It does no harm to throw the occasional man overboard, but it does not do much good if you are steering full speed ahead for the rocks." Lord Gilmour of Craigmillar

"Sometimes people don't want to hear the truth because they don't want their illusions destroyed." Friedrich Nietzsche

CHAPTER SIXTEEN:

Boris Johnson: Why is England not a racist scam?

BEDFORD, ENGLAND: District Judge, immodesty apart, the Negro's mind is finer than the system you serve. You are relevant only because England is rich and the skin colour that you neither made nor chose is irrefutably superior; apart from those, you're PURIFIED NOTHING. Your talent and the yield of your land cannot sustain your standard of living. The talent and the yield of the land of your white ancestors did not sustain their standard of living; they were very hardened PROFESSIONAL THIEVES and owners of stolen children of defenceless poor people (Black African ancestors of Meghan Markle and her white children) – Habakkuk

OYINBO OLE: THIEVES – HABAKKUK

Herod was a Jew; the very intolerant lunatic Jew removed John's head only because he spoke – Matthew 14.

The closeted racist bastards have power, but they don't have 'good brain'; they deceive their children that they have power because they have 'good brain'.

A brainless descendant of undocumented European refugees (genetic alien), with camouflage English names; he gave the game away when he approved and immortalised what his functional semi-illiterate white mother and father spoke (deductible), which his poly-educated (not a proper university - Russell Group) white supervisors in Luton authorised.

Based on available evidence, His Honour Judge Perusko studied law at Poly, not at a Russell Group University (Lower-class alternative education) – Proverbs 17:16.

Why should the white mother and father of His Honour Judge Perusko need very, very strong views about education if it is deductible that the talent of their white son was only good enough for Second Rate Alternative Poly-education – Proverbs 17:16?

Based on available evidence, GDC-Witness, British Soldier – Territorial Defence, Stephanie Twiddle, of Stephanie Twidale Limited - Dentists in Bicester OX26 6QB,

unrelentingly lied under oath. Her white ancestors were incompetent racist liars too; they were THIEVES and owners stolen children of defenceless poor (Meghan Markle's ancestors) – Habakkuk.

A WHITE WOMAN. A DISHONEST RACIST WHITE COUGAR.

WHITE PRIVILEGE: When whites, straight-faced criminals, hired Negrophobic persecutors, and Negrophobic perjurers, commit racist crimes against our people (Africans), closeted racist white bastards who oversee the administration of their law always criminally bury racial hatred.

OYINBO OLE: THIEVES – HABAKKUK

The white man is the devil - Columbia University
https://ccnmtl.columbia.edu › mmt › mxp › concepts

Referring to Whites as "devils" originates with the teachings of Master W.D. Fard and the legend of Yakub. Fard taught Elijah Muhammad who preached the ...

Only stupid Negroes believe that they are no longer inferior under English law, after the 1807 Act, ```````and only stupider Negroes do not know that whites measure whites with a very, very different yardstick, and the stupidest Negroes do not know that demons can't out demons – Matthew 12:27.

Boris Johnson: Based on available evidence, Bedford's District Judge Paul Ayers, the Senior Vice President of the Association of Her Majesty's District Judges is a functional semi-illiterate and an incompetent liar. His white ancestors were incompetent liar too; they were THIEVES and

owners of stolen children of defenceless poor people
(Black African ancestors of Meghan Markle and her white
children) - Habakkuk.

Facts are sacred.

"The truth allows no choice." Dr Samuel Johnson

"I think I will ask our legal adviser for any advice he may
have. My view is that there are six or seven of us here who
had the admission down, but we cannot find it in the
transcript and there is wordings that imply that there was,
but it is not in black and white….." Dr Shiv Pabary (NHS),
the Archetypal GDC Committee Chairman, Member of the
Most Excellent Order of our Empire (MBE), and Justice of
Peace (JP).

AN IMBECILE: AN ADULT WITH THE BASIC
SKILLS OF A CHILD – OECD.

"Yes, Sir, it does *her* honour, but it would do nobody else
honour. I have indeed, not read it all. But when I take up
the end of a web, and find it packthread, I do not expect, by
looking further, to find embroidery." Dr Samuel Johnson.

The sheep are worthless, certainly intellectually, and the
shepherds know, but cannot do anything about it because
they do not have control of genetic mix, the Holy Grail,
and education will polish only what genetic mix

Their Indian, Shiv Pabary, MBE, is the product of the
educational system of one of the richest nations on earth;
had he been the product of one of the educational systems

of one of the poorest nations on earth, he might not be read properly. In Punjab, scores of millions go to the bush to defecate.

They sadistically impose their worst fear on their fellow man and his children.

Based on available evidence, Dr Shiv Pabary (NHS), the Archetypal GDC Committee Chairman, Member of the Most Excellent Order of our Empire (MBE), and Justice of Peace (JP), unrelentingly lied under oath – Habakkuk.

Their unspoken objective is to kill, albeit hands-off.

GOOGLE: Dr Anand Kamath, dentist.

GOOGLE: Dr Richard Bamgboye, GP.

NIGERIA: SHELL'S DOCILE CASH COW.

Children with huge oil wells and gas fields near their huts eat only 1.5/day in NIGERIA; an Indian whose father and mother have never seen crude oil, there are no oil wells or gas fields in Newcastle and Punjabi, is the Archetypal GDC Committee Chairman, Member of the Most Excellent Order of our Empire (MBE), and Justice of Peace (JP).

They find a very, very dull Indian, a near perfect imitation upper-class English man, with camouflage English names, and they adorn him with very, very high titles, and he becomes Freemasons' Zombie Private Soldier (IRA of Sinn Fein).

Immortal mendacity is complicated by mediocrity.

Shiv Pabary: Mendacious Member of our Empire (MMBE) and Justice of Incompetent Racist Lies (JIRL).
They do not have any control of genetic mix, the most important basis of individual intellect, so they resort to Judicial Terrorism to save face.
Education (formal and informal) will polish only what genetic mix presents to it.

Their ancestors of used guns, not intellect, to loot Africa.

Parts of the resultant effect of several centuries of indiscriminate mass murder, racial hatred, and extremely greedy economic cannibalism is that millions of adults with the basic skills of a child thrive in Great Britain: Dr Richard Dawkins, what's great about several centuries of industrial-scale professional THIEVERY and SLAVERY?

"The truth allows no choice." Dr Samuel Johnson

Facts are sacred.

Dr Richard Dawkins, your ancestors were THIEVES. Prior to Slavery, they were landowners or feudal agricultural labourers. Gigantic yields of millions of stolen and destroyed lives immeasurably transformed their standard of living.

*****

Hyper-patriotic descendants of undocumented refugees from Europe (genetic aliens), with camouflage English names.

Lord Brittan: "A German Jew." Lord Denning (1899 – 1999).

Lord Brittan's father was from Lithuania.
Apart from creating very cushy salaried jobs for irrefutably functional semi-illiterate Judges who foreseeably FAILED in their oversaturated mediocre trade, what do millions of adults with the basic skills of a child need very, very expensive administration of the Law for?
Facts are sacred, they can't be overstated.

"The one great principle of the English law is, to make business for itself. There is no other principle distinctly, certainly, and consistently maintained through all its narrow turnings. Viewed by this light it becomes a coherent scheme, and not the monstrous maze the laity are apt to think it." Charles Dickens

The report, by the OECD, warns that the UK needs to take significant action to boost the basic skills of the nation's young people. The 460-page study is based on the first-ever survey of the literacy, numeracy and problem-solving at work skills of 16 to 65-year-olds in 24 countries, with almost 9,000 people taking part in England and Northern Ireland to make up the UK results. The findings showed that England and Northern Ireland have some of the highest proportions of adults scoring no higher than Level 1 in literacy and numeracy—the lowest level on the

OECD's scale. This suggests that their skills in the basics are no better than that of a 10-year-old.

AN IMBECILE: AN ADULT WITH THE BASIC SKILLS OF A CHILD.

White Judges (predominantly) who expend their professional lives on daily dialogues with imbeciles will be affected by their regular encounters.

OYINBO OLE – HABAKKUK.

Descendants of Alphonse Gabriel fool fools that they are Archangel Gabriel.

They accurately foresaw that their descendants, not all, will be imbeciles, so they used guns to loot Africa, directly and indirectly, and they used yield of several centuries of the greediest economic cannibalism, and the nastiest racist terrorism the world will ever know – to create an Eldorado for millions of white imbeciles; the Eldorado where overfed racist bastards ate butter-scones, drank Indian tea, and played crochet – while stolen children of defenceless poor Africans laboured for NOTHING on cane and cotton fields, at gunpoint, and they decommissioned natural selection, and they reversed evolution, and they made it affordable for millions of imbeciles of all shades to breed irresponsibly.

DELUDED BRAINLESS RACIST PAPER TIGERS: Their hairs stand on end when they are challenged by our people. We and our type are the ones closeted racist bastards will beat up without the support of the YANKS.

"Ethical foreign policy." Robin Cook (1946 – 2005). Then, there Judges, nearly all, were Freemasons; some of them were THICKER than a gross of planks.

If members of the Charitable Antichrist Racist Freemasonry Quasi-Religion (Mediocre Mafia/ New Pharisees) are as Ethical and as Brave as they seem to imply, they should use guns to evict Putin from Crimea; he stole it with guns.

If a Negro farmed thousands of white pigs with great snouts for roasted pigs' snouts curry, the stupidest of the white pigs with great snouts deserves to be killed and eaten first.

"I am very fond of my pigs, but it doesn't stop me from eating them." Archbishop Runcie (1921 – 2000)

They see a Judge, the Negro sees a very, very hardened, innately racist (hereditary), and a properly schooled impostor, and an intellectually disorientate and a mentally imbalanced expert of deception who has sold unashamed mediocrity and confusion to the undiscerning for decades; if they are not excessively stupid, the Negro must be mad.

He seemed obsessed with me, and he seemed to be the power behind almost every woe; he might tell his fellow closeted white supremacists that he knew me very well.

Financial disclosure in a divorce: How can a mere Negro have what I don't have?

Then, there, the archetypal Judge was white, white supremacist, Christian, and FREEMASON.

OYINBO OLE: A RIGHTEOUS DESCENDANT OF ULTRA-RIGHTEOUS THIEVES AND OWNERS OF STOLEN CHILDRE OF DEFENCELESS POOR PEOPLE (BLACK AFRICAN ANCESTORS OF MEGHAN MARKLE AND HER WHITE CHILDREN) - HABAKKUK.

Dr Shiv Pabary (NHS), the Archetypal GDC Committee Chairman, Member of the Most Excellent Order of our Empire (MBE), and Justice of Peace (JP).

PERCEPTION IS GRANDER THAN REALITY.

Everything is assumed in favour of the irrefutably superior skin colour that the very, very fortunate wearer neither made nor chose.

Without his irrefutably superior skin colour, the incontrovertibly functional semi-illiterate white man, albeit England's Class Judge, will be considerably diminished as a human being. White skin privilege.

The centuries-old unspoken myth that intellect is somehow related to their irrefutably superior skin colour – is the mother of all racist scams

The direct descendants of father of lies tell the mother of RACIST LIES – John 8:44.

"I do not approve of anything that tampers with natural ignorance. Ignorance is like a delicate exotic fruit; touch it and the bloom is gone. The whole theory of modern education is radically unsound. Fortunately, in England, at any rate, education produces no effect whatsoever. If it did, it would prove a serious danger to the upper classes, and probably lead to acts of violence in Grosvenor Square." Wilde

They are not immortal, and they are not the only creation of Almighty God, and the irrefutably superior skin colour that the very fortunate wearer neither made nor chose is not the only wonder of our world.

GDC: Kevin Atkinson (Scottish Kev) unrelentingly lied under oath. His Scottish ancestors were incompetent racist liars too; they were THIEVES and owners of stolen children of defenceless. Had he been black, he would have been in trouble. Racist bastards measure their own people with a very, very different yardstick – Matthew 12:27.

A properly proofed and approved Judgement by a properly educated Judge should pass through at least four separate filters: The transcript writers, the proof-readers, the Court, and the Judge.

In an open dialogue with Ruth Bader Ginsburg (1933 – 2020), Lady Hale lamented funding.

Why is paying functional semi-illiterate white Judges (predominantly) loads of other people's money to have daily dialogues with adults, of all shades, with the basic skills of a child (imbeciles), not a bloody waste of MONEY – Proverbs 17:16?

OYINBO OLE: THIEVES - HABAKKUK

"A government that robs Peter to pay Paul can always depend on the support of Paul." George Bernard Shaw

"It is incumbent upon the court and all those professionals involved to conclude court proceedings as quickly as possible. This hopefully ensures that a child has stability, love and affection and the parents working together to ensure that he has the best opportunity of developing academically and emotional." District Judge Paul Ayers, Senior Vice President of the Association of Her Majesty's District Judges – proofed and approved Judgement

AN IMBECILE: AN ADULT WITH THE BASIC SKILLS OF A CHILD.

Brainless nonsense.

The white man is not good enough; had he been black, he will not be a Judge.

Facts are sacred, they can't be overstated.

White Judges (predominantly) who expend their professional lives on daily dialogues with imbeciles are bound to be affected by their regular encounters.

The report, by the OECD, warns that the UK needs to take significant action to boost the basic skills of the nation's young people. The 460-page study is based on the first-ever survey of the literacy, numeracy and problem-solving at work skills of 16 to 65-year-olds in 24 countries, with almost 9,000 people taking part in England and Northern Ireland to make up the UK results. The findings showed that England and Northern Ireland have some of the highest proportions of adults scoring no higher than Level 1 in literacy and numeracy - the lowest level on the OECD's scale. This suggests that their skills in the basics are no better than that of a 10-year-old.

AN IMBECILE: AN ADULT WITH THE BASIC SKILLS OF A CHILD.

Adults with the basic skills of a child will succeed adults with the basic skills of a foetus, and the former will need only food and shelter.

"Natural selection will not remove ignorance from future generations." Dr Richard Dawkins

BORIS JOHNSON: Then, there, White Judges (predominantly), who believed that daily dialogues with imbeciles was a worthwhile occupation, in a finite life experience, were SCAMMERS, and those who demanded and accepted valuable consideration in exchange for having daily dialogues with imbeciles were RACKETEERS (THIEVES) – Habakkuk.

BORIS JOHNSON: Apart from creating very safe and cushy salaried jobs for Solicitors and Barristers who foreseeably FAILED in their overpopulated, grossly overrated, and mediocre trade, what do imbeciles need very, very expensive administration of the Law for?

Just as it was in Professor Stephen Hawking's School, then, at the University of Lagos, the brightest students did mathematics, physics, and chemistry, and did not attend lectures at the Faculty of Law.

"In my school, the brightest boys did math and physics, the less bright did physics and chemistry, and the least bright did biology. I wanted to do math and physics, but my father made me do chemistry because he thought there would be no jobs for mathematicians." Dr Stephen Hawking.

A grossly overrated, overhyped, overpopulated, and mediocre trade that is dying slowly and imperceptibly, and is overseen by the Antichrist Racist Freemasons (Mediocre Mafia) - Habakkuk 1:4; John 8:44; John 10:10.

"The legal system lies at the heart of any society, protecting rights, imposing duties, and establishing a framework for the conduct of almost every social, political, and economic activity. Some argue that the law is in its death throes while others postulate a contrary prognosis that discerns numerous signs of law's enduring strength. Which is it?" Professor Raymond Wacks.

https://www.youtube.com/watch?v=BlpH4hG7m1A&feature=youtu.be

"They may not have been well written from a grammatical point of view but I am confident I had not forgotten any of the facts." Dr Geraint Evans, Postgraduate Tutor, Oxford

AN IMBECILE: AN ADULT WITH THE BASIC SKILLS OF A CHILD.

Based on available evidence, the white man is a functional semi-illiterate and an incompetent liar.

https://youtu.be/rayVcfyu9Tw

"Why, Sir, Sherry is dull, naturally dull; but it must have taken him a great deal of pains to become what we now see him. Such an excess of stupidity, Sir, is not in Nature." DR SAMUEL JOHNSON

BORIS JOHNSON: Then, they foresaw that their descendants, not all, will be imbeciles, so they used guns to loot Africa, and they used the yields of several centuries of the greediest economic cannibalism to create and evilest racist terrorism the world will ever know to create an

441

Eldorado for millions of white imbeciles, and they decommissioned natural selection, and they reversed evolution, and they made it possible for millions of imbeciles to breed millions of imbeciles – Habakkuk.

"By definition therefore there needs to be a contact order for Mr B so that he knows when he is going to see his son. It is absolutely essential that this occurs and mother agrees with that. She said so several times in her evidence. Mrs Waller agreed that not only should a child have the opportunity of developing relationship with both parents, any sibling should also be there so that inter- sibling relationship could be fostered and nurtured. Obviously in this particular case the children reside in different places. That immediately puts a strain on the children having limited contact with each other. F's sister is very much older than him and she will be further advanced into her adult life. Thus it is not a matter that that sibling relationship can only be fostered by the children being together. Indeed as we all know absence sometimes makes the heart grow fonder. F should have an opportunity of seeing his sister. Wherever he does that it should be done in a friendly and loving environment. If the time comes that his sister goes to university of course his contact with her will be restricted to the time that she is home from university. In years to come when they have both grown up, with their own family they will see less of each other. But it doesn't mean that they don't still love and adore each other as much as they would if they saw each other every day." District Judge Paul Ayers of Bedford County Court, the Senior Vice President of the Association of Her

Majesty's District Judges – proofed and approved Judgement.

AN ADULT WITH THE BASIC SKILLS OF A CHILD.

"Yes, Sir, it does *her* honour, but it would do nobody else honour. I have indeed, not read it all. But when I take up the end of a web, and find it packthread, I do not expect, by looking further, to find embroidery." Dr Samuel Johnson.

The yield of a very, very elementary intellect; his spinal cord seemed to be his highest centre.

Based on available evidence, the white man is a functional semi-illiterate and an incompetent liar.

Facts are sacred.

"The truth allows no choice." Dr Samuel Johnson
Based on available evidence, our Edinburgh University Educated Prime Minister, the scholar from Fife, couldn't spell: In the Country of the blind, the partially sighted is the guide.

-----Original Message-----
From: George Rothnie <georgerothnie@hotmail.com>
To: adeolacole@aol.com
Sent: Mon, 8 Mar 2010 20:19
Subject: Re Meeting 9th March

Hi Ola,

We are scheduled to meet tomorrow evening at my surgery about 5.30ish.
Unfortunately something has cropped up which
necessytates me having to
postpone the meeting. I'm really sorry it's such short notice.

I will contact you in the week to arrange another date.

Once agaim my apologies.

George

AN IMBECILE: AN ADULT WITH THE BASIC SKILLS OF A CHILD.

Based on available evidence, our Edinburgh University Educated Deputy Postgraduate Dean, Oxford, is a functional semi-illiterate and an incompetent liar.

They were all white: Based on very proximate observations and direct experiences, the white man is the devil.

The white man is the devil - Columbia University
https://ccnmtl.columbia.edu › mmt › mxp › concepts

Referring to Whites as "devils" originates with the teachings of Master W.D. Fard and the legend of Yakub. Fard taught Elijah Muhammad who preached the ...

CREEPING DPRK: They want to ban the expression of truths. Closeted racist bastards love the irrefutably superior skin colour that they neither made nor chose, their brainless and baseless birth right, but they don't love Freedom of Expression because they don't want their mentally very gentle children to know that they are excessively stupid closeted racist bastards.

*****

The pattern is the same almost everywhere.

Geraint Evans, dentist, Rowtree Dental Care, Northampton, unrelentingly lied under implied oath - Habakkuk. Had he been black, he would have been in trouble.

Only stupid Negroes do not know that whites measure whites with a very different yardstick, and only stupider Negroes do not know that demons cannot cast out demons – Matthew 12:27.

OYINBO OLE: HABAKKUK

District Judge Paul Ayers, Senior Vice President of the Association of Her Majesty's District Judges, which part of Bedford County Court, 3, St Paul's Square, MK40 1SQ was not stolen, or which part of it preceded SLAVERY, or which part of it did the people of Bedford buy?

Bedford, England: District Judge, based on available evidence, your white ancestors were THIEVES and owners of stolen children of defenceless poor people (Meghan Markle's ancestors) - Habakkuk

A CLOSETED RACIST FOOL'S APPROVAL!

PURIFIED ROT!

"All sections of the UK Society are institutionally racist." Sir Bernard Hogan-Howe

The Judiciary is part of the UK Society.

BORIS JOHNSON: Based on available evidence, District Judge Paul Ayers of Bedford County Court, 3, St Paul Square, MK40 1SQ, the Senior Vice President of the Association of Her Majesty's District Judges is a functional semi-illiterate and incompetent liar. His white ancestors were incompetent liars too; they were THIEVES and owners of stolen children of defenceless poor people (Meghan Markle's ancestors) – Habakkuk

"Those who have robbed have also lied." Dr Samuel Johnson

Facts are sacred, they can't be overstated.

"The truth allows no choice." Dr Samuel Johnson

BORIS JOHNSON: Members of the Charitable Antichrist Racist Freemasonry Religion (Mediocre Mafia/New Pharisees) are religious-terrorists, and like terrorists, they trample on the Law that their victims must obey, and which they expect to protect them.

BEDFORD, ENGLAND: Freemason, Brother, Dr Richard William Hill fabricated reports and unrelentingly lied under oath – Habakkuk 1:4; John 8:44; John 10:10. Had he been black, he would have been in trouble.

A WHITE MAN. A DISHONEST RACIST CROOK – HABAKKUK.

"Michael Jackson would have been found guilty if he'd been black." Jo Brand

BORIS JOHNSON: Why is England not a scam?

BEDFORD, ENGLAND: Sue Gregory, Officer of the Most Excellent Order of our Empire (OBE), unrelentingly lied under implied oath.

Our Empire did not evolve; then, almost everything was actively and deliberately stolen – Habakkuk

"Affluence is not a birth right." David Cameron

BORIS JOHNSON: Freemasons are the MICRO-RULERS of the state, their people are EVERYWHERE, including inside 10 Downing Street, and they control almost everything.

BORIS JOHNSON: Elected servants of the people (Parliament) makes law, and unelected members of the Charitable Antichrist Racist Freemasonry Quasi-Religion (Mediocre Mafia/New Pharisees), our irreconcilable religious enemies, oversee the administration of English Law – Habakkuk 1:4; John 8:44; John 10:10.

CHAPTER SEVENTEEN:

BORIS JOHNSON: Why is England not a scam?

"Masonry ought forever to be abolished. It is wrong - essentially wrong - a seed of evil which can never produce any good." President John Quincy Adams (1767 – 1848).

BORIS JOHNSON: Then, there, white Judges, and white Police Officers, nearly all, were members of the Charitable Antichrist Racist Freemasonry Quasi-Religion; some of them were THICKER than a gross of planks – Habakkuk 1:4; John 8:44; John 10:10.

The Negro's dispute with Antichrist GDC is purely religious; they do not believe in the exceptionalism of Christ (John 14:6), and we are certain of it, and we have evidence, and they are not deterred by the transparent Justice of what they do not believe (John 5:22; Matthew 25: 31-46).

Met Police's 'boys club of misogyny' means it's 'no surprise' Wayne Couzens wasn't stopped." Former PC Ali Hassan Ali

"Freedom of Expression is a basic right." Lady Hale

"Freedom of Expression is the cornerstone of our democracy." Jacob Rees-Mogg.

Maria Ressa and Dmitry Muratov were awarded the 2021 Nobel Peace Prize "for their efforts to safeguard freedom of expression.

Freemasons are very, very shallow; they can only see molecules.

"The supreme vice is shallowness." Wilde

We will reveal atoms to the closeted white supremacist thugs who use very, very expensive aprons to decorate the temples of their powerless and useless fertility tool, when truths, with evidence, override all laws, including the harassment law that they use to stifle Freedom of expression.

If one is a racist crook, and if there is irrefutable evidence that one's white ancestors were racist crooks too, Freedom of Expression is not one's Friend.

GDC: Richard Hill (NHS) fabricated reports and lied under oath.

GDC: Kevin Atkinson (NHS) lied under oath

GDC: Jonathan Martin lied on record

GDC: Helen Falcon (MBE) lied on record

GDC: George Rothnie (NHS) lied on record

GDC: Stephanie Twiddle (NHS) lied under oath

GDC: Sue Gregory (OBE) lied on record

GDC: Rachael Bishop (NHS) lied under oath

GDC: Geraint Evans (NHS) lied on record.

Facts are sacred.

They were all white, and they were all closeted racist crooks. Only the irrefutably superior skin colour that they neither made nor chose is truly good, everything else is art, incompetent art that incompetently imitates life.

They don't like our people; we know.

The intellect of the individual member of the Satanic Cult (FREEMASONS) is their soft underbelly, and paradoxically our shield.

They stalk our people (Africans) like prey, and they hunt in packs.

Christ does not place Africans in the back row, white men do.

The white man is the devil.

They were all white, and they were all excessively stupid, so Freedom of Expression is not their friend.

"Many Scots masters were considered among the most brutal, with life expectancy on their plantations averaging a mere four years. We worked them to death then simply imported more to keep the sugar and thus the money flowing. Unlike centuries of grief and murder, an apology cost nothing. So, what does Scotland have to say?" Herald Scotland: Ian Bell, Columnist, Sunday 28 April 2013

OYINBO OLE: THIEVES – HABAKKUK.

Christ did not place Africans in the back row, white men did.

Based on very proximate observations and direct experiences, the white man was the devil.

They are not the only creation of Almighty God, and they are not immortal, and the irrefutably superior skin colour that the very, very fortunate wearer neither made nor chose is not the only wonder of our world.

They are not deterred by His Justice (John 5:22) because they do not believe in His exceptionalism (John 14:6); He is watching them – Proverbs 15:3. The nemesis is not extinct, and the fact that it tarries isn't proof that it will never come - Habakkuk.

Everything is assumed in favour of the irrefutably superior skin colour that the very, very fortunate wearer neither made nor chose, and without it, she will be considerably diminished as a human being

"Those who have the power to do wrong with impunity seldom wait long for the will." Dr Samuel Johnson

Based on available evidence, GDC-Witness: Richard Hill fabricated reports and unrelentingly lied under oath — Habakkuk. A DISHONEST RACIST: A HIRED PERJURER

Based on available evidence, GDC-INSIDER: Sue Gregory (OBE), Officer of the Most Excellent Order of our Empire unrelentingly lied under implied oath — Habakkuk. A DISHONEST RACIST: A HIRED PERJURER

Our Empire did not evolve; then, almost everything was actively and deliberately stolen – Habakkuk.

Which part of Bedford County Court, 3, St Paul's Square, MK40 1SQ, wasn't stolen, or which part of it did the people of Bedford buy: The building or its chattels?

OYINBO OLE: RIGHTEOUS DESCENDANTS OF ULTRA-RIGHTEOUS THIEVES.

Ignorance is bliss.

Then, there, the yields of stolen children of defenceless poor people (Meghan Markle's ancestors) were used to build magnificent courts and pay the wages of white

Judges who sent white people who stole money to prisons built with the yields of stolen and destroyed lives - Habakkuk.

"Sometimes people don't want to hear the truth because they don't want their illusions destroyed." Friedrich Nietzsche.

BEDFORD, ENGLAND: District Judge Paul Ayers, the Senior Vice President of the Association of her Majesty's District Judges; it's plainly deductible that you're worthy only because your skin colour is irrefutably superior and England is rich, apart from those, you're PURIFIED NOTHING.

"Those who have robbed have also lied." Dr Samuel Johnson

OYINBO OLE: Racist descendants of THIEVES and owners of stolen children of defenceless poor people (Meghan Markle's ancestors) – Habakkuk.

"Those who know the least obey the best." George Farquhar

"Affluence is not a birth right." David Cameron.

Then, there, Policemen, nearly all, were Masons; some of them were thicker than a gross of planks. Is Wayne Couzens a Mason?

Based on available evidence, GDC-Witness: Rachael Bishop, Senior NHS Nurse, unrelentingly lied under oath — Habakkuk.

Based on available evidence, GDC-Witness: Geraint Evans (NHS) unrelentingly lied under implied oath — Habakkuk.

Based on available evidence, GDC-Witness: Stephanie Twidale (TD) unrelentingly lied under oath — Habakkuk.

Based on available evidence, GDC-Witness: George Rothnie (NHS) unrelentingly lied under implied oath — Habakkuk.

Based on available evidence, GDC-Witness: Kevin Atkinson (NHS) unrelentingly lied under oath — Habakkuk

They were all white: Homogeneity in the administration English law is the impregnable secure mask of racial intolerance.

PERSECUTORY NEGROPHOBIA AND NEGROPHOBIC PERJURY — HABAKKUK 1:4; JOHN 8:44; JOHN 10:10.

They persecute our people for the dark coat that we neither made nor chose, and cannot change, and they steal yields of our Christ granted talents.

Christ, the only true Judge, is watching them — Proverbs 15:3; John 5:22; Matthew 25: 31–46.

The nemesis is not extinct; the fact that it tarries isn't proof that it will never come — Habakkuk.

A bastardised, unashamedly mediocre, indiscreetly dishonest, vindictive, potently weaponised, and institutionally racist legal system that is overseen by MASONS (Mediocre Mafia/ New Pharisees) — Habakkuk 1:4; John 8:44; John 10:10.

"To deny or belittle this good is, in this dangerous century when the resources and pretensions of power continue to enlarge, a desperate error of intellectual abstraction. More than this, it is a self-fulfilling error, which encourages us to give up the struggle against bad laws and class bound procedures and to disarm ourselves before power. It is to throw away a whole inheritance of struggle about the law and within the forms of law, whose continuity can never be fractured without bringing men and women into immediate danger." — E. P Thompson.

"The truth allows no choice." Dr Samuel Johnson.

Facts are sacred.

"There is not a truth existing which I fear... or would wish unknown to the whole world." President Thomas Jefferson ·

BORIS JOHNSON: My mind is finer that the system you serve; it is what I got. Your order is disorder to me. The notion of relativity that excludes the infinite is intellectually flawed: The fact that A is significantly better than B isn't proof that both aren't crap. The fellow is who He says He is, and He told the truth when He disclosed pictures His unbounded mind painted – John 14:6.

Charitable, Antichrist Racist Freemasonry Quasi-Religion (Luciferians/ Mediocre Mafia/ New Pharisees): White supremacist bastards; closeted racist descendants of ultra-righteous owners of stolen children of defenceless poor people (Meghan Markle's ancestors) - Habakkuk

Then, there, White Judges, not all, were members of the Charitable, Antichrist, Racist Freemasonry Quasi-Religion (Luciferians/Mediocre Mafia/New Pharisees); some of them were thicker than a gross of planks - Habakkuk.

BORIS JOHNSON: I am very different from you; it is what nature imposed. I am aware of the existence of the supernatural. Reasoning and vision are infinite. The fellow is who He says He is, and He told the truth before the Council when He disclosed pictures His unbounded (infinite) mind painted – John 14:6.

If the British Premier, The Right Honourable Boris Johnson, could prove that alleged Freemason, District Judge Paul Ayers of Bedford County Court, 3, St Paul's Square, Bedford, MK40 1SQ, the Senior Vice President of the Association of Her Majesty's District Judges is not a functional semi-illiterate and an incompetent racist liar, and if he could prove that GDC-Witness, Freemason, Brother, Richard William Hill did not fabricate reports and unrelentingly told lies under oath, it should confirm the belief of billions of people in our world, Charitable Antichrist Freemasonry Quasi-Religion (Mediocre Mafia/New Pharisees), and all other motley assemblies of FAITHS and RELIGIONS under the common umbrella of the Defender of the FAITH and the Governor of the Church of England are not intellectually flawed Satanic Mumbo Jumbo, and it will concomitantly confirm that reasoning and vision have finite boundaries. If reasoning and vision have finite boundaries, He must have lied, in the Council, before Jews, when He disclosed pictures His unbounded (infinite) mind painted, and He must have also lied when He audaciously stated:

The first quality that is needed is audacity." Churchill

If the fellow told the truth before the Jews, in the Council, we are FORKED, as His Knights attack Kings and Queens simultaneously and only the Queens can move, and

458

everything that is not aligned with John 14:6, is travelling in the wrong direction and heading straight for the rocks.

"It does no harm to throw the occasional man overboard, but it does not do much good if you are steering full speed ahead for the rocks." Lord Gilmour of Craigmillar

Then, there, Members of the Charitable Antichrist Racist Freemasonry Quasi-religion (Mediocre Mafia/New Pharisees) who oversee the administration of English law seem to believe that genetic mix does not have an overriding effect, and technology can make an adult with the basic skills of a child useful. So, the closeted racist white bastards issued school dropouts and racist thugs with uniforms, with several attached gadgets, to compensate for hereditary intellectual impotence.

RE: METROPOLITAN POLICE: UNDISCLOSED ALLEGED HARASSMENT.

Mon, 25 Sep 2017 7:32
(Kieran.Dempsey@met.pnn.police.uk)To:you Details
Sir,

Thank you for your expeditious response.

I can in fact confirm it was myself who called you on 21/09/2017 in regards to the content of the letter you reference below.

as explained in such letter, an allegation has been made against you.

As such, you will need to attend ILFORD POLICE STATION where you may give your version of events by means of taped interview, where all evidence will be put to you in an interview inline with the Police and Criminal Evidence Act 1984.

In interview, with the prescience of a solicitor, you are entitled to give your version of events via a prepared statement, should you decide that this is the appropriate response to questioning.

Please advise of which dates you would be able to attend for interview.

Please do not hesitate to contact myself should you have any further questions.

Sincerely,

PC Kieran Dempsey

ERT A

Ilford Police Station

EA BOCU

Brainless nonsense!

Immortal stupidity!

The yield of the educational system of one of the richest Nations on earth: The fantastic affluence was preceded by SLAVERY.

AN IMBECILE: AN ADULT WITH THE BASIC SKILLS OF A CHILD.

Had PC Kieran Dempsey been exposed to the educational system of one of the poorest Nations on earth, he might not be able to read properly.

PERCEPTION IS GRANDER THAN REALITY.

PC Kieran Dempsey immortalised what he might have heard his own mother and father, and Ms Cressida Dick, speak, which Ms Cressida Dick must have authorised.

They want superiority, their brainless and baseless birth right; they don't want Freedom of Expression because they don't want their mentally very gentle children to know that they are excessively stupid.

They want Apartheid by stealth.

Based on very proximate observations and direct experiences, the natural instinct of the white privileged dullard is Apartheid by stealth.

Based on available evidence, Mr Robert Kingston, Director Dobern Property Limited unrelentingly lied under implied oath (on record) – Habakkuk.

Facts are sacred.

"The truth allows no choice." Dr Samuel Johnson

New Herod, Matthew 2:16: They lied to their mentally gentle children that they are geniuses, and they kill all those who know that they are brainless racist bastards, albeit hands-off.

NEW HEROD: Anything that they can't control, they destroy.

The Lunatic Jew removed John's head only because he spoke – Matthew 14.

He was lynched like Gadhafi and crucified only because He spoke; He disclosed pictures His infinite mind painted.

BEDFORD, ENGLAND: Based on available evidence, District Judge Paul Ayers of Bedford County Court, Shire Hall, 3 St Paul's Square, Bedford MK40 1SQ, the Senior Vice President of the Association of Her Majesty's District Judges, implied that like his own mother and father, the mother and father of Ms Cressida Dick and PC Kieran Dempsey did not have very, very strong views about education.

Why should the white mother and father of District Judge Paul Ayers of Bedford County Court, Shire Hall, 3 St Paul's Square, Bedford MK40 1SQ, the Senior Vice President of the Association of Her Majesty's District Judges need very, very strong views about education if there is irrefutable evidence that the white ancestors of his white mother and father were THIEVES and owners of stolen children of defenceless poor people (Meghan Markle's ancestors) – Habakkuk?

"Sometimes people do not want to heat the truth because they don't want their illusions destroyed." Friedrich Nietzsche

CHAPTER EIGHTEEN:

Boris Johnson: Why is England not a scam?

"When one is dirty, one is black whether one is thinking of physical dirtiness or of moral dirtiness …………The black man is the equivalent of a sin." Frantz Fanon

WHITE PRIVILEGE: Everything is blindly and baselessly assumed in favour of the indisputably superior skin colour that the wearer neither made nor chose.

They are not the only creation of Almighty God, and they are not immortal, and their indisputably superior skin colour is not the only wonder of our world.

Based on available evidence, several centuries of barbarously racist European Commerce in stolen Africans was imposed with mercilessly sadistic, overwhelming, and very, very disproportionate extreme violence - Habakkuk.

The white man was the devil.

To survive in Great Britain, especially if you are a mere Negro, members of the Charitable Antichrist Racist Freemasonry Quasi-Religion (Mediocre Mafia/New Pharisees) must love you, and you must love them, as they oversee the administration of English Law, and they can do and undo.

WOLLASTON, ENGLAND: GDC-Witness, Ms Rachael Bishop, Senior NHS Nurse, unrelentingly lied under oath.

A RACIST CROOKED WHITE COUGAR. A DISHONEST WHITE WOMAN.

Based on available evidence, the ancestors of GDC-Witness, Ms Rachael Bishop, Senior NHS Nurse were liars too; they were THIEVES and owners of stolen children of defenceless poor people (Meghan Markle's ancestors) – Habakkuk.

When their people commit racist crimes against our people, racist bastards who oversee the administration of English Law criminally bury racial hatred – Habakkuk 1:4; John 8:44; John 10:10.

Only stupid Negroes do not know that whites measure whites with a very different yardstick, and only stupider

Negroes expect demons to cast out demons – Matthew 12:27.

Only a white person could openly destroy the life of a Negro by kneeling on his neck: Derek Chauvin killed George Floyd, and without video evidence, Members of the very, very Charitable Antichrist Racist Freemasonry Quasi-Religion (Mediocre Mafia/ New Pharisees) who oversee the administration of the law might've buried the TRUTH.

"Lies are told all the time." Sir Michael Havers

"There is in Scotland a diffusion of learning, a certain portion of it widely and thinly spread. A merchant has as much learning as one of their clergies." Dr Samuel Johnson

Charitable Antichrist Racist Freemasons (Scottish Rite) teach their members secret voodoo-handshake, not grammar, the former is easier to master.

Dr George Rothnie (Scottish George), Deputy Postgraduate Dean, Oxford: A brainless Scotsman; a racist descendant of white thieves and owners of stolen children of defenceless poor people - Habakkuk.

Dr George Rothnie (Scottish George), Deputy Postgraduate Dean, Oxford is the product of the educational system of one the richest nations on earth.

Had Edinburgh University Educated Dr George Rothnie (Scottish George), Deputy Postgraduate Dean, been exposed to the educational system of one of the poorest nations on earth, he might not be able to read properly.

Our Edinburgh University Educated Prime Minister, the Scholar from Fife, couldn't spell, in a Country of the blind, the partially sighted is the guard and guide.

Why should the father and mother Dr George Rothnie (Scottish George), Deputy Postgraduate Dean, Oxford and our Edinburgh University Educated Prime Minister, the Scholar from Fife, need very, very strong views about education if their Christ granted talents are only good enough for functional semi-illiteracy—Proverbs 17:16?

Based on available evidence, His Honour Judge Perusko studied Law at Poly (Lower Class Alternative Education)—Proverbs 17:16.

Why should one's father and mother need very, very strong views about education if one's Christ granted talent is only good enough for second rate alternative poly-education—Proverbs 17:16.

"Mr Bamgbelu clearly has very, very strong views about education and I understand those views are based upon the fact that he is a successful dentist here in Bedford which he attributes to the fact that his parents cared for him and his education when he was young. They ensured that he had a proper fee paying education ...." District Judge Paul Ayers of Bedford County Court, Shire Hall, 3 St Paul's

Square, Bedford MK40 1SQ, the Senior Vice President of the Association of Her Majesty's District Judges—proofed and approved Judgement.

Brainless nonsense!

Majestic appointee.

"There is no sin except stupidity." Wilde

When innate racial hatred (hereditary) copulates with unmanageable sadism and very ugly ENVY, insanity is their offspring.

"Dirty Nigger! …. Mama, look, a Negro!" Frantz Fanon.

Financial disclosure in a divorce: 'How can a mere Nigger have what I do not have?'

"The Negro is just a child." Frantz Fanon.

OYINBO OLE: A STRAIGHT-FACED DESCENDANT OF ULTRA-RIGHTEOUS PROFESSIONAL THIEVES AND OWNERS OF STOLEN CHILDREN OF DEFENCELESS POOR PEOPLE (MEGHAN MARKLE'S ANCESTORS)—HABAKKUK.

Indiscreet envy.

Envy is a thief.

"Envy is weak." Yul Brynner.

Brainless sarcasm.

It's clearly deducible that white father and mother of District Judge Paul Ayers of Bedford County Court, Shire Hall, 3 St Paul's Square, Bedford MK40 1SQ, our Senior Vice President of the Association of Her Majesty's District Judges did not have very, very strong views about education, and they did not care, had they, their functional semi-illiterate white son would not have settled for daily dialogues with confused people, in a District Court in Bedford, and if he selflessly did, he would not have approved and immortalised excessive stupidity at 16, and he would be a properly educated lawyer, privately educated Anthony Julius, Anthony Blair, Geoff Hoon, and Rabinder Singh's Class, and he might practice proper law in STRAND.

"Someone must be trusted. Let it be the Judges." Lord Denning.

An ignorant racist white dipstick; a righteous descendant of ultra-righteous, industrial-scale, very hardened PROFESSIONAL THIEVES, and owners of stolen children of defenceless poor people (Meghan Markle's ancestors)—Habakkuk.

"Sometimes people don't want to hear the truth because they don't want their illusions destroyed." Friedrich Nietzsche.

Why should the father and mother of Bedford's District Judge Paul Ayers, the Senior Vice President of the

470

Association of Her Majesty's District Judges, need very, very strong views about education if, for several continuous centuries, their ancestors were extremely nasty racists, murderers, THIEVES and owners of stolen children of defenceless poor people (Meghan Markle's ancestors)— Habakkuk.

Facts are sacred.

"The truth allows no choice." Dr Samuel Johnson

BEDFORD, ENGLAND: District Judge Paul Ayers of Bedford County Court, which part of Bedford County Court, Shire Hall, 3 St Paul's Square, Bedford MK40 1SQ was not stolen, or which part it did the people of Bedford buy, or which part preceded the barbarously racist commerce in millions of stolen children of defenceless poor people: The building and its chattels?

"Those who know the least obey the best." George Farquhar

Facts are sacred.

"The truth allows no choice." Dr Samuel Johnson.

Members of the Charitable Antichrist Racist Freemasonry Quasi-Religion (Mediocre Mafia/ New Pharisees) love the superiority that is associated with the irrefutably superior skin colour, which they neither made nor chose, and which is their baseless and brainless birth right; they don't love Freedom of Expression because they don't want their mentally very gentle children (deductible/OECD/Dr Richard Dawkins) to know that they are excessively stupid.

The closeted racist bastards love only Apartheid by stealth.

Which part of Bedfordshire Masonic Temple to Baal, the Keep, Bedford Road, Kempston, MK42, was not stolen, or which part of it did the transparent virtue and industry of Freemasons yield, or which part of the magnificent building preceded slavery: The building or its chattels?

Ignorance is bliss.

OYINBO OLE: THIEVES – HABAKKUK.

They want us to see the world from their perspective.

They want to ban the expression of truths accessible in the public domain.

Ignorance is bliss.

The Grand Masonic Temple to Baal, (Mother Temple), 60 Great Queen St, London WC2B 5AZ, was built in the early 18th century at a height of the barbarously racist traffic in millions of stolen children of defenceless poor African (Black African ancestors of Meghan Markle and her white children) – Habakkuk.

If Lala's husband, England's Class Biology Genius, Dr Clinton Richard Dawkins, and all the Freemasons at Bedfordshire Masonic Temple to Baal, the Keep, Bedford Road, Kempston, MK42, and all the Master Builders

472

(Stonemasons) at the Grand Masonic Temple to Baal (Mother Temple), 60 Great Queen St, London WC2B 5AZ, and Sir, Mr Justice Haddon-Cave, QC, KBE, and the British Premier, The Right Honourable Boris Johnson, could prove that British Soldier – Territorial Defence, GDC -Witness, Stephanie Twiddle (TD) did not unrelentingly tell lies under oath, and if Sir, Mr Justice Haddon-Cave, QC, KBE, could prove that he did not know, and he ought not to know that British Soldier – Territorial Defence, GDC -Witness, Stephanie Twiddle (TD) criminally unrelentingly lied under oath (Negrophobic Perjury/ Persecutory Negrophobia), it should confirm the belief of billions of people in our world, Charitable Antichrist Freemasonry Quasi-Religion (Mediocre Mafia/New Pharisees), and all other motley assemblies of FAITHS and RELIGIONS under the common umbrella of the Defender of the FAITH and the Governor of the Church of England are not intellectually flawed Satanic Mumbo Jumbo, and it will concomitantly confirm that reasoning and vision have finite boundaries. If reasoning and vision have finite boundaries, He must have lied, in the Council, before Jews, when He disclosed pictures His unbounded (infinite) mind painted, and He must have also lied when He audaciously stated:

The first quality that is needed is audacity." Churchill

If the fellow told the truth before the Jews, in the Council, we are FORKED, as His Knights attack Kings and Queens simultaneously and only the Queens can move, and everything that is not aligned with John 14:6, is travelling in the wrong direction and heading straight for the rocks.

473

"It does no harm to throw the occasional man overboard, but it does not do much good if you are steering full speed ahead for the rocks." Lord Gilmour of Craigmillar.

Boris Johnson, why is England not a scam?

Based on available evidence, the administration of English Law, almost in its entirety, is based on mediocrity and mendacity.

What they want is intellectual superiority that is associated with the indisputably superior skin colour that they neither made nor chose.

Their ancestors were very, very hardened racists, murderers, and THIEVES - Habakkuk: Then, they used guns to steal almost everything He gave to others: Movable and immovable.

"All have taken what had other owners and all have had recourse to arms rather than quit the prey on which they were fastened." Dr Samuel Johnson

WHITE PRIVILEGE: Everything is assumed in favour of the irrefutably superior skin colour that the wearer neither made nor chose.

District Judge Paul Ayers of Bedford County Court, 3 St Paul Square, Bedford MK40 1SQ: Based on available evidence, an intellectually impotent white nonentity; a racist descendant of very, very hardened professional THIEVES, racists, murderers, and owners of stolen human beings, children of defenceless poor people (Black African ancestors of Meghan Markle and her white children) - Habakkuk

An irrefutably functional semi-illiterate white District Judge of Empire of stolen affluence - Habakkuk.

BEDFORD, ENGLAND: Based on available evidence, GDC-Witness, Freemason, Brother, Richard William Hill fabricated reports and unrelentingly lied under oath – Habakkuk 1:4; John 8:44; John 10:10.

A CLOSETED RACIST CROOK. A WHITE MAN. A DISHONEST RACIST.

When their people commit racist crimes against our people, the closeted racist bastards who oversee the administration of English Law (Freemasons) criminally bury racial hatred. Demons can't cast out demons – Matthew 12:27.

Facts are sacred, they cannot be overstated.

They are scared: They fear the untamed mind of the self-educated African more than Putin's poisons.

OXFORD, ENGLAND: Based on available evidence, GDC-Witness, British Soldier – Territorial Defence, unrelentingly lied under oath – Habakkuk 1:4; John 8:44; John 10:10.

A CLOSETED RACIST CROOKED COUGAR. A DISHONEST WHITE WOMAN.

BEDFORD, ENGLAND: District Judge Paul Ayers, Senior Vice President of the Association of Her Majesty's District Judges approved and immortalised what is white mother and father spoke, which his supervisors in LUTON authorised. Poly-educated incontrovertibly functional semi-illiterate innately racist (hereditary) white rubbish was granted the platform to display irreversible familial prejudice.

"This hopefully ensures that a child has stability, love and affection and the parents working together to ensure that he has the best opportunity of developing academically and emotional." District Judge Paul Ayers, Senior Vice President of the Association of Her Majesty's District Judges – proofed and approved Judgement

PURIFIED ROT!

A properly proofed and approved Judgement by a properly educated white Judge should pass through at least four separate filters: The transcript writers, the proof-readers, the Court Clerks, and the Judges.

"Gentlemen, you are now about to embark on a course of studies which will occupy you for two years. Together, they form a noble adventure. But I would like to remind you of an important point. Nothing that you will learn in the course of your studies will be of the slightest possible use to you in after life, save only this, that if you work hard and intelligently you should be able to detect when a man is talking rot, and that, in my view, is the main, if not the sole, purpose of education." John Alexander Smith, Oxford University Professor of MORAL PHILOSOPHY.

Based on very proximate observations, all semi-illiterate white Judges are racists.

NIGERIA: SHELL'S DOCILE CASH COW.

THE VERY HIGHLY LUXURIANT SOIL OF NORWICH YIELDS ONLY FOOD. THERE ARE NO OIL WELLS OR GAS FIELDS IN BISHOP'S STORTFORD, CECIL RHODES (1853 -1902) WAS A THIEF.

"We shall deal with the racist bastards when we get out of prison." Comrade Robert Mugabe (1924 - 2019).

Children with huge oil wells near their huts eat only 1.5/day in NIGERIA; a closeted racist functional semi-illiterate former debt-collector solicitor in Norwich who white mother and father have never seen crude oil, and whose white ancestors, including John Bunyan (1628 – 1688) were fed like battery hens with the yields of stolen children of defenceless Africans (Meghan Markle's ancestors) is our District Judge in Bedford.

OYINBO OLE: RIGHTEOUS DESCENDANTS OF ULTRA-RIGHTEOUS THIEVES - HABAKKUK.

CREEPING DPRK.

Then, racist bastards carried and sold millions of stolen children (Meghan Markle's ancestors); now, they carry natural sources.

SUBSTITUTION IS FRAUDULENT EMANCIPATION.

"Moderation is a virtue only among those who are thought to have found alternatives." Henry Kissinger.

Based on available evidence, Dr Richard Dawkins and OECD implied that all the children of District Judge Paul Ayers of Bedford County Court, 3, St Paul's Square, Bedford, MK401 SQ, should be duller than their irrefutably functional semi-illiterate father.

"Natural selection will not remove ignorance from future generations." Dr Richard Dawkins

England's young people are near the bottom of the global league table for basic skills. OECD finds 16- to 24-year-olds have literacy and numeracy levels no better than those of their grandparents' generation

England is the only country in the developed world where the generation approaching retirement is more literate and numerate than the youngest adults, according to the first skills survey by the Organisation for Economic Co-operation and Development.

In a stark assessment of the success and failure of the 720-million-strong adult workforce across the wealthier economies, the economic thinktank warns that in England, adults aged 55 to 65 perform better than 16- to 24-year-olds at foundation levels of literacy and numeracy. The survey did not include people from Scotland or Wales.

The OECD study also finds that a quarter of adults in England have the maths skills of a 10-year-old. About 8.5 million adults, 24.1% of the population, have such basic levels of numeracy that they can manage only one-step tasks in arithmetic, sorting numbers or reading graphs. This is worse than the average in the developed world, where an average of 19% of people were found to have a similarly poor skill base.

The pattern is the same almost everywhere.

They love the enormous advantage that come with the irrefutably superior skin colour that they neither made nor chose, but they don't love Freedom of Expression because they don't want their mentally very gentle children to know that they are excessively stupid closeted racist bastards.

Almost everything is art, incompetent art that incompetently imitates life.

"A complaints such as Mrs Bishop's could trigger an enquiry." Stephen Henderson, LLM, Head at MDDUS, 1 Pemberton Row, London EC4A 3BG, Holborn, London.

Brainless nonsense!

"I don't want to talk grammar. I want to talk like a lady."
George Bernard Shaw

A CLOSETED RACIST CROOKED DUNCE.

Since 1984, apart from the FROTH he bought in Cardiff in 2005, the only postgraduate examinations Stephen Henderson, LLM, BDS, Head at MDDUS, didn't FAIL, are those he didn't do.

Based on available evidence, District Judge Paul Ayers of Bedford County Court, 3 St Paul's Square MK40, 3 1SQ, implied that like his own mother and father, the mother and father of Stephen Henderson, LLM, Head at MDDUS, 1 Pemberton Row, London EC4A 3BG did not have very, very strong views about education.

WOLLASTON, ENGLAND: Based on available evidence, GDC-Witness, Ms Rachael Bishop, Senior NHS Nurse, unrelentingly lied under oath – Habakkuk 1:4; John 8:44; John 10:10.

A RACIST CROOKED COUGAR. A DISHONEST WHITE WOMAN.

One of the most important tasks of Closeted Racist White Supremacist Freemason Judges was to bury racial hatred.

They hate us, with merciless sadistic passion, and we know.

NORTHAMPTON, ENGLAND: GDC, Geraint Evans, Rowtree Dental Care, Postgraduate Tutor, Oxford, unrelentingly lied under implied oath – Habakkuk

A WHITE MAN. A DISHONEST RACIST.

A bastardised, unashamedly mediocre, indiscreetly dishonest, potently weaponised, vindictive, and institutionally racist legal system that is overseen by the members of the Charitable Antichrist Racist Freemasonry Quasi-Religion (Mediocre Mafia/New Pharisees) - Habakkuk 1:4; John 8:44; John 10:10.

"To deny or belittle this good is, in this dangerous century when the resources and pretensions of power continue to enlarge, a desperate error of intellectual abstraction. More than this, it is a self-fulfilling error, which encourages us to give up the struggle against bad laws and class bound procedures and to disarm ourselves before power. It is to throw away a whole inheritance of struggle about the law and within the forms of law, whose continuity can never be fractured without bringing men and women into immediate danger." - E. P Thompson

Facts are sacred, they cannot be overstated

BORIS JOHNSON: Based on available evidence, England is a scam.

Members of the Charitable Antichrist Racist Freemasonry Quasi-Religion (Mediocre Mafia) who oversee the administration of English Law operate on the molecular level, and they are oblivious to the existence of atoms.

"The supreme vice is shallowness." Wilde

Members of the Charitable Antichrist Racist Freemasonry Quasi-Religion (Mediocre Mafia) who oversee the administration of English Law: Half-educated school dropouts and their superiors who have informal access to some very powerful white Judges. They do loads of vulgar Pharisees' Charitable works, and they use very expensive aprons to decorate the temples of their powerless and useless fertility tools, and they lie that they don't lie – Psalm 144.

Modern Freemasonry emerged in the early 18th century. They did charitable works with stolen money, yields of stolen lives. They did not do a lot of charitable works before SLAVERY.

Before SLAVERY, what?

Which part of Bedfordshire Masonic Temple to Baal, the Keep, Bedford Road, Kempston, MK42, was not stolen, or which part of it did transparent virtue yield, or which part of it preceded SLAVERY?

OYINBO OLE: THIEVES – HABAKKUK

"Those who know the least obey the best." George Farquhar

He told the rich Jew to sell the yield of transparent virtue, give the proceeds to the poor, and follow him – Matthew 19:21.

He tells Freemasons to return the yield of millions of stolen and destroyed children of defenceless poor people (Meghan Markle's ancestors) – Habakkuk.

Righteousness without equitable reparation is continuing racist fraud - Habakkuk.

Like Herod, Kim, Putin, Saddam Hussein, babies, and MBS, the closeted white supremacist thugs (FREEMASONS) expect everyone to love them and say and/or print only what they want to hear.

C of E raises serious concerns about Christian Freemasons
https://www.theguardian.com › uk-news › feb › c-of-e-...

8 Feb 2018 — Church of England warning that secret society may not be compatible with Christianity echoes concerns from 1987.

Then, there, white Judges, nearly all, were Freemasons; some of them were thicker than a gross of planks – Habakkuk 1:4; John 8:44; John 10:10.

GDC: A white man, Richard Hill fabricated reports and unrelentingly lied under oath.

GDC: A white man, Kevin Atkinson (NHS) unrelentingly lied under oath

GDC: A white man, Jonathan Martin unrelentingly lied on record

GDC: A white woman, Helen Falcon (MBE) unrelentingly lied on record

GDC: A white man, George Rothnie (NHS) unrelentingly lied on record

GDC: A white woman, Stephanie Twiddle (NHS) unrelentingly lied under oath

GDC: A white woman, Sue Gregory (OBE) unrelentingly lied on record

GDC: A white woman, Rachael Bishop (NHS) unrelentingly lied under oath

GDC: A white man, Geraint Evans (NHS) unrelentingly lied on record

They were all white, including the Judges.

They deceive imbeciles that the administration of their law is transparent, equal, colour-blind, and exact, when in actual fact theirs is a properly organised racist crime syndicate that dishonestly impersonates impartial administration of the law.

"The highest reach of injustice is to be deemed just when you are not." Plato

The administration of their law is absolutely incompatible with Christian belief - .

The affluence they brag about was STOLEN. Before SLAVERY, what?

To survive under Antichrist Racist Freemasonry Rule, we must bow to them or play closeted racist bastards

FREEMASONS' LEVERAGE: INCOMPETENT LIES GUARDED BY ILLEGAL PARALLEL POWER.

The white man is the devil - Columbia University
https://ccnmtl.columbia.edu › mmt › mxp › concepts

Referring to Whites as "devils" originates with the teachings of Master W.D. Fard and the legend of Yakub. Fard taught Elijah Muhammad who preached the ...

A bastardised, indiscreetly dishonest, unashamedly mediocre, vindictive, potently weaponised, and institutionally racist legal system that is overseen by members of the Charitable Antichrist Closeted Racist Freemasonry Quasi-Religion (Mediocre Mafia/New Pharisees) – Habakkuk 1:4; John 8:44; John 10:10

OYINBO OLE: THIEVES - HABAKKUK

"To deny or belittle this good is, in this dangerous century when the resources and pretensions of power continue to enlarge, a desperate error of intellectual abstraction. More than this, it is a self-fulfilling error, which encourages us to give up the struggle against bad laws and class bound procedures and to disarm ourselves before power. It is to throw away a whole inheritance of struggle about the law and within the forms of law, whose continuity can never be fractured without bringing men and women into immediate danger." - E. P Thompson.

BORIS JOHNSON: Freemasons are tolerant to Christians whose belief aligns with 'FAITHS' (dissenters of His exceptionalism). The closeted white supremacist bastards who use very expensive aprons

BORIS JOHNSON: Our position is absolutely incompatible with theirs (Dissenters of John 14:6/Defenders of FAITHS) because John 14:6 is non-negotiable.

"The Good Samaritan had money." Mrs Margaret Thatcher (1925 – 2013).

Mrs Margaret Thatcher implied that the Good Samaritan, like Mother Teresa, did charitable works with yields of transparent virtue.

DELUDED PAPER TIGERS: Baseless and brainless superiority that is based on the irrefutably superior skin colour that they neither made nor chose is their birth right. Their hairs stand on end when they are challenged by our people; we and our type are the one's racist bastards will beat up without the support of the YANKS.

"Ethical foreign policy." Robin Cook (1946 – 2005).

If Members of the Charitable Antichrist Racist Freemasonry Quasi-religion are as ethical and as brave as they imply, they should forcibly evict Putin from Crimea; just as Saddam Hussein forcibly annexed Kuwait, he forcibly stole Crimea.

Prior to Covid-19, what was in Norwich for irrefutably functional semi-illiterate Freemason Solicitors to do?

The only evidence of thehis purportedly higher IQ of District Judge Paul Ayers of Bedford County Court, 3 St Paul's Square, MK40 1SQ, the Senior Vice President of the Association of Her Majesty's District Judges, is the stolen affluence that his white ancestors crossed the English Channels, without luggage or decent shoes to latch onto

JUDICIAL DIVERSITY: ACCELERATING CHANGE. "The near absence of women and Black, Asian and minority ethnic judges in the senior judiciary, is no longer tolerable. It undermines the democratic legitimacy of our legal system; it demonstrates a denial of fair and equal opportunities to members of underrepresented groups, and the diversity deficit weakens the quality of justice." Sir Geoffrey Bindman, QC, and Karon Monaghan, QC.

DIVERSE MEDIOCRITY IS AKIN TO RAKING MUCK.

CHAPTER NINETEEN:

BORIS JOHNSON: Why is England not a scam?

"Mr Bamgbelu clearly has very, very strong views about education and I understand those views are based upon the fact that he is a successful dentist here in Bedford which he attributes to the fact that his parents cared for him and his education when he was young. They ensured that he had a proper fee paying education…….." District Judge Paul Ayers of Shire Hall, 3 St Paul's Square, Bedford MK40 1SQ, the Senior Vice President of the Association of Her Majesty's District Judges—proofed and approved Judgement.

Brainless nonsense!

AN IMBECILE: AN ADULT WITH THE BASIC
SKILLS OF A CHILD.

An incontrovertibly functional semi-illiterate former, mere,
debt-collector Solicitor in Norwich (coastal dole) treats the
Judiciary as if it were his father's private business. Poly-
educated functional semi-illiterate white trash rides a very,
very powerful tiger, deluded, he thinks he's it, dismounted,
he'd instantly revert to PURIFIED NOTHING (a mere
former debt-collector Solicitor in Norwich.

Irrefutably superior skin colour, stolen trust fund, and what
else?

OYINBO OLE: IGNORANT DESCENDANTS OF
ULTRA-RIGHTEOUS THIEVES AND OWNERS OF
STOLEN CHILDREN OF DEFENCELESS POOR
PEOPLE – HABAKKUK.

"There is no sin except stupidity." Wilde

Irrefutably superior skin colour that the wearer neither
made nor chose, stolen Trust Fund, and what else?

Before SLAVERY, what?

When innate racial hatred (hereditary) and unmanageable
envy copulate, insanity is their offspring.

Financial disclosure in a divorce: 'How can a mere Negro
have what I do not have?'

"Someone must be trusted. Let it be the Judges." Lord Denning (1899- 1999).

White Judges are human beings: Some human beings are institutionally racist.

BEDFORD, ENGLAND: Why should the white father and mother of District Judge Paul Ayers of Bedford County Court, of Bedford County Court, Shire Hall, 3 St Paul's Square, Bedford MK40 1SQ, need very, very strong views about education if there's irrefutable evidence that for several continuous centuries the white ancestors of his white grandparents were the greediest economic cannibals and the evilest racist terrorists the world will ever know - Habakkuk?

OYINBO OLE: AN IGNORANT DESCENDANT OF THIEVES AND OWNERS OF STOLEN CHILDREN OF DEFENCELESS POOR PEOPLE (MEGHAN MARKLE'S) – HABAKKUK.

Facts are sacred, and they can't be overstated.

BEDFORD, ENGLAND: District Judge Paul Ayers of Bedford County Court, 3 St Paul's Square MK 40 1SQ, the Senior Vice President of the Association of Her Majesty's District Judges, based on available evidence, you are LEECH; your ancestors were THIEVES. It is absolutely impossible for your talent and the yield of your land to sustain your standard of living; you are being 'carried' by others.

Did Putin poison Bob Dudley; he sits on the largest gas reserve in the world?

OYINBO OLE: THIEVES – HABAKKUK.

BEDFORD, ENGLAND: District Judge Paul Ayers of Bedford County Court, 3 St Paul's Square MK 40 1SQ, the Senior Vice President of the Association of Her Majesty's District Judges, based on available evidence, our own Money, NIGERIA (oil/gas) is by far more relevant to the economic survival of all your children than Norwich (coastal dole). You will not defend yourself on a level playing field. Had you not been a Judge, I wouldn't know you, and would certainly not voluntarily buy anything from a functional semi-illiterate genetic Eastern European with camouflage English names.

BEDFORD, ENGLAND: District Judge Paul Ayers of Bedford County Court, 3 St Paul's Square MK 40 1SQ, the Senior Vice President of the Association of Her Majesty's District Judges, the affluence that you implicitly brag about did not evolve, and your ancestors met it here. Then, affluence was actively and deliberately stolen with guns during several centuries of the greediest economic cannibalism and the evilest racist terrorism the world will ever know – Habakkuk. You are worthy only because England is rich, and your skin colour is irrefutably superior; apart from those you are PURIFIED NOTHING.

A GENETIC ALIEN WITH CAMOUFLAGE ENGLISH NAMES: A closeted racist descendant of undocumented refugees from the mainland (Eastern Europe) impersonates extinct aboriginal Britons.

In 55BC, the Romans, essentially their auxiliaries and legionnaires, slaughtered all those they couldn't tame and/or those who resisted armed robbery, of the remainder, Romans forcibly acquired the pretty ones, and they became sex-slaves, and they sold most of the ugly ones, in Slave Markets, in Rome, and they genetically modified the rest.

"Affluence is not a birth right." David Cameron

Based on very proximate observations and direct experiences, White Supremacist Freemason Judges are the most potent source of racial intolerance in Great Britain.

The scramble to conceal RACIAL HATRED is the evidence of their guilt.

"It was in 1066 that William the Conqueror occupied Britain, stole our land and gained control by granting it to his Norman friends, thus creating the feudal system we have not yet fully occupied." The Right Honourable Tony Benn (1925 – 2014)

William the Conqueror stole from others what others stole from others.

Genetically pure aboriginal Britons are extinct.

Saxe-Coburg and Gotha family crossed the English Channels.

"Sometimes people don't want to hear the truth because they don't want their illusions destroyed." Friedrich Nietzsche

Then, there, white Judges, nearly all, were Freemasons; some of them were thicker than a gross of planks.

NEW HEROD, MATTHEW 2:16: The deceive their children that they are geniuses, and they kill all those who know that they are brainless racist bastards.

"You will bow. You can't beat the system." Kemi Daramola

Esu!

Luciferians speak.

Imported devil.

A deliberate and properly calculated glorified prostitute and a THIEF.

Like her mother, she liked what her mother couldn't afford (idi ni won nta; glorified prostitutes).

I shan't. I know who will – Romans 11; 1 John 4:4

She prays to Christ, and regularly pays very handsome tithe (quasi-protection money) at a Bedford Church, more than £100, 000 since she joined Brickhill Baptist Church in Bedford, and members of the Charitable Antichrist Racist

Freemasonry Quasi-Religion (Mediocre Mafia/New Pharisees) Freemasons in Kempston answers her prayers.

A BLATANTLY FRAUDULENT ARRANGEMENT.

God is a business, a very good business, and God is good.

OYINBO OLE: RIGHTEOUS DESCENDANTS OF ULTRA-RIGHTEOUS THIEVES – HABAKKUK.

An ultra-righteous Christian and an imitation upper class English woman; a very prominent member of Brickhill Baptist Church in Bedford.

A former parasite who wore Christianity as a cloak of deceit and found her host: Ekiti ole. Only God knows her better than I do.

"A woman is the only hunter who uses herself for bait." Confucius

"Masonry ought forever to be abolished. It is wrong - essentially wrong - a seed of evil which can never produce any good." President John Quincy Adams (1767 – 1848).

"You should play them like chess." Resh Diu, dentist.

Playing closeted racist bastards who use very expensive aprons to decorate the temples of their powerless and useless fertility tools, like chess, is a variant of bowing to the closeted white supremacist thugs.

-----Original Message-----
From: resh diu <rdiu@me.com>
To: adeolacole <adeolacole@aol.com>
Sent: Fri, 11 Apr 2014 9:28
Subject: Re:

It's sad Ola

I kept telling you to play the game of chess rather than fight it

You take care

If you wish to dispose of 24 park road let me know

Regards

Resh
Dr Resh Diu BDS
www.oradi.co.uk

Defenders of FAITHS: Dissenters of John 14:6.

Based on available evidence, His Honour Judge Perusko studied law at Poly (Lower Class alternative education) – Proverbs 17:16.

LUTON, ENGLAND: Why should one's white mother and father need very, very strong views about education if one's Christ granted talent is only good enough for Second Rate Alternative Poly-education – Proverbs 17:16.

The Freemasons who oversee the administration of English Law do not believe in the exceptionalism of Christ (John 14:6), so they are not deterred by His Justice, John 5:22; they are free to believe and disbelieve whatever they like, but they are bound by equity to treat, we, their absolutely irreconcilable RELIGIOUS ENEMIES, John 14:6 Christians, equally under the administration of the law, which they overwhelmingly oversee.

OYINBO OLE: RIGHTEOUS DESCENDANTS OF ULTRA-RIGHTEOUS THIEVES – HABAKKUK.

"Freemasons and the Judicial Oath - The Supreme Court
https://www.supremecourt.uk › about › freemasons-and...

How many civil servants are freemasons??
The UK Supreme Court does not hold this
information. Freemasons swear an oath to lucifer who
do judges swear their ...

Freemasons - A secret society with powers over police ... -
iNews
https://inews.co.uk › news › uk › todays-freemasons-se..."
Internet

Google: Freemasonry intellectual flawed.

2 Mar 2018 — The society has told i that up to ten MPs and around 200 judges and policemen are paid up Masons. These pillars of the British establishment ...

CONFLICT OF INTEREST: There is a grossly unacceptable imbalance; our absolutely irreconcilable RELIGIOUS ENEMIES, members of the Charitable Antichrist Racist Freemasonry Quasi-religion (Mediocre Mafia/New Pharisees) oversee the administration of English Law,), and they CRIMINALLY CHEAT their irreconcilable religious enemies – John 14:6.

CORBY, ENGLAND: GDC-Witnesses, two, too many, racist Scots, George Rothnie and Kevin Atkinson, dentists, unrelentingly lied under oath or on record. Their Scottish ancestors were liars too, they were THIEVES and owners of stolen poor children of defenceless people.

A WHITE MAN. A DISHONEST RACIST

If members of the Charitable Antichrist Racist Freemasonry Quasi-Religion (Mediocre Mafia/New Pharisees) play with straight bats, they will lose all the time, as they see molecules, and we will show the closeted racist bastards who, vulgarly, use very expensive aprons to decorate the temples of their powerless and useless fertility tools, atoms, and uncover part of His face.

BEDFORD, ENGLAND: Based on available evidence, GDC-Expert Sue Gregory (OBE), Officer of the Most Excellent Order of our Empire, unrelentingly lied under implied oath-Habakkuk.

A RACIST CROOKED COUGAR.

BEDFORD, ENGLAND: District Judge Paul Ayers of Bedford County Court, of Bedford County Court, Shire Hall, 3 St Paul's Square, Bedford MK40 1SQ, based on available evidence, it is the absolute truth that your white ancestors were extremely nasty, opportunistic racist bastards, and THIEVES (Habakkuk). You are leech, a professionally packaged incontrovertibly functional semi-illiterate FROTH. You have enemies, and if you know what they truly feel, you will become tuned to reality. Based on available evidence, NIGERIA (oil/gas) is by far more relevant to the economic survival of your white father, your white mother, your white spouse, and all your white children than NORWICH (coastal dole).

OYINBO OLE: A righteous descendant of ultra-righteous THIEVES – Habakkuk.

TURF WAR: Racist descendants of aliens with camouflage English names oppress we the descendants of the robbed with the yields of the robbery.

Facts are sacred.

BEDFORD, ENGLAND: District Judge Paul Ayers of Bedford County Court, of Bedford County Court, Shire Hall, 3 St Paul's Square, Bedford MK40 1SQ, based on available evidence you are rich only because the descendants of the mercilessly slaughtered and robbed do not have the necessary overwhelming fire power needed to seriously demand equitable reparation, with interest, and extract it by overwhelming force, if need be.

"Affluence is not a birth right." David Cameron

Ignorance is bliss.

"Many Scots masters were considered among the most brutal, with life expectancy on their plantations averaging a mere four years. We worked them to death then simply imported more to keep the sugar and thus the money flowing. Unlike centuries of grief and murder, an apology cost nothing. So, what does Scotland have to say?" Herald Scotland: Ian Bell, Columnist, Sunday 28 April 2013.

OYINBO OLE: Ignorant descendants of extremely nasty racist murderers, THIEVES, and owners of stolen children of defenceless poor people.

"Those who know the least obey the best." George Farquhar

PERCEPTION IS GRANDER THAN REALITY.

BEDFORD, ENGLAND: District Judge Paul Ayers of Bedford County Court, 3, St Paul's Square, MK40 1SQ, the Senior Vice President of the Association of Her Majesty's District Judges, based on available evidence, it is absolutely impossible for your Christ granted talent to sustain your standard of living. Then, your white ancestors were sustained with the yields of stolen children of defenceless poor people (Meghan Markle's ancestors; now, our own Money, NIGERIA (oil and gas) is by far more relevant to the economic survival of all your white children than NORWICH (coastal dole) – Habakkuk

OYINBO OLE: A STRAIGHT-FACED DESCENDANT OF ULTRA-RIGHTEOUS THIEVES AND OWNERS OF STOLEN CHILDREN OF DEFENCELESS POOR PEOPLE (BLACK AFRICAN ANCESTORS OF MEGHAN MARKLE AND HER WHITE CHILDREN) – HABAKKUK.

BEDFORD, ENGLAND: Based on available evidence, District Judge Paul Ayers of Bedford County Court, Shire Hall, 3 St Paul's Square, Bedford MK40 1SQ, your white ancestors were extremely greedy economic cannibals, professional armed robbers, racist terrorists, drug dealers (opium merchants), THIEVES, and owners of stolen children of defenceless poor people (Meghan Markle's) – Habakkuk. If they didn't teach you all those at home (your white father and mother) and at school (all your white teachers), they lied to you.

CREEPING DPRK

Based on available evidence, white men, not all, seemingly guided and guarded by members of the Charitable Antichrist Racist Freemasonry Quasi-Religion (Mediocre Mafia/New Pharisees) are incompetent racist liars.

"A typical English man, usually violent and always dull." Wilde

BEDFORD, ENGLAND: Based on available evidence, GDC-Witness, Racist Freemason, White Man, Brother, Richard William Hill, England's Class Postgraduate Tutor, fabricated reports and unrelentingly lied under oath – Habakkuk.

A WHITE MAN. A DISHONEST RACIST.

NORTHAMPTON, ENGLAND: Based on available evidence, GDC-Witness, White Man, Welsh Racist Crook, Geraint Evans, England's Class Postgraduate Tutor, unrelentingly lied under implied oath – Habakkuk.

A WHITE MAN. A DISHONEST RACIST.

CORBY, ENGLAND: Based on available evidence, GDC-Witness, Freemason, White Man, Scottish Racist Crook, England's Class Deputy Postgraduate Dean, unrelentingly lied under implied oath – Habakkuk.

A WHITE MAN. A DISHONEST RACIST.

Based on very proximate observations and direct experiences, the white man is the devil.

******

"President Trump's administration packed Courts with mediocre white Judges." Kamala Harris.

They accurately foresaw that a functional semi-illiterate, mere, debt-collector Solicitor in Norwich (coastal dole), will become our top Judge, in Great Britain, they used, made in Birmingham, guns to loot and pillage Africa: Wherever the racist bastards mercilessly slaughtered, they dispossessed, and whenever the sadistic, economic cannibals robbed our people, they took possession; they were THIEVES, and they were guilty - Habakkuk.

OYINBO OLE: THIEVES – HABAKKUK.

"Find the truth and tell it." Harold Pinter

Ignorance is bliss.
"It is incumbent upon the court and all those professionals involved to conclude court proceedings as quickly as possible. This hopefully ensures that a child has stability, love and affection and the parents working together to ensure that he has the best opportunity of developing academically and emotional." District Judge Paul Ayers, Senior Vice President of the Association of Her Majesty's District Judges – proofed and approved Judgement

AN IMBECILE: AN ADULT WITH THE BASIC SKILLS OF A CHILD.

Our incontrovertibly functional semi-illiterate Freemason District Judge of our Empire of stolen affluence - Habakkuk.

A CLOSETED RACIST WHITE FOOL'S APPROVAL!

Based on available evidence, those who FAILED the A/Level could do Law in Great Britain. Which part of immortal mediocrity and confusion his great? Based on very, very proximate observations, only his irrefutably superior skin colour is good.

OYINBO ODE: AN IGNORANT RACIST DUNCE.

"Yes, Sir, it does *her* honour, but it would do nobody else honour. I have indeed, not read it all. But when I take up the end of a web, and find it packthread, I do not expect, by looking further, to find embroidery." Dr Samuel Johnson

The yield of a very, very elementary white mind; the spinal cord of the white man, albeit England's class Judge, seemed to be his highest centre.
Our Lords nominated and constructively appointed District Judge Paul Ayers, a closeted racist functional semi-illiterate former, mere, debt-collector Solicitor in NORWICH (coastal dole) as our District Judge.

"There is no sin except stupidity." Wilde.

PERCEPTION IS GRANDER THAN REALITY.

NIGERIA: SHELL'S DOCILE CASH COW: THE VERY, VERY HIGHLY LUXURIANT SOIL OF BEDFORDSHIRE YIELDS ONLY FOOD.

There are no oil wells or gas fields in Bishop's Stortford: Cecil Rhodes (1853 – 1902) was a thief.

"We shall deal with the racist bastards when we get out of prison." Comrade Robert Mugabe (1924 – 2019).

If the very, very highly luxuriant soil of Bedfordshire yields only food, as it does, and District Judge Paul Ayers of Bedford County Court, , the Senior Vice President of the Association of Her Majesty's District Judges, is irrefutably a white functional semi-illiterate, it is plainly deductible that his white ancestors must have been very, very hardened PROFESSIONAL THIEVES and owners of stolen human beings, millions of children of defenceless poor people (Black African ancestors of Meghan Markle and her white children) – Habakkuk.

"Time for Scots to say sorry for slavery
Herald Scotland:
Ian Bell, Columnist / Sunday 28 April 2013 / Opinion
Sunday 28 April 2013
According to the American founding father, the son of a Caithness Kirk minister had about him "an air of great simplicity and honesty'". The likes of James Boswell and Laurence Sterne also enjoyed the merchant's company. To his contemporaries, he was, as the author Adam Hochschild has written, '"a wise, thoughtful man who embodied the Scottish virtues of frugality, sobriety, and hard work'". Oswald was a scholar of theology, philosophy, and history. He collected art, particularly Rubens and Rembrandt, and gave handsomely to charity. Oswald, who learned his trade in Glasgow, also represented Britain in negotiations with the Americans after their war of liberation. He was the cosmopolitan epitome of Enlightenment success. But when he wasn't busy with good works, Oswald waded in blood. The precise number of deaths that can be laid at his door is impossible to calculate. As the leading figure in Grant, Oswald & Co, he had investments in each corner of the "'triangular trade'". In his own name, Oswald trafficked at least 13,000 Africans, although he never set foot on their continent. By the time he bought Auchincruive House and

100,000 acres in Ayrshire in 1764, he was worth £500,000. Writing in 2005, Hochschild thought this was ""roughly equivalent"" to $68 million (about £44m). This is conservative.

Oswald was remarkable, but not unique. Where Glasgow and its merchants in sugar, tobacco, and human life are concerned, there are plenty of names and no shortage of monuments: Dennistoun, Campbell, Glassford, Cochrane, Buchanan, Hamilton, Bogle, Ewing, Donald, Speirs, Dunlop. One way to understand what they wrought is simple: take pleasure in the city''s architecture today and you are likely to be admiring the fruits of slavery. Glasgow is not alone in that. London, Liverpool and Bristol also have their stories to tell. Edinburgh's once-great banks grew from foundations built on bones. The first Scottish venture into slavery set out from the capital in 1695. Montrose, Dumfries, Greenock and Port Glasgow each tried their hands. In the language of the present age, they were all in it together.

When commerce was coursing around the triangle, most of polite Scotland was implicated. The nobility (and country) rendered bankrupt in 1700 in the aftermath of the Darien Venture was by the mid-1760s contemplating big elegant townhouses and 100,000-acre estates. You could call that a reversal of fortune. Contrary to self-serving myth, it did not happen because of ""frugality, sobriety, and hard work". Certain things need to be remembered about Scotland and slavery. One is that the mercantile class got stinking rich twice over: despite fortunes made from stolen lives, they were quick to demand compensation when slavery was ended in 1833. Britain's government decided that £20m, a staggering sum, could be raised. In his 2010 book, The Price of Emancipation, Nicholas Draper reckons Glasgow's mob got £400,000 – in modern terms, hundreds of millions. Compensation cases also demonstrated that Scots were not merely following an English lead. According to Draper, a country with 10% of the British population accounted for at least 15% of absentee slavers. By another estimate, 30% of Jamaican plantations were run by Scots. For all the pride taken in the abolitionist societies of Glasgow and Edinburgh, the slave-holders did not suffer because of abolition. They were '"compensated"'.

And that wasn't the worst of it. Thanks to Hollywood movies, the slave economy of the American South is still taken as barbarism's benchmark. Few realise that the behaviour of Scots busily getting rich in the slave-holders'' empire was actually worse – routinely worse – than the worst of the cottonocracy. You need only count the corpses……………."

OYINBO OLE: RIGHTEOUS DESCENDANTS OF ULTRA-RIHTEOUS THIEVES – HABAKKUK.

Properly rehearsed ultra-righteousness and deceptively schooled civilised decorum were preceded by several centuries of the greediest economic cannibalism and evilest racist terrorism the world will ever know: Several continuous centuries of barbarously racist traffic in millions of stolen children of defenceless poor people (Meghan Markle's ancestors) – Habakkuk

"England is like a prostitute who, having sold her body all her life, decides to quit and close her business, and then tells everybody she wants to be chaste and protect her flesh as if were jade." He Manzi, Chinese Politician.

Why should the white father and mother of District Judge Paul Ayers of Bedford County Court, 3, St Paul's Square, MK40 1SQ, the Senior Vice President of the Association of Her Majesty's District Judges, need very, very strong views about education if there is irrefutable evidence that for several continuous centuries, the white ancestors of his white mother and father were extremely nasty and very, very greedy economic cannibals, sadist racist terrorists, and owners of stolen children of defence poor people (Meghan Markle's ancestors) – Habakkuk?

GDC-Expert, British Soldier – Territorial Defence, Stephanie Twiddle (TD), unrelentingly lied under oath – Habakkuk 1:4; John 8:44; John 10: 10.

A CLOSETED RACIST WHITE COUGAR.

"All sections of the UK Society are institutionally racist." Sir Bernard Hogan-Howe.

District Judge Paul Ayers of Shire Hall, 3 St Paul's Square, Bedford MK40 1SQ, the Senior Vice President of the Association of Her Majesty's District Judges and GDC-Expert, British Soldier – Territorial Defence, Stephanie Twiddle (TD) are parts of the UK Society.

OYINBO OLE: RACIST DESCENDANTS OF ULTRA-RIGHTEOUS THIEVES AND OWNERS OF STOLEN

CHILDREN OF DEFENCELESS POOR PEOPLE (MEGHAN MARKLE'S ANCESTORS) - HABAKKUK.

Indiscreet envy.

Envy is a thief.

"Envy is weak." Yul Brynner.

Patronage (Closeted White Supremacist Freemason Lords) rather than progressive, colour-blind merit granted our incontrovertibly functional semi-illiterate white District Judge the platform to display elementary wit.

"This man I thought had been a Lord of wits, but I find he is only a wit among Lords." Dr Samuel Johnson

LORDS: "Five hundred men, ordinary men, chosen accidentally from among the unemployed." David Lloyd George.

Brainless sarcasm; a functional semi-illiterate opportunist racist white dunce. Then, at boarding school, in the 70s, the probability that I'd floor the closeted racist white tall dwarf, in less than 8.46, in a fair man-to-man fist fight, would be 100 percent.

If they don't want to know what, we, their irreconcilable secret enemies, self-educated Negroes, truly feel, and regularly talk about behind their back, they should ban Freedom of Expression in exactly the same way as the unrepentant white supremacist thuggish Home Secretary,

Churchill, concealed the irrefutably superior BLACK
POWER – by banning inter-racial man-to-man fist fight.

OYINBO OLE: THIEVES - HABAKKUK

"What a wonderful Country this Morocco. This sunlight,
this wonderful air, these flowers. We English have always
needed a place like this to come to for sunshine. Now,
Pandar, why don't you give us Morocco, and we shall give
you India. We shall even give you Gandhi, and he's
awfully cheap to keep now that he's on hunger strike."
Churchill, 1943.

Churchill: A closeted white supremacist thug.

"Despite Britain's rich history of black boxers, racist
attitudes about the mental and physical dispositions of
black people permeated the game; full-time British
segregationist campaigners such as the evangelical
preacher Frederick Brotherton Meyer argued that white
athletes did not have the "animal development" of black
people and could therefore not compete with their
"instinctive passion" for violence. There were also worries
over the consequences of emboldening Britain's colonial
subjects. For a nervous British establishment, there were
far too many negative ramifications for their rule over the
Empire if even an innocent sports tournament could even
temporarily demonstrate the equality of black and white
people. This is why in 1911, Home Secretary Winston
Churchill banned interracial boxing matches, and the
BBBC followed suit. The BBBC's bar remained in place
until the 1940s." Tribune

It is plainly deducible that white father and mother of District Judge Paul Ayers of Bedford County Court, the Senior Vice President of the Association of Her Majesty's District Judges, did not have very, very strong views about education, and they did not care, had they, their functional semi-illiterate white son would not have settled for daily dialogues with adults with the basic skills of a child in Bedford County Court, and if he selflessly did, he would not have approved and immortalised excessive stupidity at 16, and he would be a properly educated lawyer, privately educated Anthony Julius, Anthony Blair, Geoff Hoon, and Rabinder Singh's Class, and he might practice proper law in STRAND, instead of daily dialogues with adults with the basic skills of a child in a District Court.

An ignorant racist leech; a righteous descendant of ultra-righteous WHITE PROFESSIONAL THIEVES and owners of stolen children of defenceless poor people (Black African ancestors of Meghan Markle and her white children) - Habakkuk.

New Herod, Matthew 2:16: They lie to their duller children and kill, albeit hands-off, all those who know that they are brainless racist white bastards.

John was jailed only because he spoke; the very, very intolerant lunatic Jew (Herod), more intolerant than mad Jihadists, removed John's head when he refused to stop speaking – Matthew 14. John was not punished for speaking, he was permanently prevented from speaking.

He was lynched like Gadhafi and crucified only because He spoke; He disclosed pictures His unbounded (infinite) mind painted. He was not punished for speaking, He was permanently prevented from speaking.

Then, like Herod, Kim, and MBS, their ancestors, lunatic barbarians, used to remove the heads of those who stated and/or printed what they didn't want their simple children to know about.

The last beheading, in England, with an axe, was in 1817, and decapitation was removed from the Statute Book in 1973, and the same year (1973), Kenneth Baker banned flogging.

Why remove the heads of those who stated and/or printed truths you don't like, if it were illegal to flog them?

"There is now less flogging in our great schools than formerly, but then less is learned there; so that what the boys get at one end, they lose at the other." Dr Samuel Johnson

BEDFORD, ENGLAND: District Judge Paul Ayers of Bedford County Court, based on available evidence, it is absolutely impossible for your talent and the best yields of your land to sustain your standard of living. You are a leech, and your white ancestors were THIEVES.

Then, racist white bastards carried and sold millions of stolen children of defenceless poor people (Black African ancestors of Meghan Markle and her white children); now, they carry natural resources

"To disagree with three – fourths of the British public on all points is one of the first elements of sanity, one of the deepest consolations in all moments of spiritual doubt." Wilde

"The Negro is an animal, the Negro is bad, the Negro is mean, the Negro is ugly; look, a nigger ……... Mama the nigger's going to eat me up ……. Where shall I hide? Frantz Fanon

"Masonry ought forever to be abolished. It is wrong, essentially wrong, a seed of evil which can never produce any good." John Quincy Adams (1767 – 1848), President of the United States of America (1825 – 1829).

Then, there, white Judges, nearly all, were members of the Charitable Antichrist Racist Freemasonry Quasi-Religion (Mediocre Mafia/New Pharisees); some of them were excessively stupid – Habakkuk 1:4; John 8:44; John 10:10.

Then, there, white Supremacist Judges guided and guarded Racial Intolerance. They are very highly civilised and ultra-righteous, so they do everything according to their law, and it is a crime only if the Freemasons did not prior authorise it in the selfless pursuance of the best interests of adults with the basic skills of a child.

BEDFORD, ENGLAND: GDC-Witness, Brother, Richard William Hill, unrelentingly lied under oath – Habakkuk 1:4; John 10:10; John 8:44. A RACIST CROOKED FREEMASON.

OYINBO OLE: RACIST DESCENDANTS OF ULTRA-RIGHTEOUS THIEVES.

In order to impede the ascent of progressive black families, racist white bastards use incompetent liars guided and guarded by power, to tyrannise the head of the Negro family.

If the British Premier, the Right Honourable Boris Johnson, could prove that GDC-Witness, Freemason, Brother, Richard William Hill did not fabricate reports and unrelentingly told lies under oath, he will confirm the belief of billions of people in our world, which is that Antichrist Freemasonry Quasi-Religion (Mediocre Mafia/New Pharisees), Antichrist Judaism, Antichrist Islam, and all other motley assemblies of exotic religions and/or faiths in Great Britain are not intellectually flawed Satanic Mumbo Jumbo.

BORIS JOHNSON: Based on available evidence, the administration of English Law is potently weaponised, vindictive, mediocre, dishonest, Negrophobic, rotten to its innermost core, and it seems overseen by members of the Charitable Antichrist Racist Freemasonry Quasi-Religion – Habakkuk.

BEDFORD, ENGLAND: District Judge Paul Ayers of Bedford County Court, the Senior Vice President of the Association of Her Majesty's District Judges, based on available evidence, it's absolutely impossible for Christ granted your talents and the best yields of your very highly luxuriant land to sustain your standard of living. You're not a Saint; your white ancestors were very, very hardened PROFESSIONAL THIEVES and owners of stolen children of defenceless poor people (Meghan Markle's ancestors). Facts are sacred; they can't be overstated.

BEDFORD, ENGLAND: District Judge Paul Ayers, the Senior Vice President of the Association of Her Majesty's District Judges, based on available evidence, you're worthy because your skin colour is very, very special and irrefutably superior and England is rich; apart from those, you're PURIFIED NOTHING.

"Sometimes people don't want to hear the truth because they don't want their illusions destroyed." Friedrich Nietzsche.

"There is no sin except stupidity." Wilde

"I am very fond of my pigs, but that doesn't stop me from eating them." Archbishop Runcie (1921 – 2000).

If one farmed some white pigs for great pigs' snouts curry, wise or dull white pig great snouts, fried pigs' snout curry is food, but the dullest of the white pigs with great snouts deserves to be butchered and eaten first.

"Though the English pride themselves on their sense of humour, they distrust humorous men." Lord Annan

District Judge, Bedford, the Senior Vice President of the Association of Her Majesty's District Judges approved and immortalised the type of stories his functional semi-illiterate father (deductible) used to tell when he returned home from Queen Victoria, at odd hours, stoned, and which his Poly-educated supervisors in Luton authorised.

His Honour Judge Perusko studied Law at Poly (lower-class alternative education) – Proverbs 17:16.

"To survive, you must tell stories …….. I believe that what we become depends on what our fathers teach us at odd moments, when they aren't trying to teach us. We are formed by little scraps of wisdom." Umberto Eco

BEDFORD, ENGLAND: GDC, Sue Gregory (OBE) Officer of the Most Excellent Order of our Empire, unrelentingly lied under implied oath – Habakkuk.

A RACIST CROOKED WHITE COUGAR.

OYINBO OLE: A RIGHTEOUS DESCENDANT OF THIEVES – HABAKKUK.

PERCEPTION IS GRANDER THAN REALITY.

"All sections of the UK Society are institutionally racist." Sir Bernard Hogan-Howe.

Bedfordshire County Court, Shire Hall, 3 St Paul's Square, Bedford MK40 1SQ, is part of the UK Society.

If the British Premier, the Right Honourable Boris Johnson, could prove that white District Judge Paul Ayers of Bedford County Court, 3 St Paul's Square, Bedford MK40

1SQ, is not a functional semi-illiterate and incompetent racist liar, and if he could prove that all functional semi-illiterate white Judges are not RACISTS, and if he could prove that Sue Gregory (OBE) Officer of the Most Excellent Order of our Empire did not unrelentingly tell lies under oath, he will confirm the belief of billions of people in our world, which is that Antichrist Freemasonry Quasi-Religion (Mediocre Mafia/New Pharisees), Antichrist Judaism, Antichrist Islam, and all other motley assemblies of exotic religions and/or faiths in Great Britain are not intellectually flawed Satanic Mumbo Jumbo.

Racist white bastards want all the gigantic advantages associated with their irrefutably superior skin colour (white privilege), the most valuable asset that they neither made nor chose; they don't want Freedom of Expression because they don't want their duller fairer skin children to know that they are excessively stupid.

BORIS JOHNSON: Based on available evidence, the administration of English Law is irreparably rotten to its innermost core, and it is overseen by the Charitable Antichrist Racist Freemasonry Quasi-Religion (Mediocre Mafia/New Pharisees) – Habakkuk

"A complaints such as Mrs Bishop's could trigger an enquiry." Stephen Henderson, GDC-Expert, LLM, Head of MDDUS, : The Protector of those who beat him in Dental School and in Practice.

"I don't want to talk grammar. I want to talk like a lady." George Bernard Shaw.

517

A CROOKED RACIST WHITE DUNCE.

When innate racial hatred (hereditary) and uncontrollable Envy copulate, insanity is their offspring.

NORTHAMPTONSHIRE, ENGLAND: GDC-Witness, Ms Rachael Bishop unrelentingly lied under oath – Habakkuk.

A CLOSETED RACIST CROOKED WHITE COUGAR.

Facts are sacred.

The truth allows no choice.

BEDFORD, ENGLAND: District Judge Paul Ayers, the Senior Vice President of the Association of Her Majesty's District Judges, based on available evidence, your white ancestors were very, very hardened PROFESSIONAL THIEVES (extremely nasty economic cannibalism) and owners of stolen children of defenceless poor people (Meghan Markle's ancestors); you're a LEECH and you know it, but your gentler children do not.

BEDFORD, ENGLAND: District Judge Paul Ayers, the Senior Vice President of the Association of Her Majesty's District Judges, based on available evidence, it's absolutely impossible for your talent and the yield of your land to sustain your standard of living.

BEDFORD, ENGLAND: District Judge Paul Ayers, the Senior Vice President of the Association of Her Majesty's District Judges, based on available evidence, our own Money, NIGERIA (oil/gas) is by far more relevant to the survival of all your children than NORWICH (coastal dole).

BEDFORD, ENGLAND: District Paul Ayers, the Senior Vice President of the Association of Her Majesty's District Judges, which part of Bedford County Court, 3 St Paul's Square, Bedford MK40 1SQ. was not stolen, or which part of it did the people of Bedford buy, or which part of it preceded several centuries of barbarously racist traffic in millions of stolen children of defenceless poor people (Meghan Markle's ancestors): The building or its chattels?

An ignorant white fool; a racist descendant of THIEVES and owners of stolen children of defenceless poor people (Meghan Markle's ancestors) - Habakkuk.

 Which part of Bedfordshire Masonic Temple to Baal, Bedford Road, Kempston, MK42, was not stolen or which part of it preceded slavery: The Magnificent building or its chattels?

The Grand Masonic Temple to Baal (Mother Temple), , was built in the early 18th century, at a height of the barbarously racist traffic in millions of stolen children of defenceless poor people (Meghan Markle's ancestors) - Habakkuk

OYINBO OLE: Ignorant descendants of ultra-righteous THIEVES AND OWNERS OF STOLEN CHILDREN OF DEFENCELESS POOR PEOPLE– Habakkuk

We must all live in great fear of members of the Charitable Antichrist Racist Freemasonry Quasi-Religion, and we must say what we truly feel only behind the backs of those who were verifiably inferiorly created by Almighty God: Closeted racist white supremacist voodoo men who use very expensive aprons to decorate the temples of their powerless and useless fertility tools. They are high class scammers, impostors, and experts of deception, who vulgar Pharisees charitable works as cloaks of deceit, and the white supremacist thugs lie that they don't lie – Psalm 144.

"Lies are told all the time." Sir Michael Havers (1923 – 1992)

How should mere Negroes defend themselves against Freemasons before Freemasons? Christ couldn't. He was lynched like Gadhafi and crucified only because He spoke; He disclosed pictures His unbounded mind painted – John 14:6.

Their people are everywhere, and they control almost everything. When their people commit RACIST CRIMES against ours, Racist White Bastards criminally bury Racial Hatred - Habakkuk.

The only evidence of their purportedly higher IQ is the stolen affluence that their wretched ancestors, mere agricultural labourers, crossed the English Channels, in dinghy boats, without luggage or decent shoes, to latch onto.

Descendants of Alphonse Gabriel impersonate Archangel Gabriel.

GDC: Richard Hill fabricated reports and unrelentingly lied under oath — Habakkuk.

A RACIST CROOK.

A MORON MASON.

https://www.youtube.com/watch?v=BlpH4hG7m1A

Daringtruths — DISTRICT JUDGE AYERS OF … — Facebook

https://pt-br.facebook.com › Daringtruths01 › photos

DISTRICT JUDGE AYERS OF BEDFORD COUNTY COURT: A BRAINLESS WHITE MAN; A RACIST DESCENDANT OF PROFESSIONAL THIEVES AND OWNERS OF STOLEN HUMAN BEINGS ALMOST…

Daringtruths — DISTRICT JUDGE AYERS OF| Facebook

https://www.facebook.com › posts › daringtruths-distric…

DISTRICT JUDGE AYERS OF BEDFORD COUNTY COURT: A BRAINLESS WHITE MAN; A RACIST DESCENDANT OF PROFESSIONAL THIEVES AND .

The Law Paralysed by Michael Coleade — YouTube

https://www.youtube.com › watch

15 Aug 2016 — … it is the absolute truth that District Judge Ayers of Bedford County Court in Bedfordshire, England, could not spell the word, …

Abiodun Bamgbelu — Medium

https://factsaresacred89.medium.com

Daily Cause Circuit Judges, 23/08/21 … Bedford. District Judge Ayers, 23/08/21. Justice, 23/08/21. Her Honour Judge Gargan, 23/08/21 .

BEDFORD: District Judge, you're worthy because England is …

https://medium.com › bedford-district-judge-youre-wor…

District Judge Ayers, Bedford. … Antichrist Racist Freemasons (Mediocre Mafia): Which part of Bedfordshire Masonic Centre, Kempston, preceded the …

Dawkins: a Deluded Antichrist Briton: God: a Good Business

https://books.google.com › books › about › Dawkins_a_…

District Judge Ayers, Bedford. ... Antichrist Racist Freemasons (Mediocre Mafia): Which part of Bedfordshire Masonic Centre, Kempston, preceded the ...

The Law, Paralysed — Incompetent Liars: Some Lawyers

https://blackwells.co.uk › bookshop › product › The-La...

Sir Winston Churchill Based on accessible information, it is the absolute truth that District Judge Ayers of Bedford County Court in Bedfordshire, England, ...

The Brain isn't the skin colour.

GDC-Witness: Richard Hill fabricated reports and unrelentingly lied under oath — Habakkuk.

GDC-INSIDER: Sue Gregory (OBE), Officer of the Most Excellent Order of our Empire unrelentingly lied under implied oath — Habakkuk.

GDC-Witness: Rachael Bishop, Senior NHS Nurse, unrelentingly lied under oath — Habakkuk.

GDC-Witness: Geraint Evans (NHS) unrelentingly lied under implied oath — Habakkuk.

GDC-Witness: Stephanie Twidale (TD) unrelentingly lied under oath Habakkuk.

GDC-Witness: George Rothnie (NHS) unrelentingly lied under implied oath — Habakkuk.

GDC-Witness: Kevin Atkinson (NHS) unrelentingly lied under oath — Habakkuk

They were all white: Homogeneity in the administration English law is the impregnable secure mask of racial hatred.

JUDICIAL DIVERSITY: ACCELERATING CHANGE. "The near absence of women and Black, Asian and minority ethnic judges in the senior judiciary, is no longer tolerable. It undermines the democratic legitimacy of our legal system; it demonstrates a denial of fair and equal opportunities to members of underrepresented groups, and the diversity deficit weakens the quality of justice." Sir Geoffrey Bindman, QC, and Karon Monaghan, QC

DIVERSE MEDIOCRITY IS AKIN TO RAKING MUCK.

A bastardised, unashamedly mediocre, indiscreetly dishonest, vindictive, potently weaponised, and institutionally racist legal system that is overseen by MASONS (Mediocre Mafia) — Habakkuk.

"To deny or belittle this good is, in this dangerous century when the resources and pretensions of power continue to enlarge, a desperate error of intellectual abstraction. More than this, it is a self-fulfilling error, which encourages us to give up the struggle against bad laws and class bound procedures and to disarm ourselves before power. It is to throw away a whole inheritance of struggle about the law and within the forms of law, whose continuity can never be fractured without bringing men and women into immediate danger." — E. P Thompson.

"The truth allows no choice." Dr Samuel Johnson.
Facts are sacred.

CHAPTER TWENTY:

Boris Johnson: Why is England not a scam?

"I do not approve of anything that tampers with natural ignorance. Ignorance is like a delicate exotic fruit; touch it and the bloom is gone. The whole theory of modern education is radically unsound. Fortunately, in England, at any rate, education produces no effect whatsoever. If it did, it would prove a serious danger to the upper classes, and probably lead to acts of violence in Grosvenor Square." Wilde

If you don't know that Charitable Antichrist Racist Freemasonry Quasi-Religion is a Satanic Business who is very, very interested in other people's money, it is proof that you can't see the closeted racist white bastards who use very, very expensive aprons to decorate the temples of their powerless and useless fertility tools, and incompetently lie that they don't lie – Psalm 144.

The Charitable Antichrist Racist Freemasonry Quasi-Religion (Mediocre Mafia/New Pharisees) has leverage: Unchecked incompetent mendacity guided and guarded by the fact that they oversee the administration of English Law – Habakkuk 1:4; John 8:44; John 10:10.

Vulgar Pharisees' charitable works in exchange for what? Theirs is not a good deal. Then, the most discerning rejected their grandest offer – Matthew 4:9.

WHITE PRIVILEGE: Losing debates against mere Negroes must be a taboo, so they all lied, incompetently, including under oath, and including some white Judges.

BEDFORD, ENGLAND: District Judge Paul Ayers, the Senior Vice President of the Association of Her Majesty's District Judges, based on available evidence, it is absolutely impossible for your talent and the yield of your land to sustain your standard of living. You are being 'carried', privileged dullards indirect dole. You are worthy only because England is rich; apart that – you're NOTHING.

Affluence did not evolve; then, it was actively and deliberately stolen - Habakkuk.

"Affluence is not a birth right." David Cameron.

BEDFORD, ENGLAND: District Judge Paul Ayers, the Senior Vice President of the Association of Her Majesty's District Judges, based on available evidence, your white ancestors were industrial-scale professional THIEVES and owners of stolen children of defenceless poor people (Black ancestors of Meghan Markle and her white children) – Habakkuk.

Before SLAVERY, what?

"Agriculture, not only gives riches to a nation, but the only one she can call her own." Dr Samuel Johnson.

BEDFORD, ENGLAND: District Judge Paul Ayers, the Senior Vice President of the Association of Her Majesty's District Judges, based on available evidence, then, there were laws as there are laws now; then, the yields of stolen children of defenceless poor people (Meghan Markle's ancestors) were used to build Magnificent Courts and pay wages of Judges who sent those who stole money to Prisons built with stolen money – Habakkuk.

OYINBO OLE: Ignorant descendants of ultra-righteous THIEVES – Habakkuk.

Ignorance is bliss.

"Those who know the least obey the best." George Farquhar.

They want to guide the education of our black children so that they can be excessively stupid like their people.

Charity should FORKING begin at home.

https://www.youtube.com/watch?v=BlpH4hG7m1A&feature=youtu.be

"They may not have been well written from a grammatical point of view, but I am confident I had not forgotten any of the facts." Dr Geraint Evans, Postgraduate Tutor, Oxford

AN IMBECILE: AN ADULT WITH THE BASIC
SKILLS OF A CHILD.

"Why, Sir, Sherry is dull, naturally dull; but it must have
taken him a great deal of pains to become what we now see
him. Such an excess of stupidity, Sir, is not in Nature." DR
SAMUEL JOHNSON

The yield of the educational system of one of the richest
nations on earth: England is a scam.

They are not the only creation of Almighty God, and their
irrefutably superior skin colour is not one of the wonders of
our world.

They love the superiority that is associated with the
irrefutably superior skin colour that they neither made nor
chose, their baseless and brainless birth right; they don't
love Freedom of Expression because they don't want their
duller children to know that they are excessively stupid.

They love Apartheid by stealth.

https://youtu.be/rayVcfyu9Tw

Based on available evidence, Geraint Evans, Postgraduate
Tutor, Oxford, of Rowtree Dental Care, Rowtree Road,
Northampton, unrelentingly lied under implied oath –
Habakkuk.

It is a crime only if it were not prior authorised by the Charitable, Antichrist Racist Freemasonry Religion (Mediocre Mafia/New Pharisees) – Habakkuk 1:4; John 8:44; John 10:10.

Then, there, white Judges, nearly all, were Masons; some of them were thicker than a gross of planks - Habakkuk 1:4; John 8:44; John 10:10.

We have inadvertently walked into their trap, and we will leave our children to endure institutionalised innate racial intolerance; it is as selfish and irresponsible as voluntarily making slave babies on their plantation. Then, there, the owners of the cows owned their calves.

Based on available evidence, lies are told all the time, and lies are regularly used to persecute our people by closeted racist white supremacist thugs, in your name.

Facts are sacred.

"The truth allows no choice." Dr Samuel Johnson

"Lies are told all the time." Sir Michael Havers (1923 – 1992)

BORIS JOHNSON: Members of the Charitable Antichrist Racist Freemasonry Quasi-Religion (Mediocre Mafia/New Pharisees) oversee administration of English Law, based on available evidence, it's irreparably rotten to its innermost core – Habakkuk 1:4; John 8:44; John 10:10.

The lunatic Jew (Herod) Jailed John only because he spoke.

Matthew 2:16: Members of the Antichrist Racist Freemasonry Quasi-Religion (Mediocre Mafia/New Pharisees): New Herod, they deceive their duller children that they are geniuses, and they kill all those who know that they are brainless racist white bastards who use very, very expensive aprons to decorate the temples of their powerless and useless fertility tools, and they lie that they don't lie – Psalm 144.

Based on available evidence, the lunatic Jew (Herod) removed John's head only because he spoke – Matthew 14

He was lynched like Gadhafi and crucified only because He spoke; He disclosed pictures His unbounded mind painted.

The Charitable Antichrist Racist Freemasonry Quasi-Religion (Mediocre Mafia/New Pharisees) supposedly orders its paying members to be a quiet and peaceful subject of the state, true to the government and just to the country. They must be disloyal or rebellious but submit totally to legal authority and abide to all the laws of the government of the country in which they live.

SATANIC B.S!

OYINBO OLE: Ignorant descendants of ultra-righteous THIEVES and owners of stolen children of defenceless poor people (Meghan Markle's ancestors) - Habakkuk.

BORIS JOHNSON: Based on available evidence, John 14:6 Christianity is absolutely incompatible with the administration of English Law and the Charitable Antichrist Racist Freemasonry Quasi-Religion.

BORIS JOHNSON: Based on available evidence, the fellow is who He says He is, and He is consistently accessible only through unalloyed faith.

BORIS JOHNSON: Members of the Charitable, Antichrist Racist Freemasonry Quasi-Religion (Mediocre Mafia/New Pharisees) are showing us, Non-Negotiable John 14:6 Christians, pepper; we do not like pepper soup.

"If life shows you pepper, make pepper soup." HRH Prince Charles

BORIS JOHNSON: The administration of English Law is irreparably rotten to its innermost core, and it is overseen by members of the Charitable, Antichrist Racist Freemasonry Quasi-Religion (Mediocre Mafia/New

Pharisees), our irreconcilable religious enemies (John 14:6) – Habakkuk 1:4; John 8::44; John 10:10.

The vindictive white woman might've made things up.

Based on available evidence, white women, not all, are incompetent liars.

BEDFORD, ENGLAND: Based on available evidence, GDC-Expert, Sue Gregory, OBE, Officer of the Most Excellent Order of our Empire, unrelentingly lied under implied oath – Habakkuk 1:4; John 8:44; John 10:10.

A CROOKED RACIST WHITE COUGAR.

"A typical English man, usually violent and always dull."
Wilde

BEDFORD. ENGLAND: Based on available evidence, our irrefutably functional semi-illiterate District Judge, Paul Ayers, of Bedford County Court, the Senior Vice President of the Association of Her Majesty's District Judges, incompetently lied under oath (approved judgement) - Habakkuk 1:4; John 8:44; John 10:10.

A waste of money fake Judge – Proverbs 17:16.

A properly schooled impostor and an expert of deception. Poly-educated racist white rubbish: Perception is grander than reality.

England is a scam.

Based on very proximate observations, only his irrefutably superior skin colour is good.

A CLOSETED RACIST CROOKED DIPSTICK.

He rides a very powerful tiger, deluded, he thinks he is a tiger, dismounted, he'd instantly revert to NOTHING (a mere former debt-collector Solicitor in NORWICH (coastal dole).

PERCEPTION IS GRANDER THAN REALITY.

Facts are sacred.

"The truth allows no choice."

OYINBO OLE: If we are not very, very smart, why are we very, very rich?

Shepherds did not bring stolen children of other people home, they lied to their own duller children that they were paragons of wisdom who, like Mother Teresa, did only virtuous works in Africa - Habakkuk.

OXFORD, ENGLAND: Based on available evidence, GDC-Expert, British Soldier – Territorial Defence, Stephanie Twiddle (TD), unrelentingly lied under oath - Habakkuk 1:4; John 8:44; John 10:10.

A RACIST CROOKED WHITE COUGAR: ENGLAND IS A SCAM.

BEDFORD, ENGLAND: Based on available evidence, GDC-Witness, Freemason, Brother, Richard William Hill fabricated reports and unrelentingly lied under oath - Habakkuk 1:4; John 8:44; John 10:10.

A RACIST WHITE CROOK: ENGLAND IS A SCAM.

"You will bow. You can't beat the system." Kemi Daramola

Esu: Imported devil.

I shan't. I know who will.

Christianity was the camouflage, and everything was based on 'calculation'. A glorified prostitute and a thief. A parasite who found a host, and then told everyone that she was the host.

"I was born here." Kemi Daramola

Ekiti ode.

Just like her mother, she liked what her mother couldn't afford, so she used her body to get it.

Then, the sole source of money for six dependants (five children and their mother), and countless extended family, was 'begging' and her father's income.

A properly schooled schemer: Then, relative poverty induced confused Christianity. Now, propped up by the Charitable Antichrist Racist Freemasons, she removed her mask.

I am still alive; some Nigerians kill their husbands.

A lunatic Born Again Christian.

Google: Hypothyroidism and psychosis.

To deny the child access to his sister, and his father, he made him sleep alone in a bedroom with a woman who didn't kill her husband, when she 'travelled' for 'business'.

She spins everybody except Christ and me; almost everything is incompetent art that incompetently imitates life.

The Negro is a very bad human being, only the money is good.

She corroborated incompetent racist lies and professional jealousy by closeted racist bastards.

The white man is the devil - Columbia University
https://ccnmtl.columbia.edu › mmt › mxp › concepts

Referring to Whites as "devils" originates with the teachings of Master W.D. Fard and the legend of Yakub. Fard taught Elijah Muhammad who preached the ...

"A complaint such as Mrs Bishop's could trigger an enquiry." Stephen Henderson, LLM, Head of MDDUS.

A CLOSETED RACIST CROOKED WHITE DUNCE: ENGLAND IS SCAM.

"I don't want to talk grammar. I want to talk like a lady." George Bernard Shaw

When innate racial hatred and professional envy copulate, insanity is their offspring.

NIGERIA: SHELL'S DOCILE CASH COW.

Children with huge oil wells and gas fields near their huts eat only 1.5/day; a bellyful genetic alien, with camouflage English names, whose white father and mother have never seen crude oil,

She prays to Christ and regularly pays hefty tithe (quasi-protection money) at Brick Hill Baptist Church, in Bedford, and members of the Charitable Antichrist Racist Freemasonry Quasi-Religion (Mediocre Mafia/New

Pharisees) at the Bedfordshire Masonic Temple to Baal, the Keep, Bedford Road, Kempston, MK42, answer her prayers.

A BLATANTLY FRAUDULENT ARRANGEMENT.

"A government that robs Peter to pay Paul can always depend on the support of Paul." George Bernard Shaw

We must bow and/or play the white supremacist thugs who use very expensive aprons to decorate the temples of their powerless and useless fertility tools - like chess.

-----Original Message-----
From: resh diu <rdiu@me.com>
To: adeolacole <adeolacole@aol.com>
Sent: Fri, 11 Apr 2014 9:28
Subject: Re:

It's sad Ola

I kept telling you to play the game of chess rather than fight it

You take care

If you wish to dispose of 24 park road let me know

Regards

Resh
Dr Resh Diu BDS

If all the 33rd Degree Freemasons (Scottish – Rite) at the Bedfordshire Masonic Temple to Baal, the Keep, Bedford Road, Kempston, MK42, and all the Master Builders at the Grand Masonic Temple to Baal, 60 Great Queen St, London WC2B 5AZ, and the British Premier, The Right Honourable Boris Johnson, and Sir, Mr Justice Haddon-Cave, QC, KBE, could prove that Sue Gregory, OBE, Officer of the Most Excellent Order of our Empire, did not unrelentingly tell lies under implied oath, and if they could prove that irrefutably functional semi-illiterate District Judge Paul Ayers, of Bedford County Court, the Senior Vice President of the Association of Her Majesty's District Judges, did not incompetently tell lies under oath (approved judgement), and if they could prove that GDC-Expert, British Soldier – Territorial Defence, Stephanie Twiddle (TD), did not unrelentingly tell lies under oath, and if they could prove that GDC-Witness, Freemason, Brother, Richard William Hill did not fabricate reports and unrelentingly told lies under oath, it will confirm the belief of billions of people in our world, which is that Charitable Antichrist Freemasonry Quasi-Religion (Mediocre Mafia/New Pharisees), and all other motley assemblies of FAITHS and RELIGIONS under the common umbrella of the Defender of the FAITH and the Governor of the Church of England are not intellectually flawed Satanic Mumbo Jumbo, and it will concomitantly confirm that reasoning and vision have finite boundaries. If reasoning and vision have finite boundaries, He must have lied, in the Council, before Jews, when He disclosed pictures His unbounded (infinite) mind painted, and He must have also lied when He audaciously stated:

The first quality that is needed is audacity." Churchill

If the fellow told the truth before the Jews, in the Council, we are FORKED, as His Knights attack Kings and Queens simultaneously and only the Queens can move, and everything that is not aligned with John 14:6, is travelling in the wrong direction and heading straight for the rocks.

"It does no harm to throw the occasional man overboard, but it does not do much good if you are steering full speed ahead for the rocks." Lord Gilmour of Craigmillar.

CHAPTER TWENTY-ONE:

Boris Johnson: Why is England not a scam?

"A feeling of inferiority? No, a feeling of nonexistence. Sin is Negro as virtue is white. All those white men in a group, guns in their hands, cannot be wrong. I am guilty. I do not know of what, but I know that I am no good.

Google: Dr Anand Kamath, dentist.

Google: Dr Richard Bamgboye, GP.

England is a scam: Based on available evidence, the administration of English Law is irreparably rotten to its innermost core, and it is overseen by the Charitable Antichrist Racist Freemasonry Quasi-Religion (Mediocre Mafia/New Pharisees) - Habakkuk

BORIS JOHNSON: I am very, very different from you. The mind that I got in finer than the system you serve. I am a foetus, as what I see is clearer than a vision – Act 2:17;

the fellow is who He says He is, and He is consistently accessible, but only through unalloyed faith.

"It is incumbent upon the court and all those professionals involved to conclude court proceedings as quickly as possible. This hopefully ensures that a child has stability, love and affection and the parents working together to ensure that he has the best opportunity of developing academically and emotional." District Judge Paul Ayers, Senior Vice President of the Association of Her Majesty's District Judges – proofed and approved Judgement

An intellectually disorientated and mentally imbalanced white man.

PURIFIED ROT!

"Yes, Sir, it does *her* honour, but it would do nobody else honour. I have indeed, not read it all. But when I take up the end of a web, and find it packthread, I do not expect, by looking further, to find embroidery." Dr Samuel Johnson

A CLOSETED RACIST WHITE FOOL'S APPROVAL!

AN IMBECILE: AN ADULT WITH THE BASIC SKILLS OF A CHILD.

Based on very proximate observations and direct experiences, only his irrefutably superior skin colour is good, and he neither made nor chose it, and without it, he will be considerably diminished as a human being.

Had the incontrovertibly functional semi-illiterate white man been black, he will not be a Judge.

Irrefutably superior skin colour, stolen trust fund, and what else?

Before SLAVERY, what?

"Affluence is not a birth right." David Cameron.

If District Judge Paul Ayers, Senior Vice President of the Association of Her Majesty's District Judges, of Bedford County Court, 3, St Paul's Square, MK40 1SQ, read his approved Judgement, he must have been excessively stupid, and if he didn't, he must have lied as he implied that he did.

"Gentlemen, you are now about to embark on a course of studies which will occupy you for two years. Together, they form a noble adventure. But I would like to remind you of an important point. Nothing that you will learn in the course of your studies will be of the slightest possible use to you in after life, save only this, that if you work hard and intelligently you should be able to detect when a man is talking rot, and that, in my view, is the main, if not the sole, purpose of education."
John Alexander Smith, Oxford University Professor of MORAL PHILOSOPHY.

IN ORDER TO SELL UNASHAMED MEDIOCRITY
AND CONFUSION FOR VALUE, SOME PRIVILEGED
DULLARDS ATTACH IT TO A DEVOUT CHRISTIAN
SOVEREIGN.

JUDICIAL DIVERSITY: ACCELERATING CHANGE.
Sir Geoffrey Bindman, QC Karon Monaghan QC "The
near absence of women and Black, Asian and minority
ethnic judges in the senior judiciary, is no longer tolerable.
It undermines the democratic legitimacy of our legal
system; it demonstrates a denial of fair and equal
opportunities to members of underrepresented groups, and
the diversity deficit weakens the quality of justice."

DIVERSE MEDIOCRITY IS AKIN TO RAKING MUCK.

"I do not approve of anything that tampers with natural
ignorance. Ignorance is like a delicate exotic fruit; touch it
and the bloom is gone. The whole theory of modern
education is radically unsound. Fortunately in England, at
any rate, education produces no effect whatsoever. If it did,
it would prove a serious danger to the upper classes, and
probably lead to acts of violence in Grosvenor
Square." Oscar Wilde

BORIS JOHNSON: Based on available evidence, the mind
that I got unsolicited is finer than the system you serve.

BORIS JOHNSON: Better than crap could also be crap, so
the notion of relative good, which is not aligned to infinity

543

(John 14:6) is akin to doing a simultaneous equation with only one equation.

"You will bow. You can't beat the system." Kemi Daramola

Bow to who?

Esu: Imported devil.

I shan't bow to closeted racist bastards who use very expensive aprons to decorate the temples of their powerless and useless fertility tools, and I will not play chess with closeted racist descendants of undocumented refugees (genetic aliens), with camouflage English names . I know who will – Romans 11; 1 John 4:4.

Facts are sacred; they can't be overstated.

"By definition therefore there needs to be a contact order for Mr B so that he knows when he is going to see his son. It is absolutely essential that this occurs and mother agrees with that. She said so several times in her evidence. Mrs Waller agreed that not only should a child have the opportunity of developing relationship with both parents, any sibling should also be there so that inter- sibling relationship could be fostered and nurtured. Obviously in this particular case the children reside in different places. That immediately puts a strain on the children having limited contact with each other. F's sister is very much older than him and she will be further advanced into her adult life. Thus it is not a matter that that sibling relationship can only be fostered by the children being together. Indeed as we all know absence sometimes makes

the heart grow fonder. F should have an opportunity of seeing his sister. Wherever he does that it should be done in a friendly and loving environment. If the time comes that his sister goes to university of course his contact with her will be restricted to the time that she is home from university. In years to come when they have both grown up, with their own family they will see less of each other. But it doesn't mean that they don't still love and adore each other as much as they would if they saw each other every day." District Judge Paul Ayers of Bedford County Court, the Senior Vice President of the Association of Her Majesty's District Judges – proofed and approved Judgement.

Facts are sacred, and they can't be overstated.

"Yes, Sir, it does *her* honour, but it would do nobody else honour. I have indeed, not read it all. But when I take up the end of a web, and find it packthread, I do not expect, by looking further, to find embroidery." Dr Samuel Johnson.

Unashamed, immortal, and idiotic nonsense.

Our semi-illiterate Freemason District Judge of our Empire of stolen affluence - Habakkuk.

PERCEPTION IS GRANDER THAN REALITY.

Better than crap could also be crap.

The yield of very, very elementary intellect; his spinal cord seemed to be his highest centre. His education within one of the richest on earth was bloody waste of money – Proverbs 17:16.

Immortal brainless nonsense.

BEDFORD, ENGLAND: District Judge Paul Ayers of Bedford County Court, the Senior Vice President of the Association of Her Majesty's District Judges, based on available evidence, it's absolutely impossible for your Christ granted talent and the yield of your land to sustain your standard; you're being carried. Based on available evidence, you're a leech and your white ancestors were THIEVES and owners of stolen children of defenceless poor people (Meghan Markle's ancestors) – Habakkuk.

OYINBO OLE: A closeted racist descendant of ultra-righteous THIEVES and owners of stolen children of defenceless poor people (Meghan Markle's ancestors) – Habakkuk.

No brain.
Poor in natural resources.
Several centuries of stealing and slavery preceded the huge Trust Fund. Only his indisputably superior skin colour is good; he neither made nor chose it.

The only evidence of his purportedly higher IQ is the stolen affluence that his ancestors crossed the English Channels, without luggage or decent shoes, to latch onto;

the changed their names, blended, and by deception, they became the rightful inheritors of the yields of several centuries of the greediest economic cannibalism and the evilest racist terrorism the world will ever know – Habakkuk.

BEDFORD, ENGLAND: District Judge Paul Ayers of Bedford County Court, the Senior Vice President of the Association of Her Majesty's District Judges, which part of Bedford County Court, Shire Hall, 3 St Paul's Square, Bedford MK40 1SQ, was not stolen or which part of it preceded SLAVERY: The building or its chattels?

Ignorance is bliss.

"Those who know the least obey the best." George Farquhar

BORIS JOHNSON: The fact that District Judge Paul Ayers of Bedford County Court, the Senior Vice President of the Association of Her Majesty's District Judges is superior to the Junior Vice President of the Association of Her Majesty's District Judges, certainly theoretically, isn't proof that both aren't crap.

District Judge Paul Ayers of Bedford County Court, the Senior Vice President of the Association of Her Majesty's District Judges approved and immortalised the type of stories his functional semi-illiterate white father (deductible) used to tell when he returned home from Queen Victoria, at odd hours, stoned.

"To survive, you must tell stories ….. I believe that what we become depends on what our fathers teach us at odd moments, when they aren't trying to teach us. We are formed by little scraps of wisdom." Umberto Eco

Charitable, Antichrist Racist Freemasonry Quasi-Religion (Mediocre Mafia/New Pharisees) teaches its members secret handshakes, not grammar, and the former is considerably easier to master.

Alzheimer's disease is considerably more common than ordinarily realised.

Alzheimer's disease is incompatible with the competent administration of English Law.

The competent administration of English law should be an inviolable basic right.
"Freedom of Expression is basic right." Lady Hale

Google: Alzheimer's disease.

Our irrefutably functional semi-illiterate Freemason District Judge of our Empire of stolen affluence immortalised the yield of his very, very elementary intellect.

The white man's spinal cord seemed to be his highest centre.

BORIS JOHNSON: The white man, albeit England's Class Senior District Judge, is not good enough; he is a properly schooled impostor and an expert of deception, and he seemed to have sold unashamed mediocrity and confusion to the undiscerning, for decades.

BORIS JOHNSON: I am, non-consensually, bound by your system, but I know a different and vastly superior one.

BORIS JOHNSON: The fellow is who He says He is, and He will get what He wants – Proverbs 16:33.

OYINBO OLE: An ignorant descendant of ultra-righteous thieves and owners of stolen poor black children of defenceless Africans (Black African ancestors of Meghan Markle, a Mulatto, and her white children) – Habakkuk

"Sometimes people don't want to hear the truth because they don't want their illusions destroyed." Friedrich Nietzsche.

Facts are sacred; they can't be overstated.

"The English think incompetence is the same thing as sincerity." Quentin Crisp

OYINBO ODE: A CLOSETED RACIST FUNCTIONAL SEMI-ILLITERATE DUNCE – PROVERBS 17:16.

A scatter-head white man; an ultra-righteous descendant of WHITE THIEVES – Habakkuk.

"The great enemy of the clear language is INSINCERITY (DISHONESTY). When there is a gap between one's real and one's declared aims, one turns as it were instinctively to long words and exhausted idioms, like a cuttlefish squirting ink. In our age there is no such thing as 'keeping out of politics'. All issues are political issues, and politics itself is a mass of lies, evasions, folly, HATRED and schizophrenia. When the general atmosphere is bad, language must suffer." – George Orwell

"Someone must be trusted. Let it be the Judges." Lord Denning.

Judges are human beings. Some human beings are racists.

Facts are sacred.
It's plainly deductible that Racist white Judges are the most potent racists; they have power.

Based on available evidence, England is a scam.

District Judge Paul Ayers of Bedford County Court, Shire Hall, 3 St Paul's Square, Bedford MK40 1SQ, the Senior Vice President of the Association of Her Majesty's District Judges, based on available evidence, it is absolutely impossible for your talent and the yield of your land to sustain your standard of living; your white ancestors were industrial-scale PROFESSIONAL THIEVES and owners of stolen children of defenceless poor people (Meghan Markle's ancestors). Then, the yields of stolen and destroyed children of defenceless poor people were used to build Magnificent Courts and pay the wages of white Judges who sent white people who stole money to prisons built with stolen money - Habakkuk.

OYINBO OLE: THIEVES – HABAKKUK.

"The truth allows no choice." Dr Samuel Johnson

Facts are sacred.

Your Majesty, based on available evidence, white men, not all, are incompetent racist liars.

Google: Incompetent Liars: Some Lawyers.

BEDFORD, ENGLAND: Based on available evidence, GDC-Witness, Freemason, Brother, Richard William Hill fabricated reports and unrelentingly lied under oath – Habakkuk 1:4; John 8:44; John 10:10.

A CLOSETED RACIST CROOKED WHITE MAN.

Based on available evidence, whites measure whites with a very, very different yardstick.

Only imbecile Negroes expect demons to cast out demons – Matthew 12:27.

A properly organised racist crime syndicate that is overseen by the Freemasons incompetently impersonates colour-blind and impartial administration of the law: Incompetent art incompetently imitates life – Habakkuk 1:4; John 8:44; John 10:10.

Then, if castration was the deserved punishment for Negroes who smashed white women, now, crooked white men such as GDC-Witness, Freemason, Brother, Richard William Hill also, deserves to be castrated.

"We know historically that the Negro guilty of lying with a white woman is castrated." Frantz Fanon

Your Royal Highness, based on available evidence, white women, not all, are incompetent racist liars.

A white woman, Ms Rachael Bishop, Senior NHS Nurse, unrelentingly lied under oath – Habakkuk 1:4; John 8:44; John 10:10.

A CLOSETED RACIST CROOKED WHITE COUGAR.

Your Majesty, based on available evidence, white men, not all, are incompetent liars.

"A complaints such as Mrs Bishop's could trigger an enquiry." Stephen Henderson, BDS (the rest is froth), Head of MDDUS, .

A CROOKED RACIST WHITE DUNCE.

"I don't want to talk grammar. I want to talk like a lady." George Bernard Shaw

He who can, does. He who cannot, protects.

"He who can, does. He who cannot, teaches." George Bernard Shaw.

STEPHEN HENDERSON THE DENTAL PROTECTOR: Having nearly passed or just passed almost everywhere else, Stephen Henderson protects those who beat him in Dental School and in Clinical Practice (Quasi-communism). A brainless pencil pusher: Based on very proximate observations and direct experiences, only his irrefutably superior skin colour is good; he neither made nor chose it.

"This and no other is the root from which a tyrant springs; when he first appears he is a protector." Plato

NIGERIA: SHELL'S DOCILE CASH COW.

Children with huge oil wells near their houses eat only 1.5/day in NIGERIA; Stephen Henderson, a bellyful, closeted racist functional semi-illiterate white man whose white father and mother have never seen crude oil, and whose white ancestors were fed like battery-hens with the yields of stolen children of defenceless poor people (Meghan Markle's ancestors) is a Head at MDDUS, .

OYINBO OLE: An ignorant descendant of ultra-righteous THIEVES and owners of stolen children of defenceless poor people (Meghan Markle's ancestors) – Habakkuk.

It is a crime only if members of the Charitable Antichrist Racist Freemasonry Quasi-Religion (Mediocre Mafia/New Pharisees) did not prior authorise it.

Then, there, many Judges, and many more Policemen where members of the Charitable, Antichrist Racist Freemasonry Quasi-Religion (New Pharisees/Mediocre Mafia) – Habakkuk.

"Sometimes people don't want to hear the truth because they don't want their illusions destroyed." Friedrich Nietzsche

Members of the Charitable Antichrist Racist Freemasonry Quasi-Religion do not believe that everything is subservient to John 14:6, and everything that is not aligned to it is travelling in the wrong direction and heading straight for the rocks.

Members of the Charitable Antichrist Racist Freemasonry Quasi-Religion are free to believe and disbelieve anything. The problem is that their members oversee the administration of English, and they use the leverage thereof to trample on the basic rights of, we, their absolutely irreconcilable Religious Enemies.

BORIS JOHNSON: Members of the Charitable Antichrist Racist Freemasonry Quasi-Religion (Mediocre Mafia/New Pharisees) are very powerful in England because they are above all laws (Man and God), they oversee the administration of English Law, and we, their irreconcilable Religious Enemies, do not have legal tools to return the fire of the racist white bastards for fire.

BORIS JOHNSON: They are FROTH, impostors, and properly schooled experts of deception who wear vulgar Pharisees' charitable works as cloaks of deceit, and use very, very expensive aprons to decorate the temples of their powerless and useless fertility tools and lie that they don't lie – Psalm 144. Give us the legal tools and we will deal closeted white supremacist bastards. They are bluffers and weirdos who use colourful aprons to decorate the temples of their powerless and useless fertility tools; without measurable objectivity, they awarded themselves the supreme knowledge, and become impervious and very intolerant to other views, particularly the exceptionalism of Christ.

They are more intolerant to John 14:6 than lunatic Jihadists.

High-class racist criminals who seem to desire a world where human beings are graded according to vulgar embroideries on aprons, they use to decorate the temples of their powerless and useless fertility tools.

OYINBO OLE: RIGHTEOUS DESCENDANTS OF ULTRA-RIGHTEOUS THIEVES – HABAKKUK.

BORIS JOHNSON: "Give us the tools, and we will finish the job." Churchill
BORIS JOHNSON: Based on available evidence, the administration of English Law is irreparably rotten to its innermost core; and it is a potent weapon of war between we, John 14:6 Christians, and Members of the Charitable

Antichrist Racist Freemasonry Quasi-Religion (Mediocre Mafia/ New Pharisees) who oversee the administration of English Law – Habakkuk 1:4; John 8:44; John 10:10.

Your Royal Highness, based on available evidence, white women, not all, are incompetent liars.

Facts are sacred, and they can't be overstated.

"The truth allows no choice." Dr Samuel Johnson

OXFORD, ENGLAND: Based on available evidence, British Soldier- Territorial Defence, Stephanie Twiddle (TD), unrelentingly lied under oath - Habakkuk 1:4; John 8:44; John 10:10.

A CROOKED RACIST WHITE COUGAR.

"You will bow. You can't beat the system." Kemi Daramola

Shallow and myopic imported devil who wears confused Christianity as a cloak deceit: Esu. An imported devil with tubes and precociously collapsed (wilted mammary gland): Hypermetabolism of hyperthyroidism. Ignorance is bliss.

I shan't. I know who will – Romans 11; 1 John 4:4.

She prays to Christ and pays hefty tithe at Brick Hill Baptist Church in Bedford (quasi-protection money); members of the Antichrist Racist Freemasonry Quasi-

Religion (Mediocre Mafia/New Pharisees) in Kempston answer her prayers.

A BLATANTLY FRAUDULENT ARRANGEMENT.

"A government that robs Peter to pay Paul can always depend on the support of Paul." George Bernard Shaw

Re:

Fri, 11 Apr 2014 9:28

resh diu (rdiu@me.com)To:you Details

It's sad Ola

I kept telling you to play the game of chess rather than fight it

You take care

If you wish to dispose of 24 park road let me know

Regards

Resh
Dr Resh Diu BDS
www.oradi.co.uk

In exchange for regular bread, I shan't play closeted racist bastards who use very expensive aprons to decorate the temples of their powerless and useless fertility tools, and who have informal access to some very powerful white Judges (FREEMASONS), like chess.

The closeted racist bastards who use very, very expensive aprons, with vulgar embroideries, to decorate the temples of their powerless and useless fertility tools always tell lies, but they lie that they don't lie - Psalm 144.

"Lies are told all the time." Sir Michael Havers (1923 – 1992).

BORIS JOHNSON: Based on available evidence, Freemasons are self-promoting, vulgarly charitable impostors, expert of deception, and white supremacist thugs who, without measurable objectivity, awarded themselves the monopoly of knowledge, and are extremely intolerant to those who disagree with their brainlessly and baselessly self-awarded higher IQ.

Like Herod, Putin, Saddam Hussein, MBS, Kim, and babies, the closeted racist bastards who use very, very expensive aprons to decorate the temples of their powerless and useless fertility tools – expect everyone to love them and say and/or print only what they want to hear: The New Herod, Matthew 14: The lunatic Jew removed John's head only because he spoke: John was not punished for speaking, he was permanently prevented from speaking.

The closeted racist bastards who use very, very expensive aprons to decorate the temples of their powerless and useless fertility tools are not the only creation of Almighty

God, and their irrefutably superior skin colour is not the only wonder of our world.
DELUDED PAPER TIGERS: "England will fight to the last American." American saying

Brainless and baseless superiority is their birth right; only the irrefutably superior skin colour that they neither made nor chose is truly good. Their hairs stand on end when they are challenged by our people; we and our type are the ones closeted racist bastards will beat up without the support of the YANKS.

"Ethical foreign policy." Robin Cook (1946 – 2005).

If members of the Charitable Antichrist Racist Freemasonry Quasi-Religion (Mediocre Mafia/New Pharisees) are as brave and as ethical as they imply, they should use guns to evict Putin from Crimea; he stole it with guns.

Did Putin poison Rob Dudley: The former KGB sits on the largest gas reserve in the world. There no oil wells or gas fields in Kempston. The very highly luxuriant of Bishop's Stortford yields only food.

CECIL RHODES (1853 – 1902) was an armed robber in Africa: The English man used guns to appropriate properties of others: Movable and immovable.

OYINBO OLE: THIEVES – HABAKKUK.

"All have taken what had other owners, and all have had recourse to arms rather than quit the prey on which they were fastened." Dr Samuel Johnson.

"We shall deal with the racist bastards when we get out of prison." Comrade Robert Mugabe (1924 – 2019).

GDC: Richard Hill fabricated reports and unrelentingly lied under oath. A white man. A dishonest racist bastard. It is a crime only if members of the Charitable Antichrist Racist Freemasonry Quasi-Religion (Mediocre Mafia/New Pharisees) did not prior authorise it. OYINBO OLE: THIEVES – HABAKKUK.

GDC: Kevin Atkinson (NHS) unrelentingly lied under oath. A white man. A dishonest racist bastard. It is a crime only if members of the Charitable Antichrist Racist Freemasonry Quasi-Religion (Mediocre Mafia/New Pharisees) did not prior authorise it. OYINBO OLE: THIEVES – HABAKKUK

GDC: Jonathan Martin unrelentingly lied on record. A white man. A dishonest racist bastard. It is a crime only if members of the Charitable Antichrist Racist Freemasonry Quasi-Religion (Mediocre Mafia/New Pharisees) did not prior authorise it. OYINBO OLE: THIEVES – HABAKKUK.

GDC: Helen Falcon (MBE), unrelentingly lied on record. A white woman. A dishonest racist bastard. It is a crime only if members of the Charitable Antichrist Racist Freemasonry Quasi-Religion (Mediocre Mafia/New Pharisees) did not prior authorise it. OYINBO OLE: THIEVES – HABAKKUK.

GDC: George Rothnie (NHS) unrelentingly lied on record. A white man. A dishonest racist bastard. It is a crime only if members of the Charitable Antichrist Racist Freemasonry Quasi-Religion (Mediocre Mafia/New Pharisees) did not prior authorise it. OYINBO OLE: THIEVES – HABAKKUK.

GDC: Stephanie Twiddle, TD, (NHS) unrelentingly lied under oath. A white woman. A dishonest racist bastard. It is a crime only if members of the Charitable Antichrist Racist Freemasonry Quasi-Religion (Mediocre Mafia/New Pharisees) did not prior authorise it. OYINBO OLE: THIEVES – HABAKKUK.

GDC: Sue Gregory (OBE) l unrelentingly lied on record. A white woman. A dishonest racist bastard. It is a crime only if members of the Charitable Antichrist Racist Freemasonry Quasi-Religion (Mediocre Mafia/New Pharisees) did not prior authorise it. OYINBO OLE: THIEVES – HABAKKUK.

GDC: Rachael Bishop (NHS) unrelentingly lied under oath. A white woman. A dishonest racist bastard. It is a crime only if members of the Charitable Antichrist Racist Freemasonry Quasi-Religion (Mediocre Mafia/New Pharisees) did not prior authorise it. OYINBO OLE: THIEVES – HABAKKUK.

GDC: Geraint Evans (NHS) unrelentingly lied on record. A white man. A dishonest racist bastard. It is a crime only if members of the Charitable Antichrist Racist Freemasonry Quasi-Religion (Mediocre Mafia/New Pharisees) did not prior authorise it. OYINBO OLE: THIEVES – HABAKKUK.

Ignorant racist FOOLS: Righteous descendants of ultra-righteous thieves.

The closeted racist bastards were all white, including the Judges, and they were incompetent liars — Habakkuk.

The white man is the devil - Columbia University
https://ccnmtl.columbia.edu › mmt › mxp › concepts

Referring to Whites as "devils" originates with the teachings of Master W.D. Fard and the legend of Yakub. Fard taught Elijah Muhammad who preached the ...

OYINBO OLE: IGNORANT DESCENDANTS OF ULTRA-RIGHTEOUS THIEVES – HABAKKUK

Racist descendants of the father of lies use the mother of lies to continue to conceal the centuries-old unspoken myth, which is that intellect is unrelated to the irrefutably superior skin colour that the very, very fortunate wearer neither made nor chose.

Closeted racist bastards use incompetent mendacity to conceal hereditary intellectual impotence. Their ancestors, extremely greedy economic cannibals, used overwhelming violence to steal what God gave to others, and they use incompetent racist lies to cancel the lifetime sacrifices of others. If one's ancestors were racists, THIEVES, and owners of stolen children, it will be naive not to expect racial intolerance and incompetent mendacity to be part of one's genetic inheritances. Christ did not place our ancestors in the back row, white people did. Christ does not place AFRICANS in the back row, white people do. It is selfish and irresponsible to leave one's children at the mercy of these extremely wicked savages.

Closeted racist bastards were not deterred by his Justice (John 5:22) because they do not believe in his exceptionalism (John 14:6).

OYINBO OLE: STRAIGHT-FACED DESCENDANTS OF ULTRA-RIGHTEOUS THIEVES — HABAKKUK

"Those who have the power to do wrong with impunity seldom wait long for the will." Dr Samuel Johnson

OYINBO OLE: THIEVES — HABAKKUK.

A bastardised, indiscreetly dishonest, unashamedly mediocre, vindictive, potently weaponised, and institutionally RACIST legal system that is overseen by the FREEMASONS — Habakkuk

"To deny or belittle this good is, in this dangerous century when the resources and pretensions of power continue to enlarge, a desperate error of intellectual abstraction. More than this, it is a self-fulfilling error, which encourages us to give up the struggle against bad laws and class bound procedures and to disarm ourselves before power. It is to throw away a whole inheritance of struggle about the law and within the forms of law, whose continuity can never be fractured without bringing men and women into immediate danger." — E. P Thompson.

CHAPTER TWENTY-TWO:

Boris Johnson: Why is England not a scam?

The lunatic Jew (Herod) removed John's head only because he spoke – Matthew 14.

The fellow was lynched like Gadhafi and crucified only because He spoke; He disclosed pictures His unbounded mind painted – John 14:6.

"Freedom of Expression is basic right." Lady Hale

Then, there, when Solicitors and Barristers FAILED in the very, very competitive law practice, very many did, if they were members of the Charitable Antichrist Racist Freemasonry Quasi-Religion (Mediocre Mafia/New Pharisees), many were, they were likely to become Judges, if not, they became Politicians or something else.

"The one great principle of the English law is, to make business for itself. There is no other principle distinctly, certainly, and consistently maintained through all its narrow turnings. Viewed by this light it becomes a coherent scheme, and not the monstrous maze the laity are apt to think it. Let them but once clearly perceive that its grand principle is to make business for itself at their expense, and surely they will cease to grumble." Charles Dickens

Apart from creating very cushy salaried jobs (quasi-communism) for incontrovertibly functional semi-illiterate white Judges (predominantly) who foreseeably FAILED in the very, very competitive Law Practice, what do white imbeciles (predominantly) need very, very expensive administration of the law for?

OYINBO OLE: THIEVES – HABAKKUK.

"Sometimes people don't want to hear the truth because they don't want their illusions destroyed." Friedrich Nietzsche

Your Royal Highness, based on available evidence, white women, not all, are incompetent racist liars.

BEDFORD, ENGLAND: Sue Gregory, Officer of the Most Excellent Order of our Empire (OBE), unrelentingly lied under oath.

A RACIST CROOKED WHITE COUGAR.

"To disagree with three – fourths of the British public on all points is one of the first elements of sanity, one of the deepest consolations in all moments of spiritual doubt." Wilde

Based on available evidence, when their people (whites) commit racist crimes against ours, racist white bastards (Freemasons) who oversee the administration of English law criminally bury racial hatred.

Based on available evidence, whites measure whites with a very, very yardstick.

They were all white: Homogeneity in the administration of English law is the impregnable secure mask of merciless racial hatred.

JUDICIAL DIVERSITY: ACCELERATING CHANGE. Sir Geoffrey Bindman, QC Karon Monaghan QC "The near absence of women and Black, Asian and minority ethnic judges in the senior judiciary, is no longer tolerable. It undermines the democratic legitimacy of our legal system; it demonstrates a denial of fair and equal opportunities to members of underrepresented groups, and the diversity deficit weakens the quality of justice."

BORIS JOHNSON: Reasoning and vision are unbounded. The supernatural exists, and it is consistently accessible. Based on available evidence, the fellow is who He says He is.

BORIS JOHNSON: The mind that I got is finer than the system you serve. You are travelling in the wrong direction and heading straight for the rocks. You are doing simultaneous equations with only one set of equations; it's easier, but it is wrong.

"It does no harm to throw the occasional man overboard, but it does not do much good if you are steering full speed ahead for the rocks." Lord Gilmour of Craigmillar (1926 – 2007).

"To disagree with three – fourths of the British public on all points is one of the first elements of sanity, one of the deepest consolations in all moments of spiritual doubt." Wilde

Members of the Charitable Antichrist Racist Freemasonry Quasi-Religion are dogmatically opposed to the exceptionalism of Christ (John 14:6), and for that reason, we are their irreconcilable religious enemies.

Our dispute is based solely on John 14:6; everything else is a deceptive smokescreen.

They are cowards and cheats as they pretend to be the impartial referee in a religious dispute that they are a party to – John 14:6.

Politicians are employed and sacked by the people, so they make laws, and they come and go.

Freemasons are answerable only to Baal, and they oversee the administration of English law, and they never leave.

Many Judges and many more Policemen are members of the Charitable Antichrist Racist Freemasonry Quasi-Religion; some of them are thicker than a gross of planks.

Members of the Charitable Antichrist Racist Freemasonry Quasi-Religion (Mediocre Mafia/New Pharisees) have weaponised the administration of English law, and they unfairly use the leverage thereof to persecute we, their irreconcilable religious enemies – John 14:6.

Based on available evidence, the administration of English law is irreparably rotten to its innermost core.

Verdicts, probably in Stonemasons' Temples to Baal almost always precede hearings; in open hearings, incompetent art often incompetently imitates life.

Facts are sacred.

"The truth allows no choice." Dr Samuel Johnson

Based on very proximate observations and direct experiences, members of the Charitable Antichrist Racist Freemasonry Quasi-Religion (Mediocre Mafia/New Pharisees) are always certain about the Negrophobic destruction they desire to cause, and they seem to have unchecked and unbounded power to criminally invent racist lies to justify innate, uneducated, unintelligent, and uncontrollable racial hatred – Habakkuk 1:4; John 8:44; John 10:10.

OYINBO OLE: THIEVES – HABAKKUK

Based on available evidence, Cambridge University educated rich man's son, Sir, Mr Justice Haddon-Cave, QC, KBE, and Shiv Pabary, MBE, Member of the Most Excellent order of our Empire, Justice of Peace, and the Archetypal GDC Committee Chairman, and Mary Harley, Anthony Kravitz, Jacques Lee, and David Swinstead – all constructively lied under implied oath when they implied that they did not know that GDC-Witness, Freemason, Brother, Richard William Hill, GDC-Witness, British Soldier, Stephanie Twidale (TD), GDC-Witness Rachael Bishop, Senior NHS Nurse, GDC-Witness, Kevin Atkinson, Postgraduate Tutor, and GDC-Expert, Sue Gregory (OBE) did not unrelentingly tell lies under oath or on record.

OYINBO OLE: RACIST DESCENDANTS OF ULTRA-RIGHTEOUS THIEVES AND OWNERS OF STOLEN CHILDREN OF DEFENCELESS POOR PEOPLE (BLACK AFRICAN ANCESTORS OF MEGHAN MARKLE AND HER WHITE CHILDREN) – HABAKKUK.
What is left when the white District Judge is a functional semi-illiterate, a closeted racist, and an incompetent liar?

John 14:6 is absolutely incompatible with all forms of Charitable Antichrist Racist Freemasonry Quasi-Religion – Habakkuk 1:4; John 8:44; John 10:10.

Vulgar Pharisees' charitable works in exchange for what?

BORIS JOHNSON: Theirs is not a good deal.

Then, the grandest offer of their ruler was rejected – Matthew 4:9

"The Good Samaritan had money." Margaret Thatcher (1925 – 2013)

Mrs Thatcher implied that the money of the Good Samaritan was the yield of transparent virtue.

Based on available evidence, the Grand Masonic Temple to Baal (The Mother Temple), 60 Great Queen St, London WC2B 5AZ, was built in the early 18th century, at a height of the barbarously racist traffic in millions of stolen children of defenceless poor people (Meghan Markle's ancestors) – Habakkuk

"Find the truth and tell it." Harold Pinter

He ordered the ultra-righteous rich Jew to sell all he had, the yields of transparent virtue, give the proceeds to the poor, and follow him - Matthew 19:21. Had the Jew stole his loot, He would have told him to return stolen goods.

He tells members of the Charitable Antichrist Racist Freemasonry Quasi-Religion (Mediocre Mafia/New Pharisees) to return stolen goods (equitable reparation); deluded closeted racist bastards who use expensive aprons to decorate the temples of their powerless and useless fertility tools seem to believe that vulgar Pharisees' charitable works with the yields of centuries of selling millions of stolen children of defenceless poor people (Meghan Markle's ancestors) will make them the inheritor of Heaven.

Then Britons used STOLEN MONEY to do charitable works.

Do Freemasons use the yield of transparent virtue to do charitable works?

Based on observations and direct experiences, the most important basis of the power of members of the Charitable Antichrist Racist Freemasonry Quasi-Religion (Mediocre Mafia/New Pharisees) is their control of the administration of English Law -complicated by unbounded and unchecked incompetent mendacity.

They have prior knowledge of the Negrophobic Perjury and the Persecutory Negrophobia they desire to impose on Negroes, and they have unchecked and unbounded power to criminally invent incompetent racist lies to justify unintelligent and uneducated racial hatred – Habakkuk 1:4; John 8:44; John 10:10.

The only proper Judge is watching them – Proverbs 15:3; John 5:22

They are motivated by uncontrollable, unintelligent, and uneducated innate racial hatred and religious intolerance. They fear John 14:6 more than Putin's poisons, and they are more intolerant to the exceptionalism of living Christ than lunatic Jihadists; Prophet Mohammed is dead.

MATTHEW 14: The lunatic Jew (Herod) removed John's head only because he spoke.

He was lynched like Gadhafi and crucified like a criminal only because He spoke; He disclosed pictures His unbounded mind painted.

We are guilty because we do not believe the Satanic Mumbo Jumbo of members of the Charitable Antichrist Racist Freemasonry Quasi-Religion (Mediocre Mafia/New Pharisees), so our irreconcilable religious enemies seek to destroy us, and concomitantly our children, because our religious belief, we, their eternal religious enemies, is irreconcilable with theirs; they have leverage over us because they, our irreconcilable religious enemies, oversee the administration of English Law.

A BLATANTLY UNBALANCED AND UNFAIR ARRANGEMENT.

BEDFORD, ENGLAND: GDC-Witness, Freemason, Brother, Richard William Hill, Postgraduate Tutor Bedfordshire, fabricated reports and unrelentingly lied under oath – Habakkuk 1:4; John 8:44; John 10:10.

A crooked racist Freemason thug.

Only excessively stupid people immortalise mendacity on record; some Freemasons are excessively stupid.

"If life shows you pepper, make pepper soup." HRH Prince Charles.

Your Majesty, members of the Charitable Antichrist Racist Freemasonry Quasi-Religion (Mediocre Mafia/New Pharisees) are showing us pepper and we do not like pepper soup.

It is a crime only if members of the Charitable Antichrist Racist Freemasonry Quasi-Religion (Mediocre Mafia/New Pharisees) did not prior authorise it.

A BLATANTLY UNFAIR ARRANGEMENT.

They are the true rulers of the State, and they can do and undo, including immortal dishonesty on record.

WHITE PRIVILEGE: White Police Officers kill Negroes, in America, for fun; there, only lunatic Black Police Officers will kill white people.

In Great Britain, only a lunatic Negro will fabricate reports and tell lies under oath (persecutory Negrophobia and Negrophobic perjury) against those with indisputably superior skin colour that they neither made nor chose.

Abuse of temporary power is the fullest definition of evil.

"Those who have the power to do wrong with impunity seldom wait long for the will." Dr Samuel Johnson
Based on available evidence, white Freemason Judges and/or white racist Judges measure whites with a very different yardstick: Demons can't cast out demons – Matthew 12:27.

Freemasons are very, very powerful charitable criminals who have informal access to very, very powerful white Judges - Habakkuk 1:4; John 8::44; John 10:10.

There people are everywhere, and they control almost everything.

They are extremely wicked people.

They are extremely intolerant to other religious views, especially the views of innately inferior mere Africans.

They are more intolerant to John 14:6 than Jihadists.

They are professional hands-off racist killers who wear vulgar Pharisees' charitable works as a cloak of deceit, and they lie that they don't lie – Psalm 144.

They stalk our people like prey, and they hunt and kill our people, in packs, albeit hands-off.

Google: Dr Anand Kamath, Dentist.

Google: Dr Richard Bamgboye, GP

A society based on progressive colour-blind merit does not suit them, as they must have control, and as education, formal and informal, can only polish what genetic mix presents to it, and as Freemasons do not and cannot control genetic mix, like witches in the African bush, their security and continuing survival depends on the destruction of what they cannot control.

He, with the Divine genetic mix (Y-chromosome), was lynched like Gadhafi and crucified like a criminal because He disclosed pictures His unbounded mind painted.

"You will bow. You can't beat the system." Kemi Daramola.

Esu!

Imported devil.

Then, relative poverty imposed fake Christianity. Escape from relative poverty unshackled the true self.

Then, the source of the Daramola's survival was Begging and their Brilliant Father's income. Their mother, a kept woman, was an impotente.

She prays to Christ and pays hefty tithe at Brick Hill Baptist Church, Bedford (quasi-protection money) and members of the Charitable Antichrist Racist Freemasonry Quasi-Religion (Mediocre Mafia/ New Pharisees), in Kempston, answer all her prayers – Habakkuk 1:4; John 8:44; John 10:10.

A BLATANTLY FRAUDULENT ANTICHRIST ARRANGEMENT.

A very, very racist Country that is effectively ruled by members of the Antichrist Racist Freemasonry Quasi-Religion (Mediocre Mafia/New Pharisees), our irreconcilable religious enemies - Habakkuk 1:4; John 8:44; John 10:10; John 14:6.

Prophet Mohamed is dead.

Freemasons fear only the living; they fear John 14:6 more than Putin's poisons, and they are more intolerant to it than Jihadists.

CREEPING DPRK.

There is Freedom of Expression in North Korea, there, one is free to say and/or print only what Kim wants to hear.

577

The ancestors of Kim did not kidnap and imprison all the people of North Korea overnight, they did gradually, and the basic right to disclose pictures the mind paints was the first to be withdrawn.

The charitable, closeted racist, white supremacist thugs who have informal access to some very, very powerful white Judges, and who use very expensive aprons to decorate the temples of their powerless and useless fertility tools, and who wear vulgar Pharisees' charitable works as cloaks of deceit want to use illegal parallel (unelected) to FORCE us to state and/or print only what they want to hear.

Freemasons lie that they don't lie – Psalm 144.

Then, there, white Judges, nearly all, were Freemasons; some of them were thicker than a gross of planks.

DELUDED PAPER TIGERS: "England will fight to the last American." American sating

Their hairs stand on end when they are challenged by our people. Brainless and baseless superiority is their birth right. We and our type are the ones they will beat up without the support of the YANKS.

They are not the only creation of Almighty God, their indisputably superior skin colour is not one of the wonders of the world, and they are not immortal.

"Ethical Foreign Policy." Robin Cook (1946 – 2005).

If members of the Charitable Antichrist Racist Freemasonry Quasi-Religion (Mediocre Mafia/New Pharisees) are as brave and as ethical as they seem to imply, they should forcibly evict Putin from Crimea, he stole it with guns.

"You will bow. You can't beat the system." Kemi Daramola

She pays hefty tithe (quasi-protection money) and prays to Christ inside Brick Hill Baptist Church, Bedford, and members of the Charitable Antichrist Racist Freemasonry Quasi-Religion in Kempston answer her prayers.

A BLATANTLY FRAUDULENT ARRANGEMENT.

Facts are sacred; they can't be overstated.

I shan't bow to Baal.

I know who will defeat the Antichrist Racist System that is overseen by members of the Charitable Antichrist Racist Freemasonry Quasi-Religion (Mediocre Mafia/New Pharisees), who are more intolerant to John 14:6 than Jihadists – Romans 11; 1 John 4:4

I shan't play chess with closeted racist bastards who use very expensive aprons, with vulgar embroidery, to decorate the temples of their powerless and useless fertility tools.

It's sad Ola

I kept telling you to play the game of chess rather than fight it

You take care

If you wish to dispose of 24 park road let me know

Regards

Resh
Dr Resh Diu BDS
www.oradi.co.uk

OXFORD, ENGLAND: GDC-Expert, British Soldier – Territorial Defence, Stephanie Twiddle (TD) unrelentingly lied under oath - Habakkuk 1:4; John 8:44; John 10:10.

A closeted racist white cougar.

OYINBO OLE: THIEVES – HABAKKUK.

It is a crime only if members of the Charitable Antichrist Racist Freemasonry Quasi-Religion did not prior authorise it – Habakkuk 1:4; John 8:44; John 10:10.

Had she been black, she would have been in trouble.

Demons will not cast out demons – Matthew 12:27

"Michael Jackson would've been found guilty if he'd been black." Jo Brand

Based on available evidence, it is not the TRUTH that former Judge, Negress, Constance Briscoe, is the only incompetent liar Judge in Great Britain; had she been Caucasian, truly English (Mrs Thatcher didn't believe Michael Portillo was), male, and Freemason, she might've 'WALKED'.

Without video evidence, Derek Chauvin would have 'WALKED'.

"A complaints such as Mrs Bishop's could trigger

NEW HEROD, MATTHEW 2:16: Freemasons deceive their duller children that they're geniuses, and they kill, we, their irreconcilable RELIGIOUS ENEMIES who know that they are brainless racist white bastards.

They love the superiority that is attached to their irrefutably superior skin colour, their baseless and brainless birth right; they don't love Freedom of Expression

If a John 14:6 Christian refuses to bow down to Baal through the Charitable Antichrist Racist Freemasonry Religion, especially if he were a mere Negro, the closeted racist bastards will economically strangulate the rebellious Negro and concomitantly destroy the future of his children.

They are not the only creation of Almighty God, and they are not immortal; we will go, and they must come – 2 Samuel 12:23.

Any number added to infinity is infinity. Everything is meaningless, we are mere travellers passing through, and the endless state of non-being is our common destiny.

Google: Dr Anand Kamath, dentist.
Google: Dr Richard Bamgboye, GP.

BEDFORD, ENGLAND: Based on available evidence, GDC-Expert, Sue Gregory, OBE, Officer of the Most Excellent Order of our Empire, unrelentingly lied under implied oath – Habakkuk 1:4; John 8:44; John 10:10.
A CROOKED RACIST WHITE COUGAR.

Had she been black, she would have been in trouble.
OYINBO OLE: THIEVES – HABAKKUK.

Only stupid blacks do not know that white Judges measure whites with a very different yardstick, and only stupider

Negroes expect demons to cast out demons – Matthew 12:27.

If one's ancestors were THIEVES and owners of stolen children of defenceless poor people (Meghan Markle's ancestors), it will be naïve not to expect Racial Hatred complicated by incompetent mendacity to be part of one's genetic inheritances – Habakkuk.

"Those who have robbed have also lied." Dr Samuel Johnson

They hate us; we know.

Then, there Judges, nearly all, were members of the Charitable Antichrist Racist Freemasonry Quasi-Religion (Mediocre Mafia/ New Pharisees); some of them were thicker than a gross of planks – Habakkuk 1:4; John 8:44; John 10:10.

If all the 33rd Degree Freemasons (Scottish Rite) at the Grand Masonic Temple to Baal (Mother Temple), , and all the Master Masonic Builders at Bedfordshire Masonic Temple to Baal, the Keep, Bedford Road, Kempston, MK 42, could prove that their brother, GDC-Witness, Freemason, Brother Richard William Hill, Postgraduate Tutor Bedfordshire NHS, did not fabricate reports and unrelentingly told lies under oath, it will confirm the belief of billions of people in our world, which is that Antichrist Freemasonry Quasi-Religion (Mediocre Mafia/New Pharisees), Antichrist Islam, Antichrist Judaism, and all other motley Assemblies of Religions under the common umbrella of the Governor of the Church of England and the Defender of THE FAITH (John 14:6) are not intellectually flawed Satanic Mumbo Jumbo, and it will also confirm that reasoning and vision have finite boundaries, and if reasoning and vision have finite boundaries, our own Messiah (John 14:6) must have lied when He disclosed pictures his unbounded mind painted, and He (Christ) must have also lied when He audaciously stated: "I am the way and the truth and the life. No one comes to the Father except through me." John 14:6

"The first quality that is needed is audacity." Churchill.

If the fellow told the truth before Jews, in the Council, when He disclosed pictures His infinite mind painted, everything that is not aligned with John 14:6 is intellectually flawed, and travelling in the wrong direction, and heading straight for the rocks.

"It does no harm to throw the occasional man overboard, but it does not do much good if you are steering full speed ahead for the rocks." Lord Gilmour of Craigmillar (1926 – 2007).

Freemason Judges must be compelled to remove their masks, and when that happens, our people (Negroes) will feel safer in Great Britain.

Based on observations and direct experiences, not all white Judges are openly racists, but nearly all white Judges are white supremacists - Habakkuk 1:4; John 8:44; John 10:10.

"White supremacy is real, and it must be shattered." Dr Cornel West.

BORIS JOHNSON: Reasoning and vision do not have finite boundaries. The fellow is who He says He is, and He will inevitably get what He wants – Proverbs 16:33. He told Jews the truth in the Council when He disclosed pictures His unbounded mind painted.

"You will bow. You can't beat the system." Kemi Daramola.

Bow to who?

For better for 'STAY', for worse, for 'GO'.

Had I won millions in the lottery, the born-again Christian wouldn't have left; she'd have stayed with the money.

Obinrin!

Owo ni koko!

One must be thankful that one's situation was the case of a job that became incompatible with one's Christian belief, and which one withdrew from. Had one faced serious medical challenges, the Ekiti girl would have bailed.

She loved money, not the challenges.

Had Christ been married, she would have left when He was kidnapped, tried in a Kangaroo Court, lynched like Gadhafi, and crucified like a criminal. Those who were there when He woke up the dead, disappeared when trouble came, and the Jew, Judas Iscariot took bribe.

"Jews are very good with money." President Donald Trump
Whose money?

Judas Iscariot, Ján Ludvík Hyman Binyamin Hoch, Ghislaine Maxwell's Dad, and Bernard Madoff were Jews.

The Jewish 'model' is intellectually flawed.

Then, the Corporal knew Jews were very good with other people's money, so he flipped

BORIS JOHNSON: The fellow is who He says He is, and Faith, only pure, unalloyed, and suicidal FAITH, consistently brings Him to scene.

Google: Freemasonry is intellectual flawed.
On June 19, 2009, Members of Charitable Antichrist Racist Freemasonry Quasi-Religion invited the Negro to a GDC hearing in London, and on the same day, and at the same time, the racist white bastards invited the Negro to a Divorce Hearing in Bedford.

They wanted to kill me, and the Born-Again Christian (the straight-faced devil that was imported from Lagos) wanted to rob me, before Masons kill me, albeit hands-off.

"You will bow. You can't beat the system." Kemi Daramola.

Ekiti ole.

Ekiti ode.

I shan't. I know who will – Romans 11; 1 John 4:4.

She gave white supremacist thugs and hands-off racist killers the alibi they desired. They can't be racists if they act in the interest of one Negro against the other.

MONEY, MY MONEY WAS THE 'MEAT'.

A je ni mo mu.

Idi ni Ekiti nta.

A glorified prostitute and a thief that wears Christianity as a cloak of deceit.

Christian Freemasons guide and guard her, albeit for a fee.

She pays tithe (quasi protection money) at Brick Hill Baptist Church, Bedford, and the Charitable Antichrist Racist Freemasons in Kempston answer her prayers.

"By definition therefore there needs to be a contact order for Mr B so that he knows when he is going to see his son. It is absolutely essential that this occurs and mother agrees with that. She said so several times in her evidence. Mrs Waller agreed that not only should a child have the opportunity of developing relationship with both parents, any sibling should also be there so that inter- sibling relationship could be fostered and nurtured. Obviously in this particular case the children reside in different places. That immediately puts a strain on the children having limited contact with each other. F's sister is very much older than him and she will be further advanced into her adult life. Thus it is not a matter that that sibling relationship can only be fostered by the children being together. Indeed as we all know absence sometimes makes the heart grow fonder. F should have an opportunity of seeing his sister. Wherever he does that it should be done in a friendly and loving environment. If the time comes that his sister goes to university of course his contact with her will be restricted to the time that she is home from university. In years to come when they have both grown up, with their own family they will see less of each other. But it doesn't mean that they don't still love and adore each other as much as they would if they saw each other every day." District Judge Paul Ayers, the Senior Vice President of the Association of Her Majesty's District Judges—proofed and approved Judgement.

Brainless nonsense.

AN IMBECILE: AN ADULT WITH THE BASIC
SKILLS OF A CHILD.

Our irrefutably functional semi-illiterate Freemason
District Judge of our Empire of stolen affluence.

OYINBO ODE: A CLOSETED RACIST BRAINLESS
WHITE MAN.

"Yes, Sir, it does her honour, but it would do nobody else
honour. I have indeed, not read it all. But when I take up
the end of a web, and find it packthread, I do not expect, by
looking further, to find embroidery." Dr Samuel Johnson.

The immortal yield of a very, very elementary intellect; his
spinal cord seemed to be his highest centre.

He approved and immortalised what his functional semi-
illiterate (deductible) white father and mother spoke, which
his Poly-educated supervisors in Luton authorised.

Antichrist Racist Freemasons want to guide the education
of our children; charity should FACKING begin at home,
in the very, very beautiful Shires.

When hypothyroidism (psychosis) copulates with
Alzheimer's disease, insanity is their offspring.

GIGANTIC yields of millions of stolen children of
defenceless poor people seemed to have distorted the

realities of closeted racist bastards, genetic Eastern Europeans with camouflage English names who seem to control the weaponised Judiciary and Police Force. Seemingly motivated by RACIAL HATRED, they damaged the boy, and passed him back to his parents to repair.

When, trouble comes, let there be joy – James 1.

When Freemasons expectedly created trouble for the first ever and only Negro to set up a Dental Surgery in Bedford, since He merely spoke and the Universe became, the shallow fake Christian, Kemi Daramola, indirectly, sought refuge in the Temple of the Antichrist Racist Freemasonry Quasi-Religion.

Then, there, Judges, nearly all, were members of the Charitable Antichrist Racist Freemasonry Quasi-Religion

She prays to Christ inside Brick Hill Baptist Church in Bedford, members of the Charitable Antichrist Racist Freemasonry Quasi-Religion (Mediocre Mafia/New Pharisees) in Kempston answer her prayers.

Based on very proximate observations, direct experiences, and available evidence, the administration of English law is mediocre, racist, rotten to its core and irreparable, and it is overseen by Masons.

New Herod, Matthew 2:16: Members of the Charitable Antichrist Racist Freemasonry Quasi-Religion (Mediocre

Mafia/New Pharisees) deceive their duller children that they are geniuses, and they kill, we, their enemies who know that they are brainless racist bastards – Habakkuk 1:4; John 8:44; John 10:10.

Based on available evidence, Charitable Antichrist Racist Freemasonry Quasi-Religion is a scam – John 14:6. Based on available, the administration of English Law is tyrants' tool, a scam.

"Dirty nigger! Mama, look, a Negro!" Frantz Fanon.

What does a woman want? In Nigeria, everyone knows that women, not all, are glorified prostitute and thieves who, without words, demand payment for use of their nafaq.

'The great question that has never been answered, and which I have not yet been able to answer, despite my thirty years of research into the feminine soul, is "What does a woman want?" Sigmund Freud

"You will bow. You can't beat the system." Kemi Daramola

I shan't. I know who will – Romans 11; 1 John 4:4.

A shallow fool!

"The supreme vice is shallowness." Wilde

Ekiti ode!

Ekiti ole!

She loved what her mother couldn't afford, so, like her
mother, the contractor's wife, she used her tool to get it.

A bloody waste of life. Some born Again(st) Christians
(the evil mask of deceit) pray on their knees, for two hours
every Sunday, and without fail, at Brick Hill Baptist
Church, Bedford, and 666 spend the remainder 166 preying
on God's children.

"A Welshman is the man who prays on his knees on
Sundays and preys on his friends the rest of the week."
English saying

Your Royal Highness, based on available evidence,
women, not all, are incompetent liars.

Facts are sacred.

"The truth allows no choice." Dr Samuel Johnson

The Judge is watching all – John 5:22.

"You will bow. You can't beat the system." Kemi
Daramola

Esu!

Satanic words of a demon possessed who deceptively wears Christianity as a cloak of deceit.

Then, the source of the Daramolas' money was their very brilliant father and 'begging'. Their mother was a kept woman.

She loved her own father, then, apart from begging, he was the only sources of income for her family. She hates the father of her children, but loves his money, and desired to help white supremacist thugs to kill the father of her own children, albeit hand's off.

Google: Dr Anand Kamath

Google: Dr Richard Bamgboye

https://www.youtube.com/watch?v=BlpH4hG7m1A&feature=youtu.be

"They may not have been well written from a grammatical point of view, but I am confident I had not forgotten any of the facts." Geraint Evans, Postgraduate Tutor, Oxford

https://youtu.be/rayVcfyu9Tw

"Why, Sir, Sherry is dull, naturally dull; but it must have taken him a great deal of pains to become what we now see

him. Such an excess of stupidity, Sir, is not in Nature." DR
SAMUEL JOHNSON

They don't know how to repair the scatter-heads of their
own people, but they are experts when it comes to
destroying our people (Negroes).

Derek Chauvin, a racist bastard and a coward used his
knees to destructively stretch the spinal cord of a poor
creation of his ancestors.

White Europeans, not God, created Black Americans.

Racist bastards Decommissioned Natural Selection

In the USA, they use bullets and knees to destroy the lives
of our people. In the UK, they use incompetent racist lies
to destroy the livelihood of our people.

They are not the only creation of Almighty God, and they
are not immortal, and their irrefutably superior skin colour
is not one of the wonders of our world.

If we must go, they must come – 2 Samuel 12:23.

GDC- Witness: Based on available evidence, Geraint
Evans of Rowtree Dental Care, Rowtree, Road,
Northampton, unrelentingly lied under implied oath –
Habakkuk 1:4; John 8:44; John 10:10.

If the crooked Welshman didn't, he must sue the Negro; he wouldn't because he did.

"The earth contains no race of human beings so totally vile and worthless as the Welsh ...... " Walter Savage Landor.

A closeted racist Welsh crook.

They love the superiority that is baselessly and brainlessly attached to their indisputably superior skin colour; they don't love Freedom of Expression because they don't want their duller children to know that they are excessively stupid racist crooks.

Charitable Antichrist Racist Freemasons (Mediocre Mafia/ New Pharisees) love soft, but durable Apartheid by stealth.

"Those who know the least obey the best." George Farquhar

BEDFORD, ENGLAND: District Judge Paul Ayers of Bedford County Court, Shire Hall, 3 St Paul's Square, Bedford MK40 1SQ, the Senior Vice President of the Association of Her Majesty's District Judges, based on available evidence, it is absolutely impossible for your talent and the yield of your land to sustain your standard of living. You're a leech; your white ancestors were THIEVES and owners of stolen children of defenceless poor Africans (Meghan Markle's ancestors) – Habakkuk

When Alzheimer's disease copulates with hypothyroidism, insanity is their offspring.

If you don't know that the Charitable Antichrist Racist Freemasonry Quasi-Religion (Mediocre Mafia/New Pharisees) is only interested in your money, it is proof that you can't see them.

They are like rats, and like to act without being seen, and like rats, they are excessively stupid as the defecate everywhere leaving tell-tale signs.

They stalk our people like prey, and they hunt in packs.

BEDFORD, ENGLAND: GDC-Witness, Freemason, Brother, Richard William Hill fabricated reports and unrelentingly lied under oath – Habakkuk 1:4; John 8:44; John 10:10. His white ancestors were incompetent racist liars too; they were THIEVES and owners of stolen children of Africans (Meghan Markle's ancestors) – Habakkuk

OYINBO OLE: A closeted racist crook; a righteous descendant of ultra-righteous THIEVES – Habakkuk.

CREEPING DPRK.

BORIS JOHNSON: The mind that I got, unsolicited, is finer than the system you serve. The fellow who is who He says He is, He will get what He wants, and He has time to do so.

BORIS, JOHNSON: We are at war: John 14:6 Christians versus Charitable Antichrist Racist Freemasons, and our positions are set in stone.

We know that reasoning and vision do not have boundaries, and we are aware of a different dimension and reality, and we are more certain that He is who He says He is.

BORIS JOHNSON: Ours is latent, but very potent, and raging war against our irreconcilable RELIGIOUS ENEMIES, and there is a huge imbalance, and members of the Charitable Antichrist Racist Freemasonry Quasi-Religion oversee the administration of English Law, and the huge leverage thereof, is what they use to persecute, we, their irreconcilable RELIGIOUS ENEMIES – Habakkuk 1:4; John 8:44; John 10:10.

English Law is equal for whites and blacks, but the administration of the Law is the meat of the law, and it is not equal for blacks and whites.

BORIS JOHNSON: Elected servants of the people come and go, and they make laws, and are answerable to the whole people. Members of the Charitable Antichrist Racist Freemasonry Quasi-Religion (Mediocre Mafia/New Pharisees) are answerable only Baal, and they oversee the administration of the law, and the never leave, and they are closeted white Supremacists, Defenders of Faiths, and Dissenters of John 14:6.

"Rightful liberty is unobstructed action according to our will within limits drawn around us by the equal rights of others. I do not add 'within the limits of the law' because law is often but the tyrant's will, and always so when it violates the rights of the individual." Thomas Jefferson

BORIS JOHNSON: Based on available evidence, Cambridge University Educated rich man's son, Sir Mr Justice Haddon-Cave QC, KBE, lied under implied oath, when he implied that he did not know that his own white kindred, Richard Hill, the closeted racist GDC witness, fabricated reports and unrelentingly lied under oath – Habakkuk 1:4; John 8:44; John 10:10.

BORIS JOHNSON: Based on available evidence, Anthony Kravitz (OBE), Officer of the Most Excellent Order of our Empire, GDC Committee Expert lied, under implied oath, when he implied that he did not know that his own white kindred, Richard Hill, the closeted racist GDC witness, fabricated reports and unrelentingly lied under oath – Habakkuk 1:4; John 8:44; John 10:10.

Then, there, they find a very, very dull Indian, preferably an incestuously conceived one, and they adorn the Uncle Tom with very, very high titles, and he becomes their zombie private soldier (IRA of Sinn Fein).

"I think I will ask our legal adviser for any advice he may have. My view is that there are six or seven of us here who had the admission down, but we cannot find it in the transcript and there is wordings that imply that there was, but it is not in black and white.....” Shiv Pabary, the Archetypal GDC Committee Chairman, Member of the Most Excellent Order of our Empire (MBE), and Justice of Peace (JP)

AN IMBECILE: AN ADULT WITH THE BASIC SKILLS OF A CHILD.

UNCLE TOM.

A crooked closeted racist Indian; their Indian unrelentingly lied under oath (implied).

The Archetypal GDC Committee Chairman, Moron Member of our Empire (MMBE), and Justice of Incompetent Racist Lied (JIRL).

Then, the sole ambition of Indians is to be above Negroes in the pecking order.

“One witness at a Royal Commission in 1897 said the ambition of Indians in Trinidad was ‘to buy a cow, then a shop, and say: “We are no Niggers to work in cane fields.” Patrick French, The World Is What It Is, The Authorised Biography of V.S. Naipaul.

BEDFORD, ENGLAND: District Judge Paul Ayers of Bedford County Court, Shire Hall, 3 St Paul's Square, Bedford MK40 1SQ, the Senior Vice President of the

Association of Her Majesty's District Judges, based on available evidence, our own Money, NIGERIA (oil/gas) is by far more relevant to the economic survival of all your white children, your white spouse, and your white parents than NORWICH (coastal dole); then, your white ancestors, including John Bunyan (1628 – 1688) were fed like battery hens with the yields of stolen children of defenceless poor people (Meghan Markle's ancestors) – Habakkuk

OYINBO OLE: An ignorant descendant of WHITE THIEVES and owners of stolen human beings – Habakkuk

"Sometimes people don't want to know the truth because they don't want their illusions destroyed." Friedrich Nietzsche

"I know of no evil that has ever existed, nor can imagine any evil to exist, worse than the tearing of eighty thousand persons annually from their native land, by a combination of the most civilised nations inhabiting the most enlightened part of the globe, but more especially under the sanction of the laws of that Nation which calls herself the most free and the most happy of them all." Prime Minister William Pitt the Younger

OYINBO OLE: THIEVES – HABAKKUK.

Based on available evidence, then, the white man was the devil.

"Many Scots masters were considered among the most brutal, with life expectancy on their plantations averaging a mere four years. We worked them to death then simply imported more to keep the sugar and thus the money flowing. Unlike centuries of grief and murder, an apology cost nothing. So, what does Scotland have to say?" Herald Scotland: Ian Bell, Columnist, Sunday 28 April 2013

'The white man is the devil' – what the Nation of Islam taught ...
https://www.independent.co.uk › World

5 Jun 2016 — In 1974, Muhammad Ali told Michael Parkinson and a stunned chat show audience that the white man of America was "the blue-eyed, blond-headed ...

OYINBO OLE: Closeted racist descendants of ultra-righteous THIEVES and owners of stolen, and irreversibly destroyed, creations of Almighty God (the ancestors of Meghan Markle and white children) - Habakkuk.

Irreversible genetic damage is the most enduring residue of Europeans' barbaric commerce in millions of stolen children of defenceless poor Africans (The ancestors of Meghan Markle and her white children) - Habakkuk

The centuries-old unspoken myth that intellect is related to the indisputably superior skin colour that the very fortunate wearer neither made nor chose is the mother of all racist scams.

Boris Johnson: Why is England not a scam?

"By definition therefore there needs to be a contact order for Mr B so that he knows when he is going to see his son. It is absolutely essential that this occurs and mother agrees with that. She said so several times in her evidence. Mrs Waller agreed that not only should a child have the opportunity of developing relationship with both parents, any sibling should also be there so that inter- sibling relationship could be fostered and nurtured. Obviously in this particular case the children reside in different places. That immediately puts a strain on the children having limited contact with each other. F's sister is very much older than him and she will be further advanced into her adult life. Thus it is not a matter that that sibling relationship can only be fostered by the children being together. Indeed as we all know absence sometimes makes the heart grow fonder. F should have an opportunity of seeing his sister. Wherever he does that it should be done in a friendly and loving environment. If the time comes that his sister goes to university of course his contact with her will be restricted to the time that she is home from university. In years to come when they have both grown up, with their own family they will see less of each other. But it doesn't mean that they don't still love and adore each other as much as they would if they saw each other every day." Bedford's District Judge, the Senior Vice President of the Association of Her Majesty's District Judges – proofed and approved Judgement.

AN IMBECILE: AN ADULT WITH THE BASIC
SKILLS OF A CHILD.

A CLOSETED RACIST FOOL'S APPROVAL.

"Yes, Sir, it does *her* honour, but it would do nobody else
honour. I have indeed, not read it all. But when I take up
the end of a web, and find it packthread, I do not expect, by
looking further, to find embroidery." Dr Samuel Johnson

 Sincerely perceived brainless nonsense. The yield of a
very, very elementary intellect; his spinal cord seemed to
be his highest centre.

Facts are sacred.

Sheep unnaturally shepherd sheep. Shepherds know that
sheep are imbeciles, sheep do not know Shepherds are
imbeciles too.

"Mediocrity weighing mediocrity in the balance, and
incompetence applauding its brother ...." Wilde

Percentage of children in the UK hitting educational targets
at 5, in descending order:
1. Asian (Indian)
2. Asian (Any other Asian)
3. White (British)
4. White (Irish)
5. Mixed (any other)
6. Mixed (white and black African)

7. Chinese

8. Mixed (White and black Caribbean)

9. Black (African heritage)

10. Asian (Any other Asian)

11. Black (Caribbean heritage)

12. Black (other)

13. Asian (Bangladeshi)

14. White (Any other white)

15. Any other ethnic group

16. Asian (Pakistani)

17. White (Traveller of Irish heritage)

18. White (Gypsy/ Roma)

Source: Centre Forum, Daily Mail, 04.04.2016

Children in the UK hitting educational targets at 16, in descending order:

1. Chinese

2. Asian (Indian)

3. Asian (Any other Asian)

4. Mixed (White and Asian)

5. White (Irish)

6. Mixed (Any other)

7. Any other ethnic group

8. Asian (Bangladeshi)

9. Parent/pupil preferred not to say

10. Mixed (White and black African)

11. White (Any other white)

12. Black (African heritage)

13. White (British)

14. Asian (Pakistani)

15. Black (other)
16. Mixed (White and black Caribbean)
17. Black (Caribbean heritage)
18. White (Traveller of Irish heritage)
19. White (Gypsy/ Roma)

Source: Centre Forum, Daily Mail, 04.04.2016

According to Centre Forum, only Gypsies/Roma and travellers of Irish heritage were below the descendants of plantation Negroes on the list of those meeting academic targets at age 16.

Based on very proximate observations and direct experiences, genetic damage is the most enduring residue of several centuries of barbarously racist traffic in millions of stolen children of defenceless poor people (the ancestors of Meghan Markle and her white children) - Habakkuk.

Based on available evidence, GDC-Witness: Richard Hill fabricated reports and unrelentingly lied under oath—Habakkuk.

Based on available evidence, GDC-INSIDER: Sue Gregory (OBE), Officer of the Most Excellent Order of our Empire unrelentingly lied under implied oath—Habakkuk.

Based on available evidence, GDC-Witness: Rachael Bishop, Senior NHS Nurse, unrelentingly lied under oath—Habakkuk.

Based on available evidence, GDC-Witness: Geraint Evans (NHS) unrelentingly lied under implied oath—Habakkuk.

Based on available evidence, GDC-Witness: Stephanie Twidale (TD) unrelentingly lied under oath—Habakkuk.

Based on available evidence, GDC-Witness: George Rothnie (NHS) unrelentingly lied under implied oath—Habakkuk.

Based on available evidence, GDC-Witness: Kevin Atkinson (NHS) unrelentingly lied under oath—Habakkuk

They were all white. Homogeneity in the administration of English law is the impregnable secure mask of merciless racist evil.

Based on available evidence, the administration of English Law is a weapon of war: The latent, but very, very potent race and religious war.

JUDICIAL DIVERSITY: ACCELERATING CHANGE.
Sir Geoffrey Bindman, QC, and Karon Monaghan,
QC "The near absence of women and Black, Asian and minority ethnic judges in the senior judiciary, is no longer tolerable. It undermines the democratic legitimacy of our legal system; it demonstrates a denial of fair and equal opportunities to members of underrepresented groups, and the diversity deficit weakens the quality of justice."

We are trapped again, this time in a RACE AND RELIGIOUS WAR; our irreconcilable religious enemies, dissenters of John 14:6, and defenders of Faiths (FREEMASONS), seem to oversee the administration of English Law.

Members of the Charitable Antichrist Racist Freemasons are everywhere, and they control almost everything; they're not immortal, so they must leave, and leave for eternity.

They must go to their ancestors, as they will never return to them. Freemasons should 'chillax', as we are mere travellers passing through this grossly overrated transitory 'reality', and we must all leave – 2 Samuel 12:23.

It is not the truth that our people are no longer inferior under English Law; the 1807 Act was purely symbolic.

"Change occurs slowly. Very often a legal change might take place, but the cultural shift required to really accept its spirit lingers in the wings for decades." Sera Sheridan

No people will voluntarily relinquish centuries-old advantageous positions in exchange for NOTHING, substitution is likelier.

Only foolish Negroes do not know that substitution is fraudulent emancipation.

Then, closeted racist bastards carried and sold millions of stolen children of defenceless poor people (the ancestors of Meghan Markle and her white children), now, they carry natural resources.

"Meghan Markle was the subject of explicit and obnoxious racial hatred." John Bercow

OYINBO OLE: THIEVES – HABAKKUK.

"Moderation is a virtue only among those who are thought to have found alternatives." Henry Kissinger

A bastardised, unashamedly mediocre, indiscreetly dishonest, vindictive, potently weaponised, and institutionally racist legal system that is overseen by MASONS (Mediocre Mafia)—Habakkuk.

"To deny or belittle this good is, in this dangerous century when the resources and pretensions of power continue to enlarge, a desperate error of intellectual abstraction. More than this, it is a self-fulfilling error, which encourages us to give up the struggle against bad laws and class bound procedures and to disarm ourselves before power. It is to throw away a whole inheritance of struggle about the law and within the forms of law, whose continuity can never be fractured without bringing men and women into immediate danger."—E. P Thompson.

"Find the truth and tell it." Harold Pinter

Facts are sacred, they can't be overstated.

BORIS JOHNSON: We are not alone. Reasoning and vision are unbounded. The fellow is who He says He is, and He told Jews the truth in the Council when He, reluctantly, disclosed truths His unbounded mind painted.

If all the members of the Charitable Antichrist Racist Freemasonry Quasi-Religion (Mediocre Mafia/New

Pharisees) at the Bedfordshire Mason Temple to Baal, the Keep, Bedford Road, MK42, and all the 33rd Degree Freemasons (Master Builders) at the Grand Masonic Temple to Baal (the Mother Temple), and the British Premier, the Honourable Boris Johnson, and the Prime Minister of Israel, His Excellency, Mr Naftali Bennett, and the Prime Minister of India, His Excellency, Mr Narendra Modi, and all Rabbis, Imams, Bishops, Prophets, and Prophetess, in London, Jerusalem, the Vatican City, Mecca, and Medina – could prove that District Judge Paul Ayers of Bedford County Court, the Senior Vice President of the Association of Her Majesty's Judges was not, incontrovertibly, a functional semi-illiterate and an closeted racist incompetent liar, and if they could prove that Shiv Pabary, Member of the Most Excellent Order of our Empire was not a functional semi-illiterate and incompetent racist liar, and if they could prove Robert Kingston, Director, Dobern Property Limited, was not a functional semi-illiterate and an incompetent racist liar, and if they could prove that GDC-Witness: Richard Hill did not fabricate reports and unrelentingly told lies under oath, and if they could prove that GDC-INSIDER: Sue Gregory (OBE), Officer of the Most Excellent Order of our Empire did not unrelentingly tell lies under implied oath, and if they could prove that GDC-Witness: Rachael Bishop, Senior NHS Nurse, did not unrelentingly tell lies under oath, and if they could prove that GDC-Witness: Geraint Evans (NHS) did not unrelentingly tell lies under implied oath, and if they could prove that GDC-Witness: Stephanie Twidale (TD) did not unrelentingly tell lies under oath, and if they could prove that GDC-Witness: George Rothnie

(NHS) did not unrelentingly tell lies under implied oath, and if they could prove that GDC-Witness: Kevin Atkinson (NHS) did not unrelentingly tell lies under oath, and if they could prove that Cambridge University Educated Rich Man's son, Sir, Mr Justice Haddon-Cave, QC, KBE, did not deviate from the truth when he implied that he did not know that Shiv Pabary, Member of the Most Excellent Order of our Empire (MBE) did not unrelentingly tell lies under oath, they will confirm the belief of billions of people in our world, which is that Antichrist Islam, Antichrist Judaism, Antichrist Freemasonry Quasi-Religion, and all other motley assemblies of exotic religions and faiths under the common umbrella of the Defender of the Faith and the Governor of the Church of England are not intellectually flawed Satanic Mumbo Jumbo, and it will also confirm that reasoning and vision have finite boundaries. If reasoning and vision have finite boundaries, when He disclosed pictures His unbounded mind painted. He must have lied when He audaciously stated that He was exceptionalism.

"The first quality that is needed is audacity." Sir Winston Churchill

If the fellow told Jews only truths, we are FORKED, as His Knights attacks Kings and Queens simultaneously, and only the Queens can move, and anything that is not aligned to John 14:6 is heading Straight for the rocks.

"It does no harm to throw the occasional man overboard, but it does not do much good if you are steering full speed ahead for the rocks." Sir Ian Gilmour (1926 – 2007).

CHAPTER TWENTY-TWO:

Boris Johnson: Why is England not a scam?

Apart from creating very cushy salaried jobs for incontrovertibly functional semi-illiterate white District Judges (predominantly) who foreseeably FAILED in the very, very competitive Law Practice, what do white imbeciles (predominantly) need very, very expensive administration of the law for (quasi-communism)— Proverbs 17:16

The report, by the OECD, warns that the UK needs to take significant action to boost the basic skills of the nation's young people. The 460-page study is based on the first-ever survey of the literacy, numeracy and problem-solving at work skills of 16 to 65-year-olds in 24 countries, with almost 9,000 people taking part in England and Northern Ireland to make up the UK results. The findings showed that England and Northern Ireland have some of the highest proportions of adults scoring no higher than Level 1 in literacy and numeracy—the lowest level on the OECD's scale. This suggests that their skills in the basics are no better than that of a 10-year-old.

AN IMBECILE: AN ADULT WITH THE BASIC SKILLS OF A CHILD.

GOOGLE: FREEMASONRY IS INTELLECTUALLY FLAWED.

"Natural selection will not remove ignorance from future generations." Dr Clinton Richard Dawkins

How could it, if it is decommissioned?

Adults with the basic skills of a foetus will succeed imbeciles, and the former will need only food and shelter.

FORESEERS: They accurately foresaw that their descendants, not all, WILL BE excessively stupid, so they used made in Birmingham guns to pillage and loot Africa, and the racist white bastards used the yields of several centuries of the nastiest and greediest economic cannibalism and the evilest sadism, savagery, and cruellest racist terrorism the world will ever know to create an Eldorado for millions of white imbeciles, and they decommissioned natural selection, and they reversed evolution, and they made it possible for millions of imbeciles, of all shades, to breed irresponsibly.

"We have decommissioned natural selection and must now look deep within ourselves and decide what we wish to become." Professor E. O. Wilson, Harvard biologist E. O. Wilson

Genetic aliens with camouflage English names oppress, we, the descendants of the robbed with the yields of the robbery—Habakkuk

If one farmed white pigs with great snouts solely for pigs' snout curry, the stupidest of the white pigs deserved to be killed and eaten first.

"I am very fond of my pigs; it does not stop me from eating them." Archbishop Runcie (1921 – 2000).

NIGERIA: SHELL'S DOCILE CASH COW.

Children with huge oil wells and gas fields near their huts eat only 1.5/day in NIGERIA; a closeted racist functional semi-illiterate former, mere, debt-collector Solicitor in NORWICH whose white father and mother have never seen crude oil, and whose white ancestors were fed like battery hens with the yields of stolen lives – is our District Judge in Bedford.

OYINBO OLE: THIEVES – HABAKKUK.

Re Meeting 9th March

                              Mon, 8 Mar 2010 20:20
George Rothnie georgerothnie@hotmail.comHide

    To adeolacole@aol.com
Hi Ola,

We are scheduled to meet tomorrow evening at my surgery about 5.30ish. Unfortunately something has cropped up which necessytates me having to postpone the meeting. I'm really sorry it's such short notice.

I will contact you in the week to arrange another date.

Once agaim my apologies.

George

AN IMBECILE: AN ADULT WITH THE BASIC SKILLS OF A CHILD.

Dr George Rothnie: Edinburgh University Educated, Deputy Postgraduate Dean, Oxford.

A closeted racist descendant of Scottish crooks, racists, murderers, and owners of stolen children of defenceless poor Africans (Meghan Markle's ancestors) – Habakkuk

Mrs Helen Falcon, MBE, Member of the Most Excellent Order of our Empire adorned a Scottish imbecile with a very high title, and he became her zombie private soldier

They neither made nor chose their irrefutably superior skin colour.

They love the superiority that is associated with their indisputably superior skin colour, their baseless and brainless birth right; they don't love Freedom of Expression because they don't want their duller children to know that some of the finest filtrates of their people are excessively stupid.

A brainless Scot; a racist descendant of thieves and owners of stolen children of defenceless poor people (Meghan Markle's ancestors) – Habakkuk

Then, for several centuries, armed, highly civilised racist white bastards and those they armed, mercilessly rained hell fire on our people, on the land allotted to them by Almighty God, and absolutely unprovoked; now, they impede our ascent from the bottomless crater into which theirs threw ours unprovoked, during several centuries of the greediest economic cannibalism and the evilest racist terrorism the world will ever know – Habakkuk

"Many Scots masters were considered among the most brutal, with life expectancy on their plantations averaging a mere four years. We worked them to death then simply imported more to keep the sugar and thus the money flowing. Unlike centuries of grief and murder, an apology cost nothing. So, what does Scotland have to say?" Herald Scotland: Ian Bell, Columnist, Sunday 28 April 2013

CORBY, ENGLAND: GDC-Witness, George Rothnie, Deputy Postgraduate Dean, Oxford, unrelentingly lied under implied oath – Habakkuk 1:4; John 8:44; John 10:10

A SCATTER-HEAD CLOSETED RACIST CROOKED SCOTSMAN

BORIS JOHNSON: We are not alone, and we are travelling in the wrong direction. The fellow is who He says He is, and He will get what

He wants.

The notion of relativity that is unattached to infinity is intellectually flawed, akin to doing a simultaneous equation with only one equation.

Better than crap could also be crap.

BORIS JOHNSON: Reasoning and vision are unbounded (infinite); the fellow told the truth when Hrr

BEDFORD: District Judge Paul Ayers, your white ancestors were THIEVES; you're a LEECH. It's impossible for your talent and the yield of your land to sustain your standard of living. NIGERIA (oil/gas) is more relevant to the survival of your white children than NORWICH (coastal dole).

GDC: Sue Gregory (OBE) lied on record. A RACIST CROOK.

"The best opportunity of developing academically and emotional." DISTRICT JUDGE BEDFORD.

A RACIST DUNCE.

Our semi-illiterate Freemason Judge of our Empire of stolen affluence.

A MORON MASON.

https://www.youtube.com/watch? v=BlpH4hG7m1A.

*****

The University of Lagos, Akoka, Lagos.

Dearest Sir,

Re: The Vice Chancellor University of Lagos: Pre-action Notice.

The fellow is who He says He is. John 14:6 is non-negotiable. Why wasn't that known and taught at the University of Lagos? The University of Lagos was reckless, and recklessness is malice, and/or dishonest for not disclosing the most important truth under the Sun, which is that the fellow is who He says He is, and that He is exceptional – John 14:6, and He will Judge all – John 5:22; Matthew 25: 31 – 46.

The lunatic Jew (Herod) removed John's head only because he spoke.

MBS ordered the quartering, bagging, and binning Jamal Khashoggi only because he spoke and wrote.

The fellow, and only He, will Judge Jews and Gentiles – Matthew 25: 31-46; John 5:22.

Facts are sacred; they can't be overstated.

"The truth allows no choice." Dr Samuel Johnson

Then, sadistic white bastards used to remove the heads of those who disagreed with them. The last decapitation, with an axe, in England, was in 1817.
Beheading was removed from the statute book in 1973, and in the same year, one of Mrs Thatcher's (1925 -2013) disciples, Kenneth Baker, banned flogging.

Why remove the heads of those who spoke and/or printed what you did not like if it were illegal to flog them?

"There is now less flogging in our great schools than formerly, but then less is learned there; so that what the boys get at one end, they lose at the other." Dr Samuel Johnson

Then, there, white Judges, nearly all, were members of the Charitable Antichrist Racist Freemasonry Quasi-Religion (Mediocre Mafia/New Pharisees); some of them were THICKER than a gross of planks - Habakkuk.

"Find the truth and tell it." Harold Pinter

Racist White Judges are the most potent enemies of Negroes; they have power.

A Prime Minister implied that he had very, very good reasons to suspect that white Judges, not all, were closeted racist thugs, and he corroborated his suspicion by insinuating that White Judges measure white people with a very, very different yardstick, and further implied that demons will not cast out demons – Matthew 12:27.

Based on available evidence, the administration of English law, almost in its entirety, and to its innermost core, is mediocre, vindictive, indiscreetly racist, potently weaponised, and is overseen by the Charitable Antichrist Racist Freemasons – Habakkuk 1:4; John 8:44; John 10:10. "Sometimes people don't want to hear the truth because they don't want their illusions destroyed." Friedrich Nietzsche

"British Prime Minister attacks racial bias in Universities and the Justice System. 'David Cameron has persuaded a leading labour MP to 'defect' by launching a government investigation into why black people make up such a high proportion of the prison population. Mr Cameron said Mr Lammy would examine why blacks and ethnic minorities make up nearly a quarter of Crown Court defendants – compared to 14 percent of the population. He added: 'If you are black, you are more likely to be in a prison cell than studying in a university. And if you are black, it seems you're more likely to be sentenced to custody for a crime than if you are white. 'We should investigate why this is and how we can end this possible discrimination. That's why I have asked David Lammy to lead a review. Mr Lammy, who is a qualified barrister, said: 'I am pleased to accept the Prime Minister's invitation." Mr Paul Dacre, Daily Mail, 31.01.2016

The Prime Minister had full access to all classified information.

They love skin colour superiority; they neither made nor chose their irrefutably superior skin colour, their brainless and baseless birth right. They don't love Freedom of Expression because they don't want their duller children to know that they are excessively stupid.

They love Apartheid by stealth.

Based on very proximate observations and direct experiences, the natural instinct of the white privileged dullard.

https://www.youtube.com/watch?v=BlpH4hG7m1A&feature=youtu.be

"They may not have been well written from a grammatical point of view, but I am confident I had not forgotten any of the facts." Dr Geraint Evans, Postgraduate Tutor, Oxford

Brainless nonsense. The yield of a very, very elementary intellect; his spinal cord seemed to be his highest centre.

An Antichrist white supremacists' system elevates a white Welsh imbecile to the position of a postgraduate Tutor in Great Britain.

What's great about that?

"The earth contains no race of human beings so totally vile and worthless as the Welsh......" Walter Savage Landor

https://youtu.be/rayVcfyu9Tw

"Why, Sir, Sherry is dull, naturally dull; but it must have taken him a great deal of pains to become what we now see him. Such an excess of stupidity, Sir, is not in Nature." DR SAMUEL JOHNSON

"The Negro is just a child." Frantz Fanon

AFRICA: Ignorant black bastards steal money from defenceless poor people and use stolen money to buy imbecility for their imbecile children, from a Welsh imbecile, in Great Britain. What's great about that?

England is the natural resources of Wales. The natural resources of England are in Nigeria and places like that.

Then, racist bastards carried and sold millions of stolen children of defenceless poor people (the ancestors of Meghan Markle and her white children); now, they carry natural resources.

OYINBO OLE: THIEVES – HABAKKUK.

SUBSTITUTION: FRAUDULENT EMANCIPATION.

"Moderation is a virtue only among those who are thought to have found alternatives." Henry Kissinger

Dr Geraint Evans, Postgraduate Tutor, Oxford, is the product of the educational system of one of the richest nations on earth, but not in the universe; had the closeted racist and crooked bastard been the product of the educational system of one of the poorest nations of earth, he might not be able to read properly.

Boris Johnson: Why is England not a scam?

Based on available evidence, Geraint Evans, England's Class Postgraduate Tutor, from Valleys Wales, unrelentingly lied under implied oath – Habakkuk 1:4; John 8:44: John 10:10.

Had he been black, he'd have been in trouble.

Only stupid Negroes do not know that whites measure whites with a very different yardstick, and only stupider

Negroes expect demons to cast out demons – Matthew 12:27.

Wales, a mere Province of England is worthy only because England is rich.

If Wales were to be detached from England in Monmouthshire and at the River Severn, she will be poorer than Albania.

PERCEPTION IS GRANDER THAN REALITY.

European commerce in stolen children of defenceless Africans (Meghan Markle's ancestors), and all its successors, in whatever forms, are different modes of economic cannibalism.

"OJ Simpson in a knit cap is OJ Simpson." Johnnie Cochrane

Economic Cannibalism of whatever kind is Economic Cannibalism.

The poor will always be with you; the Judge did not say that they should be robbed penniless.

"For the poor you will always have with you in the land. Therefore, I command you, 'You shall open wide your hand to your brother, to the needy and to the poor, in your land.' -Deuteronomy 15:7-11.

Not all white people are openly racist; based on very proximate observations, nearly all white people are white supremacists.

Facts are sacred; they can't be overstated.

White supremacist Freemason Judges are the most potent legal racists in Great Britain; they are closeted white supremacists, with unbounded and unchecked powers.

"Those who have the power to do wrong with impunity seldom wait long for the will." Dr Samuel Johnson.

Charitable Antichrist Racist Freemasons love superiority, their baseless and brainless birth right; they don't love Freedom of Expression because they don't want their duller children to know that they're excessively stupid.

They need Apartheid by stealth.

The Brain isn't inside the indisputably superior skin colour that they neither made nor chose.

The centuries-old unspoken myth that intellect is related to their irrefutably superior skin colour is the mother of all racist scams.

England is a scam.

If closeted racist white bastards do not want the imbeciles, of all shades, they shepherd to know that England is a scam, they should ban Freedom of Expression, in the same way as a white supremacist, Home Secretary, Winston Churchill, concealed superior black power by banning man-to-man inter-racial fist fights, as our people were knocking theirs – out, too easily, and for fun.

"Despite Britain's rich history of black boxers, racist attitudes about the mental and physical dispositions of black people permeated the game; full-time British segregationist campaigners such as the evangelical preacher Frederick Brotherton Meyer argued that white athletes did not have the "animal development" of black people and could therefore not compete with their "instinctive passion" for violence. There were also worries over the consequences of emboldening Britain's colonial subjects. For a nervous British establishment, there were far too many negative ramifications for their rule over the Empire if even an innocent sports tournament could even temporarily demonstrate the equality of black and white people. This is why in 1911, Home Secretary Winston Churchill banned interracial boxing matches, and the BBBC followed suit. The BBBC's bar remained in place until the 1940s. Manchester rose with anger for Len. Demonstrations were held across the city, and a protest delegation of boxers was sent to the BBBC's London headquarters. But the situation demoralised him, and he retired from the profession in 1933, choosing instead to mentor young boxers." Tribune

****

GDC-Witness: Freemason, Brother, Richard Hill fabricated reports and unrelentingly lied under oath—Habakkuk.

GDC-INSIDER: Sue Gregory (OBE), Officer of the Most Excellent Order of our Empire unrelentingly lied under implied oath—Habakkuk.

GDC-Witness: Rachael Bishop, Senior NHS Nurse, unrelentingly lied under oath—Habakkuk.

GDC-Witness: Geraint Evans (NHS) unrelentingly lied under implied oath—Habakkuk.

GDC-Witness: Stephanie Twidale (TD) unrelentingly lied under oath—Habakkuk.

GDC-Witness: George Rothnie (NHS) unrelentingly lied under implied oath—Habakkuk.

GDC-Witness: Kevin Atkinson (NHS) unrelentingly lied under oath—Habakkuk

Facts are sacred, and they cannot be overstated.

I expect to be killed; the public must not know that England is a scam that is overseen by the Charitable Antichrist Racist Freemasonry Quasi-Religion (Mediocre Mafia/New Pharisees) – Habakkuk 1:4; John 8:44; John 10:10.

Reasoning and vision are unbounded, rather than accept the truth, He was lynched like Gadhafi, and He was crucified only because He spoke

Then, there, members of the Charitable Antichrist Racist Freemasonry Quasi-Religion awarded themselves the monopoly of knowledge, and deluded, they became impervious to other views

Like the Universe, our Empire did not evolve from NOTHING. Then, Britons, actively and deliberately used made in Birmingham GUNS to steal almost everything.

"It was in 1066 that William the Conqueror occupied Britain, stole our land and gained control by granting it to his Norman friends, thus creating the feudal system we have not yet fully escaped." The Right Honourable Anthony Benn (1925 – 2014).

William the Conqueror stole from others what others stole from others.

"All have taken what had other owners, and all have had recourse to arms rather than quit the prey on which they were fastened." Dr Samuel Johnson

Then, the Saxe-Coburg and Gotha family crossed the English Channel.
Mustafa Mehmet is Turkish, Boris Johnson.

The real name of Nigella Lawson's great grandfather was Gustav Leibson; he was from Latvia

Then, in Africa, whenever armed racist white bastards slaughtered our people, they dispossessed them, and whenever they robbed our people, they took possession - Habakkuk.

Based on available evidence, England is a scam.

BEDFORD: District Judge Paul Ayers of Shire Hall, 3 St Paul's Square, Bedford MK40 1SQ, and of our Empire of stolen affluence, and the Senior Vice President of the Association of Her Majesty's District Judges, based on available evidence, it is absolutely impossible for your Christ granted talent and the yield of your land to sustain your standard of living. You're a LEECH, and for several centuries, your white ancestors were industrial scale professional THIEVES, merciless racist murders, vicious economic cannibals, evil racist terrorists, amoral drug dealers (opium merchants), and owners of stolen children of defenceless poor people (Meghan Markle's ancestors) – Habakkuk. You shan't make HEAVEN because you are neck deep in racial hatred and fraud.

BEDFORD: District Judge Paul Ayers of Shire Hall, 3 St Paul's Square, Bedford MK40 1SQ, and of our Empire of stolen affluence, and the Senior Vice President of the Association of Her Majesty's District Judges, based on available evidence, our own Money, NIGERIA (oil/gas) is by far more relevant to the economic survival of your white spouse, and your white father, and all your white children than NORWICH (coastal dole). Based on very, very proximate observations and direct experiences, only your indisputably superior skin colour is good, and with it, your NOTHING; you will be considerably diminished as a human being.

England: White Supremacists' Scam. The Continuing Tyranny of the White Majority.

Not all Masons are openly racist, but white Masons, nearly all, are white supremacists.

Prince Hall's Masons.

"White Supremacy is real, and it needs to be shattered." Dr Cornel West.

"Racism is rife throughout most organisations across Britain." The Mayor of London

"Meghan Markle was the subject of explicit and obnoxious racial hatred." John Bercow

"All sections of the UK Society are institutionally racist." Sir Bernard Hogan-Howe

Descendants of aliens with camouflage English names oppress we the descendants of the robbed with the yields of the robbery - Habakkuk

Based on available evidence, those who nearly passed or just passed at school could become Police Officers and Judges within one of the dullest adult populations in the industrialised world: One of the least literate and least numerate countries in the industrialised world.

Ignorance is bliss.

"By definition therefore there needs to be a contact order for Mr B so that he knows when he is going to see his son. It is absolutely essential that this occurs and mother agrees with that. She said so several times in her evidence. Mrs Waller agreed that not only should a child have the opportunity of developing relationship with both parents, any sibling should also be there so that inter- sibling relationship could be fostered and nurtured. Obviously in this particular case the children reside in different places. That immediately puts a strain on the children having limited contact with each other. F's sister is very much older than him and she will be further advanced into her adult life. Thus it is not a matter that that sibling relationship can only be fostered by the children being together. Indeed as we all know absence sometimes makes the heart grow fonder. F should have an opportunity of seeing his sister. Wherever he does that it should be done in a friendly and loving environment. If the time comes that his sister goes to university of course his contact with her will be restricted to the time that she is home from university. In years to come when they have both grown up, with their own family they will see less of each other. But it doesn't mean that they don't still love and adore each other as much as they would if they saw each other every day." District Judge Paul Ayers of Bedford County Court, the Senior Vice President of the Association of Her Majesty's District Judges – proofed and approved Judgement (verbatim).

Based on observations and direct experiences, the white man, albeit England's Class Judge, seemed intellectually disorientated and mentally imbalanced.

"Yes, Sir, it does *her* honour, but it would do nobody else honour. I have indeed, not read it all. But when I take up the end of a web, and find it packthread, I do not expect, by looking further, to find embroidery." Dr Samuel Johnson.

Immortalised brainless nonsense.

"The English think incompetence is the same thing as sincerity." Quentin Crisp

OYINBO ODE: A CLOSETED RACIST SCATTER-HEAD WHITE DUNCE.

"Sir, he was dull in company, dull in his closet, dull everywhere. He was dull in a new way, and that made many people think him GREAT......" Dr Samuel Johnson

Based on very proximate observations and direct experiences, only his indisputably superior skin colour seemed good; without it, the white man will be considerably diminished as a being.

The incontrovertibly functional semi-literate white man, albeit England's Class District Judge seemed as dull as a butter knife.

His proofed and approved Judgement accurately reflects the educational system of one of the richest nations on Earth.

Had the incontrovertibly functional semi-literate white man, albeit England's Class District Judge, been the product of the Educational System of one of the poorest nations on Earth, he'd be worse, and he might not be able to read properly.

"The typical English man, usually violent and always dull." Wilde

Google: Alzheimer's disease.

Google: Incompetent Liars: Some Lawyers

Then, there, white Judges, nearly all, were Freemasons and most of them were thicker than a gross of planks.

Charitable Antichrist Racist Freemasonry Quasi-Religion teaches its members secret-voodoo-handshake, not grammar, the former is considerably easier to master.

Dr Clinton Richard Dawkins, Professor Edward O Wilson, and OECD implied that all the white children District Judge Paul Ayers of Bedford County Court, the Senior Vice President of the Association of Her Majesty's District Judges should be duller than their white father.

Facts are sacred.

"The truth allows no choice." Dr Samuel Johnson

"Natural selection will not remove ignorance from future generations." Dr Clinton Richard Dawkins

Properly proofed and approved Judgements by properly educated Judges should pass through at least four separate filters: The transcript writers, the proof-reader's, the court clerks, and the Judge.

NIGERIA: SHELL'S DOCILE CASH COW.

Urhobo babies with huge oil wells and gas fields near their huts eat only 1.5/day in NIGERIA; bellyful white nincompoops whose white fathers and mothers have never seen crude oil, and whose white ancestors were fed like battery hens with the yields of stolen and destroyed poor black children of defenceless Africans, thrive in Great Britain (Meghan Markle's ancestors) – Habakkuk.

Based on available evidence, in an open dialogue with Ruth Bader Ginsburg (1933 – 2020), Lady Hale lamented funding.

My Lady, what is the value of many layers of unashamed mediocrity and confusion?

"The English think incompetence is the same thing as sincerity." Quentin Crisp.

District Judge Paul Ayers of Bedford County Court, the Senior Vice President of the Association of Her Majesty's District Judges is, certainly, not OXBRIDGE.

District Judge Paul Ayers of Bedford County Court, the Senior Vice President of the Association of Her Majesty's District Judges seemed intellectually disorientated and mentally imbalanced, and he unashamedly immortalised the yield of his very, very elementary mind; his spinal cord seemed to be his highest centre.

District Judge Paul Ayers of Bedford County Court, the Senior Vice President of the Association of Her Majesty's District Judges is worthy only because England is rich.

Affluence did not evolve; then, it was actively and deliberately stolen with GUNS – Habakkuk.

OYINBO OLE: Racist descendants of

Based on very, very proximate observations and direct experiences, only his indisputably superior skin colour is good; he neither made nor chose it, and without it, he WILL BE considerably diminished as a human being.

Based on available evidence, it is absolutely impossible for his talent or the yield of his land to sustain his standard of living. His white ancestors were THIEVES; he is white, and he's a leech.

Which part of Bedford County Court, shire Hall, 3 St Paul's Square, Bedford MK40 1SQ, was not stolen or which part of the Magnificent Building preceded several centuries of barbarously racist traffic in millions of stolen poor black children of defenceless Africans (Meghan Markle's ancestors): The building or its chattels – Habakkuk?

OYINBO OLE: WHITE THIEVES - HABAKKUK

BEDFORD: GDC-Witness, Freemason, Brother, Richard William Hill, fabricated reports and unrelentingly lied under oath – Habakkuk 1:4; John 8:44; John 10:10.

A CLOSETED RACIST WHITE CROOKS APPROVAL.

Had he been black, he'd have been in trouble.

"Michael Jackson would have been found guilty if he'd been black." Jo Brand

"Sometimes people don't want to hear the truth because they don't want their illusions destroyed." Friedrich Nietzsche

The report, by the OECD, warns that the UK needs to take significant action to boost the basic skills of the nation's young people. The 460-page study is based on the first-ever survey of the literacy, numeracy and problem-solving at work skills of 16 to 65-year-olds in 24 countries, with almost 9,000 people taking part in England and Northern Ireland to make up the UK results. The findings showed that England and Northern Ireland have some of the highest proportions of adults scoring no higher than Level 1 in literacy and numeracy - the lowest level on the OECD's scale. This suggests that their skills in the basics are no better than that of a 10-year-old.

AN IMBECILE: AN ADULT WITH THE BASIC SKILLS OF A CHILD.

"Natural selection will not remove ignorance from future generations." Dr Richard Dawkins

Adult with the basic skills of a foetus will succeed IMBECILES, and the former will need only food and shelter.

GOOGLE: FREEMASONRY IS INTELLECTUALLY FLAWED.

GOOGLE: INCOMPETENT LIARS: SOME LAWYERS.

"Racism is alive and well and living in Tower Hamlets, in Westminster and, yes, sometimes in the judiciary." Judge Peter Herbert, Officer of the Most Excellent Order of the British Empire (OBE)

"The liberty of the individual is no gift of civilisation. It was greatest before there was any civilisation." SIGMUND FREUD

OYINBO OLE: Racist descendants of ultra-righteous THIEVES and owners of stolen children of defenceless Africans (Meghan Markle's ancestors) - Habakkuk

"FAILING SCHOOLS AND A BATTLE FOR BRITAIN: This was the day the British education establishment's 50-year betrayal of the Nation's children lay starkly exposed in all its ignominy. After testing 166,000 people in 24 education systems, the Organisation for Economic Cooperation and Development (OECD) finds that England young adults are amongst the least literate and numerate in the industrialised world." Daily Mail, 09.01.2013

Young adults have LORDS.

LORDS of morons are likelier to be morons too.

Shepherds know sheep are morons; sheep do not know that shepherds are morons too.

Sheep unnaturally shepherd sheep.

"Mediocrity weighing mediocrity in the balance, and incompetence applauding its brother ...." Wilde

RE: METROPOLITAN POLICE: UNDISCLOSED ALLEGED HARASSMENT.

Mon, Sep 25, 2017 7:32 am

Kieran.Dempsey@met.pnn.police.ukHide

To adeolacole@aol.com

Sir,

Thank you for your expeditious response.

I can in fact confirm it was myself who called you on 21/09/2017 in regards to the content of the letter you reference below.

as explained in such letter, an allegation has been made against you.

As such, you will need to attend ILFORD POLICE STATION where you may give your version of events by means of taped interview, where all evidence will be put to you in an interview inline with the Police and Criminal Evidence Act 1984.

In interview, with the prescience of a solicitor, you are entitled to give your version of events via a prepared statement, should you decide that this is the appropriate response to questioning.

Please advise of which dates you would be able to attend for interview.

Please do not hesitate to contact myself should you have any further questions.

Sincerely,

PC Kieran Dempsey

ERT A

Ilford Police Station

EA BOCU

AN IMBECILE: AN ADULT WITH THE BASIC SKILLS OF A CHILD.

Brainless nonsense!

PERCEPTION IS GRANDER THAN REALITY.

Those who FAILED at school could become Police Officers.

Almost everything is assumed in favour of the indisputably superior skin colour that the wearer neither made nor chose.

Our incontrovertibly functional semi-illiterate Police Officer of our Empire Stolen Affluence – Habakkuk

Ms Cressida Dick went to Oxford, and she employed him, so if a mere Negro thinks that he's excessively stupid, the Negro must be a lunatic.

The fact that one is better than crap is not the evidence of the fact that one is not crap.

No brain.

Poor in natural resources.

Several centuries of stealing and slavery preceded the huge trust fund.

Only their skin colour is indisputably superior; they neither made nor chose it.

Before SLAVERY, what?

Ignorance is bliss.

"Those who know the least obey the best." George Farquhar

Ignorant descendants of THIEVES and owners of stolen children of defenceless poor Africans (Meghan Markle's ancestors) – Habakkuk.

Some people are as dull as a bitter knife; and mere tools of the Charitable Racist Freemasons (Mediocre Mafia/New Pharisees), the IRA of Sinn Fein. Kitted up Zombie Private Soldiers of the closeted racist white bastards, our irreconcilable religious enemies, who use very, very expensive aprons to decorate the temples of their powerless and useless fertility tools.

They hate us; we know. Their intellects are their very, very soft underbellies, paradoxically our shields – Habakkuk 1:4; John 8:44; John 10:10.

What they want is intellectual superiority

Their skin colour is indisputably superior, and everybody knows that.

The centuries-old unspoken myth that intellect is related to the irrefutably superior skin colour that they neither made not chose is the mother of all racist scams.

We will never accept, without cogent evidence that their intellects are superior to ours, and everybody knows that their fertility tools are inferior to ours, so those who go black never go back.

A functional semi-illiterate Closeted Racist Law Enforcer, he immortalised in writing what he might have heard his mother and father speak, which Ms Cressida Dick implicitly authorised.

The yield of the educational system of one of the richest nations on Earth; one of the most expensive education on earth seems to be a bloody waste of money – 17:16.

Education will only polish what genetic mix presents to it; Oxford University will not polish the charcoal brain of imbecile closeted racist Police Officers: White Supremacist thugs in camouflage uniform.

Ms Cressida Dick went to Oxford University.

Is Oxbridge white supremacists' scam?

Ms Cressida Dick's predecessor was educated at Oxford and Cambridge Universities.

"All sections of the UK Society are institutionally racist." Sir Bernard Hogan-Howe

Bedfordshire Police and the Metropolitan Police are part of the UK Society.

CHAPTER TWENTY-FOUR:

Boris Johnson: Why is England not a scam?

"The Negro is an animal, the Negro is bad, the Negro is mean, the Negro is ugly; look, a nigger ……... Mama the nigger's going to eat me up ……. Where shall I hide? Frantz Fanon

"If life shows you pepper, make pepper soup." HRH Prince Charles

Your Royal Highness, Charitable Antichrist Racist Freemasons, our irreconcilable RELIGIOUS ENEMIES, show us pepper, in Great Britain; we do not like pepper soup.

Then, there, white Judges, nearly all, were Freemasons; some of them were thicker than a gross of planks - Habakkuk.

BORIS JOHNSON: We are at War, a latent but very potent and raging race war. Our irreconcilable Religious Enemies oversee the administration of English Law: A grossly unbalanced and unfair arrangement. In some parts of our Commonwealth, the very emotive Religious Imbalance will be forcibly balanced with armed conflict.

The elected servants of the people make laws, and they are employed and sacked by the people, so they come and go. Members of the Charitable Antichrist Racist Freemasonry Quasi-Religion – are dogmatically opposed to the exceptionalism of Christ (John 14:6), and they oversee the administration of English Law, and they are answerable only to Baal, and they never leave, as they are not employed by the people, and cannot be sacked by the people, they are an illegal parallel force that operate by stealth.

They wear vulgar Pharisees' charitable works as cloaks of deceit, and to divert attention from their air head, they use very, very expensive aprons to decorate the temples of their powerless and useless fertility tools, and they deceive their own children by lying that they don't lie – Psalm 144. They are closeted racist thugs who seek to express their uneducated innate prejudice legally.
Vulgar Pharisees' Charitable works in exchange for what?

645

They tell incompetent racist lies all the time, and they lie that they don't lie – Psalm 144.

Google: The White Judge Lied.

"Lies are told all the time." Sir Michael Havers (1923 – 1992).

BORIS JOHNSON: Theirs is not a good deal. Then, their grandest offer was rejected by the immortal fellow who knows all and sees all and is Charitable Anti-Christ Racist Freemasonry Quasi-Religion - spin proof.

Charitable Anti-Christ Racist Freemasonry Quasi-Religion is in permanent state of spin; they are Higher Class Scammers, and they tell incompetent racist lies all the time.

They are Quasi-THIEVES.

"Those who have robbed have also lied." Dr Samuel Johnson

OYINBO OLE: WHITE THIEVES – HABAKKUK

BORIS JOHNSON: Charitable Antichrist Racist Freemasonry Quasi-Religion is a properly organised higher-class scam. Give us the legal tools, and we will lift up their very, very expensive aprons, and expose their permanently wilted, powerless, and useless fertility tools.

BORIS JOHNSON: "Give us the tools, and we will finish the job." Churchill

Without colour-blind and progressive measurable objectivity closeted racist white bastards (quasi-voodoo men) who use very, very expensive ugly aprons to decorate temples of their powerless and useless fertility tools, awarded themselves the monopoly of knowledge, and they dogmatically become impervious and very, very intolerant to other views, more intolerant to different perspectives – than the Taliban, especially the views of the mere Negro (African Bombata).

"The truth allows no choice." Dr Samuel Johnson.

Reasoning and vision do not have finite boundaries; the fellow is who He says He is   - John 14:6.

Where the press is free and everyone could read, all is safe.

— President Thomas Jefferson

Closeted racist bastards love the superiority that is associated with their irrefutably superior skin colour; they don't want Freedom of Expression because they don't want their duller children to know that they are excessively

Then, in our tribe in the African bush, the white man will be treated with sticks and stones, and he will be boiled, and eaten, as like his ancestors ours were cannibals too, and he will return to mother earth as Negroes' shit.

"Stoning certainly teaches people a lesson." Ayatollah Khalkhali

Those who shipped about 200,000 made in Birmingham guns to West Africa, annually, among those who had no means of treating penetrative gunshot wounds, were neither civilised nor Christian.

The second time racist white bastards visited our tribe in the African bush, they came with made in Birmingham guns, only for self-defence, and Bibles, and they carried natural resources and raw materials, not stolen children of defenceless poor Africans (Meghan Markle's ancestors).

The first time racist white bastards visited Africa, they with thousands of guns, the currency of the carrying trade, and gin.

Then, and now, alien white Europeans' intercourse with Africa was pure business, economic cannibalism.

Then, and now, things did not turn out well for Africa.

Then, aliens carried and sold millions of stolen children of defenceless poor Africans (Meghan Markle's ancestors); now, racist white bastards carry natural resources.

SUBSTITUTION IS FRAUDULENT EMANCIPATION.

OYINBO OLE: WHITE THIEVES – HABAKKUK

"Moderation is a virtue only among those who are thought to have found alternatives."

OYINBO OLE: An ignorant descendant of ultra-righteous white thieves and owners of stolen poor black children of defenceless Africans (Meghan Markle's ancestors) - Habakkuk

Charitable, Antichrist Racist Freemasonry Quasi-Religion teaches its members secret handshakes, not grammar, and the former is considerably easier to master.

Facts are sacred; they can't be overstated.

"The English think incompetence is the same thing as sincerity." Quentin Crisp

OYINBO ODE: A CLOSETED RACIST FUNCTIONAL SEMI-ILLITERATE WHITE DUNCE – PROVERBS 17:16.

A scatter-head white man; an ultra-righteous descendant of WHITE THIEVES – Habakkuk.

"The great enemy of the clear language is INSINCERITY (DISHONESTY). When there is a gap between one's real and one's declared aims, one turns as it were instinctively to long words and exhausted idioms, like a cuttlefish squirting ink. In our age there is no such thing as 'keeping out of politics'. All issues are political issues, and politics itself is a mass of lies, evasions, folly, HATRED and schizophrenia. When the general atmosphere is bad, language must suffer." – George Orwell

"Americans messed up in Afghanistan." Oxford University Educated Imran Khan. MEANING: Fake experts, Americans, and Britons, with very, very high IQ, were myopic fools.

GDC-Witness: Freemason, Brother, Richard William Hill fabricated reports and unrelentingly lied under oath—Habakkuk.

GDC-INSIDER: Sue Gregory (OBE), Officer of the Most Excellent Order of our Empire unrelentingly lied under implied oath—Habakkuk.

GDC-Witness: Rachael Bishop, Senior NHS Nurse, unrelentingly lied under oath—Habakkuk.

GDC-Witness: Geraint Evans (NHS) unrelentingly lied under implied oath—Habakkuk.

GDC-Witness: Stephanie Twidale (TD) unrelentingly lied under oath—Habakkuk.

GDC-Witness: George Rothnie (NHS) unrelentingly lied under implied oath—Habakkuk.

GDC-Witness: Kevin Atkinson (NHS) unrelentingly lied under oath—Habakkuk.

They were all white.

Facts are sacred, they cannot be overstated.

OYINBO OLE: Closeted Racist descendants of ultra-righteous WHITE THIEVES and owners of stolen poor black children of defenceless poor Africans (Meghan Markle's ancestors) – Habakkuk

Then, there, the yields of stolen and destroyed lives of other people's children were used to build Magnificent Courts and pay the wages of white Judges who sent white people who stole money to prisons built with the yields of stolen human beings (Meghan Markle's ancestors) – Habakkuk

Members of the Charitable, Antichrist, Closeted Racist Freemasonry Quasi-Religion (Mediocre Mafia/New Pharisees) want to enjoy the yields of several continuous centuries of the greediest economic cannibalism and evilest racist terrorism the world will ever know, in perfect peace and quiet - Habakkuk.

Charitable Antichrist Racist Freemasons: Half-educated white school dropouts (predominantly) and their superiors who use very, very expensive aprons to decorate the temples of their powerless and useless fertility tools, and have informal access to some very, very powerful white supremacist Freemason Judges.

Then, the closeted racist white bastards (predominantly) lied all the time, and they lied that they lied that they didn't lie – Psalm 144.

"Lies are told all the time." Sir Michael Havers (1923 – 1992)

Based on very long, and very, very proximate observations, not all white people are openly racist, but nearly all white people are white supremacists.

In 1738, after very, very careful study, the Roman Catholic Church banned all forms of membership, direct or indirect, of the Charitable Antichrist Racist Freemasonry Quasi-Religion.

Why should the white mother and father of District Judge Paul Ayers of Bedford County Court need very, very strong views about education if there is irrefutable evidence that for several continuous centuries, his white ancestors were the greediest economic cannibals and the evilest racist terrorists the world will ever know – Habakkuk: Industrial scale professional thieves and owners of stolen poor black children of defenceless poor people (Meghan Markle's ancestors/ Kamala Harris's ancestors)?

"Trump's administration packed Courts with mediocre white Judges." Kamala Harris

BEDFORD, ENGLAND: GDC-Witness, Freemason, Brother, Richard Hill fabricated reports and unrelentingly lied under oath – Habakkuk 1:4; John 8:44; John 10:10.

A CLOSETED RACIST CROOKED WHITE MAN.

OYINBO OLE: A racist descendant of ultra-righteous industrial scale professional THIEVES and owners of stolen poor black children of defenceless poor Africans (Meghan Markle's ancestors) – Habakkuk

"We know historically that the Negro guilty of lying with a white woman is castrated." Frantz Fanon

A white woman, Sue Gregory, Officer of the Most Excellent Order of our Empire (OBE), GDC- Expert, unrelentingly lied under implied oath – Habakkuk 1:4; John 8:44; John 10:10.

The white ancestors of a white woman, Sue Gregory, Officer of the Most Excellent Order of our Empire (OBE), GDC- Expert, were incompetent racist liars too; they were THIEVES and owners of poor black children of defenceless Africans (Meghan Markle's ancestors) – Habakkuk.

A white woman, GDC-Witness, Ms Rachael Bishop, Senior NHS Nurse, unrelentingly lied under oath.

A RACIST CROOKED WHITE COUGAR.

If Ms Rachael Bishop and/or the GDC who hired the closeted racist incompetent liar could prove that 'a white woman' did not unrelentingly tell lies under oath, they must sue the Negro. They wouldn't because she did.

"There is a nigger in there, if he touches me, I'd slap his face. You never know with them. He must have great big hands; besides he's sure to be rough." Frantz Fanon.

THE PROTECTOR: "A complaints such as Mrs Bishop could trigger an enquiry." A closeted racist crooked white man, Stephen Henderson, LLM, BDS, Head of MDDUS, Holborn, London

"This and no other is the root from which a tyrant springs; when he first appears he is a protector." Plato

A CROOKED RACIST WHITE DIPSTICK.

"I don't want to talk grammar. I want to talk like a lady." George Bernard Shaw

PERCEPTION IS GRANDER THAN REALITY.

It is plainly deductible that apart from the FROTH the closeted racist white bastard bought from Cardiff, the only postgraduate examinations the white English man didn't fail are those he didn't do.

PERCEPTION IS GRANDER THAN REALITY.

Facts are sacred.

NIGERIA: SHELL'S DOCILE CASH COW.

Children with huge oil wells and gas fields near their huts eat only 1.5/day in NIGERIA; a scatter-head white man whose white mother and father have never seen crude oil and whose white ancestors were fed like battery hens with the yields of stolen poor black children of defenceless Africans (Meghan Markle's ancestors) – Habakkuk

OYINBO OLE: Ultra-righteous descendants of righteous THIEVES and owners of stolen poor black children of defenceless Africans (Meghan Markle's ancestors) – Habakkuk.

Then, on the hard labour plantations, stolen land acquired with extreme violence, where stolen children of defenceless Africans (Meghan Markle's ancestors) were imprisoned, and worked to death, at gunpoint, highly civilised, enlightened, and Christian racist white bastards used to frog march rebellious Africans to the woods, at gun point, and defenceless Negroes, mere chattels, were hanged from tall trees, without hoods - Habakkuk.

OXFORD, ENGLAND: GDC-Witness, Stephanie Twiddle, British Soldier – Territorial Defence, unrelentingly lied under oath – Habakkuk. Her white were incompetent liars too; they were THIEVES and owners of stolen children of defenceless poor people (Meghan Markle's ancestors) – Habakkuk

A CLOSETED RACIST CROOKED WHITE COUGAR.

IF THE MOTHERS AND FATHERS OF SOME WHITE PRIVILEGED DULLARDS HAD VERY, VERY STRONG VIEWS ABOUT EDUCATION, WHY DID THEIR CHILDREN TURN OUT TO BE EXCESSIVELY STUPID?

"Why, Sir, Sherry is dull, naturally dull; but it must have taken him a great deal of pains to become what we now see him. Such an excess of stupidity, Sir, is not in Nature." DR SAMUEL JOHNSON

The only black closeted racist white bastards truly love is our own money; then, racist white bastards carried and sold millions of stolen poor black children of defenceless poor people (Meghan Markle's ancestors); now, they carry natural resources.

SUBSTITUTION IS FRAUDULENT EMANCIPATION.

"Moderation is a virtue only among those who are thought to have found alternatives." Henry Kissinger

JUDICIAL DIVERSITY: ACCELERATING CHANGE.
"The near absence of women and Black, Asian and minority ethnic judges in the senior judiciary, is no longer tolerable. It undermines the democratic legitimacy of our legal system; it demonstrates a denial of fair and equal opportunities to members of underrepresented groups, and the diversity deficit weakens the quality of justice." Sir Geoffrey Bindman, QC, and Karon Monaghan, QC.

Politicians come and go, they make laws, and they are servants of the people, who have the power to sack them. Charitable Antichrist Freemasons are the masters of the people, they oversee the administration of the law, and they never leave, and they tell lies all the time.

"Lies are told all the time." Sir Michael Havers (1923 – 1992).

When their people commit racist crimes against ours, racist white bastards criminally bury racial hatred – Habakkuk

NIGERIA: SHELL'S DOCILE CASH COW.

Children with huge oil wells near their huts eat only 1.5/day in Nigeria; closeted racist nincompoops whose fathers and mothers have never seen crude oil, and whose ancestors were fed like battery hens with the yields of stolen lives – thrive in Great Britain. What's great about that?

White Privilege: The Continuing Uneducated Tyranny of the White Majority – Habakkuk.

Then, there, most powerful weapon of closeted racist Freemason Judges is incompetent lies.

Charitable Antichrist Racist Freemasons (Mediocre Mafia/New Pharisees) are by far more intolerant than the Taliban Jihadist; they are 'violently' and dogmatically opposed to the exceptionalism of Christ, and they are indiscreetly racist.

Not all Freemasons are openly racist, but nearly all Freemasons are white supremacists.

Then, there, white Judges, nearly all, were Freemasons; some of them were thicker than a gross planks.

The Taliban is Antichrist, but not Racist.

Based on available evidence, the administration of English law is Antichrist and RACIST.

Charitable Antichrist Racist Freemasons are our irreconcilable Religious Enemies.

John 14:6 is absolutely incompatible with Charitable Antichrist Racist Freemasonry Quasi-Religion.

BEDFORD, ENGLAND: GDC-Witness, White Richard Hill fabricated reports and unrelentingly lied under oath – Habakkuk 1:4; John 8:44: John 10:10.

A CLOSETED RACIST WHITE CROOK

A MORON FREEMASON,

NIGERIA: SHELL'S DOCILE CASH COW.

Children with huge oil wells near their houses eat only 1.5/day in NIGERIA; crooked closeted racist white bastards whose white fathers and mothers have never seen crude oil, and whose white ancestors were fed like battery hens with the yields of stolen children of defenceless Africans thrive in Great Britain.

What's great about indiscreet racial hatred?

Had he been black, he would have been in trouble.

"Michael Jackson would have been found guilty if he'd been black." Jo Brand

A Closeted Racist Crooked White Man.

A bastardised, unashamedly mediocre, indiscreetly dishonest, potently weaponised, vindictive, and institutionally racist legal system that is overseen by the Freemasons (Mediocre Mafia/ New Pharisees) – Habakkuk.

"The highest reach of injustice is to be deemed just when you are not." Plato.

New Herod, Matthew 2:16: They deceive to their duller white children that they are geniuses, and they kill, albeit hands-off, all those who know that they are crooked racist white bastards.

They are not the only creation of Almighty God, and they are not immortal.

Whites measure whites with a very, very different yardstick: Judicial Apartheid, the crudest and the cruellest form of white privilege.

Only excessively stupid Negroes expect demons to cast out demons – Matthew 12:27

OYINBO OLE: Racist descendants of ultra-righteous THIEVES and owners of stolen poor black children of defenceless Africans (Meghan Markle's ancestors) - Habakkuk

BEDFORD, ENGLAND: District Judge Paul Ayers, the Senior Vice President of the Association of Her Majesty's District Judges, based on available evidence, it is absolutely impossible for your talent and the yield of your land to sustain your standard of living. You're a leech, and your white ancestors were THIEVES – Habakkuk

District Judge Paul Ayers, the Senior Vice President of the Association of Her Majesty's District Judges, which part of Bedford County Court was not stolen or which part of it preceded the barbarously racist traffic in millions of stolen poor black children of defenceless Africans (Meghan Markle's ancestors): The building or its chattels?

"Sometimes people don't want to hear the truth because they don't want their illusions destroyed." Friedrich Nietzsche.

Shallow racist white bastards see molecules, and they kill, albeit hands-off, all those who see atoms – Matthew 12:27.

"The truth allows no choice." Dr Samuel Johnson.

Then, there, gigantic yields of merciless racist evil (SLAVERY) were used to build magnificent courts and pay the wages of white Judges who sent white people who stole money to grand prisons built with stolen money – Habakkuk

"Those who know the least obey the best." George Farquhar

Before SLAVERY, what?

"England is like a prostitute who, having sold her body all her life, decides to quit and close her business, and then tells everybody she wants to be chaste and protect her flesh as if it were jade." He Manzi, Chinese Politician

BEDFORD, ENGLAND: District Judge, a closeted racist descendant of extremely nasty murderers, racists, liars, THIEVES, drug dealers (opium merchants), and owners of stolen poor black children of defenceless Africans (Meghan Markle's ancestors) – Habakkuk.

"Those who have robbed have also lied." Dr Samuel Johnson

Ignorant descendants of very hardened industrial-scale professional THIEVES and owners of stolen poor black children of defenceless Africans (Meghan Markle's ancestors) – Habakkuk.

Facts are sacred; they can't be overstated.

Those who nearly passed or just passed the A/Level could do Law within one of the dullest adult populations in the industrialised world (among the least literate and least numerate - OECD), and they are among likeliest to struggle with grammar.

PERCEPTION IS GRANDER THAN REALITY.

BEDFORD, ENGLAND: Our incontrovertibly functional semi-illiterate white District Judge of our Empire of Stolen Affluence; an ignorant descendant of extremely nasty racist murderers, greedy economic cannibals, THIEVES, drug dealers (opium merchants), and owners of stolen poor black children of defenceless Africans (Meghan Markle's ancestors) – Habakkuk.

District Judge Paul Ayers of Bedford County Court, the Senior Vice President of the Association of Her Majesty's District Judges, based on available evidence, you're being CARRIED; it absolutely impossible for your Christ granted talent and the yield of your land to sustain your standard of living. You're a leech, and your white ancestors were THIEVES. Our own Money, NIGERIA (oil/gas) is by very, very far more relevant to the economic survival of all your white children than Norwich (Coastal dole) – Habakkuk

OYINBO OLE: A closeted racist descendant of ultra-righteous WHITE THIEVES and owners of stolen poor black children of defenceless Africans (Meghan Markle's ancestors) - Habakkuk

NIGERIA: SHELL'S DOCILE CASH COW.

Children with huge oil wells near their huts eat only 1.5/day; a closeted racist, bellyful, functional; semi-illiterate white man, a mere former debt collector Solicitor in Norwich (Coastal dole) whose white mother and father have never seen crude oil, and whose white ancestors were fed like battery hens with the yields of stolen poor black children of defenceless Africans is our District Judge in Bedford, Great Britain - Habakkuk.

OYINBO OLE: Racist descendants of THIEVES and owners of stolen poor black children of defenceless Africans (Meghan Markle's ancestors) – Habakkuk.

"FAILING SCHOOLS AND A BATTLE FOR BRITAIN: This was the day the British education establishment's 50-year betrayal of the Nation's children lay starkly exposed in all its ignominy. After testing 166,000 people in 24 education systems, the Organisation for Economic Cooperation and Development (OECD) finds that England young adults are amongst the least literate and numerate in the industrialised world." Daily Mail, 09.01.2013

Young adults have LORDS.

LORDS of morons are likelier to be morons too.

NEW HEROD, Matthew 2:16: Racist white bastards (charitable Antichrist Racist Freemasons) see molecules and they kill all their irreconcilable enemies who see atoms.

"This man I thought had been a Lord of wits, but I find he's only a wit among Lords." Dr Samuel Johnson

LORDS: "500 men, ordinary men, chosen accidentally from among the unemployed." David Lloyd George

The report, by the OECD, warns that the UK needs to take significant action to boost the basic skills of the nation's young people. The 460-page study is based on the first-ever survey of the literacy, numeracy and problem-solving at work skills of 16 to 65-year-olds in 24 countries, with almost 9,000 people taking part in England and Northern Ireland to make up the UK results. The findings showed that England and Northern Ireland have some of the highest proportions of adults scoring no higher than Level 1 in literacy and numeracy - the lowest level on the OECD's scale. This suggests that their skills in the basics are no better than that of a 10-year-old.

AN IMBECILE: AN ADULT WITH THE BASIC SKILLS OF A CHILD.

Shepherds of imbeciles are likelier to be imbeciles too.

Apart from creating cushy salaried jobs for those (closeted racist functional semi-illiterate white Judges) who foreseeably FAILED in the very, very competitive law practice (quasi-communism), what do imbeciles need very, very expensive administration of the law for?

SEERS: They accurately foresaw that their descendants will be imbeciles, so they used, made in Birmingham, GUNS to loot Africa, and they used the yields of several centuries of the greediest economic cannibalism and the evilest racist terrorism the world will ever know to create an Eldorado for millions of white imbeciles, and they decommissioned natural selection, and they reversed evolution, and they made it possible for millions of imbeciles to breed irresponsibly.

Millions of imbeciles breed millions of imbeciles, accelerating extinction.

Why breed millions of imbeciles, man, or beast, if you are not going to eat them?

If one farmed thousands of white pigs with great snouts for white pigs' great snout curry, the dullest of the white pigs with great snouts deserves to be killed and eaten first.

"I am very fond of my pigs, but it doesn't stop me from eating them." Archbishop Runcie (1921 – 2000).

"Natural selection will not remove ignorance from future generations." Dr Richard Dawkins

"We have decommissioned natural selection and must now look deep within ourselves and decide what we wish to become." Professor Edward. O. Wilson

If members of the Charitable Antichrist Racist Freemasonry Quasi-religion (Mediocre Mafia/New Pharisees) are as clever as they imply, why are the sheep they shepherd among the dullest in the industrialised world (some of the least numerate and least literate) in the industrialised world - Habakkuk.

Andreas Schleicher, the OECD's deputy director for education and skills, said Japan was good at developing skills but its "education system works in silos and productivity growth is so-so. Compare this to the UK and US, where they are no longer good at developing talent but very good at extracting value from the best workers.

"If aliens visit us, the outcome would be much as when Columbus landed in America, which didn't turn out well for the Native Americans." Dr Stephen Hawking.

Then, white aliens visited Africa, and they are still there. Then, they carried and sold human beings (Meghan Markle's ancestors; now, they carry natural resources.

SUBSTITUTION IS FRAUDULENT EMANCIPATION.

"Moderation is a virtue only among those who are thought to have found alternatives." Henry Kissinger

Then, racist white bastards used, made in Birmingham, guns to loot AFRICA, and they used the yields of several centuries of the greediest economic cannibalism and the evilest racist terrorism the world will ever know to create an Eldorado for millions of white imbeciles, and they decommissioned natural selection, and they reversed evolution, and made it possible for millions of imbeciles, of all shades, to breed irresponsibly.

"Racism is alive and well and living in Tower Hamlets, in Westminster and, yes, sometimes in the judiciary." Judge Peter Herbert, Officer of the Most Excellent Order of the British Empire (OBE)

THE JUDICIARY IS NOT A BRANCH OF THE CHARITABLE ANTICHRIST RACIST FREEMASONRY QUASI-RELIGION.

https://youtu.be/rayVcfyu9Tw

RE: Outstanding statutory annual registration fee invoice: payment due – FINAL REMINDER

Thu, 3 Sep 2015 20:00

cqc (NHS SHARED BUSINESS SERVICES LTD (BRISTOL)) SBS-B.cqc@nhs.netHide

Hello,

Thank you for your below email

Kindly request you to provide your contact details
(telephone number) so we can contact you and explain.

If any query please let me know

Thanks and Regards,

Kanchan Jaisinghani

Collections
Debt Management Team

Shared Business Services

Tel 0303-123-1155

Fax 0117-933-8890

E-mail: sbs-b.cqc@nhs.net

Website: www.sbs.nhs.uk

Government Business Award Winner

Central Government Supplier of the Year 2011.

AN IMBECILE: AN ADULT WITH THE BASIC
SKILLS OF A CHILD.

Almost everyone in Great Britain is a winner. Sir Major was a winner too; he smashed the very ugly, Oxford University Educated Jew, Egg Winner.

District Judge Paul Ayers of Bedford County Court, the Senior Vice President of the Association of Her Majesty's District Judges implied that the father and mother of Kanchan Jaisinghani, CQC Executive, not a Taliban, did not have very, very strong views about education.

"Mr Bamgbelu clearly has very, very strong views about education and I understand those views are based upon the fact that he is a successful dentist here in Bedford which he attributes to the fact that his parents cared for him and his education when he was young. They ensured that he had a proper fee paying education…….." District Judge Paul Ayers of Bedford County Court, the Senior Vice President of the Association of Her Majesty's District Judges – proofed and approved Judgement.

An opportunist RACIST: Poly-class brainless nonsense.

Poly-educated (second-class), opportunistic white supremacist sarcasm.

Based on very, very proximate observations and direct experiences, most white people are not openly racist, but most white people are white supremacists.

Then, there, white Judges, nearly all, were members of the Charitable Antichrist Racist Freemasonry Quasi-religion (Mediocre Mafia) – Habakkuk 1:4: John 8:44; John 10:10.

PERCEPTION IS GRANDER THAN REALITY.

Then, in our tribe in the African bush, the opportunist racist white thug would be treated with coarse stones.

"Stoning certainly teaches people a lesson." Ayatollah Khalkhali.

Had the closeted racist white man not been our Judge in Bedford, I'd not know him; he has nothing to sell and can never have anything to sell that I'd voluntarily buy.

An overpromoted Freemason (Mediocre Mafia/New Pharisee); a mere former debt-collector Solicitor in Norwich (Coastal dole/the departure lounge of life).

What was in Norwich prior Covid-19 for closeted racist functional semi-illiterate Solicitors to do?

Based on very proximate observations and direct experiences, perception is grander than reality.

The only evidence of his purportedly higher IQ is the stolen affluence that his ancestors, mere peasants and agricultural labourers (Serfs) from Eastern Europe crossed the English Channels, in dinghy boats, without luggage or decent shoes, and they changed their names, blended, and latched onto the yields of several centuries of merciless racist evil, the greediest economic cannibalism, and the evilest racist terrorism the world will ever know, and deceive their duller children that their ancestors were aboriginal Britons that the Romans used violence to beat up and rob, in 55BC.

Ignorance is bliss.

"Those who know the least obey the best."

"It was in 1066 that William the Conqueror occupied Britain, stole our land, and gained control by granting it to his Norman friends thus creating a feudal system that we have not yet fully escaped." Tony Benn (1925 – 2014).

William the Conqueror used violence to take from others what others used violence to take from others.

"A typical English man, usually violent and always dull." Wilde

Then, almost everything was actively and deliberately stolen with guns – Habakkuk.

"All have taken what had other owners and all have had recourse to arms rather than quit the prey on which they were fastened." Dr Samuel Johnson

Facts are sacred.

"Affluence is not a birth right." David Cameron.

The cretins, of all shades, who sit before the closeted racist functional semi-illiterate white man, albeit England's Class District Judge did not know that his nomination and constructive appointment, as our District Judge, by some Lords, was not based on progressive, colour-blind, and measurably objectivity.

If we are not very, very smart, why are we very rich?

Shepherds did not bring stolen Africans back home; they lied to their duller children (Sheep) that they were paragons of wisdom who, like TARZAN, did only virtuous works in Africans.

They tell lies all the time.

"Lies are told all the time." Sir Michael Havers

Based on available evidence, His Honour Judge Perusko studied Law at Poly (Lower-class alternative education) – Proverbs 17:16.

Why should white mother and father of His Honour Judge Perusko need very, very strong views about education if his Christ granted talent is only good enough for Second-rate alternative Poly-education – Proverbs 17:16?

Why should the white father and mother of District Judge Paul Ayers of Bedford County Court, the Senior Vice

President of the Association of Her Majesty's District
Judges need very, very strong views about education if
there is irrefutable evidence that his white ancestors were
THIEVES and owners of stolen poor black children of
defenceless Africans (Meghan Markle's ancestors) –
Habakkuk?

OYINBO OLE: THIEVES – HABAKKUK.

CHAPTER TWENTY-FIVE:

Boris Johnson: Why is England not a scam?

"Dirty Nigger! Mama, look a Negro! ...... The Negro is going to eat me up, where shall I hide?" Frantz Fanon

White Privilege: The Continuing Uneducated Tyranny of the White Majority – Habakkuk. The Taliban is Antichrist, but not Racist. Based on available evidence, the administration of English law is Antichrist and RACIST.

When their people commit racist crimes against ours, half-educated school dropouts and their superiors who have informal access to very, very powerful white Freemason Judges criminally bury racial hatred – Habakkuk 1:4; John 8:44; John 10:10.

A properly organised racist crime syndicate impersonates colour-blind and impartial administration of the law.

BEDFORD, ENGLAND: Based on available evidence, GDC-Witness, Brother, Richard William Hill fabricated reports and reports and unrelentingly lied under oath – Habakkuk 1:4; John 8:44; John 10:10.

A CLOSETED RACIST WHITE CROOK.

The only BLACK the closeted racist white bastards truly love is our money; everything else is deceit.

NIGERIA: SHELL'S DOCILE CASH COW.

There are no oil wells or gas fields in Norwich (Coastal dole); the very highly luxuriant soil of Bishop's Stortford yields only food.

CECIL RHODES (1853 – 1902) WAS A THIEF.

"We shall deal with the racist white bastards when we get out of prison." Robert Mugabe (1924 – 2019).

OYINBO OLE: Ignorant descendants of THIEVES and owners of stolen poor black children of defenceless Africans (Meghan Markle's ancestors) – Habakkuk.

Then, racist white bastards carried and sold millions of stolen poor black children of defenceless Africans (Meghan Markle's ancestors); now, they carry natural resources.

SUBSTITUTION IS FRAUDULENT EMANCIPATION.

Righteousness is absolutely impossible because, prior to Covid-19, equitable and full reparation, with full interest, is unaffordable in this world and the next.

Righteousness without full and equitable reparation is continuing racist fraud – Habakkuk.

"Moderation is a virtue only among those who are thought to have found alternatives." Henry Kissinger

Facts are sacred; they can't be overstated.

BEDFORD, ENGLAND: Based on available evidence, GDC-Expert, Sue Gregory, OBE, Officer of the Most Excellent Order of our Empire, unrelentingly lied under implied oath.

A CLOSETED RACIST CROOKED WHITE COUGAR.

Our Empire did not evolve from NOTHING; then, almost everything was actively and deliberately stolen with GUNS – Habakkuk.

Ignorance is bliss.

Before SLAVERY, what?

"Affluence is not a birth right." David Cameron.

White Privilege (Charitable Antichrist Racist Freemasonry Quasi-Religion): A properly organised racist crime syndicate deceptively impersonates impartial and colour-blind administration of the law.

HIGH HOLBORN, LONDON: "A complaints such as Mrs Bishop's could trigger an enquiry." Stephen Henderson, LLM, Head of MDDUS.

"I don't want to talk grammar. I want to talk like a lady." George Bernard Shaw

A CROOKED RACIST WHITE PRIVILEGED DULLARD.

OYINBO OLE: A racist descendant of THIEVES and owners of stolen poor black children of defenceless Africans (Meghan Markle's ancestors) - Habakkuk

Apart from the froth he bought in Cardiff, the only postgraduate examinations the closeted racist envious white thug did not FAIL are those he did not do.

Facts are sacred.

"The truth allows no choice." Dr Samuel Johnson

SEERS: They accurately foresaw that a closeted racist crooked white bastard will be the Head of MDDUS, High Holborn, London, so they used, made in Birmingham, GUNS to loot Africa, and they used the yields of several centuries of the greediest economic cannibalism and the evilest racist terrorism the world will ever know to create an Eldorado for millions of white imbeciles – Habakkuk, and they decommissioned natural selection, and reversed evolution, and made it affordable for millions of imbeciles of all shades to breed irresponsibly.

NIGERIA: SHELL'S DOCILE CASH COW.

Children with huge oil wells and gas fields near their huts eat only 1.5/day in Nigeria; a closeted racist functional semi-illiterate white man, whose white father and mother have never seen crude oil, and whose white ancestors were fed like battery hens with the yields of stolen poor black children of defenceless Africans is the Head of MDDUS High Holborn, London.

676

WOLLASTON, ENGLAND: Based on available evidence, GDC-Witness, Rachael Bishop, Senior NHS Nurse, albeit England's class, unrelentingly lied under oath – Habakkuk 1:4; John 8:44; John 10:10.

A CLOSETED RACIST CROOKED WHITE COUGAR.

"Find the truth and tell it." Harold Pinter

NORTHAMPTON, ENGLAND: Based on available evidence, GDC-witness, Geraint Evans, Postgraduate Tutor, Oxford, unrelentingly lied under implied oath.

A CLOSETED RACIST WELSH CROOK.

How should our people (Negroes) defend themselves against white people who had the power to tell lies under oath – before white referees (Judges)?

"The earth contains no race of human beings so totally vile and worthless as the Welsh ….." Walter Savage Landour

https://www.youtube.com/watch?v=BlpH4hG7m1A&feature=youtu.be

"They may not have been well written from a grammatical point of view, but I am confident I had not forgotten any of the facts." Dr Geraint Evans, Postgraduate Tutor, Oxford

They see a Postgraduate Tutor, Oxford; I see an imbecile. If they are not excessively stupid, I must be mad.

677

https://youtu.be/rayVcfyu9Tw

Based on very proximate observations and direct experiences, then in the Valleys of Wales, there were millions of white sheep and people, and all the white sheep, not all the white people were incestuously conceived, and all the white sheep, but not all the white people were excessively stupid.

Based on very proximate observations and direct experiences, England is essentially a properly organised Antichrist Racist Scam.

The belief of the Charitable Antichrist Racist Freemasonry Quasi-Religion (Mediocre Mafia/New Pharisees), our irreconcilable religious enemies – is incompatible with our belief, the exceptionalism of Christ, John 14:6.

The closeted racist, grossly overrated, white bastards who use very expensive aprons to decorate the temples of their powerless and useless fertility tools, are very, very, powerful in England only because they are above all laws (Man's and God's) – Habakkuk. They have real enemies; in order parts of our Commonwealth, their enemies will stand their grounds and summarily deal with them if they made wrong moves.

BORIS JOHNSON: Give us the legal tools and we will deal with half-educated school dropouts and their SUPERIORS who have informal access to some very, very powerful white Judges.

BORIS JOHNSON: Freemasons are our irreconcilable religious enemies; their people are everywhere, and they control almost everything.

BORIS JOHNSON: "Give us the tools, and we will finish the job." Churchill

Based on available evidence, District Judge Paul Ayers of Bedford County Court, the Senior Vice President of the Association of Her Majesty's District Judges, unrelentingly lied under oath (implied) – Habakkuk 1:4; John 8:44; John 10:10. A Crooked Racist Freemason Dipstick.

Facts are sacred; they can't be overstated.

"The truth allows no choice." Dr Samuel Johnson

District Judge Paul Ayers of Bedford County Court, the Senior Vice President of the Association of Her Majesty's District Judges, based on available evidence, it is absolutely impossible for your talent and the yield of your land to sustain your standard of living.

District Judge Paul Ayers of Bedford County Court, the Senior Vice President of the Association of Her Majesty's District Judges, based on available evidence, your white ancestors were THIEVES and owners of stolen poor black children of defenceless Africans (Meghan Markle's ancestors), and you are a leech - Habakkuk

Based on very proximate observations and direct experiences, not all white people are openly racist, but nearly all white people are white supremacists.

"Racism is rife throughout most organisations across Britain." The Mayor of London

"All sections of the UK Society are institutionally racist." Sir Bernard Hogan-Howe

"Megan Markle was the subject of explicit oblivious racial hatred." The Right Honourable John Bercow, then, the Speaker

"White supremacy is real, and it needs to be shattered." Dr Cornel West

The Brain isn't inside the irrefutably superior skin colour that the wearer neither made nor chose. They are not the only creation of All Mighty God, and their indisputably superior skin colour is not the only wonder of our World.

If one is incontrovertibly a functional semi-illiterate, and if one's land yields only food, and if one is rich, it's plainly deductible that one's white ancestors must have been THIEVES - Habakkuk.

"It was our arms in the river of Cameroon, put into the hands of the trader, that furnished him with the means of pushing his trade; and I have no more doubt that they are British arms, put into the hands of Africans, which promote universal war and desolation that I can doubt their having done so in that individual instance. I have shown how great is the enormity of this evil, even on the supposition that we take only convicts and prisoners of war. But take the subject in another way, and how does it stand? Think of 80,000 persons carried out of their native country by we know not what means! For crimes imputed! For light or inconsiderable faults! For debts perhaps! For crime of witchcraft! Or a thousand other weak or scandalous pretexts! Reflect on 80,000 persons annually taken off! There is something in the horror of it that surpasses all bounds of imagination." – Prime Minister William Pitt the Younger.

NIGERIA: SHELL'S DOCILE CASH COW

Then, they accurately foresaw that their descendants will be excessively dull, so they used, made in Birmingham, guns to loot Africa, and they used the yields of several centuries of the greediest economic cannibalism and the evilest racist terrorism the world will ever know to create an Eldorado for millions of white imbeciles, and they decommissioned natural selection, and reversed evolution, and made it affordable for millions of imbeciles of all shades to breed irresponsibly.

"Sometimes people don't want to hear the truth because they don't want their illusions destroyed." Friedrich Nietzsche

GDC-Witness: British Soldier – Territorial Defence, Stephanie Twidale (TD), unrelentingly lied under oath— Habakkuk. A Crooked Racist Cougar. She looked like someone who regularly visited THE GAMBIA to sit on black rocks.

When their people commit racist crimes against ours, their people, referees or Judges, criminally bury racial hatred, as they are closeted racists too.

Only foolish Negroes expect demons to cast out demons – Matthew 12:27.

DELUDED PAPER TIGERS: Brainless and baseless superiority is their birth right. Their skin colour is indisputably superior; they neither made nor chose it.

Their hairs stand on end when they are challenged by our people; we and our type are the ones they'd beat up without the support of the YANKS.

"England will fight to the last American." American saying

"Ethical foreign policy." Robin Cook (1946 – 2005).

If members of the Charitable Antichrist Racist Freemasonry Quasi-Religion (Mediocre Mafia/New Pharisees) are as ethical and as brave as brave as they imply, they should forcibly evict Putin from Crimea; he stole it with guns.

Did Putin poison Bob Dudley; he sits on the largest gas reserve in the world?

GDC-Witness: George Rothnie (NHS) unrelentingly lied under implied oath—Habakkuk. Scottish crooked imbecile: Edinburgh University Educated Scatter-head white man.

Our Edinburgh University Educated Prime Minister, the Scholar from Fife, couldn't spell; in the Country of the blind, the partially sighted is a guide.

OYINBO OLE: Ignorant descendants of THIEVES and owners of stolen poor black children of defenceless Africans (Meghan Markle's ancestors) – Habakkuk

"You will bow. You can't beat the system." Kemi Daramola.

Imported devil: Antichrist Christian. She liked what homunculus Eunice couldn't afford, like her, mother, the very, very rich contractor's wife, she used her tube-tools to get it: A glorified prostitute and a THIEF.

"Yinka, you make my life feel secure." Kemi Daramola.

She prays to Christ and pays tithe (quasi-protection money) at Brickhill Baptist Church, Bedford; Charitable Antichrist Racist Freemasons in Kempston answer her prayers.

Then, there, white Judges nearly were Christians and Freemasons; some of them were THICKER than a gross of planks – Habakkuk 1:4; John 8:44; John 10:10.

The DNA of the administration of English Law is Racial Hatred and Incompetent Lies: The administration of English Law is overseen by Freemasons - Habakkuk

Merciless descendants of the greediest economic cannibals and evilest racist terrorists the world will ever know impede our ascent from the bottomless crater in which their ancestors threw ours, in the African bush, unprovoked, during several centuries of sadism and savagery: The barbarously racist traffic in millions of stolen and destroyed poor children of defenceless poor Africans (Meghan Markle's ancestors) – Habakkuk.

They were all white: Homogeneity in the administration English law is the impregnable secure mask of merciless racial hatred.

A bastardised, unashamedly mediocre, indiscreetly dishonest, vindictive, potently weaponised, and institutionally racist legal system that is overseen by MASONS (Mediocre Mafia/ New Pharisees)—Habakkuk.

"To deny or belittle this good is, in this dangerous century when the resources and pretensions of power continue to enlarge, a desperate error of intellectual abstraction. More than this, it is a self-fulfilling error, which encourages us to give up the struggle against bad laws and class bound procedures and to disarm ourselves before power. It is to throw away a whole inheritance of struggle about the law and within the forms of law, whose continuity can never be fractured without bringing men and women into immediate danger." - E. P Thompson.

"The truth allows no choice." Dr Samuel Johnson.

Reasoning and vision are unbounded; the fellow is who He says He is   - John 14:6.

Where the press is free and everyone could read, all is safe.

— President Thomas Jefferson

CHAPTER TWENTY-SIX:

Boris Johnson: Why is England not a scam?

White Privilege: The Continuing Uneducated Tyranny of the White Majority – Habakkuk. The Taliban is Antichrist, but not Racist.

Based on available evidence, the administration of English law is Antichrist, mediocre, and RACIST.

Mother Teresa of Africa: If we are not very smart, why are we very rich? Shepherds did not bring stolen poor black children of defenceless Africans back home; they lied to their moron sheep that they were paragons of wisdom who, like Mother Teresa, did only virtuous works in Africa.

OYINBO OLE: Ignorant descendants of ultra-righteous THIEVES and owners of stolen poor black children of defenceless Africans (Meghan Markle's ancestors) - Habakkuk

They know how to steal for their people, but they don't know how to repair their scatter-heads.

The Statement of Robert Kingston, Accountant, Director, Dobern Property Limited, and England's Class Solicitor.

"This statement is about a series of letters and emails I have been recieving. I am the above named person. I live at an address provided to police. In this statement I will also mention XXXXXXXXXXXXXXXXXXXXXXXXXXX a leaseholder for a property I manage at my place work. I am the company director of DOBERN properties based in Ilford. These emails have been sent to my company email address of mail@debern.co.uk, and also letters have been sent to myself at our company ADDress of P.O BOX 1289, ILFORD, IG2 7XZ over the last Two and a half years, I have recieving a series of letters and emails from DR BAMGeLu. DR BAMGBELU is a leasholder for a property I manage at my place of work. Over the period of his leaseholding, DR BAmGelu has continually failed to pay arrears for the property. In march 2016 my company took DR to court and he was ordered to pay outstanding costs of around £20000 since that time and lead up to the case, DR BaMGBelu has been emailing me and posting me letters that are lengthy and accuses me repeatedly of being a racist in emails and letters tact are regularly Ten to twelve pages long, DR BAMGBELU. lists numerous quots from google searches all refrencing ham I am a bigot and a racist. The most recent letter I received from DR BAMGBELU opens with you are jealous and racist Evil combination you hate us we know it" he goes on to say "I would not have knowingly had anything to do with white supremicists." In the last email I recieved from him on 02/09/2016 DR BaMGBELU stated "you are restricted by poor Education within one of the least literate countries in the world". I would be perfectly happy for DR BAMGBElu to contact myself or my company if he has relevant enquiries to his lease holding, however these continuous letters and emails are causing me distress and I feel intimidated. I am not a racist and these accusatios make uncomfortable. All I want is to conduct between us in a normal manner. I want BambGlu to stop emailing me and sending me letters accusing me of being racist and harassing me." ROBERT KINGSTON, SOLICITOR, ACCOUNTANT, AND DIRECTOR DOBERN PROPERTY LIMITED.

A seemingly incestuously conceived scatter-head white man; only his indisputably superior skin colour was good.

Shocking!

"Why, that is, because, dearest, you are a dunce." Dr Samuel Johnson

"There is no sin except stupidity." Wilde

"Yes, Sir, it does *her* honour, but it would do nobody else honour. I have indeed, not read it all. But when I take up the end of a web, and find it packthread, I do not expect, by looking further, to find embroidery." Dr Samuel Johnson

NIGERIA: A little child with huge oil wells and gas fields near her house eats 1.5 (thrice in two days); incontrovertibly functional semi-illiterate Jew, Mr Robert Kingston (Claimant), whose mother and father might have never seen black crude oil – is a Solicitor in Great Britain. What's great about that?

Freemasons teach their members secret handshakes, not grammar; the former is considerably easier to master – Habakkuk 1:4

Conflict of interest: "We have the power to turn against our creators." Dr Richard Dawkins

Based on observations and direct experiences, too many Solicitors/Lawyers in Great Britain are functional semi-illiterates. What's great about that?

Based on available evidence, those who failed the A/Level could do law, albeit with the graduate educational system of one of the dullest

The legal trade: A mediocre dying trade clings on straws.

"Some argue that the law is in its death throes while others postulate a contrary prognosis that discerns numerous signs of law's enduring strength. Which is it?" Professor Raymond Wacks

Based on available evidence, a functional semi-illiterate solicitor could become a District Judge in Great Britain. What's great about that?

Then, there, White Judges, nearly all, were Freemasons; some of them were thicker than a gross of planks.

Printed in Great Britain
by Amazon